THE SCOTTISH ENLIGHTENMENT

THE SCOTTISH ENLIGHTENMENT

A SOCIAL HISTORY

ANAND C. CHITNIS

CROOM HELM LONDON

ROWMAN AND LITTLEFIELD TOTAWA, N.J.

First published 1976
© 1976 Anand C. Chitnis

Croom Helm Ltd
2-10 St John's Road, London SW 11

ISBN 0-85664-349-1

First published in the United States 1976
by ROWMAN AND LITTLEFIELD, Totowa, New Jersey

Library of Congress Cataloging in Publication Data

Chitnis, Anand C
  The Scottish enlightenment.

  Bibliography: p. 261
  1. Scotland — Intellectual life. 2. Enlightenment. 3. Philosophy, Scottish. I. Title.
DA812.C48 1976 941.1 76-17279
ISBN 0-87471-857-0

Printed and bound in Great Britain by
REDWOOD BURN LIMITED
Trowbridge and Esher

CONTENTS

for my Mother and in memory of my Father

PREFACE

The Scottish Enlightenment has become an increasingly popular field of study, interest, and research in recent years. There have already been celebrated the first distinguished bicentennials of births, deaths, and publication dates associated with the movement, and others will occur during the last quarter of this century. The interest aroused has been international, for German, Italian, and North American scholars have often given leads to their Scottish and English colleagues who have joined them in this rich area of multi-disciplinary study.

This is a social history of the Scottish Enlightenment. Naturally, it will not satisfy all those who specialise in particular aspects of the subject, but it does attempt to give coherent shape to the wide range of scattered writings by others as well as incorporating my own research. It is not intended as a definitive study but to summarise the research of the 'sixties and early 'seventies and, hopefully, to interest a wider audience in its results.

ACKNOWLEDGEMENTS

I have incurred many debts in writing this book and I have met with
immense kindness from scholars and friends whose help I have sought.
It is difficult, not to say invidious, to attribute more to one person than
another but I must mention first Professor Malcolm Thomis, University
of Queensland, who, while he was at Stirling, pored over several versions
of the entire manuscript several times, helping me especially to elimin-
ate obscurities and to improve the style. His friendship has been
invaluable from the day I first met him and his help with the present
study is a testament to it. Professor Roy Campbell, University of
Stirling, read most of the early drafts and in rewarding discussion, set
me on the way to what I hope were and are improved later versions.
Professor Christopher Smout, University of Edinburgh, read first drafts
of the first half of the study at a particularly difficult time in its
composition. He took immense trouble in providing me with criticisms,
suggestions, advice and, above all, encouragement and I would wish
here to record his kindness to me. If it had not been for Professor
David Waddell, I would never have taught a special subject on Scotland
and the Enlightenment at the University since 1971. The idea for the
book was that of Bruce Hunter, who has had much concern for it since,
and whose efforts have ensured that it is now reaching the general
public. The students who have studied the subject with me in sessions
1971-4 and 1975-6 were able and helpful. They will recognise passages
in the book which were formulated as a result of our discussions, and
I have acknowledged in the notes individual contributions.

I consulted some specialists on particular themes and thank in
particular for their help Mrs Monica Clough; Jack Morrell, University
of Bradford, who thoroughly vetted a long and diffuse first draft of
Chapter Six; Roy Porter, Churchill College, Cambridge, for some
comments on my account of James Hutton; Dr George Davie, University of Edinburgh, for permission to use his ideas and writings so
liberally throughout the book; and Rev. Dr Ian Clark, Bishop's College,
Calcutta, for permission to use his published and unpublished work on
the Moderates and for some perceptive comments and observations on
Chapter Three, only some of which I have been able to take up in the
present study.

I would like to acknowledge gratefully the contributions of Steve
Richard, The Bodleian Library, Oxford; Mrs Catherine B. Richard,

formerly librarian, Science Studies Unit, University of Edinburgh; Iain McIver, National Library of Scotland and Ian Cornelius, University of Stirling Library. They are among many librarians whose help was so unstinting. Miss Margaret Hendry, with help from Miss Betty Neech and Mrs Brenda Wilson, displayed the patience of Job when it came to typing, re-typing and correcting the manuscripts, and I cannot convey adequately my appreciation of the efforts they put into the text and into a multitude of other associated matters.

The University of Stirling granted me sabbatical leave in the session 1974-5, during the first part of which I completed the manuscript. I acknowledge, too, the award of a research grant from the Social Science Research Council for that same session to study the Scottish Enlightenment and the Evolution of Victorian Society. I have incorporated some preliminary findings in the current work but the substantive results await the completion of a second monograph.

The most important debt I wish to record is to my wife, Bernice, who, in between her teaching duties in the French Department of the University of Stirling, her studies of French Renaissance funerary rhetoric, her domestic responsibilities, her giving birth and ministering to our children in 1972 and 1974 and gestating our third due in May 1976, still found time to give parts of the book the benefit of her penetrating mind, to give me comfort when the problems of writing were acute and to display much forebearance of my moods. Rajendra and Lucia Chitnis, unwittingly maybe, played their parts too, by tolerating a frequently preoccupied father whose mind was on institutions and ideas in the eighteenth century, rather than family life and recreation in the twentieth.

The end result, though, is entirely my responsibility. The errors, misjudgements and inadequacies that remain are not to be associated with the large number of named and unnamed people who together have shown an immense fund of goodwill, consideration and friendship that I have much appreciated and here acknowledge.

Bridge of Allan, March 1976.

1 THE SCOTTISH ENLIGHTENMENT

The European Enlightenment of the eighteenth century occurred during that epoch in the history of man when he realised that he could both understand and control his environment. By his environment is meant society, political, social and economic arrangements, as well as the natural world, his health, the climate, the fabric of the earth itself. Hence the era of the Enlightenment in the history of civilisation is crucial: it was a period distinguished by some remarkable works in the history of thought and cultural expression which laid some of the critical foundations of the modern world.

The Enlightenment was the period that in science saw the rise to considerable influence and acceptance of the experimental method of Isaac Newton and the extension of that method to the study of society itself. It was the period that saw the emergence of the social sciences from moral philosophy, and their pursuit as disciplines in themselves, namely economics, history, sociology, psychology. Similar strides forward were evident in natural and physical sciences, physics, chemistry, geology, medicine. The eighteenth century was also an era that witnessed the perceptible though gradual triumph of reason, reason applied to knowledge, to religion, to political and social arrangements. Tradition, faith and divine right could no longer expect to prevail as unquestioned authorities in the affairs of men.

The roots of the Scottish Enlightenment lay deep in the nation's history, since the expression of the movement depended on the Church, the law, the lawyers and the universities. The Church and universities at least had very long histories. Nonetheless, if there had been much growth below ground by the mid to late seventeenth century, the first shoots of the Enlightenment began to appear from then, to bud in the 1730s and to bloom from about 1750 to the 1780s. From then on it by no means withered, but most of the more celebrated authors were dead or dying, the pioneering work was now more in natural philosophy and medicine than moral philosophy, and the institutions which supported the movement one by one began to sag. Certainly by the 1820s the Scottish Enlightenment was on the point of demise and did not survive the third decade of the century.

Despite the ascription 'Scottish', the Enlightenment was not apparent all over Scotland; nor did it flower with equal vigour in those parts of the country where it appeared. Its location was essentially that limited geographical area of the central, lowland belt bounded by Glasgow in the west and Edinburgh in the east but also taking in the city and universities of Aberdeen. It was an urban movement and its intimacy was prompted, and its progress facilitated, by the forms of social and intellectual expression that towns and urban living encouraged. That the milieu of the Scottish Enlightenment lay in the universities and the legal and ecclesiastical professions not only emphasises its urban-ness but also underlines the importance of Edinburgh over the other university towns; the capital was the seat of the law courts, the annual venue of the General Assembly of the Kirk, but more important, it became a city of considerable economic and social attraction for men of letters.

Scotland experienced a new era in the eighteenth century for which the way had been paved in the seventeenth century. The social, economic and general cultural awakening was evident more commonly in the Lowlands than in the Highlands. Historians have described the period generally as an 'age of improvement' which ultimately led to 'the rise of an industrial society'. The Scottish Enlightenment was a particular and distinctive part of the new era with its origins likewise lying in the seventeenth century. The interests of the Enlightenment were confined to specific intellectual matters and its setting and media of expression were limited to certain institutions and centres.

The whole era of which the Scottish Enlightenment was a part included such cultural expressions as paintings, with the younger Allan Ramsay and Henry Raeburn as portrait painters, and also William Aikman, David Allan, Alexander and Patrick Nasmyth and David Wilkie; there was the Glasgow printer Robert Foulis, renowned for his professional work and for the development of an academy of Arts that produced James Tassie, the fashioner of portraits in paste; Scotland provided too such notable architects as Robert Adam and his brothers, John and William, Colin Campbell and James Gibb. The Golden Age was especially evident in literature, the poetry of Robert Burns, the elder Allan Ramsay, James Thomson and Robert Ferguson; the novels of Walter Scott, James Hogg, Tobias Smollett and Henry Mackenzie. The other side of the general cultural development was less artistic but no less inventive for all that: it can be seen in the general schemes of agricultural and economic improvement and also in the activities of James Watt, the inventor of the steam engine and related devices, or those concerned in the transport revolution of the era, canals, bridge-

building, marine engineering, lighthouse building and shipping, like
Thomas Telford, John Rennie, John Smeaton, Robert Stevenson,
Such a catalogue of achievements conveys that Scotland was experiencing an era of broad social, cultural and economic activity of some
distinction in the eighteenth century. The concern of the present study,
however, is not with the general scene. The concern here is rather with
the smaller but no less remarkable phenomenon, the Scottish Enlightenment, which shared some of the same origins and concerns but whose
essential characteristic was philosophical not merely literary, and whose
sphere of action was not society at large but the elite professions and
their resorts.

As with the European Enlightenment as a whole, The Scottish philosophers were concerned with their environment as earlier defined, and
consequently, the subjects of their disquisitions ranged from philosophy
as it is conventionally understood to a particular form of social philosophy which was influenced by the methodology of Isaac Newton
and by the approach of the French *philosophe,* Montesquieu, all the
way through to the natural sciences and medicine. The social philosophy comprehended intellectual approaches that subsequent to the
eighteenth century became disciplines in their own right, such as
sociology, history, economics. The pioneering of social science was a
major achievement of the movement.

The study of man as a social and sociable being was a central interest
of the philosophers of the Scottish Enlightenment. They were not only
active in social institutions such as the Church, the legal profession,
universities and clubs, but they were interested in the mechanisms
whereby society operated and their analyses were historically based.
Accordingly, their social philosophy must receive attention of a
different character from other aspects of the movement in any social
history. Several of them were lawyers, and since lawyers played
particular parts in the Scottish society of their own time, the law and its
practitioners linked the Enlightenment to concerns that were current.
The early history of Scots Law, eighteenth-century lawyers and their
multifarious activities, let alone their coincidence with the Enlightenment, is a subject much in need of investigation and present discussion must remain speculative.

Education in Scotland's universities was a further important preoccupation: in Arts it was distinctively philosophical, designed to
encourage generalisation and the habit of thoughtfulness, the
reduction of a mass of facts to a few general principles. The philosophic character of the Scottish Enlightenment was thus underpinned.

In many subjects taught in the Scottish universities of the Enlightenment, much concern appears to have been shown for effective teaching
and this meant at times that distinguished teaching was achieved.
Since the Universities comprised more than Arts Faculties, the concern
for education was equally apparent in medicine and science. Medicine
in the Scottish Enlightenment was as concerned with teaching aspiring
doctors as with caring and curing. Most of the developments in medicine had an educational purpose behind tham. From the rise and
development of Scottish medicine from the late seventeenth century
came a stimulus to sciences that were at first ancilliary to medicine but
which, in time, became independent of it, such as chemistry and
botany. Scottish chemistry in the Enlightenment, through the work of
Joseph Black especially, was yet another considerable feature. Natural
History, the most obviously environmental of the sciences, and also
shaped in the eighteenth century, was of considerable interest and
itself spawned sub-sciences such as meteorology, minerology and
geology, in all of which areas of knowledge Scotland's Enlightenment
figures were deeply interested and undertook original work.

It will subsequently be argued that in the seventeenth century the
basis began to be laid in various ways for the eighteenth century's age
of improvement. Among the central agencies of improvement were
three institutions that had traditionally played conspicuous parts in
Scottish life and history, the Kirk, and the legal and educational
systems. So sound a basis was laid that by the eighteenth century, and
aided by the catalyst that was the Treaty of Union in 1707 (which,
along with the accompanying Act of Security. left untouched the
three institutions) Scotland was in an increasingly strong position to
take advantage of the secular opportunities that presented themselves.
In the 1750s, a party became active in the Church which, far from
exerting any restrictive influence on Scotland's seizing of those opportunities, positively sought to harmonise and integrate the Church
and society. Part of the general climate of improvement included an
interest in intellectual developments from England and Holland
especially, which was expressed and elaborated in the traditional
institutions. That philosophy was fundamental to Scottish university
education facilitated the acceptance of the new thought. Consequently,
the Enlightenment arose in Scotland out of improvement in a country
that had the human ability and the social institutions to support it.
In the jargon of the economic historians, the Scottish Enlightenment
"took off" from the basis of a sympathetic environment and a sound
infrastructure. The themes of this book are, therefore, improvement,

leading by way of secularisation to enlightenment, and the centrality of the refurbished traditional institutions, and, much later, the establishment of new ones during the Scottish Enlightenment. The interaction of the Enlightenment with the society in which it flourished was crucial: consequently, it is often difficult to distinguish as clearly as might be ideally desirable between improvement and enlightenment.

A particular historical approach was common to the social philosophy of Scottish thinkers, but others amongst their   contemporaries also were interested in the past. In order to distinguish, therefore, between the writings of the philosophers and others, it is necessary to indicate some writers working largely outside of the philosophical tradition and more in the antiquarian, who were more preoccupied with sources and records than with explanations. The philosophical approach would be here considered as enlightened and the antiquarian as outside of the Enlightenment. Robert Wodrow, a presbyterian minister and sometime Glasgow University librarian, who wrote amongst a number of other works, *History of the Sufferings of the Church of Scotland;* James Anderson, author of *Diplomata Scotiae;* Thomas Ruddiman, the grammarian, Keeper of the Advocates' Library and Edinburgh University printer who undertook two volumes of *Epistolae Regum Scotorum* (1739); Thomas Innes, the Roman Catholic priest after whom *The Innes Review* is named, who wrote the critical *Essay on the Ancient Inhabitants of the Northern Parts of Britain or Scotland* (1729); and Walter Goodall, editor in 1759 of John of Fordun's *Scotichronicon,* were all meticulous scholars in the sense that they were concerned with historical documents, editing them, collecting them, appending them to their writings. Much of their work was a far cry from the more speculative endeavours of the philosophers, who were prepared to sacrifice, neglect or ignore facts that were not in tune with their conjectures. Nonetheless, in some instances, the line between the enlightened and the antiquarian is again not as simple to draw as may sometimes seem to be suggested.

Finally, there were those who wrote in the era of the Scottish Enlightenment on matters of direct relevance to the movement's work, but who are not considered to be in its philosophical tradition. First, in order to illustrate the points prevailing among the *literati* and which were common to them, much selectivity of matters and men has been used in subsequent pages, and there was an implicit ranking of writers at the time which has led to the exclusion or relative neglect of certain authors. Secondly, there are individuals who, while writing of enlightened topics, rarely appear in any list of distinguished thinkers.

To illustrate both these points, Sir James Steuart's *Inquiry into the Principles of Political Economy* (1767) and the Earl of Lauderdale's *Inquiry into the Nature and Origin of Public Wealth* (1804) might be mentioned, since the subject of their prelections, political economy, was a new discipline produced by the Scottish Enlightenment, and because they have suffered in comparison to the more familiar Adam Smith.

In short, the work of neither was of the stature of Smith's, which was immensely broad and systematic in purpose and cast in a philosophic framework. Both Steuart and Lauderdale also had avowedly political purposes which contrasted with Smith's more covert intellectual Whiggism. Steuart was a Jacobite and concerned in his book to point up the limitations and insularity of England and, consequently, of the English connexion in comparison to Scotland and the Continent, and also to attack English pragmatism. He contrasts with Smith and others who were not concerned with economic matters in that, to quote Dr George Davie, he was anglophobe and they were anglophil. Smith saw that the industrial society heralded by England would be imitated in Scotland; Steuart considered England a most unsuitable model. Lauderdale, who wrote some forty years later, was a Whig; his whole analysis was designed to influence contemporary policy and was strongly expressed. Consequently, in the political climate of the time and the simplicity of the then popular economic ideas, such as those of David Ricardo, as well as the accurate attacks made on his actual economic theories and analysis, he was virtually neglected in his day. Nonetheless, certainly in Steuart's works, there appear ideas and considerations of problems that were also to be found in the writings of the philosophical tradition; economic development, the proximity of a developed and an underdeveloped country, and the historical stages of the economy are examples. Both men could also be original or improve on the philosophers' work in specific matters. Steuart improved on Smith in dealing with banking, public credit, paper money; Lauderdale has been justly criticised for his erroneous oversaving theory but he made important contributions in his comprehensive explanation of the theory of value and his analysis of the function of capital. He also analysed demand, which he saw entirely controlling production in a free economy and as being of great significance for the distribution of income, and consequently, of economic progress.[1]

To rescue the distinctive and impressive movement that was the Scottish Enlightenment from the broader social, cultural and economic awakening of the eighteenth century of which it was a part, it has here been necessary to define it quite strictly and to discuss some weighty matters pertaining to the definition. In fact, the lines between areas of improvement, mere awakening and enlightenment, are often blurred as the subsequent analysis will indicate. A strict definition can be modified and compromised in specific instances as the examination unfolds. Pure intellectual content is subsequently diluted by the enmeshing of the ideas with society, since what makes the Scottish Enlightenment so attractive an area of study is that its thinkers were both in the world and of it.

Notes

1.   G. E. Davie, 'Anglophobe and Anglophil', *Scottish Journal of Poltical Economy*, XIV (1967), pp. 291-302; Sir James Steuart, *An Inquiry into the Principles of Political Economy,* 2 vols., ed. Andrew S. Skinner (Scottish Economic Society, Oliver and Boyd, Edinburgh and London, 1966) and A. V. Cole, 'Lord Lauderdale and his "Inquiry" ', *Scottish Journal of Political Economy,* III (1965), pp. 115-25.

2   THE PRELUDE AND THE SETTING

I

It is remarkable, on the surface, that a major group of contributors to
the European Enlightenment were to be found not only in the entour-
ages of the enlightened despots, French salons, and the coterie of
encyclopaedists but also in the urban settings of lowland Scotland,
in the classrooms of the Scottish universities, in Scottish legal and
ecclesiastical circles, and in the membership of the Royal Society of
Edinburgh. For the circumstances of Scotland in the eighteenth
century were not apparently propitious: at the turn of the century,
not many years had passed since the famine years of the 1690s, and it
is difficult for a society to countenance and support a movement such
as the Scottish Enlightenment on an empty stomach or the threat of
one. Secondly, at the turn of the century Scotland still bore the scars
of a divided society. The prelude to and the results of the Revolution
of 1688-9 accentuated the religious divisions of Presbyterian, Roman
Catholic and Episcopalian. The divisions between the Jacobites and
the supporters in Scotland of the new Dutch king likewise persisted.
The geographical division in Scotland between the Highlands and the
Lowlands was linked to the political and religious ruptures and, in turn,
led to great personal differences between the two areas. There is every
reason to suggest that the descent from the Highlands by the supporters
of the Stuarts in the '15 and the '45 was not exactly welcomed by the
Lowlanders who had begun, well before those years, to turn their
attention to the cause of improvement, were by then settling down to
taking the new opportunities presented by the Union, and were somewhat embarrassed by the extravagant behaviour of their northern
countrymen. Yet Highlanders had little economic or social basis to
enter upon an era of improvement themselves, little to distract them
from the ancient causes which they had always espoused and continued to espouse almost up to the middle of the eighteenth century.

The union of the crowns in 1603 appears to have been the first political social cultural and economic stimulus to the era of improvement
which was evident periodically in the seventeenth century, boosted by
the 1688 Revolution and by the union of the parliaments in 1707, and
which, thereafter, made possible an age of enlightenment. Social and
economic historians have been in the forefront of those who have

11

countered the impression that seventeenth-century Scottish history is
an entirely dark age. Religious and ecclesiastical feuding was, indeed,
bitter and bloody but it did not consume all the energy and time at
the Scots' disposal. The Kirk was even prominent in initiating several
educational measures which created, by the beginning of the eighteenth
century, a society in the Lowlands that for its day was remarkably
literate. An economic and a cultural example of the effects of the
departure of the Crown can be seen in the loss sustained by those who
serviced the Court and its entourage, and in the loss of a cultural
standard which a national court provided. The burgesses of Edinburgh,
being composed of the City's tradesmen and merchants, forever sought
new means of generating business and ultimately found them, at least
in part, in the building of a New Town, in the generous funding of the
town's college and medical school, in judicious appointments made to
chairs which enhanced the reputation of the college, and in the business
of publishing the books of those men of letters attracted to their city,
and in all the ancillary occupations involved in the printing, publishing
and bookselling enterprise. All this was accomplished by the middle of
the eighteenth century. The rediscovery of the cultural fortunes took
as long, and forlorn-ness took the form of sensitivity to Scottish speech,
writing style and vocabulary that dogged even the most celebrated of
philosophers David Hume. In a letter written in 1757, he remarked:

> Is it not strange that, at a time when we have lost our Princes, our
> Parliaments, our independent Government, even the Presence of
> our chief Nobility, are unhappy in our accent and Pronunciation,
> speak a very corrupt Dialect of the Tongue which we make use of;
> is it not strange, I say, that, in these Circumstances, we shou'd
> really be the People most distinguish'd for Literature in Europe?

Eleven years earlier, when writing to the historian, William Robertson,
on words used in Robertson's book on the Emperor Charles V, Hume
had been specific:

> *Maltreat* is a Scotticism which occurs once. What the devil had you
> to do with that old-fashioned dangling word *wherewith*? I should
> as soon take back *whereupon, whereunto*, and *wherewithal*. I think
> the only tolerable decent gentleman of the family is *wherein*, and
> I should not choose to be often seen in his company. But I know
> you affection for *wherewith* proceeds from your partiality to Dean
> Swift, whom I can often laugh with, whose style I can even approve,

but surely can never admire . . . But what a fancy is this you have taken of saying always *an hand, an heart, an head*? Have you *an ear*? Do you not know that this *n* is added before vowels to prevent cacophony, and ought never to take place before *h* when that letter is sounded? It is never pronounced in these words, why should it be wrote? Thus, I should say, *a history*, and *an historian*; and so would you too, if you had any sense!

The Scottish Enlightenment took place in the context and atmosphere of a society that was improving and developing. To set the scene for the later rise and expression of the Scottish Enlightenment, through a particular milieu and institution, three areas of more general economic and cultural development may be examined, which are not of them-selves exhaustive examples of Scotland's age of improvement nor do they account on their own for the later Enlightenment. They do, however, give an indication of the spirit and nature of improvement that was abroad in Scotland, in the century prior to the period of High Enlightenment (1750-80), and explain a good part of the economic and social infrastructure on the basis of which the Scottish Enlighten-ment might 'take off'. The three examples are agricultural improve-ments, education and literacy and the building of the Edinburgh New Town.

The preparation for agricultural improvement was undertaken in the seventeenth century by a series of acts which had encouraged the division, consolidation and enclosure of land. An act of 1695 authorised the division of all common land not held by the king or the royal burghs among proprietors, according to the value of the rents of their existing holdings. Owners of land that was adjacent to common land acquired the right to use it by custom. Another act of 1695 permitted sheriffs to divide lands that were held as a series of detached holdings (runrig) and, as with the other legislation of 1695, that land, too, had to be allocated on the basis of who was adjacent to it. So more land was being handed over to individuals, which encour-aged an increase in the area under cultivation, fostered consolidation of land holdings and so promoted economies of scale by the various provisions relating to adjacencies. Enclosure was facilitated by yet more seventeenth-century legislation (1661, 1669 and 1685) which permitted the erection of fences along the boundaries of holdings.

All these measures were necessary preludes to new methods of agricultural production in the eighteenth century in terms of both equipment and methods such as crop rotation. The legislation was not of itself sufficient to permit agricultural improvement, but it did create a framework within which the agents of agricultural improvement, the landowners, could operate.[2] They did so not only for their own profit, or even, sometimes, more selflessly, for the profit of future generations (since agricultural improvement could sometimes be a very long-term investment) but because traditionally, landowners had certain duties to carry out, not least in providing a living and employment for their tenants and servants. They also, for example, administered local justice, could nominate, according to the particular historical period, the local kirk minister and schoolmaster, and act as the agent for dispensing poor relief.

It is possible that the Treaty of Union modified the conditions in which the traditional duties and occupations of the landowners were carried out: before and immediately after the Union, the spur to profit was lacking; agricultural improvement was a pioneering venture; incomes and demand low. Such investment in agriculture by early eighteenth-century landowners has been seen by Professor Christopher Smout as the Scottish equivalent of that conspicuous consumption for fashionable or patriotic purposes that in England took the form of elegant building, landscape gardening or undertaking the Grand Tour.[3] John Ramsay of Ochtertyre, himself an improver and an intimate friend of the intellectuals, wrote of two of his fellow Stirlingshire farmers and gentry that improved crop yields and the reputation of being good farmers were their important motivating forces.[4]

The Union acted as a stimulus to areas of economic life such as agriculture, which were already improving. Agriculture became increasingly important, too, with a rise in the number of mouths to be fed. For some of the landowners agriculture had, furthermore, to be treated with more seriousness than amusement, because it was now one of the few spheres in which they could carry out their patriotic duties, since national political responsibilities were considerably limited. Yet another sphere in which the landed classes could be active was the Scottish Enlightenment which, along with others such as town councils, church leaders and lawyers, they actively patronised.

The reformed Scottish Church of the sixteenth century had laid great emphasis on education, since it was in schools that children might be taught the ways of God. Only a universal school system could help to achieve the objective. Consequently, in the seventeenth century, several Acts were passed which were designed to realise the ideal: the legislation that has been assumed to have been most effective was the 1696 Act for Settling of Schools but in fact the effects of

earlier acts to establish parochial schools, in 1616, 1633 and 1646 have
been underestimated, at least in certain counties. The provision appears
to have been best in Fife, East Lothian, Midlothian, Angus and West
Lothian so that it has been said that the act of 1696 was not required
there to establish the schools, but as a measure of security for the
schoolmasters.[5]

The development of what can very generally be termed literacy
makes it possible to see the Scottish thinkers not as solitary geniuses
whose contemporaneous contributions to knowledge were coincidental,
but as the products of a society equipped and prepared to countenance
and support a movement such as the Scottish Enlightenment was. The
literacy, in a broad sense, is indicated not simply by the provision of
schools and schoolmasters, but in such other matters as a rise in the
number of people employed in the processes of paper-making, publishing and printing, and in increasing library provision. An invaluable
historical source for such social matters, albeit photographing a particular decade rather than illustrating a trend, and establishing the greater
affluence of the 1790s as much as the period's greater literacy, is the
first *Statistical Account of Scotland*. The work was inspired and conducted by Sir John Sinclair, first President of the Board of Agriculture;
in May 1790, when a lay member of the General Assembly of the
Church of Scotland, he prevailed upon parish ministers to act as
agents of an inquiry into the general state of Scotland. So valuable and,
in some cases, minutely detailed were the accounts of the parishes
that, rather than collate all the material or present it in another form
as an account of Scotland, Sinclair presented the material in parish
form.

There are many caveats to be borne in mind when using the *Statistical Account*, both in general and to illustrate the particular argument of
concern here. In the particular instance, it may be reiterated that the
source does not necessarily indicate a trend or historical development,
and that it as much reveals a country growing more wealthy as more
literate. Nonetheless it does demonstrate what use had been made of
the legacies of the Reformation and the seventeenth century, what
impact the union of the parliaments and the increasing secularity and
prosperity of the eighteenth century had had, and what was the state
of Scotland on the eve of industrialisation which, probably for a while,
caused Scottish standards of literacy to deteriorate. In general, each
parish account, for example, will depend for its accuracy and thorough-
ness on the care and attention devoted to its compilation by the minister
concerned; the account will also depend, in terms of what is inserted and

what is omitted, on the personality, predilections, prejudices and interests of the minister himself. Quite often the reader is treated more to descriptions of flora and fauna in a given locality than to indications of parishioners' employment or leisure activities; such descriptions do, nonetheless, indicate the general interest in natural history, which was treated on an intellectual level in the Enlightenment, and relate to the work in botanical classification of the Swede, Charles Linnaeus, and the popularity of Buffon's *Natural History*. Frequently, ministers preach sermons, in their accounts, on the virtues of industriousness and the evils of idleness and drink, with valuable time and space allotted to such encouragement or blame at the expense of more vital historical evidence. Sometimes the ministers are concerned to take credit for their own achievements, and incline to omit some features of parishes from their accounts that were obvious to them but not to outsiders. Despite these limitations, the source can be of immense value in studying Scottish society in the decade of the 1790s.

In his *Analysis of the Statistical Account of Scotland*, published more than twenty years after the last volume of evidence, Sinclair himself stressed that in Scotland, literature was an industry and, therefore, it was part of Scotland's material wealth, just as important as the goods of any other branch of industry. There was also no place where literary undertakings were carried on to such an extent in proportion to its population as in Edinburgh; furthermore, out of a population of one and a half million in 1795, 5,000 Scottish families, or 20,000 people, depended on literature for their subsistence, while 3,500 families or 10,500 people were dependent on teaching. Of Scottish domestic manufactures, only woollens, linen and hemp, iron and liquors employed more people than the paper industry.[6] Elsewhere in his analysis, Sinclair noted that reports from thirty parishes indicated that even the poor were eager for education, that they saved to receive it, that in some parishes all children over twelve could read and write, and that people sold clothes to buy books for their children.[7]

Consider now the evidence on particular themes, namely paper manufacturing and printing, libraries and education, taken from individual parish accounts in the central lowland belt of Scotland. Several ministers noted that paper mills had been erected in their parishes in recent years to the 1790s: Ayton in Berwickshire was one; Currie in Midlothian boasted the paper manufacture of Messrs Nisbet and Macniven which was the most extensive, on one waterfall, of any at present in Britain. It was the only new form of employment to be introduced at Currie and had increased the population by two hundred. New

Kilpatrick in the counties of Dunbarton and Stirling had a paper-mill as
did Penicuik in Midlothian, whose population increase was attributed
by the minister to the spirit with which two paper-mills have been carried on. In 1763, the erection of a paper-mill at Crieff, in Perthshire, was
only the second north of the Forth at the time, and a further one was
founded there in 1780. Paper was the only manufacture to be established at Urr, in Kircudbrightshire in 1794 in Dalbeaty and 'this work
has prospered abundantly'.

Certain other accounts were more forthcoming about the paper-
making enterprise: the minister of Lasswade, near Edinburgh, for
example, reported that five paper-mills had been erected in the fifty
years prior to 1794. The number of people employed in them had
risen from thirty or forty to 260. Three hundred tons of rags were
consumed for paper making, and a Mr Simpson, who owned two of
the mills, was the first paper manufacturer in Scotland to apply the
liquor recommended by Berthollet in his new method of bleaching.
He also introduced to Scotland the drying of paper by means of flues
on the principle of hot houses, which was of great value during the
winter. Simpson had also made other improvements relating to the
quality of paper, the cleanliness of manufacture and the cutting of
costs. In Methven, Perthshire, two mills owned by Messrs Morison and
Lindsay manufactured, weekly, sixty reams of superfine post, fools-
cap and the like, ninety reams of fine and common printing papers
and fifty reams of cartridge blue and wrapping papers. In other words,
the bulk of their products was for writing and printing. In Perth itself,
there were three mills producing between nine and ten thousand reams
of writing and printing paper, and between seven and eight thousand
reams of blue, cartridge, brown, grey and packing papers. The minister noted that the value of the products increased with the quantity
of fine paper produced. In 1750, a paper-mill had been erected at
Peterculter, in Aberdeenshire, by an Englishman, Bartholomew Smith.
It was the first of its kind in the north and was a successful enterprise,
even though it made insufficient superfine paper and paper for the
Aberdeen banks. Indeed, the Peterculter production, when taken
together with that of another paper-mill on the Don, could not satisfy
the requirements. Most striking of all the accounts, however, was that
for Edinburgh: in 1763, there had been three paper-mills in the city.
By 1790, their number had grown to twelve, and the minister commented that some of these paper mills were more extensive than any
in Britain. Of their production (6,400 reams in 1763; 100,000 reams in
1791) a vast quantity was sent for printing in London, whence formerly

it used to be brought.[8]

Naturally, it would be expected thatm with those figures, there would
be an accompanying rise in Edinburgh of printing houses. In 1763, there
were six. In 1790, their number had grown to sixteen. Similarly in Perth
there was clearly a thriving publishing trade: a letter dated 10 June
1794, from James Morison, the Perth publisher, was quoted in the
Statistical Account as saying that since the previous January he had
printed about 14,000 volumes, so that except for Edinburgh and
Glasgow, Perth was the only town in Scotland where books were
printed annually.[9] Other than these two instances, the *Account* was
remarkably reticent about the printing and publishing business. From
the Glasgow account, the wages of various journeymen tradesmen can
be discovered: printers' compositors earned between 52p and 90p a
week; pressmen 50p to 60p and bookbinders 35p to 52p. This compared with carpenters 40p to 60p and weavers 60p to 70p. Hence it is
known that printing and publishing thrived in Glasgow (the firm of
Foulis was the most celebrated).[10] The title pages of many contemporary books indicate that publishing also took place in such unexpected
places as Haddington, Montrose and Coupar Angus, but their ministers
and the ministers of yet other, albeit small, centres of publishing, may
have considered that the printed word in the hands of the common man
was a dangerous thing, unless that printed word was the word of God.
Finally, Hugo Arnot, the lawyer, writing of Edinburgh in 1779, noted
how within forty years the number of printing houses had increased
from four to twenty-seven.[11]

The provision of libraries matched the growth of the printing and
publishing business. Consider, for example, Duns in Berwickshire
whose public library was established in 1768. Sixty shareholders paid
£2 a share and 30p a year. The money was used to buy £150 worth of
books in the first year, and £12 to £15 worth annually ever since.
If the library in Duns sounds as though it was for the affluent, it can
be contrasted with the library of Leadhills, near Crawford in Lanarkshire. There the lead mines employed 200 men, pickmen, smelters,
washers, labourers, carpenters and smiths, who worked six out of
twenty-four hours in the mine. The minister noted that the employees
had a great deal of spare time, and so employed themselves in reading,
and for this purpose had fitted up a library, out of which every one
who contributed to the expense received books. According to Ramsay of
Ochtertyre, the library was one of many schemes to improve the lot
of the Leadhill miners designed by James Stirling, manager of the
Scottish Mining Company for some thirty years from 1734.[12]

Montrose, in Angus, acquired in 1758 a flourishing public library which purchased publications not readily available in the town. It was also used by schoolteachers and university students and many valuable books had been presented to it. In 1783, gentlemen in Greenock, Renfrewshire, had embarked on a similar enterprise which, by 1793, had 200 volumes. Tranent, near Haddington, also had 200 volumes in its library, established in 1793, which was dependent on the support of the richer people. Other towns which followed the late eighteenth-century trend were Campbeltown, in Argyll (where the minister commented that controversial books were read with avidity by the common people in Scotland), Kelso, Roxburghshire, Cambusnethan, Lanarkshire, and, as might be expected, Perth, which had a general library, well supplied with books, especially on history, as well as a collection of books in the Literary and Antiquarian Society, founded in 1784.[13]

The most remarkable of the mid- to late-eighteenth-century Scottish public libraries was at Innerpeffray, near Crieff in Perthshire. For the social historian concerned with the number of readers and the nature of their reading, the survival of the eighteenth-century Innerpeffray borrowing registers is an enormous boon. From that register, it is clear that the Library operated from at least 1747 as a lending library, and the following range of occupations (in alphabetical order) took advantage of its facilities: barber, bookseller, (army) captain, Cooper, dyer, dyer's apprentice, factor, farmer, flaxdresser, gardener, glover, mason, merchant, miller, minister, quarrier, schoolmaster, servant, shoemaker, students (of various subjects), smith, surgeon, surgeon's apprentice, tailor, watchmaker, weaver and wright. The books they borrowed were not all, by any means, religious but included popular as well as 'enlightened' works of the day such as William Robertson's *History of Charles V,* Locke's *Works* and Buffon's *Natural History*. Out of the 370 loans made between 1747 and 1800 199 were of non-religious books, namely works of history, law and politics, literature, agriculture, travel, mathematics and science, and other miscellaneous works.[14] Innerpeffray Library's borrowing register shows the capacity of ordinary people in central, lowland Scotland of the mid- to late-eighteenth-century to support and countenance an intellectual movement in the university towns and cities. If William Robertson, regarded as one of the great European intellectuals of his day, was regularly read by artisans in Perthshire, the intellectual elite of Scotland were not operating in a sphere totally above that of their fellow countrymen.

Before any employment or profit might be given to the printers and publishers, and before any of the libraries had books to lend, there were schools to teach reading. Observations on the Scottish educational system have already been made. In the mid- to late-eighteenth century it appears that, in the opinion of the parish ministers, there was still a fairly general interest in school provision and in the importance of education. The *Statistical Account* had much to say about schools: in Renfrew, for example, the minister commented that not only tradesmen, but even day labourers, gave their children a good education. There was scarcely a boy who was not taught reading, writing, arithmetic, and a little church music. Similarly, the minister at Leadhills noted that there was a very good school in the place. Even as far north as Petty, Inverness-shire, where the school was built in 1784, a great number of scholars attended the school, as even the poorest people were becoming sensible of the importance of giving some education to their children. At Cleish, Kinross-shire, there was scarcely an eight or nine year old who could not read quite well. From the beginning of the eighteenth century, there were four schools in the Barony of Glasgow, Lanarkshire, and education was so inexpensive that it was not beyond the access of the poorest. In Coupar Angus, where the school was rebuilt in 1792, sixty scholars from 520 families in Coupar itself attended.

As to the purpose of education, the minister of Auchtertoul wrote in tones consonant with those of the Enlightenment thinkers that education was of prime importance in a well-regulated state because it made man the superior animal, advanced his happiness and interests, brought political blessings such as good and stable government and countered forces that tended to anarchy.

Occasionally the impact of the Enlightenment itself can be discerned, as in the case of the western isles of Gigha and Cara, where the minister, Rev. William Fraser, who had been educated in Aberdeen, showed a distinct comprehension of the division of labour, which Smith and others had elaborated in the prime of the Scottish Enlightenment. Fraser was concerned that, while his parishioners might not merit being called industrious, neither were they lazy: 'Division of labour, which is the highest improvement in society has not yet been carried to such a length, as to entitle the people of Gigha to the character of being industrious'. There was no market to stimulate the farmers to produce more, everyone worked to supply all their own wants, and entire attention could not be given to individual professions; even the shoemaker, the smith, and the tailor had also to farm and fish to keep their families.

Families had to be attended to, employment was not constant, returns for labour were not punctual, and no one thought of making fishing, which was open to all, a profession, so that industry and improvement were held back. The time taken between the different occupations was almost equal to the actual time given to labour, and all the Western Isles were in a similar situation. Their inhabitants were not lazy but they could not be compared with the lowlanders, who were 'accustomed to a proper division of labour and to marketing their products'.

In conclusion, therefore, it can fairly be said that Scotland's age of improvement was not only to be seen in economic (mainly agricultural) terms, but also in the whole social and economic enterprise that has broadly been defined here as literacy. In the lowland central belt fairly general provision appears to have been made for educational advance, for reading and for a perceptible increase from the seventeenth to the late eighteeneth centuries in the amount of paper manufactured and books printed. No wonder Edinburgh was to be called the Birmingham of literature. [16] On the evidence here presented, it is only remarkable that a county town such as Perth, little known perhaps before the railway age, should not have merited the same description. What is evident is that, on the basis of seventeenth-century developments, a society sympathetic to knowledge had grown up, and had become secularised in the eighteenth century, so that many people had graduated from reading bibles (as Defoe had seen in early-eighteenth-century crowds) and were now aspiring to Buffon.

II

To a recent historian of Scotland, the building of a new town in Edinburgh from the mid-eighteenth century 'was the cold, clear and beautiful expression of the rational confidence of the eighteenth-century middle-class'. For David Daiches, the same construction was the realisation of the heavenly city of the philosophers in stone.[17] Certainly, the plans to build the Edinburgh New Town and the first steps in the realisation of those plans coincided with the beginning of the heyday of the Scottish Enlightenment. However, there is ample argument to suggest that the link was coincidental, not that the New Town was the architectural expression of an otherwise predominantly philosophic movement. For many decades the Town Council had been aware of the need of some major developments which would once again bring both dignity and wealth to the Scottish capital, and, by 1752,

they had already set in motion such other schemes as the development
of the town's colleges and medical school. The purpose of examining
the construction of the New Town, and its consequential effects, is to
illustrate how economic motives could intimately affect the Scottish
Enlightenment, to a degree sufficient even to cause later historians to
see the Enlightenment and the New Town as coincidental. There
follows, as a result, an attempt to correct the record, and to point up
the thin line between improvement and enlightenment as well as the
interaction of the Enlightenment with society. The other object is to
discuss the social background to the Enlightenment in Edinburgh,
with the intention not of compounding the past imbalance whereby
studies of the Scottish Enlightenment have been, in fact, studies of the
Edinburgh Enlightenment, nor simply of repeating what has often
been written. Rather the objective is to recognise Edinburgh's importance as one of the settings, as the centre where the lawyers, for
example, could display the increasing wealth and influence that they
had in mid-eighteenth-century Scotland, and to facilitate a definition
of the Scottish Enlightenment by arguing that the 'making of classical
Edinburgh' was not part of it.

   *The Proposals for carrying on certain Public Works in the City of
Edinburgh* (hereafter referred to as the *Proposals*) emerged from a
meeting of the Convention of Royal Burghs held on 8 July 1752, and
were published as a pamphlet which is still extant. The Convention,
which dated from the sixteenth century, was one of the few institutions of Scottish society which, under Article 21, survived intact the
Treaty of Union. The sixty-six Royal Burghs were those which, like
all self-regulating Scottish burghs, had privileges granted by the King
enabling them to promote trade within and without their boundaries.
They had greater commercial privileges than other burghs, which included dealing with imports and exports. In the area immediately surround-
ing a royal burgh only its burgesses might do business, and only a royal
burgh was entitled, in the days before the union of parliaments, to be
represented separately in the Scottish parliament. Before and after the
Treaty of Union, only royal burghs might send commissioners to the
Convention of Royal Burghs, which was a body that legislated on
economic and financial matters of interest to them all. In other words,
it is important to note that the Convention was essentially a self-
protecting commercial organisation and any resolutions it might make
would be designed to promote the financial well-being of its members.

   The motivation behind the proposals to build Edinburgh New Town
lay ostensibly in Edinburgh's lack of appointments: there was no

meeting room suitable for the annual Convention of Royal Burghs, no reception room for dignitaries, no robing nor retiring room for the judges of the courts of Session and Exchequer, no offices for various senior legal officials. The Lord Register's office was now too small for all the records and papers which required to be housed, and one room in particular was not suitable for the purpose because of dampness. The reputable lawyers' library was increasing in size and yet had no appropriate quarters; there was no merchants' exchange in which people of business might meet; there were no roads or bridges to connect the town with those fields to the south and north that were suitable for building development. The most important motive of all was not stated, namely that the old town was overcrowded and insanitary, and in need of expansion. But then physical expansion to accommodate a larger population of all classes was not, of itself, an investment leading to higher profits for legal and commercial gentlemen.

The Convention believed that 1752 was the best opportunity for remedying Edinburgh's deficiencies, because many appropriate sites for the required buildings were in a ruined state or in the hands of the Edinburgh magistrates who were quite willing to hand them over for the specified purposes. To carry out the undertakings, it was proposed that a voluntary subscription be raised to cover the cost and that the scheme be conducted by thirty-three directors, three chosen by the Senators of the College of Justice, two by the Barons of Exchequer (guardians of the Crown revenue in Scotland), three by the Faculty of Advocates, three by the Clerks to the Signet, ten by those who subscribed £5, eight by the Magistrates and Town Council of Edinburgh, with four *ex officio* directors being the Lord Provost, the Dean of Guild, the Treasurer, and Deacon-Convenor. It can be seen that just as the defined needs of Edinburgh were seen to be in legal and commercial quarters, so the Directors were very largely to be found from amongst the legal and commercial men of the City.

The practical delineation of what was required and who would see the scheme realised was accompanied by a more than thirty-page justification of the plan, which was the burden of the *Proposals*. The justification revealed even more the self-interested legal and commercial motives behind the plans of the Convention. The *Proposals* also demonstrated the lawyers' and merchants' sense of inferiority in economic matters to England and a desire to raise Scotland to a supposed level with other European countries. Consider the contents of the document: they began with the theory that the facilities and beauty of a capital city could percolate prosperity down throughout a nation and should naturally become the centre of trade and commerce, of learning and the arts, of politeness, and of refinement of every kind. London was given as the most striking example of this notion, yet when London was described it appears to bear no relation to that sink of dirt, disease and delinquency which has since been described so graphically by historians of the eighteenth century English capital: 'we cannot fail to remark its healthful, unconfined situation, upon a large plain, gently shelving towards the Thames'. The presence in London of those very facilities which Edinburgh lacked was pointed up, the commodious family houses, wide streets, bridges, a merchants' exchange, courts of justice, the theatre. Indeed, Edinburgh was compared very unfavourably with London, as well it might have been, not least because Edinburgh citizens had the habit of throwing 'foul water, filth, dirt and other nastiness' out of their windows, and because all urban refuse, butchers' offal and other town guano flowed down from the hill on which the town was built into the North Loch, a foul pool that occupied the present site of Princes Street gardens. As John Wesley commented of the city in 1759, 'How long shall the capital city of Scotland, yea, and the chief street of it, stink worse than a common sewer?'[18]

However, the following statement that 'To enlarge and improve this city, to adorn it with public buildings, which may be a national benefit, and thereby to remove at least in some degree, the inconveniences to which it has hitherto been liable, is the sole subject of these proposals' masks the self-interested motives for developing Edinburgh on the part of the capital's legal and commercial men. A lengthy, historical consideration of Scotland's trade and commerce, and a review of the trading relationship of Scotland and England followed on immediately after the expression of the objective. For example, the *Proposals* noted that, after the Union of the Crowns, Scotland was little better than a conquered province. The nation was dispirited; the little trade there was languished and decayed; and England discouraged every proposal. The beneficial effects on trade of the union of the parliaments was then delineated. If the sole object of the *Proposals* had been to provide grand public buildings to boost the dignity of the City, it seems unlikely that so much space would immediately have been given to trade considerations. The professed objective in carrying out constructional activity was followed by a long history of Scottish trading fortunes, how they recovered after the union of the parliaments, and because the Treaty of Union specified that certain funds were to be set aside to promote Scottish fisheries, manufactures and trade. It was pointed out how the provision in the treaty was neglected for some twenty years and how it took until 1727, when the first trustees of the money were appointed, before a better spirit began everywhere to exert itself. Yet, the success of the trustees in promoting economic life was minimal in Edinburgh and its neighbourhood until after the quelling of the Jacobite rebellion in 1746. Then, progress was rapidly achieved in trade, husbandry and manufacture, and the whole nation, not just individual towns, exerted itself.

To support these assertions, the *Proposals* continued by detailing the improved fortunes of the linen trade in the eighteenth century, of the malt and distilling industries, and the increase in tonnage of shipping belonging to the port of Leith. And in the face of such an economy and such an economic performance, the state of the capital city, Edinburgh, was seen to be particularly mean. It seemed a most appropriate point in time to remedy that deficiency, and the buildings that were required were all detailed, namely a merchants' exchange, accommodation for the law courts and other legal departments, the Convention of Royal Burghs and the town council. The arguments for each of the buildings were all rehearsed: Edinburgh was the only city which pretended to an extensive trade which had no exchange. The merchants met in the streets to carry out their negotiations in public, amid passing coaches, carriages and people. The inevitable contrast with London was given, how prior to 1566 London merchants met in Lombard Street until Sir Thomas Gresham built at his own expense, the Royal Exchange.

The Advocates' Library was of too great a value to Scotland not to merit a new building, let alone the number of books and valuable historical manuscripts it contained which were beginning to exceed existing accommodation. A long list of different kinds of legal register was given, the records of the Kingdom of Scotland, the acts and proceedings of the Scottish Parliament, the registers of Seisins, Incumbrances, the Signet Office, Privy Seal and Chancery, and the inconceivably bulky records of the Clerks of Session. The bulk had swelled in relatively recent years not least by the enormous number of land transactions, transactions which had also so swelled the incomes of Edinburgh lawyers that they sought more commodious domestic and business premises which would not be paid for by them, but which would match their new-found wealth. Furthermore, there remained unopened, for want of room, ten hogshead of papers, which, with the other records, had been taken away by Oliver Cromwell, and were brought back from London in 1660; various records were scattered in rented property all over the town and not the least of the dangers to which they were susceptible was fire.

The *Proposals* recommended the enlargement of the town, not because of the crowded and insanitary state in which the mass of ordinary Edinburgh citizens were required to live, but because the city should be made attractive to the Scottish aristocracy. Few of them had moved to London since the Treaty of Union, and when others of them visited the British capital their expenditure was a financial drain that Scotland could ill afford. If Edinburgh were made more congenial for them, people of rank would hardly prefer an obscure life at London, to the splendour and influence with which they might reside at home. The argument was continued in a vein wholly constant with the burden of the *Proposals:*

> Wealth is only to be obtained by trade and commerce, and these are only carried on to advantage in populous cities. There also we find the chief objects of pleasure and ambition, and there consequently all those will flock whose circumstances can afford it. But can we expect, that persons of fortune in Scotland will exchange the handsome seats they generally possess in the country, for the scanty lodging, and paltry accommodations they must put up with in Edinburgh?

So the presence of the native aristocracy would buttress the commercial activities of the City and, lest anyone might fear that moving the centre of gravity of Edinburgh would cause the old centre to be deserted, commercial good sense would prevent that:

> People of fortune, and of a certain rank, will probably chuse to build upon the fine fields which lie to the north and south of the town: but men of professions and business of every kind, will still incline to live in the neighbourhood of the exchange, of the courts of justice, and other places of public resort; and the number of this last class of men will increase in a much greater proportion, than that of the former.

It will be seen later that these were pious hopes and the increasingly well-to-do lawyers soon moved in to the spacious accommodation of the New Town.

The *Proposals* gave several examples from other contemporary European cities (Turin, Berlin) and from history (Venice, Genoa) of the kind of economic and social developments which were seen to spring from such plans as were being suggested: the greater consumption of products and rapid circulation of money would increase prosperity generally, and raise the level of trade, land prices and general morale.

The document voiced the opinion that now peace was generally established in Scotland, now that the rage of faction had been dispersed, no more peaceful exercise than the development of the capital city could be undertaken. The authors likened the situation of mid-eighteenth-century Scotland to that of Elizabethan England, called for the same busy, patriotic spirit, and concluded with the following rhetorical flourish:

In the reign of Queen Elizabeth, England was but a forming state, as Scotland is now. It was then that the spirit of the English began to exert itself. Ships were fitted out, navy fleets were equipped by private gentlemen. In the same manner public buildings were erected, colonies were settled, and new discoveries made. In a lesser degree, the same disposition begins to discover itself in this country. Building bridges, repairing high-roads, establishing manufactures, forming commercial companies, and opening new veins of trade, are employments which have already thrown a lustre upon some of the first names of this country. The little detail of an established commerce, may ingross the attention of the merchant: but it is prosecution of greater objects, that the leading men of a country ought to exert their power and influence. And what greater object can be presented to their view, than that of enlarging, beautifying, and improving the capital of their native country? What can redound more to their own honour? What prove more beneficial to Scotland and by consequence, to a United Britain?

Thus concluded a thoroughgoing commercial call to action. No hint was given that the building of a glorious capital was related to the age of distinguished letters of which Scotland was on the eve in 1752. There was no consciousness then of constructing 'the Athens of the North'. Rather were Edinburgh's legal and businessmen unashamedly calling upon the nation to finance accommodation which would make the carrying out of their business more pleasant, convenient and profitable. They were seeking the support of the Scottish aristocracy in the venture, rather as the dignified element in Scottish society (to anticipate Walter Bagehot's nineteenth-century constitutional terminology) who would evoke money and co-operation for the schemes which would duly be used for the profit and comfort of the efficient element in Scottish economic life. There is no hint that the New Town or the functional buildings should necessarily be masterpieces of architecture, so that if Edinburgh was a heavenly city for the philosophers it was not so by design. The public works proposed for Edinburgh in 1752 were either to help line the pockets of the Edinburgh traders, or to facilitate the business and provide handsome dwellings for the increasingly powerful and wealthy Edinburgh lawyers. No idealistic or architectural vision was in the minds of the initiators. Nonetheless as will be seen, the very construction of the type of new town and buildings did create an ambience and economic mechanisms which attracted and maintained the writers of the Scottish Enlightenment, and caused them to prosper. This was not, however, planned by the burgesses and tradesmen of the Edinburgh City Council. Their fellows in the other royal burghs subscribed £1,500 for the undertaking through the Convention, although the paucity of that sum can be seen when the cost of the Royal Exchange building alone, £31,457, is borne in mind.[19]

So the Edinburgh New Town was built and the story of its development between 1750 and 1840 has been told by Professor A.J. Youngson in *The Making of Classical Edinburgh*.[20] Competitions for designs and plans were held; publicly and privately financed schemes were undertaken and fine buildings, of a domestic, public and business nature, arose. Even to this day, residences are quite common in some parts of central, Georgian Edinburgh, though many town houses are rapidly surrendering to that commercial spirit that lay behind Edinburgh's development in the first place, and are being converted into offices. The most celebrated plan was that of James Craig whereby two squares (Charlotte Square in the west, St. Andrew's in the east) were to be linked by three wide parallel streets (Queen Street being to the north, George Street in the middle and Princes Street to the south). The symmetry was to be maintained by building a church in each square, one on the west side of Charlotte Square, the other on the east side of St Andrew Square. The first of these churches was duly constructed, but the site for the second was found to be occupied by the mansion of one Sir Laurence Dundas, who had moved quickly to ensure that one of the finest New Town situations and buildings should not be supplanted by a church; thus was the symmetry ruined. Personal desires early asserted superiority over town planning.

In general, feelings then and now about the architecture and plan-

ning of the New Town have been mixed. The nineteenth-century
Scottish judge and Whig, Henry Cockburn, in his *Memorials,* was one
of those who felt that the contrast between the crowded wynds of the
old town and the long straight lines of new town streets was too stark
and his views are worth quoting at length:

> Our escape from the old town gave us an unfortunate propensity to
> avoid whatever had distinguished the place we had fled from. Hence
> we were led into the blunder of long straight lines of street, divided
> to an inch, and all to the same number of inches, by rectangular
> intersections, every house being an exact duplicate of its neighbour
> with a dexterous avoidance, as if from horror, of every ornament
> or excrescence by which the slightest break might vary the surface.
> What a site did nature give us for our New Town! Yet what insig-
> nificance in its plan! What poverty in all its details!

He considered that Scottish architecture in the hundred years after the
Union was deplorable, not least in its tendency to extinguish all that
was picturesque and to reduce everything to dullness and bald uniformity. Ancestral and contemporary European examples were rejected.
Indeed, when there was a divergence in New Town architecture, it
caused a wonderful effect on people, so that people went to stare at
Abercromby Place, the first curved street.

Cockburn also bemoaned another accompaniment to New Town
building:

> We massacre every town tree that comes in a mason's way; never
> sacrificing mortar to foliage . . . I do not know a single instance in
> which the square and the line have been compelled to accommodate
> themselves to stems and branches . . . and there was no Scotch city
> more strikingly graced with individual trees and by groups of
> them than Edinburgh, since I knew it, used to be . . . But the sad
> truth is that the extinction of foliage, and the unbroken display
> of their bright free-stone, is of itself a first object with both our
> masons and their employers . . . It is our horror of the direct com-
> bination of trees with masonry, and our incapacity to effect it,
> that I complain of.[21]

Others thought Craig's plan to be unoriginal and the other private
developments in the City to be haphazard and whimsical. Yet others
bemoaned the destruction of the older ports and porches which

accompanied demolition when space in the old town was cleared for new buildings.[22] Nonetheless, Edinburgh New Town, from Craig's plan in the centre to the Moray developments in the west, was a major architectural achievement, and one which houses some of the finest Georgian and classical designs, such as those of Robert Adam, whose most celebrated work in Edinburgh was probably the north side of Charlotte Square.

The man who presided over the major development and extensions of the City of Edinburgh was George Drummond (1687–1766). He was Lord Provost no less than six times during his life and was responsible for several new ventures in the City: the Royal Infirmary, founded in 1729, the Royal Exchange in the old town, the New Town, and the establishment of chairs in the University. He has been said to have been more alive to the social reforms necessary in his day than endowed with aesthetic tastes for the beautiful in the buildings he erected.[23] The Town Council over which he presided for so much of the eighteenth century was exclusively elected by and composed of merchants and tradesmen. Other significant sections of the Edinburgh population, such as professors, physicians and men of letters, had no place on it and can, therefore, be said to have influenced developments in the City only marginally in its highest counsels.[24] The Town Council also elected its successor at the end of its period of office and was, therefore, self-perpetuating. Drummond was assisted in his Edinburgh public works venture by the author of the *Proposals* who was a lawyer. Sir Gilbert Elliot, a Lord of Justiciary and appointed a director of the scheme by the Court of Session.[24] The hopes, dreams and ambitions of this accountant and lawyer appear to have been realised, if posterity judges from letters which William Creech, the bookseller to the philosophers of the Enlightenment, wrote to Sir John Sinclair on the occasion of the compilation of the *Statistical Account.*[26]

Creech was struck by the immense changes that had taken place in the city of Edinburgh in the twenty years between 1763 and 1783, and, in some instances, during the following ten years. He took 1763 as being the last year in which the City still maintained its traditional appearance and extent, and 1793 was the year in which the *Letters* were first published. Modern man assumes that it is only in the twentieth century that the appearance and size of a town, and the occupations and recreations of its inhabitants, can be so revolutionised in the space of twenty or thirty years. Creech's *Letters* belie that assumption. Further, it is clear from them that the public works that were being carred on in Edinburgh bore no small responsibility for the pace and character of the changes.

One of the first points Creech noted was the end of the old town pattern of residence whereby representatives of all classes of society might be found living in apartments off a common stair in the closes and wynds of the High Street.[27] Such shoulder rubbing of peer, preacher and pauper gave way to the more modern pattern of residential segregation by class, income or occupation. By 1783, for example, it was quite clear that the lawyers were moving to expensive and fashionable New Town houses that the *Proposals* had envisaged would be the domains of the aristocracy. To quote Creech, 'In 1763 people of quality and fashion lived in houses, which, in 1783, were inhabited by tradesmen or by people in humble and ordinary life. The Lord Justice Tinwald's house was possessed by a French teacher — Lord President Craigie's by a Rouping wife or Sales-woman of old furniture'.[28] Further evidence of the same trend has been adduced by Professor Youngson from his analysis of Peter Williamson's *Street Directory of Edinburgh,* feu charters and vassalage books. Whereas in the mid-1770s only one out of dozens of those powerful and influential Writers to the Signet, and one advocate, lived in the New Town, by the late 1780s, the majority, some two-thirds, did so. To take one example, in Heriot Row, to this day peopled heavily by lawyers, they took a third of the first twenty-seven feuings, and in other prominent streets they built a quarter or a fifth of the houses for themselves.[29]

The move to the New Town became fairly common among all the well-to-do in the last quarter of the eighteenth century. A wheelwright owned a house in 1793 that at the Union had belonged to the Duke of Douglas; an ironmonger now possessed the house of the late President Dundas; a tailor now inhabited the dwelling of one of the Lords of Session. Titles became twice as common in the list of New Town addresses, George Street, Princes Street, Frederick Street, Thistle Street and, especially, in St Andrew Square, so that only a minority of the aristocracy by the 1790s were still living in or near the Royal Mile. The law and the aristocracy together predominated amongst the new townsmen, above all other groups.[30] Consequent upon the creation of a fashionable quarter of the City came a multiplicity of changes in customs and modes of behaviour. In 1763, for example, people of tone dined at two o'clock, having closed their shops at one o'clock, and they resumed their business in the afternoon. Wine was seldom to be seen at the tables of the middle rank. Gentlemen attended ladies' drawing-rooms for tea, and mixed and conversed with them. In the 1780s and 1790s, however, the fashionable and bourgeois classes dined at four or five o'clock:

> No business was done in the afternoon, dinner of itself having
> become a very serious business . . . Every tradesman in decent cir-
> cumstances presents wine after dinner; and many in plenty and
> variety . . . The drawing-rooms were totally deserted; invitations to
> tea in the afternoons were given up; and the only opportunity gentle-
> men had of being in ladies' company, was when they happened to
> mess together at dinner or supper; and even then an impatience
> was sometimes shewn, till the ladies retired. Card parties, after a
> long dinner; —and also after a late supper were frequent.[31]

In terms of peoples' appearance, no such profession as haberdasher was
known in 1763; there were no perfumers and only a few hairdressers. In
the 1780s, almost the commonest profession in Edinburgh was that of
haberdasher, including mercer, milliner, linen-draper, hatter, hosier,
glover and many others. The number had multiplied even more since
then. Perfumers had fine shops in the principal streets; they advertised
the keeping of bears, which were killed to provide grease for ladies'
and gentlemen's hair, bear fat being superior for that purpose to that
of any other animal. Hairdressers had tripled in number, and their
previous reluctance to work on a Sunday had given way to Sunday
becoming their busiest day. Barbers and wigmakers were not only
numerous but were not numbered among the burgesses of the
City.[32]

The quality of life in Edinburgh changed in many ways, not least
in the character and type of entertainment that became available as the
town developed. In 1788 a circus was built to exhibit feats of horse-
manship and pantomimes. Four years later it was converted into a
playhouse and Edinburgh had two regular theatres. Times changed
from 1763, when Rev. John Home had been suspended for writing his
play, *Douglas,* and when Saturday night was considered the most improper in the week for playgoing. In the 1780s, no one considered the
morality or otherwise of stage plays; Saturday was the most popular
night of the week and boxes for the night were booked for a season:
the galleries always applauded what they formerly would have hissed
as improper in sentiment or decorum.[33] Dancing and appropriate
dress for dancing underwent a revolution. Whereas minuets, country
dancing, strict regularity in dress and decorum, and great dignity of
manners were the rule of 1763, in the 1780s and 1790s the provision
of more space for dancing coincided with the abolition of minuets,

the substitution of romps for country dances, and the neglect of dress, and men went inebriated on wine from the tavern to assemblies of as elegant and beautiful women as any in Europe. Early fixed hours for dancing (6 p.m.–11 p.m.) were replaced by 'the young Masters and Misses, who would have been mortified not to have seen out the ball, thus returned home at three or four in the morning, and yawned and gaped, and complained of headaches all the next day'. Private balls and elegant suppers thereafter, ending at dawn, were highly fashionable. By the 1790s concerts were the most crowded places of amusement, whereas earlier only the subscribers tended to go.[34]

The number of newspapers in Edinburgh trebled between 1760 and 1790, despite the duty levied on them, which might have been compensated by the large number of advertisements they contained. Clearly, the city's population and activities permitted the survival of such a press. The communications with the outside world also developed rapidly in the late-eighteenth century: few stage coaches left Edinburgh in 1763 and only one a month for London. By 1783, six every half hour, rather than two every hour, went to Leith and conveyances to every considerable town in Scotland now existed. Fifteen coaches a week went to London in a quarter of the time (four instead of sixteen days). Within Edinburgh itself, by 1783 many and elegant hackney-chariots had replaced those considered Britain's worst in 1763. Private citizens such as merchants, physicians and surgeons came to keep their own carriages in increasing numbers, and even ministers did so.

The Moderate clergyman, Alexander Carlyle, wrote that Edinburgh's size and geographical position made it possible for Hume or Smith or Robertson or Ferguson to assemble together from the country in a tavern by 9 p.m., the chief time of convivial entertainment in 1760.[35] That ministers had joined the carriage-keeping class was due in no small measure, Creech believed, to their literary abilities. Many ministers were among the ranks of the intellectuals, and the rise of authors acquiring money by their writings, was another feature of the late-eighteenth century. Creech noted, too, the contemporary foundation of magnificent new buildings for the University and its general prosperity in terms of student numbers. He also pointed to several other features of Edinburgh's improved economic life: the establishment in 1786 of a Chamber of Commerce and, in 1790, a society for the improvement of wool. The increase and development of paper-mills in the Edinburgh area was seen earlier; to support these and other ventures were the local banks which, on the whole, appear to have prospered. In 1763, Royal Bank of Scotland stock sold at the rate of £160 per cent, whereas by 1791 it was selling for £240 per cent. The Bank of Scotland was permitted to double its capital by an Act of Parliament in the 1790s, and the British Linen Company's stock which, in 1763 was 40 per cent below par, sold, in 1792, for over £162 per cent. The port of Leith likewise entered a boom period in the latter part of the eighteenth century: shore dues multiplied by eight; the number of sailings to and from England and the Baltic ports increased from a few to hundreds. The amount of soap and candles manufactured and exported increased massively. The increased tonnage of Leith shipping was such the the harbour was having to be enlarged. The markets now sold immense quantities of strawberries in season and fresh vegetables and provisions, which compared most favourable with the 1760s, when Musselburgh supplied Edinburgh and the Musselburgh women sold the foods from baskets on their backs and were easily exhausted of supplies if there was any sudden increase in demand. The improved provision meant that at Leith, the Jamaica fleet, dreadfully afflicted with scurvy, was soon restored to health by the plentiful supplies.[36] Creech also remarked, in his economic observations, that the new custom of using an umbrella had led to the opening of a number of umbrella warehouses, the conducting of a considerable trade in umbrellas, and, consequent upon the improved communications, the spread of the fashion throughout Scotland.

Creech would not have been such a typical eighteenth-century Scot if he had not inserted a mixture of philosophic history and calvinistic caution mid-way through his comparisons to the effect that as nations grew more wealthy so they inclined to decadence.[37] The sentiments were akin to many expressed by clergy in the *Statistical Account*. For Creech, such decay was evident in the alteration of the dress of maids, whose wages in 1763 and 1783 were the same, but who had changed their dress from blue or red cloaks or plaids to dresses as fine as their mistresses'. More seriously, the accompaniment of opulence and decay was to be seen in the neglect of church-going, especially by men, in 1783 as compared with 1763, the degeneration of Sunday into a day of relaxation, and the abandonment of the practice whereby families took their domestics to church with them. Indeed, at the times of services, the behaviour in the streets was loose and riotous. Not lease to blame for the decay were the clergy, who now ceased to visit, catechise and instruct, and were content to leave in ignorance those who did not attend church. The church censure

of adultery was not used, and divorces and separations were more
common. Divorced women were happily received back into fashionable
society. Fines collected by the Church for illegitimate children had
trebled. The number of brothels had increased twenty-fold and the
number of prostitutes by a hundred times: whereas in 1763, a person
might have gone from the Castle to Holyroodhouse, 'the then length of
the city' at any hour of the night, without being accosted by a single
street-walker, now every part of the city and suburbs was infested
with multitudes of vicious females, a great many of whom were too
young to know right from wrong. Young ladies were consequently not
allowed on the streets unattended. Other forms of crime such as theft,
street robbery and pickpocketing had also increased. Cock-fighting,
previously unknown, was common in 1783 and a regular cockpit had
been built; in 1790, a professional bruiser opened a school of boxing,
which 'branch of education does not correspond with the mild genius
of Christianity, which we profess; and it can be looked on only with
pity, even when practised among savages and barbarians'. swearing had
increased greatly among the lower orders. To counterbalance the
nostalgia for former times made evident in his observations, Creech did
remark that intemperance had declined among the genteel: hospitality
had much increased, and excess on the occasions of it had much
decreased. Creech could not suppress all his prejudices, however, and he
found that the sobriety and decorum of the lower orders on the
occasion of the King's birthday and Hogmanay, which in 1763 were
attended with peace and harmony, in 1783 were devoted to drunken-
ness, folly and riot.

As for young people, boys were by the 1790s frequenting taverns
too often and behaving insolently as a result. Apprentices' behaviour
was not checked by their masters, who no longer had them stay in
their homes. An equally sad decline in the conception of their
duty was evident among the girls: whereas in 1763 their education
and attention were devoted solely to domestic duties, in the 1780s and
1790s, a housekeeper was employed by tradesmen to undertake them.
Their daughters spent all morning on their appearance and other time
reading from the circulating library or being taught music at great
expense, whether or not they liked it. An interesting change had taken
place in the meaning of 'fine fellow': whereas in 1763 it denoted an
accomplished, well-mannered, moral man of principle, by 1783 it denoted one who could drink three bottles, who swore, seduced, ridiculed
religion and who was active in all the fashionable follies.[38]
Despite these largely unfavourable comparisons, Creech had none-

theless to admit that the amenity of the City had much improved. Strangers coming to Edinburgh need no longer find a lack of hotels and have to put up at an uncomfortable or dirty inn, but might now find many public hotels with luxurious and princely accommodation. More important, especially in view of Edinburgh's earlier insanitary state a new iron pipe of five inches diameter was laid in 1787 to bring spring water to the increased number of Edinburgh citizens. A pipe of seven inches was laid in 1790, taking in three springs, three miles further south of the City, and a new reservoir was built.[39] In general, Edinburgh had become in a very short time a prosperous and fashionable city, with all the vices and virtues of any other European town at the time. It had responded to the blows delivered to its status as a capital by the departure of both Crown and Parliament by developing the mechanisms and ambience required to take advantage of increased business, trade and commerce. The enormous growth in the number of private teachers of a wide range of subjects, including the social graces, also testified to the development of 'fashionable' Edinburgh. In the City could be learned not only reading, writing and arithmetic but classical and modern languages, geography, navigation, surveying, dancing, fencing, music, cookery and art.[40] By 1826, when the Enlightenment was over, Walter Scott suggests that an income of £3,000 a year in Edinburgh was opulence, £2,000 brought ease and wealth, £1,000 'a handsome competence' and £500, well managed, would maintain a large family with all the necessaries and decencies of life, and permit them to take quite a high place in society.[41]

Yet the intimate character of the City, which had been prompted earlier in the Age of Enlightenment by the crowded pattern of Old Town living, was maintained when Edinburgh broke her bounds and when wealth tended to reside in the New Town. Outside of Edinburgh, geography was in no way responsible for the intimacy of the central, lowland, urban area in which the Scottish Enlightenment thrived. Common interests also bound together those that participated in and contributed to the Enlightenment. Edinburgh was where the General Assembly of the Kirk was held and was the pivot of the Scottish legal system, where the Courts were housed. The City also maintained the leading Scottish university and medical school of the day. Hence were congregated in the City, particular professions, all of which had a university education in common. Shared intellectual interests and pursuits led to the formation of learned societies in eighteenth-century Edinburgh, where divines, doctors, advocates and professors met for mutual cerebral stimulation. As they were similar kinds of people, they also enjoyed relaxing together and formed many a social club, alongside more serious corporate organisations. The old town taverns became favourite haunts and meeting places.

The common bond of a university education was not the only spur to intimacy among the social groups on which the Enlightenment depended. There were close familial, social and economic links between the aristocrats and lawyers: it has been shown how in the years 1707-51, 96 per cent of those entering the Faculty of Advocates were either from landed families, or had close connections with landed families. The percentage was 88 for 1752 to 1811. It has similarly been shown that one half or more new Writers to the Signet came from legal or gentry families.[42] The prosperity of the landed and legal gentlemen was linked, for the successful prosecution of agricultural improvement meant, for the nobility or gentry, the financial ability to own and maintain a New Town house. As more and more conveyancing was required for landowners undertaking land consolidation, so the lawyers would profit, and in their turn, be able to afford similar accommodation.

Churchmen and professors were closely associated, not only because churchmen were also often professors, but because of contacts between the Faculty of Divinity and the Church, and because in the age of High Enlightenment, the Church leadership was taken by a group that was open-minded on intellectual matters and numbered authors in its ranks. Lawyers and professors shared a similar relationship through the existence of the Law faculty, but the more intimate connection between them lay in shared intellectual concerns. Most of the philosophical thinkers were professors; those that were not were more than likely in the legal profession. Their prime concern was the science of society, whereby the adaptation of social arrangements to the changing circumstances of mankind was studied historically. Law was closely connected with most social arrangements; the regular revision of Law so that it was in tune with human circumstances, was vital. Hence, lawyers, such as Lord Kames and John Millar, were prominent among the writers of the Scottish Enlightenment. The association between law and moral philosophy was mutually enriching. Societies were a forum where the interchange between legal and professional men of letters could take place. The presence of a university in three major Scottish towns was a powerful stimulus to the cementing together of influential social and economic groups. Intimacy was forged by identity of interests.

Edinburgh was not a city of manufactures, even though those responsible for its tone and spirit were highly motivated towards com-

mercial objectives. In 1835, when overspending by the Town Council
(not least on the New Town) led to the city's bankruptcy, it was proposed by the city fathers that manufactures be introduced. Henry
Cockburn's reaction to the suggestion was predictable; it led him, in
his *Journal*, to remember the glorious days and he almost envisaged
the great men turning in their graves. He did not believe that the city
whose law, college and church had almost subsided, could be excited
by steam:

> We must try to survive on better grounds, on our advantages as the
> metropolis, our adaptation for education, our literary fame,
> and especially on the glories of our external position and features;
> improved by the bluish smoke of human habitation, and undimmed
> by the black dirty clouds from manufactures, the absence of which
> is one of the principal charms of our situation.[43]

Thinkers had not only thrived but had been attracted by the wealth,
congeniality and security generated by the social and economic developments in Edinburgh. The congregation in Edinburgh of Lawyers,
churchmen, physicians and professors of like minds, made the city a
particularly pleasant place for them to live and work. The societies and
taverns mingled work with pleasure. Furthermore, various accompani-
ments to the developments of the commercial and fashionable Scottish
capital worked to the profit of the thinkers: publishers and booksellers
began to abound and to offer substantial advances for their works. The
publishers' and booksellers' businesses, such as those of Creech and
later Archibald Constable, were closely related to the increase in printing houses and paper manufacture.

In the eighteenth century the terms bookseller and publisher were
not used in the exclusive sense of the twentieth century; nor was there
such a clear division of labour between them. The bookseller would
transfer manuscripts to a printer, who printed, tied, folded and bound
the manuscript, and the bookseller would then store, distribute and
retail the book.[44]

The familiar atmosphere among the Scottish writers facilitated the
financing of their works. It was a common practice for eighteenth-
century authors to collect subscriptions to pay for the proposed publication; the subscriptions would be raised by appeals to friends, who
would expect the compliment to be returned, or by public advertise-
ment in newspapers. Alternatively, a steady and dependable sale of
books would put publishers in a position to make the enormous ad-

vances they did. Not only were even relatively humble people able and anxious to read, and read widely, but the nobility and gentry, their appetites whetted by at least a smattering of knowledge gleaned by attendance at a university, would keep up the acquired tastes and buy books from their ample purses. The intimacy of urban life especially in Edinburgh encouraged the mutual profit and security of author and publisher.

Yet another attraction of Edinburgh for the intellectuals in terms of satisfying their mental drives and the natural desire for security and profit, lay in the success of Edinburgh's university in the heyday of the Scottish Enlightenment. There were factors intimately connected with the University itself which accounted for its appeal. Edinburgh's university was an institution which could afford new buildings and the latest scientific apparatus, which were attractions in themselves. Certainly, major figures of the Scottish Enlightenment were so tempted by prospects in Edinburgh that they forsook Glasgow University where they had originally made their names. Whatever the factors indigenous to the University, there can be little doubt that the City and its economic possibilities were real magnets. When the French wars, in 1793, effectively cut off the Continent from English aristocrats who formerly would have made the Grand Tour, they flocked to the 'Athens of the North' and, hence, the social composition of Edinburgh had added to it yet another vital ingredient. Furthermore, the professors were paid by means of class fees; a prospective student paid his fee at the first class of the session or he could even buy his class ticket at Creech's bookshop. The higher the enrolment, the greater the professorial income. The size of the classes at Edinburgh, in some subjects, were such that class fees were necessarily greater than any of the Scottish universities. Hence legal or professorial thinkers would find Edinburgh in the Enlightenment congenial, socially, intellectually, economically.

The New Town, as Creech indicated, became sufficiently prosperous and fashionable for the leaders of Scottish society to settle there, and for leading English families to make it a place of resort when European hostilities began in the later years of the Scottish Enlightenment. The legal, commercial and trading purposes for which it had originally been built were more than served. The upper and middle class groups, whose work or improved financial status led to their congregation in the centre of the Church and Law, were inextricably intertwined by family or economic ties, and by their shared educational and intellectual interests. Hence an intimacy was fostered which, in its turn, made possible so much of the Scottish Enlightenment.

In short, Edinburgh was not the heavenly city of the philosophers, unless their conception of heaven on earth was a city where financial security could accompany their intellectual predilections and pursuits. The New Town and public works in Edinburgh were not stimuli to the philosophers in their designs but in their capacity for generating congenial economic mechanisms.

Notes

1. *The Letters of David Hume*, ed. J. Y. T. Greig, 2 vols. (Oxford, Clarendon Press, 1932), I, p. 255 and II, p. 194. Other interesting examples of Hume's dislike of Scotticisms can be found *ibid*., I, p.182, and in the list of Scotticisms he annexed with a glossary to his *Political Discourses* in 1752 which were published in the *Scots Magazine*, XXII (1760), pp. 686-7.
2. R. H. Campbell, *Scotland since 1707: The Rise of an Industrial Society* (Blackwell, Oxford, 1965), pp. 24-8.
3. T. C. Smout, *A History of the Scottish People 1560-1830* (Collins/Fontana, London, 1972), p. 277.
4. *Scotland and Scotsmen in the Eighteenth Century, from the mss. of John Ramsay of Ochtertyre*, ed. Alexander Allardyce, 2 vols. (Edinburgh and London, 1888), II, p. 236.
5. Donald J. Withrington, 'Lists of Schoolmasters teaching Latin, 1690', *Miscellany of the Scottish History Society*, X (T. and A. Constable, Edinburgh, 1965), pp. 124-30, and 125.
6. John Sinclair, *Analysis of the Statistical Account of Scotland* (Edinburgh, 1826), Part One, pp. 149, 212, 213, 219, 321. There is no explanation to be given for Sinclair's allowance of four per family for those dependent on literature, and only three per family for those dependent on teaching.
7. *Ibid*., Part Two, Appendix No. V, pp. 19-21 which was entitled 'Proofs of Zeal for Education in Scotland' and taken from the *Digest of Parliamentary Returns*, printed by the House of Commons.
8. *The Statistical Account of Scotland* (hereafter *O.S.A.*), 21 vols. (Edinburgh, 1791-99), I (1791), p. 83; V (1791), p. 323; VII (1793), p. 103; X (1794), p. 422; IX (1793), pp. 592-3; XI (1794), p. 75; X, pp. 279 and 617; XVIII (1796), p. 517; XVI (1795), p. 373; VI (1793), p. 595.
9. *Ibid*., VI, p. 596; XVIII, p. 521.
10. *Ibid*., V, p. 505.
11. Hugo Arnot, *The History of Edinburgh* (Edinburgh and London, 1779), pp. 437-8. Arnot's figures and those of the *O.S.A.* conflict and it is not now possible to say which is the most accurate. Both, however, indicate the conclusion that late-eighteenth-century Edinburgh was able to support a rapidly growing number of printers and publishers.
12. Ramsay, II, pp. 306-16.
13. *O.S.A.*, IV (1792), pp. 391, 511-2; V, pp. 34, 583; X, pp. 99, 561, 597; XII (1794), p. 574; XVIII, p. 538.
14. I am indebted for their hospitality on several occasions to the current librarian of Innerpeffray and his wife, Mr and Mrs W. Pickersgill, and for their permission to consult the borrowing register. The alphabetical list of borrowers and the subject analysis of books borrowed are taken from Paul Kaufman, 'A Unique Record of a People's Reading', *Libri*, XIV

(1964-5), pp. 227-42.

15.   *O.S.A.*, II (1792), p. 169; IV, p. 512; III (1792), pp. 33, 559; XII, p. 122; XVII (1796), p. 9; VIII (1793), pp. 117-8 and 67-69. I am grateful to Desmond Brogan for the reference to Gigha and Cara.

16.   L. Simond, *Journal of a Tour and Residence in Great Britain, during the years 1810 and 1811*, 2 vols., (Edinburgh, 1815), I, p. 375.

17.   Smout, p. 347 and David Daiches, *The Paradox of Scottish Culture* London, Oxford University Press, 1964), p. 70. The same connection between the Enlightenment and the building of the Edinburgh New Town is made throughout in A. J. Youngson, 'The City of Reason and Nature', *Edinburgh in the Age of Reason* (Edinburgh University Press, 1967), pp. 15-22.

18.   John Wesley, *Journal*, ed. N. Curnock, 8 vols. (London, 1938), IV, p. 452.

19.   Robert Chambers, *Traditions of Edinburgh*, 2 vols. (Edinburgh, 1815), I, p. 31 and William Baird, 'George Drummond: An Eighteenth Century Lord Provost', *Book of the Old Edinburgh Club*, IV (Edinburgh, 1911) p. 46.

20.   Edinburgh University Press, 1966.

21.   Henry Cockburn, *Memorials of his Time* (Edinburgh, 1856), pp. 286-7, 291-4.

22.   See Baird, p. 52, for a twentieth-century echo of Cockburn.

23.   *Ibid.* George Drummond was an accountant, who worked for a committee of the Scottish Parliament on the rating and valuation of the country prior to the Union and after the Union was made Accountant-General of Excise. Commissioner of Customs from 1715. Edinburgh City Treasurer from 1717 to 1726. Commissioner to General Assembly. A Protestant and a Whig, organised abortive defence of Edinburgh against Bonnie Prince Charlie 1745. Grand Master of Freemasons in Scotland 1753. Married four times, twice apparently for children (14) and twice for money — the dowries of wealthy widows being worth more than £40,000.

24.   The merchants were all organised in their Guilds and the tradesmen in separate, privileged corporations. The fourteen incorporated Edinburgh trades were surgeons, goldsmiths, skinners, furriers, hammermen, wrights, masons, tailors, baxters, fleshers, cordiners, weavers, waulkers, bonnet-makers.

25.   Gilbert Elliot 1693-1766; MP for Roxburgh 1722-6; 1726 raised to bench; 1733 Lord of Justiciary (Lord Minto); 1763 Lord Justice Clerk. A man of culture, an eager agriculturist and an improver, and a Whig.

26.   William Creech 1745-1815. At first worked with Alexander Kincaid, bookseller, publisher, HM Printer for Scotland and from 1733 concerned with principal authors and literary works in Scotland including Hugh Blair, William Cullen, Adam Ferguson and Robert Burns. An original founder of the Speculative Society, member of Edinburgh Town Council and Lord Provost 1811-13. His breakfast room in his High Street shop was used by the *literati* as a lounge and was known as Creech's Levée. A hard-headed businessman in dealing with the *literati*.

27.   'On the same building lived families of all grades and classes, each in their flats in the same stair — the sweep and caddie in the cellars, poor mechanics in the garrets, while in the intermediate stories might live a noble, a lord of session, a doctor, or city minister, a dowager countess,, or writer; higher up, over their heads, lived shop-keepers, dancing masters, or clerks.' (H. G. Graham, *The Social Life of Scotland in the Eighteenth Century* (London, 1899), I, p. 85.)

28.   William Creech, *Letters addressed to Sir John Sinclair, Bart., respecting the mode of living, arts, commerce, literature, manners etc. of Edinburgh*

in 1763 and since that period (Edinburgh, 1793), p. 7.

29.   A. J. Youngson, *The Making of Classical Edinburgh,* pp. 227-9.
30.   Creech, pp. 7 and 7n; Youngson, *The Making of Classical Edinburgh,* pp. 228-9.
31.   Creech, pp. 32-3.
32.   *Ibid.,* p. 17. Bears' grease was used to prevent baldness, in the belief that as the bear was a hairy animal, the use of its fat would promote hair growth.
33.   *Ibid.,* pp. 15-16, 41-2.
34.   *Ibid.,* pp. 41, 42, 43.
35.   National Library of Scotland, Ms. 3464, f. 17.
36.   Creech, pp. 10-11, 16, 13-14, 20-1, 25-6, 28-9.
37.   *Ibid.,* p. 31.
38.   *Ibid.,* pp. 26-7, 33, 34, 35, 36, 37, 38, 39, 40, 41.
39.   *Ibid.,* Ibid., pp. 27, 23-4.
40.   Alexander Law, 'Teachers in Edinburgh in the Eighteenth Century', *Book of the Old Edinburgh Club,* XXXII (Edinburgh, 1966), p. 112, from an analysis of advertisements in local newspapers.
41.   Walter Scott, *Provincial Antiquities and Picturesque Scenery of Scotland,* 2 vols. (London, 1826), I, p. 82.
42.   N. T. Phillipson, *The Scottish Whigs and the Reform of the Court of Session, 1785-1830,* Ph.D. Dissertation (University of Cambridge, 1967), p. 352, and Smout, pp. 351-2.
43.   *Journal of Henry Cockburn.* 2 vols. (Edinburgh, 1874), I, p. 87.
44.   The information contained thus far in this paragraph is taken from Ian Watt, 'Publishers and Sinners: The Augustan View', *Studies in Bibliography,* XII (1959), pp. 5-6.

3 THE CHURCH

I

The intellectual elite, with a prominent exception in David Hume, were overwhelmingly either churchmen, lawyers or professors. That gave the Scottish Enlightenment a distinctly vocal character for its main actors were professional pleaders, preachers or teachers. That only their books remain inevitably deprives posterity of the movement's volubility, a potent form of its expression. William Robertson (1721-93) who is a central figure in the history of the Scottish Enlightenment and, therefore, ubiquitous in this study, was reputed to be an insatiable talker and dominator of conversations. Not only was he one of its leading thinkers because of his historical writings but he also played a leading part in two of the institutions of Scottish society crucial to the generation and expression of the Scottish Enlightenment. He was the leader of the Moderate party from 1752 and rose to be Moderator of the General Assembly of the Church of Scotland between 1766 and 1780, during which years he dominated and deftly managed not simply his party but the Assembly and Church as well. In 1762 he also became Principal of Edinburgh University, which, by inspired leadership and administration, he made into one of the most distinguished institutions of higher learning of its age and itself a major contributor to the Scottish Enlightenment. He was also a leading light and founder of several of the learned societies of his time, most notably the Select Society and the Royal Society of Edinburgh.[1] He reputedly preferred male to female company 'which we laughingly used to say was owing to their rivalship as talkers' but his friends found his great love of dissertation tedious because they knew all his topics.[2] In Henry Cockburn's words, 'It was a discussing age':[3] the General Assembly of the Church, the law courts, university senates and lectures. but especially the learned clubs and convivial societies, can never be recreated in the same way as the written works of the philosophers can be analysed and reprinted. Their physical presence, intimacy and interaction as well as their rhetoric and conversations are dimensions which it is impossible for the historian to convey adequately.

That David Hume was not a professor was in no small way attributable to the heresy-hunters of the Edinburgh and Glasgow presbyteries. Yet despite them never before nor since has the Scottish Church

produced so many distinguished and enlightened men of letters as in
the eighteenth century, although ironically they contributed not at all
to original theological thought. To account for the clerical distinction
albeit in secular philosophy and literature, the historian can offer
three explanations: first, that the association between the Scottish
Church and the Scottish Enlightenment can be attributed to the
comparative decline in religious bitterness that marks eighteenth century ecclesiastical history off from the seventeenth. Banning tended to
replace bloodshed. The wish not to stir old and dying embers prompted
the clergy, an educated elite in Scottish society, to divert their abilities
from polemic to polite literature, not only as a means of indulging
intellectual pursuits but as a way of showing that even Scottish clerics
could sustain the general ethos of Hanoverian peace, toleration and
security. A second explanation is that the writings of a knowledgeable
body of divines in the eighteenth century was simply a continuum and
marked no break with the past. Theology in Scotland was the original
social science, had been stressed and elaborated throughout the seventeenth century to encourage the transformation of the individual who,
through his conduct in life towards others, was endeavouring to attain
salvation. That conduct towards others expressed itself in the multifarious relationships and categories of relationship (political, legal,
economic) that existed in society, and ideally was a precondition for
social change. Theology was, therefore, a social science, which in the
seventeenth century paved the way for the secular social sciences of
the eighteenth century. The contribution of churchmen to the Scottish
Enlightenment, which was so productive of works on social philosophy,
was well founded and in a sound tradition. Earlier, for example, George
Buchanan (1506-82) had graced Scottish church history (being a Moderator of the General Assembly as well as holding other distinguished
posts) and had been renowned for such scholarly works of political
theory as *De Jure Regni apud Scotos* (1579) and a history of Scotland.
In this explanation can be seen how the seventeenth century paved the
way for the Enlightenment of the eighteenth as far as the Kirk was
concerned.

A third, more mundane explanation is the paucity of careers open
to educated men in pre-industrial Scotland. The number was fewer
still if the young man had an aptitude for learning and an academic
turn of mind. If one were of the right lineage landowning was one
obvious opening; for those more humble but talented the armed forces,
church, law, medicine and teaching alone were left.[4] The Church,
therefore, necessarily recruited those who lacked a religious vocation

but who saw in the ministry a way of life which permitted them to indulge their interests (the *Statistical Account* illustrates marvellously not only the attitudes but the ways of life of late-eighteenth-century Kirk ministers) to consort with leisured gentry and noble classes, and to be respected members of society. Writing of the mid-eighteenth century, the advocate Henry Mackenzie commented that the clergy were one of the most respectable and happy of people. Their education made them at least the equal of any man in their parish, their influence was correspondingly great, and their incomes, given the value of money and living patterns at that period, were much more adequate to all the purposes of comfort and appearance than their stipends in 1822. Unlike those of the 1820s, when Mackenzie was writing, clergy of the mid-eighteenth century did not have as social rivals younger sons of proprietors in the parish who brought back great wealth. Hence, they had rank and could offer plain and cordial hospitality, which gave them all the advantages of gentlemanly society. The annual meetings of the General Assembly took the clergy to Edinburgh, where they mixed for a time with the upper classes, and it was the fashion for the inexpensive meals of tea and supper to be the occasions of social intercourse.[5] Whatever Mackenzie might say, however, the clergy of the Church of Scotland in the 1750s behaved all too humanly when they expressed strongly the view that their stipends required augmentation.

A committee of the General Assembly presented figures which showed that 650 out of 800 livings surveyed bore stipends of often much less that £60 a year. Clerical salaries compared favourably with those of Scottish schoolmasters at the time. Five hundred out of 900 schoolmasters earned £16 including all emoluments and perquisites. Of that only £8 was stated salary and the rest was uncertain. The schoolmaster did receive a house but this was often too small and unsuitable for the climate. However, the salaries compared very unfavourably with those of professors who could, in certain favourable circumstances, earn sums approaching £1,000 a year and several hundred pounds was not uncommon. The total cost of paying the clergy's stipends was £50,000 whereas £60,000 worth of teinds (tithes) still lay unappropriated in the lands of the landed proprietors. The late-eighteenth century saw many attempts against the Government and landed proprietors to raise the stipends but nothing was achieved until 1810 when £150 was made the norm.[6]

To a select few, the Church was an *entrée* to the intellectual world; an author could not survive, at lease at the beginning of his career, on his writings alone; several clerical authors seem to have forsaken the ecclesiastical concerns of their early life in outlying parishes, upon appointment to university chairs in other than Divinity faculties. A Church career could pave the way to a university chair which, once attained, made possible an exclusive involvement in secular philosophy and affairs. Certainly there are examples, some eminent, of those whose status as ordained ministers might not be inferred from their later life and work. What must certainly be emphasised is that the Church was a career and a profession as is quite evident from the lives of distinguished Scottish churchmen in the Age of Enlightenment. If they had been less aware of the secular and less susceptible to human appetites then the connections between some parties in the Church and the Scottish Enlightenment would not have been as close.

Two of several examples which illustrate the type of church minister who played prominent parts in the history both of the Church and Scottish society generally in the Age of Enlightenment are Robert Wallace (1697-1771) and Alexander 'Jupiter' Carlyle (1722-1805).[7] If Carlyle's *Autobiography* were considered alone, it would appear that he and his close associates, whose influence over the Kirk in the last half of the eighteenth century was immense, spent their time in various Edinburgh taverns, imbibing burgundy only slightly less frequently than claret. Typical of the impression given by Carlyle in his book of the attitudes and behaviour of churchmen, lay and ordained, was his account of the custom whereby patrons of parish livings, whose nominations were not being readily accepted and which were, therefore, coming before the General Assembly for a decision, opened the public houses to entertain members of the Assembly. In 1749, for example, the Duke of Douglas offered a table daily for twenty people, which vied with the Lord Commissioner's for dinners, and surpassed it in wine. In 1756 began the frequenting by Carlyle and his associates of the first of two premises managed by one Thomas Nicholson: for the General Assembly of that year, it was proposed that twelve dozen bottles of claret be laid in at the Carriers' Inn for Assembly parties— 'but we could not be concealed; for . . . the out-of-the-way place and mean house, and the attempt to be private, made it the more frequented'. Six years later, when the same group founded the Poker Club to advocate the cause of a Scottish militia, they met in Nicholson's new inn. Dinner was at two o'clock in the afternoon, it cost one shilling a head, and wine was confined to sherry and claret. Members displayed no inebriety in the first seven years of the Club, which moved to the most fashionable tavern in Edinburgh, Fortune's, where the dinners were more showy, not better, and the wines dearer.[8]

Robert Wallace turns out to have been even more surprising a
Presbyterian minister than the vinolent Carlyle and his companions,
and reflects in other ways how the Church was 'improving' in the early
eighteenth century so as to permit some sections of it to participate
in the Enlightenment later in the century. For example, in 'A Letter
to a Reverend Clergyman in Scotland Concerning Submission to the
Church' written in 1730, Wallace urged on a minister whose views
may have changed since his original subscription of faith, to keep his
new views hidden. Any thinking man was bound to undergo changes
of view and it was expedient in the circumstances to be discreet.
There has recently been reprinted from the manuscripts housed in the
Edinburgh University Library an undated essay by Wallace entitled
'Of Venery, or of the Commerce of the two Sexes'.[9] In a comment
written on the outer cover of the essay, Wallace regarded it as
'needless & by no means proper to publish . . . att least att present'
since its contents were 'so contrary to our present notions & manners'.
It has been surmised that Wallace's unorthodox religious views were
shared by many other clergymen and that so too were the ideas expressed in 'Of Venery'. However, discretion, as he himself perceived,
was of the essence in his time and only in the present more tolerant
(or, it might be argued, permissive) age is it possible to reveal them.
Let some, albeit mild, excerpts from the essay speak for themselves:

> But in truth love & lust are very nearly allied, & the most bashful
> virgin or chastest matron has often more lust or inclination to
> Venery than the greatest prostitute, who often has an aversion
> to her trade & only consents & submits the drudgery of the Act
> in the view of money.

Wallace rejected the notion of platonic love:

> Seldom I believe can a man admire the good qualities of a fine
> woman's mind and conduct without a secret wish to be familiar
> with her person. Virtue, honour, prudence, may restrain him from
> any indecency, but his regard is allwayes mixed with something
> sensuall. If his health & the temperament of his body be vigorous
> he would gladly rush into her embraces: What women feel I know
> not but perhaps the most bashfull virgin or chastest matron may
> not be without the same sort of passionate Desires. I imagine where
> ever there is any secret desire after Venery, this desire is moved by

every object which has not something so ugly or Dissagreeable as is sufficient to extinguish the Desire altogether.

In another passage that almost presaged many very modern sentiments Wallace remarked:

I think fornication should be Disscouraged, but be only gently punished. It ought not to be accounted a very great blot even upon a woman's character . . . According to our manners it is no stain upon a woman to marry; it is not any stain upon her to marry twice or thrice. Her commerce with a former husband is not thought to pollute her. The most squeemish & Delicate among the men can marry with as much gout, tast, and relish as if she were the purest virgin. Those who profess to make love an art, those who study it, often prefer a married woman even during her marriage, to their own wives or to virgins. The world have certainly gone into foolish, whimsicall, unnaturall, absurd, ill founded conceits on this head. It would be much better if fornication gave less scandall & there was less jealousy of wives & mistresses. I dare say there is no foundation in nature for placing so much happiness in the sole enjoyment of a woman. The *concubitus vagus* [promiscuity] is bad & must be prevented: But a woman's being enjoyed by a Dozen in proper circumstances can never render her less fit or less agreeable to a thirteenth, if proper care is taken of all necessary decencies. I would therefor prohibit the concubitus vagus, but encourage a much more free commerce of the sexes than is allowed by our customs & permitt women to make proposals as well as men.

It must be recalled that Wallace was a Moderator of the General Assembly of the Church of Scotland, during the meetings of which, according to a well-known Edinburgh working-class tradition, the prostitutes of Rose Street, Edinburgh, never had so much custom. More sound support for the tradition comes from the following passage in a letter of a whisky agent, who was also a magistrate, to his manufacturer, dated 20 May 1814: 'I have the Police Court at present, and I will be needed very much to keep the whores and Ministers in order during the sitting of the Assembly.'[10]

Church-going played an important part in times which contained relatively few opportunities for recreational pursuits and other means of social contact. It made possible business, and mild pleasure as well as devotion; and it brought together the community more regularly than did any other event, as well as providing an opportunity for the exchange of news and gossip'.

Writing of Edinburgh before the lax times that William Creech so bewailed, the traveller Edward Topham noted how everyone went to Church:

> Pass thro' Edinburgh during the time if service, and you will not meet with a human creature; the streets are silent and solitary; and you would conclude, from the appearance of them, that some epidemic disorder had depopulated the whole City. But from the moment prayers are over, the scene changes: they pour from the Churches in multitudes, which nothing but having seen can give you any idea of. Even with every care possible you are driven from one side to another, till your shoulders are almost dislocated; for they are so intently employed with meditating on the good things they have heard, and the enjoyments of another life, that they have no time to look before them.[12]

John Gibson Lockhart, however, writing a physiognomical analysis in 1819, found the preoccupation much the same:

> The best place to study their [Scotch] faces is in the kirk; it is there that the sharpness of their discernment is most vehemently expressed in every line—for they are all critics of the sermon, and even of the prayers; but it is there also that this sharpness of feature is most frequently seen to melt away before emotions of a nobler order, which are no less peculiarly, though far less permanently theirs. It is to me a very interesting thing to witness the struggle that seems to be perpetually going on between the sarcastic and reverential elements in their disposition.[13]

That the Church was a vital and integral part of Scottish life could also be seen in its responsibilities for the provision of education and poor relief and in the composition and activities of the General Assembly in the Age of Enlightenment. The basic unit of the Church was the local kirk session; a number of kirk sessions in a locality comprised a presbytery and a number of presbyteries a synod. The General Assembly was the supreme body. It was comprised in Robertson's day of 364 members, 202 of whom were clergy and the rest laymen. Their origin was as follows:

Presbyteries sent	290 members (201 ministers, 89 lay elders)
Royal burghs sent	57 members (all lay)
Universities sent	5 members (who might be laymen or clergy from the universities)
Scottish Church at Campvere, Holland sent	2 members (1 lay, 1 minister)[14]

The interests represented in the Assembly are not obvious from a mere account of how a person technically happened to find himself in Edinburgh in May of any year. The Government was represented through the nominated Royal Commissioner (who was not technically a member of the Assembly) and by the Lord Advocate, Solicitor-General and other Crown officers and judges who sat as a result of being elected in their more local capacity as elders of the kirk. The second most important influence in the Assembly, as can be seen from the occupations of those who *de facto* represented the Government, was the Law. Not only were lawyers often elected as elders and from that position could be elected in force to go to the Assembly but the advocates were closely connected with the landed class. Here was to be found one of the important situations where the close interconnections between the Church and the Law could be seen, and between the Church, the Law and politics. The third interest represented was the Universities, which were to varying degrees in the hands of the clergy but whose considerable patronage was wielded by the Government, the landed interest and the town councils. Finally, of course, the clergy were an interest in the General Assembly, but the clergy throughout the Age of Enlightenment were divided as they had always been in Scottish history. They were split into parties, and each party sought and possessed lists of reliable lay elders for the presbyteries to elect in the spring to the General Assembly in May.[15]

After the Union, a wide variety of Scottish matters that were not overtly ecclesiastical or religious came to be aired at the General Assembly. It will be recalled how Sir John Sinclair was inspired at a General Assembly to use ministers as the best means of collecting the very general information that was incorporated in the *Statistical Account* . The presence of the interests delineated above would have ensured that role for the Assembly let alone the absence of an alternative such as a parliament. As Rev. Dr John Hill, William Robertson's successor both as leader of the Moderate party and as Moderator, put it, lay participation in the Assembly had a powerful influence in

maintaining that connection between Church and State which necessary
for the peace, security, and welfare of both.[16] Young lawyers used the
Assembly as a theatre in which they could display their eloquence and
excercise their talents—in the words of one historian it was 'the only
field left for Scotch oratory and statesmanship'.[17] When John Wesley
visited the General Assembly in the course of a visit to Scotland in
1764 he noted that the main speakers were lawyers.[18] The lack of an
alternative forum, the almost statutory presence of Scotland's leading
laymen, and the close involvement in Assembly business by lawyers
all pointed to a similar intimate connection between the kirk and
politics. The basis of the Church's involvement in eighteenth-century
politics stemmed from the re-introduction of lay patronage in 1712.
Thereafter, vacant livings were filled by patrons who, after con-
sulting with the congregation, presented the nominee to the presbytery which ordained and inducted him if his qualifications were deemed
satisfactory. The Patronage Act of 1712 replaced William III's abolition
of lay patronage in 1690 and his vesting the right of nomination in
the heritors (landowners) and elders (members of the governing body of
a congregation) or kirk-session of the parish. The heritors paid teinds
(tithes) which provided the clergy's stipends and went towards the
upkeep of the churches. Landowners were opposed to popular pressure
in the parishes to have the 1712 Act repealed and replaced either by
popular election or by election confined to heritors and elders.
The Government were dependent on the landed interest for electoral
support and so were unlikely to agree to the repeal of the Patronage
Act. Opposition to the Act was not the only contentious matter liable
to be raised in the Assembly; the Kirk's involvement as an institution
and through lay elders in the general life of Scotland, and the absence
of alternatives made the annual Assembly a place where opinion on a
wide range of matters might be expressed. As such it was potentially
dangerous, in the sensitive post-Jacobite decades, since heated debates
might suggest that all was not harmonious in the Scottish nation.
Because the Government was most concerned that this impression
should not be given, it tended to interfere in Church affairs through its
representatives in the General Assembly. An example of Government
control over the Church was their suppression in 1749-50 of the
clergy's demands for the augmentation of their stipends.[19] The suppression of the demand for increased stipends led to the formation of
the Moderate Party.

The 'improvement' in the Church, which paved the way for at least
some of its members to contribute to the Enlightenment from 1750

can be illustrated in two ways. First, until the Moderates took over in
the 1750s, the Government was concerned to keep a firm hand on the
Church, and in effect, controlled it from outside. The Government
maintained a tight reign so that the bitterness and contentiousness of
seventeenth-century Scottish ecclesiastical politics, which had been
effectively smothered, should not reappear. Improvement was the
inevitable consequence of such smothering. The Government's control
was to be seen in its foisting of an unpopular patronage act on the
Church in 1712 and in its ability to withstand demands for increases
in clerical pay.That the bonds between Church and Government should
have been severed by the Moderates on so secular a matter as pay is
revealing, as is equally the resumption of good relations on the grounds
of social harmony and law. Secondly, the Moderates were, by the
1750s, in a position to assert themselves not least because two secessions had carried out of the Kirk some of their most energetic and
powerful opponents. Between 1731 and 1740 Ebenezer Erskine,
minister of Stirling, and his evangelical followers battled against the
restriction of the election of ministers to heritors and elders till
finally in 1740 they were deposed by the General Assembly. A second
apparently similar deposition took place in 1752 when Thomas Gill-
espie, a minister from near Dunfermline, refused to take part in the
induction of an unpopular appointee, but he was of much more liberal
and independent thinking than Erskine's evangelicals, having more in
common with the radical outlook of eighteenth-century English dissent.
Not that evangelicals of Erskine's ilk were incapable of 'secular' endeavour, as can be seen in the demographic work of Rev. Alexander
Webster, whose charge was the Tolbooth Church in Edinburgh, and
who from the 1740s produced his reasonably reliable *Account of the
Number of People in Scotland,* completed in 1755. He engaged in the
excercise not only because it interested him but because the Government commissioned him to do it and because he was working on an
annuity scheme for the widows and children of the clergy.

The Kirk was central, therefore, to Scottish life and the rooting of
the Enlightenment in the state of eighteenth-century Scotland necessarily was to imply a close connection between the Church and the
Enlightenment.

II

In the heyday of the Enlightenment the Church of Scotland was
clearly divided into two parties, the Moderates and the Evangelicals.

The significance of the differences between them was in essence a battle
over how, if at all, the Kirk was to respond to the Enlightenment and
the more secular age of which it was a part and which of the two
parties was to predominate in the Kirk. It was members of the Moderate
party who, among churchmen, contributed to the *corpus* of Enlightenment literature. The Moderates have, by and large, received a bad
press, and the study that does most to rehabilitate them and explain
the rationale behind their origins and the inherent contradictions that
became apparent the longer they survived unfortunately remains
largely inacessible in thesis form in the Cambridge University
Library.[21] Hence, even now little has been published to argue against
the traditional view of the Moderates. That view was best expressed
(albeit as a satire) in 1752 by John Witherspoon, subsequently
President of Princeton University and the only ordained man to sign
the Declaration of Independence, in his *Ecclesiastical Characteristics:
or the Arcana of Church Policy, being a humble attempt to open up
the Mystery of Moderation, wherein is shewn a plain and easy way of
attaining to the Character of a Moderate Man, as at present in repute
in the Church of Scotland*. Thirteen maxims of the Moderate Man
were given—including that all clergymen suspected of heresy, whatever their rank or dignity, were 'to be esteemed men of great genius,
vast learning, and uncommon worth' and were to be given all support;
that orthodoxy was to be made a term of contempt and reproach;
that in preaching a Moderate minister must confine himself to social
duties, to recommend them only because they were rational not because they pertained in any way to eternity, and to base his views on
heathen authorities and on scriptures not at all; that a Moderate minister must be very unacceptable to the common people; that he must
put on the airs and graces of a gentleman, condemn all but sceptical
learning, shun appearances of devotion, pander to patrons and heritors,
regard those ministers opposed by the people as of great worth,
castigate his adversaries as knaves and fools; and that he should regard
the unbeliever more than those professing religion. An article from the
'Athenian Creed' supposedly ran:

> I believe that there is no ill in the Universe, nor any such things
> as virtue absolutely considered; that those things vulgarly called
> *sins* are only errors of judgement, and foils to set off the beauty
> of Nature, or patches to adorn her face; that the whole race of
> intelligent beings, even the devils themselves (if there are any) shall
> finally be happy; so that Judas Iscariot is by this time a glorified
> saint, and it is good for him that he hath been born.[22]

The traditional and commonly held beliefs that the Moderates were
great eaters and drinkers who hobnobbed solely with the upper strata
of society at the expense of their duties among the more humble have
also been given currency by the tales of high life recounted in Alexander Carlyle's *Autobiography.*

Perhaps the most celebrated episodes where Moderates and Evangelicals displayed their mutual antagonism was over the play *Douglas,*
a tragedy written by Rev. John Home, a Moderate minister, of the
parish of Athelstaneford, near Edinburgh.[23] Elements in the Kirk had
for some two hundred years regarded the theatre as a sink of iniquity
and it was only successive chipping away at old attitudes that permitted the licensing of theatres, their eventual popularity, and even the
altering of the timetable at the General Assembly in 1784 whereby
important business was fixed for alternate days to permit members to
attend performances in the City by Mrs Siddons—all the younger
members, clergy and laity, were in the theatres on those days by three
in the afternoon.[24] But in 1756 a very different climate prevailed and
the theatre, let alone the fact of a minister writing a play for production
could be counted on to raise much opprobrium in evangelical circles.
Of the situation Topham wrote that it was considered immoral for a
minister to go to a play or assembly, and that his congregation would
disdain him if he did. As a result, many clergy consoled themselves with
a bottle.[25]

When Home had completed the play, Evangelicals would have been
horrified to learn, he rehearsed it in the house of a professional actress,
Sarah Ward, with a most eminent cast of intellectuals and ministers.
William Robertson played the part of Lord Randolph; David Hume was
the young hero Glenalvon; Carlyle old Norval; Home himself Douglas;
Adam Ferguson, a minister and professor of Moral Philosophy in the
University of Edinburgh, Lady Randolph; and Hugh Blair, minister of
the High Kirk, Greyfriars, and later Professor of Rhetoric in the
University, Anna the maid.

When the play was performed publicly in Edinburgh in 1756 it
received an enthusiastic and patriotic welcome from all except Evangelical ministers. It was, as might be expected, condemned by both
the Edinburgh and Glasgow presbyteries. The condemnations were
followed by formal accusations against John Home, Carlyle, and
others. Home was being upbraided for his authorship of the play,
the others for their attendance at it. A pamphlet war ensued between
the supporters of Home and his Evangelical opponents. In the end,
Home left the Church and entered the world of the professional play-

wright, London life and the circle of Lord Bute. Carlyle successfully
fought off the summons he received from the Presbytery of Dalkeith;
to be defeated, he believed, would have set progress in the church back
fifty years, and greatly discouraged aspirants to the ministry.[26]

The other and earlier cases involving Moderate-Evangelical disputes
concerned David Hume and Lord Kames. Hume had from fairly early in
the century been the object of clerical attacks and *veto* as a result of his
alleged scepticism as evidenced by his *Treatise of Human Nature*. At the
beginning of the heyday of the Enlightenment in Scotland, in the mid-
1750s, he and Kames again became subject to charges of religious
infidelity. There were two occasions when they were effectively delat-
ed to the General Assembly, in 1755 and 1756, for heresy. On the
first occasion two Evangelical clergymen, Rev. George Anderson
(described by David Hume as 'godly, spiteful, pious, splenetic, charitable, unrelenting, meek, persecuting, Christian, inhuman, peace-making,
furious Anderson') in a pamphlet published in 1753 and Rev. John
Bonar of Cockpen in another pamphlet published two days after the
meeting opened in May 1755, urged on the General Assembly that
Hume and Kames (the latter specifically for his *Essays on Morality and
Natural Religion*) were seducing members of the Church (the Moderates);
their excommunication should be considered, and it should be decided
whether the excommunication should take place in local church courts
or the General Assembly and whether the matter should be dealt with
expeditiously or after the two men had been given a chance to
repent.[27]

In the first assault, Anderson was trying to tar Kames in particular
with the brush of heresy, suspicion and infidelity, and the attack was
the more wounding because Kames had sat as a commissioner to the
Assembly. Bonar summarised what in his opinion were Kames' views
in eleven propositions and Hume's in six, for example that 'all distinction between virtue and vice is merely imaginary' and 'Of all the
modes of Christianity Popery is the best, and the reformation from
thence was only the work of madmen and enthusiasts.' The manner
and content of the Moderate defence of their associates will shortly
be examined. The matter of prosecuting Kames and Hume in 1755
was considered by the Committee of Overtures, led by William Robertson. He succeeded in having merely a very general and anonymous
resolution passed from his Committee for unanimous acceptance
by the Assembly, which expressed 'the utmost abhorrence of those
impious and infidel principles which are subversive of all Religion
Natural and Revealed and have such pernicious Influence on life and

morals' and concern over the avowal of infidel and immoral principles
in several books lately published in Scotland. The conclusion of what
what was merely the first battle in a war did not, however, lift the
pressure from either man: David Hume reported that the Evangelicals
intended to pray for Kames in all the churches of Scotland for six
months. As for himself, Hume said that his opponents intended to
give him over to Satan, which they thought they had the power of
doing. 'My friends, however, prevailed, and my damnation is post-
poned for a twelvemonth'.[28]

The Government in London, vigilant as has been seen for any signs
of disharmony in crucial areas of Scottish life which might be construed
as rocking the Hanoverian ship of state, were delighted with Robertson's
formula.

> I am allways very glad when Ecclesiastical Assemblies pass over in
> a Manner consistent with the Quiet both of Church and State.
> It was certainly prudent to parry the Attack . . . tho' both the
> authors . . . have caus'd much observation in this Country as well
> as in Scotland

wrote the Lord Chancellor to the Lord Advocate.[29]

In the intervening period before the second encounter, Kames
partially shifted the pressure on him by recanting on one contentious matter but he by no means did an about face. However, by the
time of the second onslaught prior to the 1756 General Assembly the
Evangelicals' ire was more obviously directed at David Hume. At the
time of the Assembly's meeting Anderson issued two pamphlets, one
of which once more called for the censure of infidel writers. Other
Evangelicals wrote other works attacking the Homes and the associated Moderates. The case against Hume especially was pressed once
more in the Committee of Overtures which, in its turn, proposed the
establishment of a committee to inquire into Hume's writings. The
Moderates successfully beat down the motion mainly by another
piece of successful debate management by Robertson and the maiden
Assembly speech of a lay moderate and future Lord Chancellor, Alexander Wedderburn. Wedderburn's argument simply and briefly put
was that little good would come from censuring Hume since he could
not be convinced of opposite arguments to his own nor was he likely
to admit the error of his ways. There would be no secular consequences
upon an ecclesiastical censure. At the end, the decision was taken not
to transmit the overture to the Assembly by 50 to 17 and Wedderburn's motion to take no action was passed.[30]

In the Edinburgh University manuscripts, Hume's biographer found Robert Wallace's unpublished views of the matter and of the debate, the value of which Professor Mossner sees as being not least its insight into the state of Enlightenment in Scotland in 1756. Wallace noted how it was mainly ministers of all kinds and ages who took part in the debate and the main question was the expediency of inquiring into Hume's writings or prosecuting him. Wallace believed motions of censure should not be confined to writers but to all who act against Christian law—adulterers as much as supposed infidels. Furthermore, if Hume was prosecuted his writings would become more objects of curiosity than they were and thus become known and read. (It might incidentally here be noted that the advocate John Ramsay of Ochtertyre, an intimate of the philosophers, considered that the attacks, even as far as they went, served to make the books of Hume and Kames more read and longer talked of than they would otherwise have been. He wrote of the process that 'this rash and feeble attempt to check the progress of free thinking, convinced the philosophers of Edinburgh that they no longer had anything to dread from the Church courts'.)[31] He considered that clergy who consorted with Hume were being attacked unwarrantably and he even defended them.[32]

Wallace proposed that Hume might be wrongheaded rather than wronghearted and sincerely troubled that he could not regard nature and providence as others did. It would be a pity for such people to be cut off from conversation with the clergy. Finally, Wallace made a point of some importance in understanding the Moderate outlook: he argued that clergy were part and parcel of society and not separate from it, simply because society was the object of their influence. Hence they were to partake of all that society offered if they so chose and conversation even with heretical intellectuals was one of society's offerings. The revealing Evangelical-Moderate debates in the General Assembly over Kames and Hume were the prelude to the even more cathartic row over *Douglas*. What the three episodes illustrated was a fundamental institution of Scottish society, the Kirk, coming to terms with the Age of Enlightenment.

The Moderates were that body of clergy and lay elders who from the 1750s, certainly until the impact of the French Revolution was felt, fought successfully to ensure that the Church and the Enlightenment could co-exist to their mutual benefit. There had always been a 'Moderate' tradition amongst Scottish Presbyterian clergymen but it cannot be said that there was a Moderate 'party' in the sense of 'a disciplined and organised group of clergy' (Ian Clark) until after 1752.

The origin of the spirit that moved William Robertson and his cohorts can perhaps be found in the outlook and teaching of two eminent Glasgow University men, William Leechman and Francis Hutcheson. Moderatism grew in part because of the reaction to the narrow spirit and bitter strife of the seventeenth century. This negative stimulus, however, could not last for a century and other social and intellectual influences that were brought to bear on the development of Moderatism included the rapid changes in eighteenth-century Scottish society and the intermingling of the latitudinarianism of seventeenth-century Scottish Calvinism, in the sense of its intimate involvement with society, and the growing interest in the philosophy of Shaftesbury and Locke which Hutcheson popularised.

Hutcheson and Leechman urged their students to avoid theological speculations in their sermons and concentrate on personal conduct. As in so much else, there was nothing particularly novel in their approach for it could have been seen in the seventeenth-century writings of such Scottish divines as Robert Leighton (1611-84), principal of Edinburgh University 1653-62, bishop of Dunblane 1661-9 and archbishop of Glasgow 1669-74 and Henry Scougal (1650-78) professor of Divinity at King's College, Aberdeen, and a student of Leighton's. Leighton's commentary on the first epistle of St Peter is a case in point where detailed attention is drawn to the importance of personal conduct in life and to the working out of a godly life through relationships to others in society and even in submission to government (a clear pointer to later Moderate attitudes):

> The main ground of submitting to human authority, is the interest that Divine authority hath in it, God having both appointed civil government as a common good amongst men, and particularly commanded his people obedience to it, as a particular good to them, and a thing very suitable with their profession: it is *for the Lord's sake* . . . God hath in general instituted civil government for the good of human society, and there is still good in it. Tyranny is better than anarchy.

Scougal's best known work is *The Life of God in the Soul of Man* where again personal behaviour is stressed as also charity towards men— the social transformation that should ensue from individual attention to the spiritual life. Just as Christ loved all men, not just his relatives or particular friends so too should those who wished to imitate him have universal charity:

inward goodness and benignity of spirit reflects a certain sweetness
and serenity upon the very countenance, and makes it amiable and
lovely: it inspireth the soul with a holy resolution and courage, and
makes it capable of enterprising and effecting the highest things.
Those heroic actions which we are wont to read with admiration
have, for the most part, been the effects of the love of one's country,
or of particular friendships: and, certainly, a more extensive and
universal affection must be much more powerful and efficacious.[33]

If even such brief excerpts of seventeenth-century religious writings
are borne in mind, and they are typical of much more by Leighton and
Scougal, then it can be appreciated how theology was a social science;
how in the more secular eighteenth century it paved the way for other
more secular social sciences; and how the religious message itself, in
the hands of the Moderates, was made to concert with the world: was
itself secularised. The Moderates adapted an already well-defined
tradition.

Hutcheson laid the intellectual foundations for eighteenth-century
Scottish moral philosophy during his tenure of the Glasgow University
chair for seventeen years from 1729; between 1743 and 1785 Leechman was in more or less intimate contact with all the clergy who
studied at Glasgow—one quarter of the total ministry. He met with the
students every Friday from 5 p.m. to 8 p.m. in his own library and,
according to Carlyle, opened the minds of his students, and encouraged
full enquiry while avoiding heresy.[34]

It is difficult both to explain the emergence of the Moderate *party*
as such and to rescue the Moderates from the aspersions of Witherspoon
and misinterpretation of Carlyle's *Autobiography* without giving an
account of their views and the conclusions which they drew from them.
In this way, however, can be demonstrated the intimate connection
between the Moderates and the Enlightenment, of which they were
so vital a part of the expression. The key notion is integration. The
self-contained compartmentalisation of various aspects of human
existence was a notion totally foreign to them. They believed, in
common with eighteenth-century thinkers, that man was social by
nature and that religion was an indispensable sanction for social stability
and effective government. The intimate and inseparable connection of
church and society ensured social control, and sermons of the Moderate
minister and Royal Chaplain, Thomas Somerville, and of the Professor
of Divinity at Aberdeen, Alexander Gerard, powerfully advocated
that view.[35]

If the Moderates regarded the good order of society as essential, and saw for the Church a crucial part in the maintenance of that order, then they saw good order in the Church as equally fundamental. The Church was a society within society. It had its own courts and its members had to submit to those courts, which were the instruments of the Kirk's discipline. The Moderates said that they were returning to the first principles of Presbyterianism when they tried to revive the old authority of the Assembly and insisted that its decisions be carried out by synods and presbyteries. It is important to stress the Moderate outlook on the Church's function of discipline in society, the Church as a society within society and, consequently, the necessity for discipline within the Church. For historically the Moderates have been regarded as placing the issue of patronage and adherence to the prevailing system of ecclesiastical appointments before all else. It has furthermore been pointed out that they consorted socially with the aristocracy and gentry, who received Moderate encouragement to appoint ministers of a superior manner and education to the people, thus provoking secessions in the eighteenth century and ultimately the Disruption in 1843. Furthermore, as Witherspoon, Anderson and Bonar alleged, the Moderates consorted in intellectual circles with heretics. Yet, as Dr Ian Clark's work has shown, the second change arose from the Moderates' belief that the Kirk must be involved in the secular world if it was to have any influence in it: as far as patronage and social exclusivity were concerned, the social composition of both clerical parties was similar; both owed their livings to the same relatively small circle of patrons and in the eighteenth century, indeed, the only two baronets to be ordained were Evangelicals. The first change arose from the Moderate desire to restore uniform procedure in church courts and ecclesiastical discipline, instead of the anarchy inherent in a variety of practices. By so doing, the Moderates were carrying out their objectives of integration and providing the Kirk with leadership. What was really important to them was discipline and, therefore, patronage was a side-issue, merely the area of dispute over which the principle of order was fought.[36]

'The Moderates as a party . . . were the only group who could *possibly* have provided the *milieu* for the transmission and development of a distinctive Scottish culture in the 18th century'[37]—the quotation could, however, equally well be written of the Scottish lawyers and professors. All three fields were integral to Scottish life. All three made possible distinguished contributions to the *corpus* of Scottish Enlightenment literature. In many ways, though, the Moderates'

objectives, the sermons and pamphlets written and battles fought in
the attainment of those objectives, were also part of the Scottish Enlightenment and as such deserve further examination. The reason for
this is that the objectives of the Robertsonian Moderates were enlightened, rational and utterly in tune with the intellectual movement and
the society in which the intellectual movement operated. The Moderates, for example, were preoccupied like the *literati* with society.
They wished Christianity to be a crucial influence in society—especially
a society that was undergoing all the economic and social change of
mid-eighteenth-century Scotland. For the Church to relate to the
changing society the Moderates saw that the Church would have to
ally with disciplines of thought outside of theology—disciplines that
were actually influencing society. The flexible Scottish university
system of courses made the alliance not only possible but easy. It
should not surprise the student of the general Scottish awakening, therefore, to find Moderate clergymen involved in agriculture, history,
drama and the like.[38] Rather than a sign of their secularity, it is a sign
of their practising the fundamental Moderate principle of integration.
Religion was to appeal to the 'whole' man, just as Leighton and Scougal
had preached in the seventeenth century.

The fundamental cause of the Moderates as a party being called into
existence was secular control over the Kirk for political ends. Such, in
the Moderates' view, was the Kirk's central problem and it expressed
itself in the questions of clerical stipends and patronage. It has been
seen earlier how the Government wished to keep the General
Assembly at least superficially harmonious for political reasons and
so introduced a powerful secular interest in Church affairs. By 1749-50
the demand for augmented stipends not only threatened the harmony
but also the Government's control over Scottish electoral politics.
If the stipends were augmented the landed interest would have to
pay. If the landed interest (which included many who were elders,
heritors, MPs and Scottish peers all at the same time) were forced
to pay they would withdraw support from the Newcastle-Pelham
ministry. Hence when the clergy's deputation went to London, they
were told that if they pressed for the augmenting of stipends, the law
of patronage would be bound more strictly on the Church. Such a
quid pro quo was the least the Government could offer to the heritors
in return for making them pay more in stipends. Neither option satisfied the ministers but they were powerless in the face of this external
control. In the very early 1750s, therefore, the ground was well prepared for a party in the Church strong enough to assert independence.

In the view of a Moderate, Alexander Ranken, writing almost fifty years later, a religious establishment created such a close link with civil government that the interests of both were secured. The most perfect establishment was one where interference was minimal but co-operation easy.[39]

At the same time, if the Kirk was to be strong and master in its own house, capable of dealing with the civil power on equal terms, the power and authority of the General Assembly had to be asserted. The battle for its assertion was the issue of patronage: this was to be the *quid pro quo* with the civil authority. The Assembly would insist on co-operation with the law of the land in return for freedom from interference. Hence, within the Church, the Moderates, under William Robertson, fought to assert the law of patronage and the authority of the supreme court, the General Assembly, over recalcitrant synods and presbyteries. Robertson's view was that patronage was the legal method of appointing ministers to vacant parishes and there was little prospect of, in the short term, altering the method. The Kirk would be in a stronger position to assert control over its own affairs if it accepted and enforced the patronage system. Following on from that, Robertson believed that the most should be gained from the *status quo*: the legal system of ministerial appointments could make possible the appointment of particular kinds of clergyman—those, for example, of a more liberal education and higher social status than in the past. Such individuals would not be appointed if the popular will was to be expressed. This was not a justification of patronage but rather a benefit which could be gained from abiding by the law of the land.[40] Robertson's expedient line was part of his successful campaign to free the Church of external and political manipulation, as well as to re-introduce discipline and the authority of the General Assembly internally.

Some fourteen years, however, before Robertson's 'rule' over the General Assembly came the manifesto of the emerging Moderate party. It was entitled *Reasons of Dissent from the Judgment and Resolution of the Commission, March 11th 1752, resolving to inflict no censure on the presbytery of Dunfermline for their disobedience in relation to the Settlement of Inverkeithing.*[41] The title of the 'manifesto' explains partially the circumstances of its writings by, among others, William Robertson: the town council, kirk session and people of Inverkeithing, Fife, refused to accept the presentation of Rev. Andrew Richardson in 1751 and the presbytery of Dunfermline refused to induct him despite being so instructed by the Assembly. The pushing of Richardson's case ultimately led to a secession but for present purposes a consideration of Moderate views expressed in the *Reasons of Dissent* is of importance.

The first reason expressed clearly the view that man is a social being and gains benefit from that condition. Hence regulations for public order have to be established—regulations agreed by either the majority or by those entrusted with legislative power, and which must be accepted as both final and superseding private judgment. While there were extraordinary circumstances under which a man might resist the regulations or seek to dissolve civil society, as long as he continues in civil society, accepts and benefits from it, then he must obey its laws. Failure so to do is dishonest and disorderly and for anyone to maintain that such disobedience requires no censure is to deny, in effect, that there should be government and order. 'They deny those first principles by which men are united in society; and endeavour to establish such maxims, as will justify not only licentiousness in ecclesiastical, but disorder and rebellion in civil government'.[42]

Having established a general point about societies in general, the Moderate authors moved on to the application of the point, particularly to ecclesiastical society. The Church is a voluntary society founded on the laws of Christ:

> to his laws we conceive it to be most agreeable, that order should be preserved in the external administration of the affairs of the church . . . There can be no union, and, by consequence, there can be no society where there is no subordination: and therefore, since miracles are now ceased, we do conceive, that no church or ecclesiastical society can exist, without obedience required from its members, and inforced by proper sanctions.

Every Church historically has had some discipline and authority; again there can be private judgement or conscientious objection but not on those matters which are tantamount to Independency, anarchy and confusion. Every Church has agreed its form and method of external administration and no one ought to join a Church without being prepared to conform to that administration:

> if a judicature which is appointed to be the guardian and defender of the laws and orders of the society, shall absolve them who break these laws, from all censure, and by such a deed encourage and invite to future disobedience . . . they have exceeded their powers, and betrayed their trust in the most essential instance.[43]

The failure to censure the presbytery of Dunfermline's disobedience particularly offended against Presbyterian church government, which had two capital articles, the parity of its ministers and the subordination of its judicatures. The second capital article especially guarantees against anarchy and confusion. Under it, there must be a supreme court, whose judgements are absolute and final. The General Assembly is that supreme judicature in the Church of Scotland and if lesser courts disobey the Assembly with impunity, then the entire Presbyterian constitution is overturned. Ministers at their ordination subscribe to the principle of subordination of judicatures, it has been historically upheld and re-asserted, and so should not in this, or any other, instance be ignored.

The fourth reason of dissent, taken from an important instance from 1646, showed that not only in principle but also in practice had the principle of subordination of judicatures been upheld, and censures inflicted. The fifth reason pointed out that once disobedience to Church decisions was allowed to pass uncensured, it would only be a matter of time before doctrines were contradicted. The sixth asserted that the Commission had exceeded the powers given to it by the Assembly and by their failure to censure were contradictory to the acts, dangerous to the constitution, and subversive of the present establishment of the Church. They acted without the authority of and inconsistently with the ruling of the Assembly. By so doing, asserted the seventh reason, the Commission undermined the authority of the Assembly, and finally, no excuse whatever had been given to the Assembly by the presbytery of Dunfermline as to why they should be exempt from censure:'if presbyteries assume to themselves a right of superseding at pleasure the authority of the general assembly, injoining a settlement to be made effectual, no man can see an end of this confusion'.[44] There is no clearer or more comprehensive statement of Moderate principles than the *Reasons of Dissent*.

Such were the intellectual foundations of the Moderate party. The prime issues for them were integration, authority and freedom from political interference. The General Assembly of 1751 was the first occasion when the practical and tactical gathering of the party's leading personnel took place. They met in a tavern to consider the matter of voting on a case of nomination which would impose the authority of the General Assembly. Of the eleven whom it is known were present, eight ministers among them were all under 36 years of age and one of the three lay elders was only 29. Of the three laymen was first Provost Drummond, then 64, reputedly a man of deep piety and father-in-law

of one of the ministers, John Jardine. He was the only man present
who, in 1751, had any official standing. The next in 'seniority' was
Andrew Pringle (died 1776) who became Solicitor-General in 1775 and
was raised to the bench of the Court of Session as Lord Alemoor in
1759. The one layman among the 'Young Turks' was the son of a
close associate of Drummond's in the Edinburgh New Town project too,
Gilbert Elliot of Minto, who was called to the bar in 1742 and whose
subsequent career included a seat in Parliament and several minor offices.
The Moderate clergymen were strengthened by the legal capabilities of
sympathetic lay elders.

Of the eight ministers brief accounts have already been given of
Robertson, Carlyle and John Home. The others included Adam Dickson
(1721-76), an able ecclesiastic much skilled and informed in agriculture
and George Logan (1723-52), a reputed metaphysician. John Drysdale
(died 1788) was probably at the meeting: he was minister of Lady
Yester's, Edinburgh, for three years from 1763 and then of the Tron
Church, Edinburgh. He was Moderator of the General Assembly in 1773
and 1784 and its Clerk in 1778. The two most important ecclesiastics
remaining were Hugh Blair and John Jardine.[45] Carlyle, both in his
Autobiography and in surviving MSS in the National Library of Scotland left a fascinating comparison between Robertson and Blair, the
two leading thinkers among the Moderates. Robertson was sagacious,
selfish and ambitious, Blair naive, fussy and timid, seeming 'to have no
wish but to be admired as a preacher, particularly by the ladies . . . He
was as eager about a new paper to his wife's drawing room, or his own
new wig, as about a new tragedy or a new epic poem'. Both lacked wit,
and felt unhappy away from home in rainy weather as neither could
play golf, bowls, cards or backgammon as they were then considered
indecorous in the clergy. Carlyle revealed that 'As I had set the first
example of playing at cards at home with unlocked doors, and so
relieved the clergy on that side, they both learned to play at whist
after they were sixty. Robertson did very well. Blair never shone.'[46]
Jardine was a man of sound understanding who acquired a rich fund of
political information. He was worldly wise and while he rarely spoke
publicly, was thus invaluable for the private counsels of the Moderates
in, one feels, their smoke-filled taverns. He strengthened Moderate
bargaining power from his active superintendence of all the public
charitable institutions under the management of the city ministers,
for that gave him a source of patronage. He persuaded the Edinburgh
Town Council to resume the presentation of ministers rather than
filling benefices through the votes of kirk-sessions. A contemporary

wit, Lord Dreghorn, wrote of Jardine and Provost Drummond:

> The old provost, who danced to the whistle
> Of that arch-politician, the Dean of the Thistle[47]

There is no question that even from the very early years of the party's existence the General Assembly was gingered up. Indeed by 1753 the 'old guard' were losing control for the practice of calling up the principals of the universities, professors and judges to give their opinions was abandoned in that year and anyone might speak freely. Of the opportunity the young clergy and laity took full advantage to the improvement of the debates.[48] The early 1760s saw the further displacement of the old leadership as Jardine was made Dean of the Chapel Royal in 1761. 1762 saw Robertson's Principalship and Carlyle made Almoner Royal in Scotland, and 1763 saw Robertson made Historiographer Royal for Scotland and Jardine Dean of the Thistle. They pushed hard to assert the Church's independence of external political control and the subordination of judicatures in the interests of order. They supported their speech-making by astute political manoeuvres to ensure their control over the body for whose supremacy they were fighting, the General Assembly. Robertson rose to be Moderator by the mid-1760s by way of able committee work such as was seen earlier in the delations of Hume and Kames. He and other Moderates controlled the Assembly by capturing the various elective offices of the Church—the posts of Moderator, Clerk and Procurator for example. Thirty-nine out of fifty-four Moderators who were elected between 1752 and 1805 were Moderates. As far as the manipulation of ecclesiastical and private patronage was concerned, in the same period twenty-four out of forty-one appointments to offices (deaneries, chaplains to the Crown, almoner) were made from Moderates. In the Edinburgh taverns where their tactics were planned, they could produce a list of sympathetic laymen prepared to sit as commissioners for any presbytery who would elect them. Their organisational ability as much as anything else ensured their control.[49] Yet if the Moderate leadership seemed to be based in Edinburgh and district and if their tactics might tend to give the impression that nationally they had little support, it is important to note that while indeed the majority of presbyteries were evangelical or incapable of classification, the Moderates were strong in three very different areas—Fife and the east coast burghs up to Aberdeen, the Lowlands from the Synod of Lothian and Tweeddale to Galloway, and Ayrshire.[50]

The coming together of the Moderates not merely impinged but had an impact on the expression of the Scottish Enlightenment, as well as on the purely internal affairs of the Kirk. The fact, as this chapter has argued, that the Church and Scottish society were as interwoven and inseparable in practice as the Moderates wished them to be in theory ensured that their activity in church affairs would affect the intellectual movement then consuming the Scottish and especially the Edinburgh intellectual elite. There are three matters to be considered here: first, the events of 1755-6, the founding of the short-lived first *Edinburgh Review* and the Moderate defence of Hume and Kame; secondly, a brief reiteration of the close links between Moderatism and the society and thought of the Scottish Enlightenment and, thirdly, a consideration of the Moderates as pastors—their sermons as further examples of the thought of the Scottish Enlightenment as well as of views which so affected the internal history of the Kirk.

The first *Edinburgh Review* relates both to the Enlightenment and to the Moderates. Robertson, Blair, Jardine, Adam Smith, the moral philosopher and the author of the *Wealth of Nations,* and Alexander Wedderburn were its founders—Wedderburn being particularly responsible.[51] It was he who wrote the Preface, noting how timely was the appearance of such a venture, in imitation of other similar works elsewhere in Europe and in view of the revival of letters following the violence and disorder that prevailed in the seventeenth century. The aim of the work was to show men the gradual advances of science, as a means of inciting them to the pursuit of learning, which would do honour to their country. To this end notice would be given each half year to the books published in Scotland. Only two numbers of the *Review* appeared: Robertson, Blair, Jardine and Wedderburn wrote virtually every article. The last contribution to appear was a letter from Adam Smith which indicated that limiting the attention of the *Review* to books published in Scotland was unduly narrow and provincial in the cosmopolitan age of the Enlightenment. The fact, too, that the contributors were also from a very limited and intimate circle also supports the view of several historians that, as a literary and critical production, the *Edinburgh Review* was prematurely born. The Enlightenment in Scotland was not yet sufficiently broad in outlook or interest or sufficiently numerous in participants to sustain such a work. The time was much more propitious in 1802 when its successor began so successful a publishing run, but that was too late for so many of the distinguished *literati* and the second *Edinburgh Review* was largely written at first by students of the second generation of *literati* known more for their ability as teachers and synthesisers than as original minds.

The first *Edinburgh Review* lasted long enough, however, and was published in a sufficiently crucial year to permit the Moderates, who were behind it, to take notice of the Evangelicals' pamphlet attacks on Hume and Kames. Two articles in the first number were directed first to Bonar's pamphlet and then to Blair's reply.[52] The author notes that for Bonar to sustain his case he had to reproduce faithfully and exactly those quotations from Hume's and Kames' work. In fact he mangled quotations, directly misrepresented the meaning of the texts, and even invented quotations and ideas.[53]

The pamphlet received half a page of attention—extremely short shrift and, therefore, insulting as compared to the fourteen pages devoted to a review of Hutcheson's moral philosophy. Blair had made a good sound Moderate point in his *Scots Magazine* article when he noted, with reference to the attacks on Hume and Kame:

> The proper objects of censure and reproof are not freedom of thought, but licentiousness of action; not erroneous speculations, but crimes pernicious to society. Against these ought the clergy to exert their utmost efforts; and by such a conduct they will more advance the cause of religion, than by engaging in metaphysical disputes, which may perplex the understandings, but can never impair the morals of men.[54]

The close relationship between the Moderates and the thought of the Enlightenment needs to be stressed. Dugald Stewart, Robertson's first biographer, noted how, in three surviving commonplace books of the historian, the motto was prefixed 'Vita sine literis mors est'— life is death without literature.[55] The Moderates appealed to all facets of man, his reason, his emotions, his sociability. For them, the Church was not only to interpenetrate society, but itself bore an analogy to society. Their ideal was a broad-based and undogmatic Kirk, with the Assembly being the focus for all aspects of national life. Their notions concorded well with the thought of the Scottish Enlightenment.[56]

The Moderates' sermons were also opportunities to express an ecclesiastical ideal that harmonised with the social philosophy of the age, and to demonstrate that pastoral commitment, which tradition has denied they had. Many volumes exist of published Moderate sermons, especially those of Hugh Blair. It will be recalled how he was minister of St. Giles, the High Kirk which drew in the aristocrats and

professional men of the capital city. To them he preached the inter-
dependence of men in society and their mutual rights and duties that
were dictated as much by nature as by religion.[57] Examples of other
sermons by Moderates, Gerard and Somerville, were noted earlier also
concerning themselves with the integration of society. Most revealing
of all, judged not least from the many times he was asked to preach
it, was William Leechman's 'The temper, character and duty of a
minister of the gospel'—the words of the man who heavily influenced a
good quarter of ordained ministers in the Age of the Enlightenment.
In the sermon, he impressed upon his auditors the kind of upright
behaviour they were expected to show in a variety of contexts and
how they should cultivate contemplation and width of study. 'The
most perfect character of a teacher of true religion', however, 'is that
of one who lives among mankind, converses with them, and at the
same time retains as much purity of mind, and discovers as much dis-
engagement of heart from the world, as if he were entirely separated
from it.'[58]

In the same volume of sermons, the much maligned Carlyle is also
found to be concerned with the character of clergy in his sermon
preached in 1767 on 'The tendency of the Constitution of the Church
of Scotland to form the temper, spirit, and character, of her ministers.'[59] He even spoke sentiments before the General Assembly which
historians, who have misinterpreted his outlook by misunderstanding
the nature of an autobiography, have regarded as totally foreign to him
when he said 'vox populi is the vox Dei'.[60]

III

William Robertson retired in 1780. The world external to Scotland was
much changed with the American war being fought and the French
revolution less than a decade away. With that cataclysm, the cult of
reason in Europe came under a cloud. After he had departed, the
Moderates, under the impact of changed political and social conditions,
became a very different group from that coterie of youthful idealists
who had met in an Edinburgh tavern in 1752. The post-1780 period
saw less contact between the Church and the Enlightenment in Scotland and the contrast illustrates how vital a period Robertson's heyday
was. In the concluding chapter it will be seen how the generation and
expression of the Scottish Enlightenment ended as, one by one and not
simultaneously, the props that supported it were removed. The prop of
the Church began to collapse after the 1780s and while the Enlighten-

ment continued after that time, much of the support it had earlier received from the Kirk was lost. It would be fitting to think that the Moderate notion of the integration of religion and society was responsible for the most distinguished era of creativity in the Scottish Enlightenment between the 1750s and and 1780s.

Notes

1. Minister of Gladsmuir, East Lothian, 1743-59; minister of Greyfriars Kird, Edinburgh, 1759-62; Principal of Edinburgh University from 1762 until his death; Historiographer Royal for Scotland from 1763; author of *History of Scotland* (1759), *History of the Reign of Charles V* (1769) *History of America* (1777) and *Historical Disquisition concerning the Knowledge which the Ancients had of India* (1791).

2. *The Autobiography of Dr Alexander Carlyle of Inveresk, 1722-1805,* ed. John Hill Burton (London and Edinburgh, 1910), p. 302 and National Library of Scotland MS 3464, f. 15.

3. Henry Cockburn, *Memorials of his Time* (Edinburgh, 1856), p. 27.

4. Henry Cockburn, the Scottish judge and Whig, wrote in his vivid and invaluable *Memorials* (p. 235) of the seventeenth century 'The Church was the greatest field which our poor country contained for native talent and influence' and there was little change until the economic and social impact of the Industrial Revolution was felt. Alexander 'Jupiter' Carlyle, in his *Autobiography* (pp. 57-8) wrote of his toying with the army, law and medicine before his grandfather urged him to enter the Church in view of his position as the eldest of eight in the family.

5. Henry Mackenzie, *An Account of the Life and Writings of John Home* (Edinburgh, 1822), pp. 8-10.

6. See John Cunningham, *The Church History of Scotland,* 2 vols., 2nd ed. (Edinburgh, 1882), II, pp. 332-3n. On p. 333n is given the following table drawn up by the committee giving the value of livings in more than 800 parishes.

		£		£
1	under	25	not	
3	above	25	higher	30
12	"	30	than	35
25	"	35		40
106	"	40		45
126	"	45		50
84	"	50		55
119	"	55		60
94	"	60		65
119	"	65		70
38	"	70		75
27	"	75		80
22	"	80		85
7	"	85		90
9	"	90		95
12	"	95		100
3	"	100		105
2	"	105		110

	£	£
8 "	110	
16	138 17s. 9.66d.	

For schoolmasters' salaries some forty years later see N.K., 'A Letter to Sir John Sinclair, Bart., on the state of National Education in Scotland', *The Statistical Account of Scotland,* 21 vols., XXI (Edinburgh, 1799), pp. 308, 308n and 309.

7. Wallace was appointed minister first, in 1733, of New Greyfriars Church, Edinburgh and then in 1739 of New North Church; 1737 refused to read the Porteous Riot Act from his pulpit; subsequently in charge of church patronage in Scotland and from 1744 one of the Royal chaplains in Scotland and Dean of the Chapel Royal; 1743 Moderator of the General Assembly. Member of several early societies devoted to literary and other 'enlightened' matters such as the Rankenian (named after a tavern owner) and the Select. Author of *Dissertation on the Numbers of Mankind* (1753), *Doctrine of Passive Obedience and Non-Resistance Considered* (1754), *Characteristics of the Present Political State of Great Britain* (1758) and *Various Prospects* (1761). Carlyle was known as 'Jupiter' because of his appearance: Walter Scott spoke of him as 'the grandest demigod I ever saw', Educated at Edinburgh, Glasgow and Leyden universities and minister of Inveresk, near Musselburgh (near Edinburgh) from 1748 until his death. One of the defenders of Edinburgh against Bonnie Prince Charlie 1745. A member of that inner and vital group of Moderates led by William Robertson who came to hold sway over the General Assembly. His *Autobiography* is a fundamental source but, as is discussed below, is deliberately of its *genre* and alone gives an unfair picture of the life style and beliefs of Moderate ministers.

8. Carlyle, pp. 239, 324, 440-1.

9. I base all the information I give on this topic on a paper given by Norah Smith to the seminar of Scottish Cultural History in the Eighteenth Century, at the University of Edinburgh's Institute of Advanced Studies in the Humanities, on 17 March, 1972. Her paper is published as 'Robert Wallace's 'Of Venery', *Texas Studies in Literature and Language,* XV (1973), pp. 429-44. The 'Letter to a Reverend Clergyman' is in Edinburgh University Library, MS. La II 62017. I am grateful to Mrs Smith for permission to use her material here. The subsequent quotations from her article are taken from pp. 435 and 439.

10. Scottish Record Office, R.H. 15-1856. I am very grateful to Professor Christopher Smout who first drew the attention of the above seminar to this information and to Mr R. Weir, University of York, for permission to use the quotation, which he originally found.

11. Donald J. Withrington, 'Non-Church-Going, *c.* 1750—*c.* 1850. A Preliminary Study', *Records of the Scottish Church History Society,* XVII (1970), p. 99.

12. Edward Topham, *Letters from Edinburgh written in the years 1774 and 1775,* (London, 1775), pp. 235-6.

13. J. G. Lockhart, *Peter's Letters to his Kinfolk,* 3 vols., 2nd ed., (Edinburgh, 1819), I, pp. 40-1

14. Dugald Stewart, *Account of the Life and Writings of William Robertson,* (London, 1801), pp. 105-6.

15. For the delineation of interests represented in the Assembly see Ian D. L. Clark, 'From Protest to Reaction: The Moderate Regime in the Church of Scotland 1752-1805', *Scotland in the Age of Improvement,* ed. N. T. Phillipson and R. Mitchison (Edinburgh U.P., 1970), p. 203.

16.   Stewart, p. 185.
17.   Carlyle, pp. 260-1, Cunningham, II, p. 368.
18.   John Wesley, *Journal*, ed. N. Curnock, 8 vols. (London, 1938), V, p. 71
       I am grateful to George MacKenzie for this reference.
19.   David Hume attempted to revenge himself somewhat on the clergy when the
       issue of augmentation of stipends arose. He wrote a skit on their request
       entitled *Petition of the Grave and Venerable Bellmen, or Sextons, of the
       Church of Scotland, To the Honourable House of Commons* (1751).
       Among the reasons supporting the petition were: 'That the present poverty
       of your Petitioners in this kingdom is a scandal to all religion, it being
       easy to prove, that a modern Bellman is not more richly endowed than a
       primitive apostle, and consequently possesseth not the twentieth part of
       the revenues belonging to a Presbyterian Clergyman.' 'That the instru-
       mental music allotted to your Petitioners being the only music of that
       kind left in our truly reformed churches, in a necessary prelude to the
       vocal music of the Schoolmaster and Minister, and is by many esteemed
       equally significant and melodious.' (quoted in E. C. Mossner, *The Life of
       David Hume* (London, Nelson, 1954), p. 236.
20.   J. G. Lockhart, III, pp. 22-5 gives a graphic description of how the General
       Assembly brought to Edinburgh representatives of the Kirk from the whole
       country.
21.   Ian D. L. Clark, *Moderatism and the Moderate Party in the Church of
       Scotland 1752-1805*, Ph.D. dissertation (University of Cambridge), 1964. I
       have drawn heavily on Dr Clark's thesis for my exposition below. A sum-
       mary of some of Dr Clark's work can be more readily found in his article
       'From Protest to Reaction: The Moderate Regime in the Church of Scot-
       land 1752-1805', *Scotland in the Age of Improvement*, ed. N. T. Phillip-
       son and R. Mitchison (Edinburgh U.P., 1970), pp. 200-24. In subsequent
       references I refer either to 'Clark thesis' or 'Clark article'.
22.   John Witherspoon, *Ecclesiastical Characteristics* . . . , 2nd ed (Glasgow,
       1753), pp. 8-45 in summary. The quotation is from page 27.
23.   John Hume 1722-1801. Also wrote other tragedies such as *Agis and The
       Fatal Discovery*. Owner of a farm in Kilduff, East Lothian. Secretary to
       Lord Bute 1758-63. Merited the following mention in a codicil to David
       Hume's will: 'I leave to my friend Mr John Home, of Kilduff, ten dozen
       of my old claret at his choice; and one other bottle of that other liquor
       called port. I also leave him six dozen of port, provided that he attest,
       under his hand, signed John HUME, that he has himself alone finished
       that bottle at a sitting. By this concession he will at once terminate the
       only difference that ever arose between us concerning temporal matters.'
24.   Carlyle, p. 339.
25.   Topham, p. 237.
26.   *Ibid.*, p. 332
27.   Detailed accounts of the attacks on Kames and Hume can be found in E.
       C. Mossner, *The Life of David Hume* (London, Nelson, 1954), pp. 336-55
       and I. S. Ross, *Lord Kames and the Scotland of his Day* (Oxford, Clarendon
       Press, 1972), pp. 152-9 and I have here drawn from them.
28.   *The Letters of David Hume*, ed. J. Y. T. Greig, 2 vols. (Oxford, Clarendon
       Press, 1932), I, p. 224.
29.   Quoted in Ross, p. 156.
30   Mossner, pp. 347-8.
31.   *Scotland and Scotsmen in the Eighteenth Century from the MSS of John
       Ramsay, Esq. of Ochtertyre*, ed. Alexander Allardyce, 2 vols. (Edinburgh
       and London, 1888), pp. 315 and 317.

32. Mossner, p. 351.
33. *The Whole Works of Robert Leighton, D.D.*, 2 vols. (London, 1846), I, p. 295 and Henry Scougal, *The Life of God in the Soul of Man* (Inter-Varsity Fellowship, London, 1961), pp. 42-3.
34. Carlyle, pp. 93-4.
35. See *The Scottish Pulpit; a Collection of Sermons by Eminent Clergymen of the Church of Scotland*, ed. Robert Gillan (Edinburgh, 1823), pp. 57-8, and *The Scotch Preacher: or a Collection of Sermons by Some of the Most Eminent Clergymen of the Church of Scotland*, 2 vols. (Edinburgh, 1776), p. 311.
36. Clark thesis, p. 24.
37. *Ibid.*, pp. 373-4.
38. *Ibid.*, pp. 202, 255-6.
39. Alexander Ranken (1755-1827), *The Importance of Religious Establishment* Edinburgh, 1799), p. 3
40. Clark thesis, pp. 30-1.
41. The document was published in full in *Scots Magazine*, XIV (1752), pp. 191-7.
42. *Ibid.*, XIV, p. 191.
43. *Ibid.*, XIV, pp. 191-3.
44. *Ibid.*, XIV, p. 196.
45. Hugh Blair (1718-1800) was also one of the *literati*. He was a minister at three important Edinburgh churches—Canongate, Lady Yester's and for over 40 years at the High Kirk of St Giles. He was the first Professor of Rhetoric and Belles Lettres at Edinburgh from 1768 and author of several works especially his *Lectures on Rhetoric*. His sermons, excerpts from which are given below, indicate the close interconnection between Moderate ecclesiastical and enlightenment thought. John Jardine (1715-66) was the supreme politician of the Moderate party and has no reputation as a preacher or *literatus*. Minister at Liberton from 1741-50, then of Lady Yester's, Edinburgh 1750-4 and then of the Tron Church (almost next to St Giles) from 1754. Chaplain to the King from 1759, Dean of Chapel Royal from 1761 and Dean of the Thistle from 1763. Not only was he Drummond's son-in-law but his daughter married Kames' son, thus illustrating another facet on the intimacy of various circles connected with the Scottish Enlightenment. He dropped dead at the General Assembly of May 1766.
46. Carlyle, pp. 305 and 307; N.L.S. MS 3464, f. 13.
47. Thomas Somerville, *My Own Life and Times 1741-1814* (Edinburgh, 1861), pp. 91-2.
48. Carlyle, p. 284.
49. Clark thesis, pp. 145-58 *passim*.
50. *Ibid.*, pp. 164 and 167.
51. Alexander Wedderburn (1733-1805) became a judge of the Court of Session as Lord Chesterhall in 1756 after being admitted an advocate in 1754; left the Scottish Bar and was called to the English Bar in 1757; MP for the burghs of Rothesay and Inverary, 1762; Solicitor-General 1771-8, created Lord Loughborough, 1780; the first Scotsman to become Lord Chancellor 1793-1801; Earl of Rosslyn, 1801.
52. Published in *Scots Magazine*, XVII (1755), p. 23.
53. *Edinburgh Review*, I (1755-6), p. 53.
54. *Scots Magazine*, XVII, p. 233.
55. Dugald Stewart, 'Account of the Life and Writings of William Robertson D.D.', *Collected Works of Dugald Stewart*, ed. Sir William Hamilton, 10 vols. (1754-1860) X (1858), p. 104.

56. Clark article, pp. 207 and 222.
57. Clark thesis, p. 21.
58. *The Scotch Preacher, II,* pp. 136-87. The quotation is from p. 151.
59. *Ibid.,* II, pp. 1-27.
60. *Scots Magazine,* XLI (1779), p. 313.

4 THE LAW

There is a vast field of virgin territory still waiting to be tilled for a
social historian of the Scottish Law, its practitioners, and the legal
system from the seventeenth to the nineteenth centuries. It is clear that
all three were crucial not merely to the Scottish Enlightenment but to
agricultural improvement, industrial and commercial development,
politics and manners, indeed most spheres of Scottish social life in that
period. The law, lawyers and legal system were like a hub of a wheel in
the eighteenth century, with spokes going out to touch most areas of
élite activity. Because of the relative lack of research that has been
undertaken on the social history of the Scottish Law, what follows will
regrettably be briefer than the treatment of other matters in the book,
but the brevity does not reflect the relative importance to the subject
at hand.

From important research that has been undertaken, though largely
unpublished in detail, it has been confirmed that, from the early
eighteenth century at least, the upper reaches of the Law were a field
of employment for the landed aristocracy and gentry of Scotland.
Between 1707 and 1751, 96 per cent of the entrants to the Faculty of
Advocates (barristers) came from landed families or from families with
close landed connections, and the number declined only to 88 per cent
in the years 1752-1811. Of those 18 per cent came from the peerage or
from families of significant political influence, 38 per cent from the
baronetcy or from families of lesser political influence and 35 per cent
from minor landed families between 1707 and 1751, and the figures
were respectively 8 per cent, 24 per cent and 47 per cent between 1752
and 1811. Apart from the significance of the decline of aristocratic
entry into the Law and the rise of numbers coming from the professional classes in the late-eighteenth and early-nineteenth centuries, it
is clear that in the age of the Scottish Enlightenment the personnel of
the Scottish legal system were intimately connected with the landed
aristocracy and gentry, and even previously non-landed professional
classes were purchasing small estates in the later period.[1]

The reasons for the Law being so aristocratic and landed a preserve
are financial and social. Prior to 1707 and until 1740, most aspiring
lawyers were required to study on the Continent and even after 1740,
when the numbers studying abroad declined in response, no doubt, to

developing provision within Scotland, the entrance fee to the Faculty
of Advocates rose from £30 in 1707 to £150 in 1790.[2] By then, the
Law was still a preserve of the wealthy, but those classified as wealthy
by the end of the eighteenth century were not necessarily aristocrats
and gentry but professional and commercial classes too. Socially the
Law appears to have been regarded as a fashionable but useful and
respected career in public service, rather as Anglican livings were considered for the younger sons of aristocrats and gentry in nineteenth-
century England. However, not only younger sons became Scottish
lawyers since the combination of wealth, power, prestige and a seat on
the bench was irresistible to some aristocrats. Of much more ancient
custom was the edict of James I and an Act of Parliament of James IV
which laid down that the eldest sons of all barons and freeholders
should have a knowledge of law if they were to carry out their local
duties in a suitable manner.

Henry Cockburn, himself a nineteenth-century judge, educated in
the era of the Scottish Enlightenment and author of some of the most
lively accounts of Scotland at that time, wrote of the legal
profession as:

> the highest profession that the country knows; its emoluments and
> prizes are not inadequate to the wants and habits of the upper
> classes; it has always been adorned by men of ability and learning,
> who are honoured by the greatest public confidence . . . Its higher
> practice has always been combined with literature, which, indeed,
> is the hereditary fashion of the profession. Its cultivation is en-
> couraged by the best and most accessible library in this country,
> which belongs to the bar.

(The latter part of the quotation can serve for the present as a connection between law and the Scottish Enlightenment.) Elsewhere Cockburn
also wrote:

> Ever since the Union, the Parliament House has been the great
> native scene for Scotch ability and learning, and speaking and
> patriotism; and a brilliant scene it has been . . . To the lawyer
> that scene gave fees and honours—to the studious, books and
> leisure; to the idle, an intellectual club; to the gay, fun; to the
> partisan his faction; to all talk, society, friendship and excitement.[3]

Describing the early nineteenth century, John Gibson Lockhart (whose familiarity with the Law and with Edinburgh arose not least from his being Walter Scott's son-in-law) wrote in his satirical *Peter's letters to his Kinsfolk* how it was a way of life for some advocates to wait for public office, which they might reasonably expect from their blood or marriage ties, or from patrons. Thus they were 'the chief community of loungers and talkers in Edinburgh'. By Lockhart's time, however, the chief wealth lay with the Writers to the Signet, of whom there was an abundance in Edinburgh. Indeed, there was scarcely an estate in Scotland whose owner did not employ a Writer to manage it, thus giving them a very intimate connection with the landed interest.[4]

The changing social composition of the Faculty of Advocates, the implication that Scotland's wealth was, towards the end of the eighteenth and the beginning of the nineteenth centuries, increasingly in the hands of the *bourgeoisie*, the general increase in the number of advocates and Lockhart's observation that, by his time, the chief wealth lay in the Writers to the Signet all point to the increasing social and economic importance of the legal profession. Only a career at the Bar gave such social, political and financial advantages. James Boswell, the companion and biographer of Samuel Johnson, wrote in 1785 that the high society of Edinburgh consisted of lawyers, and they set the social tone.[5]

As far as patronage was concerned, the Law offered plenty of places which had to be filled, for as Henry Cockburn said, in every country where there was no Parliament, the Bar necessarily became the next most important political element. In support of the statement Lockhart made, Cockburn accepted that the Bar (again at the end of the Enlightenment, in the early 1820s) was prodigiously overcrowded. Yet, for every three advocates actually in practice there was a 'job'. The Faculty roll in 1823 listed 374 names of whom 150 were ineligible because of age, existing occupation, peerage, bad health, and other such reasons, and a further 53 who were too junior to be expecting yet any public office. For the remaining 171 there were 78 places, the salaries for which together were worth nearly £81,000 a year. The offices open to nomination by the Crown were judgeships in the Court of Session and Justiciary, Exchequer, Jury, Admiralty and Commissary Court, Sheriffs, clerks of Session and Jury Court, Deputy Clerk Register, Solicitor of Tythes, Lord Advocate, Solicitor-General and Professor of Public Law in Edinburgh University. Other nominations included the Lord Advocate, the Faculty of Advocates and the General Assembly, in whose hands were posts such as Deputy Advocates, Crown Counsel, Law Professors, Collectors of Decisions, Counsel for the Boards of Excise

and Customs, and Procurator for the Church.[6] Yet more grist to the
legal mill was the volume of litigation which passed through the Court
of Session: 1,358 causes were enrolled in the Outer House (where they
were processed before going before all the law lords in the Inner House)
in 1761, and by 1791 their number had swollen to 2,948.

In short, the social history of the legal profession in the Age of the
Enlightenment was one of growing prestige, wealth and power: it was
the highest profession that the country knew, lawyers set the tone of
society, and as will subsequently be seen, they prospered from the land
and commercial developments of the time so that they bought themselves those trappings crucial to social acceptance, such as a New Town
house and a country estate. Added, however, to all this, as will also be
seen, was their place at the centre of the Scottish political process, and
it was from within the ranks of Edinburgh lawyers too that formulation
of the new politics of the late-eighteenth and early-nineteenth centuries
was to come.

II

As with the Church and the university system, the Scottish law had
strong historical connections with the Continent. First, the spirit of
Scots law was Roman-Dutch, as opposed to the common law system of
England. Thus, by sharing a legal basis with the continental countries
rather than with England, Scotland had been open in a crucial area of
her social organisation to European thought, practice and education.
For example, the infiltration and penetration of Roman Law in Scotland began through the Roman Church in medieval times, and the close
association with Continental countries in the sixteenth and seventeenth
centuries accounted for much of the form of Scottish law which
began to take shape at that time. The College of Justice (as the supreme
Court, the Court of Session, was styled) was founded in 1532, and was
based on an Italian model. Many Scots lawyers in the sixteenth, seventeenth and early-eighteenth centuries undertook their courses in law in
France and Holland, where the main content of the syllabus was Roman Law. Roman Law's position in Scotland was strengthened by the
removal of Canon Law at the time of the Reformation and Calvin's
Institutes were clearly influenced by Roman Law. Hence, by the time
of Lord Stair's *Institutions* in 1681 (the first clear definition and
systematisation of Scots Law), while Scottish examples were given
where available, there was a clearly defined place in Scottish legal
thought and practice for the Emperor Justinian's code and for more

recent Dutch elaborations.[7]

Sir James Dalrymple (1619-95), first Viscount Stair, taught Logic at Glasgow University in the early 1640s, was prominent in the conduct of university business and in 1648 was called to the Scottish Bar. He became Lord President of the Court of Session in 1671 and had considerable experience of public life. His *Institutions* are the major example of that seventeenth-century improvement in Scottish law which preceded the part played by law and lawyers in the eighteenth-century Enlightenment. Prior to his work, the College of Justice relied on *Practicks,* compilations of law decisions, arranged alphabetically by subject, and containing abridgments of old laws. They were practical, encyclopaedic manuals not concerned with fundamental principles. The *Institutions,* which were followed three years later in 1684 by Sir George Mackenzie's slighter work of the same title confined largely to the Criminal Law, were not a compendium but a philosophic and practical treatise which evolved from Stair's studies of the original sources of Roman Law and the subsequent Dutch and French commentators. Whether it was sufficiently philosophical is a matter to be seen later. As one historian has commented, Scotland entered the post-Union era with a scientific system of law which was founded on philosophical principles, that contrasted with the precedents that constituted English Law.[8] The absence of records reinforced the tendency of Scots Law to be like Roman civil law in being based on principles rather than precedent. Stair differed from two highly influential continental jurists, the Dutchman Hugo Grotius (1583-1645) and the German Samuel Pufendorf (1632-94) in not regarding a rational theory of law as possibly independent of theological assumptions, and so he was adding a distinctively Scottish element to legal thought by allying it to religious belief. Stair secondly diverged from the natural lawyers by adding the importance to reason of authority in the construction of legal principles. Thirdly, and here the posthumous *Institute of the Law of Scotland* (1773) by John Erskine (1695-1768), professor of Scots Law at Edinburgh, 1737-65, might also be considered, the institutional writers regarded law as natural (as had Grotius and Pufendorf) and believed that both law and adherence to agreements were dictated by reason. Nature also imposed on property holders various restrictions in the public interest, and thus was stressed the social context in which law operated—in this instance the communal interest in private property.[9] That philosophers who were not lawyers were preoccupied with the connection between law and society too gives added importance to legal developments in eighteenth-century Scotland.

If Stair's *Institutions* were one example of improvement in the seventeenth century that necessarily preceded enlightenment in the eighteenth a second example was preparation to facilitate legal education in Scotland, which would permit Scots Law to be taught and which would obviate the need for legal students to go to continental universities. Legal education prior to the eighteenth century, necessitated by the lack of provision in Scotland and convenienced by the similarity of the law elsewhere, took place in Leyden, Bourges, Utrecht, Orleans and other universities. Stair's *Institutions* marked the beginning of Scots Law as an independent system; in the year of the Treaty of Union the chair of public law and the law of nations and nature was founded in the University of Edinburgh, and the chair of Law at the University of Glasgow was revived. In a matter of a few subsequent years further chairs were established in the Scottish universities: Edinburgh founded a chair of Civil Law in 1709 and of Scots Law in 1722, for example. From then on there was, in a sense, competition between the old Roman-Dutch Law and Scots Law, with some members of the Scottish legal profession being keen on developing Scots Law, and others to introduce Roman Law. The perceptive decline in the influence of Roman Law was not really evident until the end of the eighteenth century. From then on, the practice of Scottish law students studying in the Netherlands was not only interrupted by the French wars but ceased to be attractive in the face of the Dutch law faculties' adoption of the new Civil Code in the place of Roman-Dutch Law. Furthermore, as has been seen, provision had been made for studying the emerging Scots Law in Scotland. Another reason for the decline of Roman Law in the nineteenth century was the impact of industrialisation—Roman Law being better suited to the social and economic conditions of eighteenth-century Scotland.[10]

The Jacobite Rebellions of 1715 and 1745 were further *stimuli* to the development of Scots Law. The Law grew as a result of various acts (such as the Clan Act of 1715, and the act abolishing the old Courts of the Lords of Regality, 1747) being passed and decisions of the Courts being made on the basis of those acts. A complex system of conveyancing (which in Scotland comprises land law as well as the legal instruments by which rights are transferred) was also growing up, simultaneous with all the social and economic development on the land. Roman Law was referred to less because by statute or custom it did not apply. The changes were reflected in procedures for qualifications as an advocate: in 1692 Scots Law was merely an optional subject of examination for prospective advocates whereas in 1750 an examination in Scots Law became imperative. A separate commercial law was yet another outcome of eighteenth-century developments, such as an increase in commercial activity.

As far as the actual working of the legal system was concerned, the Court of Session consisted of the Lord President and fourteen Lords of Session, who held their posts for life. Six of the fourteen were named by the Crown as Lords of Justiciary, one with the title of Lord Justice-Clerk, and were the most superior judges. In between the Edinburgh sessions of June to August (summer) and November to March (winter) the Lords of Justiciary travelled to particular centres in Scotland trying criminal cases. The College of Justice was housed in Parliament House, Edinburgh: only advocates might plead before the supreme courts, and judges of the Court of Session had to have served five years as an advocate first. As far as the location of other legal work was concerned, it was, like Church management, in taverns.[11]

III

The Treaty of Union of 1707 merely boosted an existing situation in which the Law and its practitioners in Scotland were beginning to thrive. There are five ways in which the centrality of the Law to eighteenth-century Scottish life can be seen—agricultural improvement, political management, the importance of property, commercial development and the relationship in law with England. As far as agricultural improvement is concerned, it has already been seen that in the early period the actual legal personnel in the Faculty of Advocates came from landed families. Hence, numbered among the country's agricultural improvers were many lawyers; they 'were particularly effective in directly searching out or propagating . . . new farming techniques'.[12] But their role was more profitable than that of simple improver. They acted professionally for other improvers, seeing through the many land transactions, the conveyancing, that necessarily took place in an era of agricultural improvement.

Secondly, lawyers became vital to the post-Union political process. Among a number of tasks that devolved upon lawyers was the requirement that they comment on legislation which pertained to Scotland and which Wstminster needed to pass. This gave to Edinburgh lawyers an effective say in crucial political affairs; they were essentially the arbiters of Scottish politics in the new situation of union and were to remain so probably until the appointment of the first Secretary of State in 1885.[13] Any legislation pertaining to Scotland (such as the

Election Act of 1743, the Entail Act of 1770 and the Bankruptcy Act of 1772) was reviewed within Scotland largely by the judges, advocates and writers before it went on to Westminster for largely formal approval. More important was the political management of Scotland itself and its parliamentary seats. Patronage and placemen oiled the machinery of the whole system of British politics in the eighteenth century. The loss of the Scottish Parliament saddled Scotland with the system of management that operated the political process throughout Britain. Cockburn wrote in 1824 that the purely political functions of the office of Lord Advocate gave it the principal dignity and influence because of the extent of his patronage:

> ... the Lord Advocate is the Privy Council of Scotland,—the Grand Jury of Scotland,—the Commander-in-Chief of the forces of Scotland — the guardian of the whole police of the country, — and that, in the absence of higher orders, the general management of the business of Government is devolved upon him.[14]

Lawyers were central to the Scottish political process of the time: they managed the electoral machine. What were at stake were the forty-five Scottish MPs who were to be delivered up to the Government interest.[15] Cockburn described the situation of the late-eighteenth and early-nineteenth centuries as one where in the whole of Scotland there were only 1,500 or 2,000 county electors, because of the qualifications imposed, and no opposition member could ever be returned.[16]

Hence, Ramsay of Ochtertyre could comment that 'lawyers are never paid so handsomely as in election causes'.[17] The system was structured in such a way that there was a manager of Scottish affairs whose place during lengthy absences in London was taken by one or more *sous-ministres*. The *sous-ministres* were lawyers and had been chosen for the position because of their particular expertise in local affairs.[18]

An example of how the system worked can be seen in the case of Henry Home, later Lord Kames. In 1750, when a vacancy occurred on the Scottish Bench, the leader of the Government, Henry Pelham, wrote to the Lord President of the Court of Session saying that he had heard of him as a good lawyer and a zealous Whig. Kames failed nonetheless to gain an appointment on this occasion because his earlier Jacobitism and Episcopalianism were remembered in Scotland, and, in the words of David Hume, he was opposed by the Earl of Marchmont, who controlled Scottish patronage at the time and whom Kames had not sufficiently wooed.[19] The system of management that permeated Scottish politics and legal appointments extended to the conduct of the Law itself. It has been noted how in litigation political or family loyalties and bribery as much as reason were used to influence judges. It is here that the social composition of the legal profession related to the political function of lawyers: family or clan loyalty was strong in Scotland and Scottish landed society was small and tightly-knit by marriage. (In 1798 there were only 88 families of peerage and 253 of baronage.) Hence, litigation was conducted on the basis of family interest, and the litigious class was encouraged by the system, especially in the first half of the eighteenth century, to ensure their success at law by entering members of their families in the Faculty of Advocates.[20]

The involvement of the Law in politics meant that it was within the Law that Scottish political battles were often fought out. The Faculty of Advocates, for example, became politicised and it can be appreciated that the importance of the Law in the operation of Scottish politics would lead to such a development. The system of Scottish political management by England through a Scottish 'manager' and *sous-ministres*, with its accompanying corruption, began to come under more vocal and active attack with the rise to the office as Lord Advocate and 'manager' of Henry Dundas in the 1770s, which coincided with the beginning of a whole change of climate not only for the operation of the Law, but also for the Scottish Enlightenment.[21] Henry Cockburn was a lively reporter of the situation, admittedly writing well over fifty years later: in the late-eighteenth-century Scotland had 'no popular representation, no emancipated burghs, no effective rival of the Established Church, no independent press, no free public meetings, and no [impartial] trial by jury'. The political system reposed on the town council, small, self-elected and self-interested, and in no way involving the people. Cockburn concluded: 'Thus, politically, Scotland was dead'. Under Dundas judges, sheriffs, clergy, professors and all bureaucratic posts increased greatly.[22]

The era of the American War, which was followed so closely afterwards by the French Revolution and its consequential wars and stimulus to political discussion and activity, saw the first challenge to so moribund a state. The leaders of the reforming Whigs were Sir Thomas Dundas and Henry Erskine, son of the Earl of Buchan.[23] Erskine was a witty man, popular even in circles opposed to his views and a capable barrister in all departments of litigation. In the General Election of 1784, fifteen of the Scottish seats went to supporters of Erskine and

Dundas, and the following year Erskine was elected to the Deanship of the Faculty of Advocates and remained so until 1796. In other words, just as the Law operated the *status quo*, so it was within a crucial body of the Law, the Faculty, that the political opposition to the *status quo* grew up. Cockburn's delineation of centres of power outside of the Law in Scotland, which accompanied his list of those supporting Erskine (Thomas Dundas became reconciled in 1794 with his kinsman Henry in the wake of the French Revolution), is valuable not least because these centres were vital contributors to the Enlightenment as a whole: The Church, the medical profession and the University in Edinburgh.[24] The sole object of the Scottish Whigs at this time was to breathe life and propriety into the corrupt Scottish political system.[25] Lawyers were in the van of the struggle throughout the troubled era in Scotland during which the impact of the French Revolution and the subsequent repression were felt. Erskine lost his Deanship of the Faculty in January 1796, for example, because he had presided at a public meeting to petition against the war. On a more positive note, it was that generation of Whigs who were educated under the foremost teachers of the Scottish Enlightenment who founded the second *Edinburgh Review* in 1802, part of the purpose of which was to blazon forth articles of the Whig creed. The first editor was a lawyer, Francis Jeffrey, and the *Review* was a new institution created during the Scottish Enlightenment. It emerged from a particular political situation and was connected at least in part with lawyers. More important for the Scottish Enlightenment, the increase of party politics and the rise of frequent and intense political issues from the 1770s, was ultimately a cause of its demise. Politics throttled the Scottish Enlightenment.

Property was an important concept for the social thought of the Scottish Enlightenment but it was, and always had been, of everyday importance, especially in a society that was creating new owners of property as the economy developed. In such a situation lawyers were obviously crucial because it was they who actually conferred the documents of legal entitlement upon an owner. The rise of a new class of wealthy men was due, in part, to increasing commercial activity in the eighteenth century; as Lockhart discerned, the more the commercial towns thrived the more business was created for the legal town of Edinburgh: 'every great merchant in Glasgow pays large salaries to some two or three members of the law in Edinburgh, who conduct the numerous litigations, that arise out of a flourishing business with great civility'. Indeed 'every house which a man, not a lawyer, builds out of Edinburgh, enables a man, who is a lawyer, to build another equally

comfortable in Edinburgh'. Consequently, the control of the law and
the social life of Edinburgh was in the same hands and the advocates'
influence extended over almost the whole of Scotland.[26]

One of the leading philosophers and a professor of law, John Millar,
wrote in his celebrated work, *An Historical View of the English Government,* that Scotland borrowed some of the Roman procedures and
some English ones too, because of its proximity. Consequently, Scotland
has, for example, the jury trial in criminal prosecutions, but no jury in
most civil actions.[27] The situation Millar outlined, which prevailed long
before any union of Crown or Parliament, was reinforced by the Treaty
of Union of 1707. It has been shown that as far as company legislation
was concerned, in the nineteenth century and under the Bubble Act of
1719, certain acts were required to be passed in England to facilitate
business enterprise. In fact, there was much less need for the acts in
Scotland. There the Law already provided for such modern measures
as the transferability of shares, the ability for a company to sue and be
sued in its own name, and limited liability. Nonetheless, despite the
superiority of Scots Law on these and related questions, the legal
system became assimilated to the English despite a decision in 1757
which asserted that superiority. English economic domination soon
came to mean at the very least modification of areas of Scottish life
apparently far removed from the subject of the economy.[28]

The result of the lawyers becoming embroiled in agriculture, politics,
property and commerce, despite assimilation, was that as the century
wore on they became influential, powerful, arbiters of politeness and
social tone, but above all, wealthy. What was seen of their part in and
their benefits from the building of the Edinburgh New Town confirms
all that. Even those lawyers who did not originally own land were now
accruing sufficient substance to remedy the deficiency. On the basis
of the late-seventeenth-century definition of Scots Law and its rise to
prosperity in the ensuing decades, its relationship to the Scottish Enlightenment can be examined.

IV

The Scottish Law related to the Scottish Enlightenment through
individuals and through the concern that legal and non-legal intellectuals had for the Law as a social discipline. First, a number of first
and second rank thinkers were lawyers—John Millar, Lord Kames and
Lord Monboddo to name but three. They bore out the validity of
Cockburn's quotation seen earlier that the Law was a profession con-

genial to the practice of literature and philosophy. However, individual
contributions reveal little about the Law as such, as a vehicle or prom-
oter of the Enlightenment: often for quite non-professional reasons
lawyers were just as active in politics or economic development. It was
the public service career of its age. Likewise professors and churchmen
wrote no less literature and philosophy than lawyers. It cannot be
argued that it was because Kames or Millar or Monboddo were lawyers
that they were able to contribute to the corpus of Scottish Enlightenment thought. After all, Kames contributed equally to literary criticism. All that can be argued is that their particular expertise made what
the legal *literati* had to say about law in the context of social philosophy more compelling, but lawyers did not initiate the concern for
social philosophy. They merely contributed albeit vitally, to volumes written on the subject.

Hence, the concern must be for ideas on law, though any detailed
consideration must await a later discussion of social philosophy. Suffice
it to note at present that law and justice were considered to be of
great significance by legal and non-legal *literati* alike. They were necessary in society because of the institution regarded as a fundamental
determinant of so many social arrangements, namely property. William
Robertson noted how, in primitive ages, such few property disputes as
there were were settled by the authority figures—the venerable old
men, or chiefs. As disputes multiplied with the refinement or progress
of societies, precedents were appealed to as being the results of accumulated wisdom and experience.[29]

Government arose, in the predominant view of the Scottish *literati,*
to protect property, and the function of government was to administer
justice. Law and justice were the forces that enabled society to cohere.
Consequently, law, like other institutions fundamental to society, had
to be reviewed regularly so that if conformed to the prevailing circumstances of the people who were required to live by it. Adam Ferguson
was one of the intellectuals who saw that law, in its intimate connection
with property, would necessarily be an instrument in the hands of the
wealthy and powerful. As their composition changed so too might the
Law. Lockhart spoke of the predominant social and economic group in
the Edinburgh of 1819 as a 'jurisprudential aristocracy', and his use of
the adjective was particularly apt in the Scottish setting, since the
object of jurisprudence 'is to study the phenomenon of law as a
whole and its relation to society'.[30]

The thinkers, lawyers and non-lawyers alike, 'improved' on the
philosophic treatment meted out to Scots Law by Stair, in the light of

the changed circumstances through which Scotland had passed since 1681 and was passing in the period of High Enlightenment. They raised the Law from a mere social instrument to a place in advanced, philosophical thought. Consequently, they dignified Scots Law, they took an interest in it, as it was being shaped and helped to make it into a highly respected intellectual discipline. It required the detailed elaboration and study it received in the eighteenth century, because, given its social importance, it had to be able to respond to the rapid social and economic developments of the age. The Enlightenment, starting with Stair's philosophical approach which was compounded by later *literati*, made the Law what it was. The legal system and even the lawyers might be affected by external factors—England, agricultural and commercial improvement, politics—but the Law itself was *sui generis* and legitimately to be considered an achievement of the Scottish Enlightenment.

In the course of the Law being adopted by the Enlightenment, there were bound to be tensions among its practitioners, all the more so since the Law was so intimately involved with ecclesiastical and political issues of the age. The social and professional position of the Law gave the profession a significant say in the Kirk through such officials who were members of the General Assembly as the Lord Advocate, the Solicitor-General and judges, elected as elders. Other lawyers, not officials, also were elected in their capacity as elders to the General Assembly, many landed advocates naturally being among them. So were embroiled together the Church, Law, land and politics, in the management of which lawyers were so active. Consequently, in the ecclesiastical party disputes which reigned from at least mid-century, and which were by no means confined to the ordained ministers of the Kirk, the lay lawyers, now in their capacities as elders and as authors whose works were under scrutiny, necessarily were drawn in to the Moderate-Evangelical battles.

The Moderates' insistence on the law being obeyed (all law, not just the Patronage Act) so that the place of the Church in national life should be secured was an important and significant measure given the process of evolution in which Scots Law found itself at the time of their activity. Several important lawyers were active in the inner Moderate circle of the early 1750s—Andrew Pringle, later a judge of the Court of Session as Lord Alemoor, who was Solicitor-General in 1755, Gilbert Elliot of Minto, who had been called to the Bar in 1742 and who, with another lay Moderate, George Drummond, had been a moving spirit behind the project to build Edinburgh's New Town, and

the younger Alexander Wedderburn, who was called to the Scots Bar
in 1754 and raised to the bench only two years later on the road to
becoming Lord Chancellor of England. Yet another lawyer involved
was Kames, who was, as has been seen, accused of heresy but received
powerful support from the Moderates, numbered among whom
were legal colleagues. It appears, though, that it was mostly young lawyers who supported the Moderate cause, since it was their vigour that
from 1753, when the Moderates began to show their strength, caused
the free speaking in the Assembly and the abandonment of the calling
of judges, among others, to give their opinions first. Here can be seen a
generational split between lawyers, old *versus* young, judges *versus*
advocates, that would also have permeated intra-professional disputes.

As far as political tension within the profession was concerned,
that was most evident from the 1770s, when the party political temperature nationally began to rise and when the Whig-Tory rivalries and
disputes grew more and more intense, especially in the aftermath of
the French Revolution and the continued insistence of the Whigs on
political reform at home. It is this atmosphere and situation which
explain the dichotomy between the conservative judges, who saw
Jacobins under every bed in the 1790s but yet whose conduct was
almost certainly exaggerated by the Whig Cockburn in the lambasting
they received in his *Memorials*,[31] and the Glasgow professor of law,
the radical Whig and republican John Millar. Clearly the different
occupations within the profession, practical judges, academic professors, also contribute to explaining an important difference between
and among lawyers. There arose in the political circumstances of the
late-eighteenth century a battle within the profession somewhat akin to
the earlier Moderate-Evangelical battle in the Kirk. There were the conservative lawyers, in politics, in the Faculty and on the bench, who
considered that then was the time to batten down the hatches. There
were the other lawyers, Erskine and his young followers, Whigs and
those educated in Enlightened Edinburgh and Glasgow classrooms,
who saw the time as ripe for actually implementing the social theory
of the Scottish Enlightenment, for introducing reform not repression,
for bringing the country's institutions into line with new social and
economic circumstances, not for resisting all thoughts of even mild
reform. The Whigs, reformers and enlightened, were those, largely
lawyers but aided by ageing professors, who kept alight the liberal
torch in the dark days of Pitt's and Dundas' repression. Like the
Robertsonian Moderates who were prepared to be bold in a secular
age, so were the liberal lawyers prepared to be bold in a revolutionary

one. The Evangelicals and the conservative bench in each case were those who were not prepared to put their faith to the test.

The Scottish Enlightenment was intimately connected with particular milieus of Scottish society. That lawyers, because of their professional and political contributions, increasing wealth, and consequent social status, were important actors in the total scene of Scottish improvement meant that they too would be part of the Enlightenment. But added to straightforward political, social and economic history was the intellectual element, and the considerable place given to law in social thought by the philosophers. Consequently, the intellectual and practical elements in the Scottish legal profession could not be kept apart in the troubled days of the 1790s and early 1800s. However, the resilience of the system and the profession had been developed to such a degree by the closing years of the Enlightenment that they survived, even if the Enlightenment, which had contributed so much to the making of the Law, did not.

Notes

1.   N. T. Phillipson, *The Scottish Whigs and the Reform of the Court of Session 1785-1830*, Ph.D. dissertation (University of Cambridge, 1967), Appendix B, Tables I-V, pp. 349-58 which explain in detail the figures, the method of compilation, and the various qualifications to be made in assessing them. John Shaw, University of Stirling, has important work in progress on the place of lawyers in eighteenth-century Scottish society.

2.   *Ibid.*, pp. 17 and 348.

3.   Henry Cockburn, *Life of Lord Jeffrey with a selection from his correspondence*, 2 vols. (Edinburgh, 1852), I, pp. 84-5, and Henry Cockburn, *Journal of Henry Cockburn being a continuation of the Memorials of his Time*, 2 vols. (Edinburgh, 1874), II, p. 230.

4.   J. G. Lockhart, *Peter's Letters to his Kinsfolk*, 3 vols., 2nd ed. (Edinburgh, 1819), I, pp. 210-12.

5.   James Boswell, *A Letter to the People of Scotland on the alarming attempt to infringe the articles of the Union and introduce a most pernicious innovation by diminishing the number of Lords of Session* (London, 1785), pp. 46-7.

6.   Henry Cockburn, 'Office of Lord Advocate of Scotland', *Edinburgh Review*, XXXIX (1823-4), pp. 377 and 377n-379n.

7.   The following articles in two volumes of the Stair Society's publications emphasise and detail the close links between Scotland and the Continent in the field of Law: A. C. Black, 'The Institutional Writers, 1600-1829', *An Introductory Survey of the Sources and Literature of Scots Law* (Edinburgh, 1936), pp. 59-69; D. B. Smith, 'Roman Law', *ibid.*, pp. 171-82 J. C. Gardner, 'French and Dutch Influences', *ibid.*, pp. 226-34; J. Irvine Smith, 'The Transition to the Modern Law 1532-1660', *An Introduction to Scottish Legal History* (Edinburgh, 1958), pp. 25-43; J. Irvine Smith, 'The Rise of Modern Scots Law 1660-1707', *ibid.*, pp. 44-9.

8.   H. W. Meikle, *Some Aspects of Later Seventeenth Century Scotland* (Glasgow, 1947), pp. 8-12. The quotation is from p. 12.

9.   Peter Stein, 'Law and Society in Eighteenth Century Scottish Thought', *Scotland in the Age of Improvement*, ed. N. T. Phillipson and Rosalind Mitchison (Edinburgh U.P., 1970), pp. 148-52.

10.   Peter Stein, 'The Influence of Roman Law on the Law of Scotland', *The Juridicial Review* (1963), pp. 221 and 243.

11.   See Walter Scott, *Provincial Antiquities and Picturesque Scenery of Scotland*, 2 vols. (London, 1826), I, p. 73.

12.   T. C. Smout, *A History of the Scottish People 1560-1830* (Collins/Fontana, London, 1972), p. 264.

13.   H. J. Hanham, *Scottish Nationalism* (London, Faber, 1969), pp. 52-6.

14.   Henry Cockburn, *Edinburgh Review*, XXXIX, p. 369.

15.   See Smout, pp. 201-4. See also John M. Simpson, 'Who Steered the Gravy Train?', *Scotland in the Age of Improvement*, pp. 47-72.

16.   Cockburn, *Jeffrey*, I, pp. 74-5.

17.   John Ramsay, *Scotland and Scotsmen in the Eighteenth Century*, ed. A. Allardyce, 2 vols. (Edinburgh, 1883), II, p. 473.

18.   Phillipson, p. 29.

19.   Ian S. Ross, *Lord Kames and the Scotland of His Day* (Oxford, Clarendon Press, 1972), p. 114 and *The Letters of David Hume*, ed. J. Y. T. Greig, 2 vols. (Oxford, Clarendon Press, 1932), I, p. 162. For an account of the Scottish political system in the eighteenth century and the pervasiveness of lawyers in it, see W. Ferguson, *Scotland: 1689 to the Present*, (Edinburgh and London, Oliver & Boyd, 1968), Ch.5, 8 and 9.

20.   Phillipson, pp. 23 and 25.

21.   Henry Dundas (1742-1811); 1763 entered Faculty of Advocates; 1766 Solicitor-General; 1774-90 MP for Midlothian; 1775-83 Lord Advocate; 1782 and 1784, Treasurer of Navy; 1791-94 Home Secretary; 1793 President of Board of Control with management of Indian Affairs; 1794-1801 Secretary at War; 1802 created Viscount Melville. 1804-6 First Lord of Admiralty; 1806 impeachment proceedings on grounds of his earlier mishandling naval funds, failed.

22.   Cockburn, *Jeffrey*, I, pp. 75-6, 76, 77-8.

23.   Henry Erskine (1746-1817); 1768 admitted to Faculty of Advocates; 1783 and 1806 Lord Advocate; 1758-96 Dean of the Faculty of Advocates; MP for Haddington 1806 and for Dumfries 1806-7; His reputation for integrity more than compensated for his short list of formal achievements.

24.   Cockburn, *Jeffrey*, I, p. 81.

25.   *Ibid.*, I, p. 82.

26.   Lockhart, I, pp. 210-12, 208-9, 207.

27.   John Millar, *An Historical View of the English Government from the Settlement of the Saxons in Britain to the Revolution in 1688*, 4 vols. (London, 1803), II, p. 300.

28.   R. H. Campbell, 'The Law and the Joint-Stock Company in Scotland', *Studies in Scottish Business History*, ed. Peter Payne (Cass, London, 1967), pp. 136-51.

29.   *The Works of William Robertson, D.D.*, 8 vols. (Oxford, 1825), VIII, pp. 287-8.

30.   Lockhart, II, p. 4 and Peter Stein, 'Legal Thought in Eighteenth Century Scotland', *Juridicial Review* (1957), p. 1.

31.   Henry Cockburn, *Memorials of his Time* (Edinburgh, 1856), pp. 113-25.

5 THE STUDY OF SOCIAL MAN

The capacities of the human mind have been in all ages the same, and . . . the diversity of phenomena exhibited by our species is the result merely of the different circumstances in which men are placed . . . the application of this fundamental and leading idea to the natural or *theoretical history* of society in all its various aspects; to the history of languages, of the arts, of the sciences, of laws, of government, of manners, and of religion,—is the peculiar glory of the latter half of the eighteenth century, and forms a characteristical feature in its philosophy.[1]

I

It was noted in the first paragraph of Chapter 1 that the European Enlightenment was that epoch in the history of man when he realised he could both understand and control his social and natural environment. The concern of the current chapter is that preoccupation of the Scottish philosophers with society. Among the questions and matters that absorbed them were why human beings associated with one another, what bonds held them together, what stimulated them to develop corporately and the institutions which arose in society such as language, property, government and law. The consideration given here is neither exhaustive nor designed to abbreviate, even if it were possible, the intellectual achievements in mental, moral and social philosophy of the Scottish Enlightenment. An indication will be given here of the Scottish contribution to that eighteenth-century concern for man's social environment, a concern that was highly dependent on the achievements of seventeenth-century philosophers.

The thought of the Scottish Enlightenment is connected with the social history of the movement. The writers' own environment stimulated their reflections upon it: Scotland was moving from what might be called a 'rude' state to a 'polished' one; she was modernising; she was now in close contact with an advanced neighbour, and the situation necessarily posed questions about the dynamics and mechanics of development and the value of things Scottish, what should survive and what should be laid decently to rest as having served its purpose. The fact that the philosophers relatively rarely discussed Scotland as such in their work may not mean that they were unaware of and uninvolved in Scotland's circumstances in the eighteenth century, but rather that to dwell on Scotland might have been regarded as provincial rather than cosmopolitan. Nonetheless they did write of the benefits Scotland would derive from sharing in the post-1688 English constitution and the economic opportunities which the Treaty of Union made possible, and they were also involved in advocating a separate Scottish militia.[2] Furthermore, the thought was channelled through institutions basic to Scottish life as witnessed by the development of an independent system of Scots Law, in the notions of the Robertsonian Moderates in the Kirk (see, for example, the underlying philosophy of their *Reasons of Dissent*) and in the teaching offered by the universities. Societies and journals were yet another vital, corporate expression of the Scottish Enlightenment and were due in large part to the eagerness of the writers to benefit from a sharing of ideas. Subsequent chapters on the universities, societies, journals and the like will consider the intricate relationship between the institutions of the Scottish Enlightenment and that other vital segment of ideas, on science and nature.

II

There were primarily five *literati* who dominated the social philosophy of their age, who together (and in concert with men of lesser intellectual stature and impact) can be said to constitute the Scottish school of the eighteenth century. They are David Hume, Adam Smith, William Robertson, Adam Ferguson, and John Millar.

David Hume is a philosopher for all time and not merely to be considered in the context of his own age or alongside lesser minds.[3] To his contemporaries though he was regarded as an historian. In the twentieth century, philosophers have rediscovered him, concentrating on his relevance for their contemporary studies. In any study of the Scottish Enlightenment he is central, because of his writings, his sociability, his familiarity and proximity to the other philosophers; he is central to the intellectual impact they made in their own day as seen in the lengths to which the Church went to counteract him, and to their impact in subsequent periods; and he was central in the stimulus he provided to the establishment of Thomas Reid's common sense school of philosophy with its influence in nineteenth-century England and America as well as Scotland.[4] He stands as the most celebrated and distinguished man of letters, despite his always being apart from the formal structures of Scottish society, shunned by the

Church, vetoed by the universities and only on the fringes of the Law while Librarian to the Faculty of Advocates. Yet he was highly active in the informal settings and in his social philosophy he had much in common with his contemporaries. Those shared intellectual preoccupations are the concern here while, of course, it is recognised that much more can be said about the many other aspects of the totality of his philosophy.

Adam Smith is as well known as Hume, but his writing is much more concentrated in the shared concerns and approaches of the social philosophers of the Scottish Enlightenment and so he is, in some senses, a far more typical writer.[5] The current study sets Smith's work in the context of a total philosophy of society (as Smith himself conceived it) and does not consider him mainly as the writer of a treatise on economics, which is in itself a highly limited description of the *Wealth of Nations*. His closest friends, and also his executors, were Joseph Black and James Hutton, both of whom were regarded primarily as natural philosophers.[6]

One of the most important intellectual inheritances of the philosophers was the scientific method which had so successfully, in the preceeding century, opened up the mysteries of the laws of nature. The Scots were determined to do for the science of man and society what Bacon and Newton had done for matter. Indeed, in 1786, when the heyday of the Enlightenment was over, John Millar could say that as a result of their studies of society: 'The great Montesquieu pointed out the road. He was the Lord Bacon of this branch of philosophy. Dr Smith is the Newton.'[8] More than thirty years earlier, Smith himself had written a vigorous defence of Newton's philosophy in the first *Edinburgh Review.*[8] The method on which they sought to model their enquiries was highly systematic. Man was to be studied through the workings of his mind, and in studying that the Scots were to follow Locke's empirical method of introspection. By looking at the world of their own time and at history, it became clear to them that it was natural for man to be sociable, to form societies. This is the first premise of the social philosophers to be considered here. The Scots of the eighteenth century differed from such as Hobbes of the seventeenth, who talked of society arising out of a contract made by the members of society as a measure of self-preservation against the otherwise uncontrolled, selfish passions of man leading to a nasty, brutish and short life. Ferguson wrote, on the contrary that mankind began in peace, and continued in peace, until some quarrel arose.[9] The Scots, in one of the several ways in which they showed indebtedness to the English philosopher Shaftesbury, were more positive: man was naturally social, and societies were the natural state in which to find mankind. Ferguson, for example, wrote several times in his *Essay on the History of Civil Society* of man's group propensities.[10] For Hume, in his *Treatise of Human Nature*:

> 'Tis by society alone [man] is able to supply his defects . . . By society all his infirmities are compensated: and tho' in that situation his wants multiply every moment upon him, yet his abilities are still more augmented, and leave him in every respect more satisfied and happy, than 'tis possible for him, in his savage and solitary condition, ever to become.[11]

A clear statement of the same belief, which also pointed to man's capacities as being meaningless outside a social context, was provided in 1730 by Francis Hutcheson in his inaugural lecture entitled 'The Natural Sociability of Man' as Glasgow University's Professor of Moral Philosophy.[12] Finally, in another work, Adam Ferguson, had some qualifications to make on the naturally social character of man, namely that man might sometimes be disposed to break the peace. He argued that if a social character were natural, there would be no need for fences, locks, bars, magistrates, troops, prisons and instruments of torture. Nonetheless, he wrote: 'Man is made for society and the attainments of reason'.[13]

The second matter to be considered here is the philosophers' analysis of the evolution of society because, their observation informed them, man had clearly developed from a primitive or rude state to a sophisticated or polished condition. Such change and development was prompted by the state of man, as an active being, which caused him to satisfy 'natural' and 'insatiable' wants by improving his material conditions. To quote Adam Smith:

> It is this which first prompted [mankind] to cultivate the ground, to build houses, to found cities and commonwealths, and to invent and improve all the sciences and arts which ennoble and embellish human life, which have entirely changed the whole face of the globe, have turned the rude forests of nature into agreeable and fertile plains, and made the trackless and barren ocean a new fund of subsistence, and the great high road of communication to the different nations of the earth.[14]

John Millar wrote likewise:

> One of the most remarkable differences between man and other
> animals consists in that wonderful capacity for the improvement
> of his faculties with which he is endowed. Never satisfied with
> any particular attainment, he is continually impelled by his desires
> from the pursuit of one object to that of another; and his activity
> is called forth in the prosecution of the several arts which render
> his situation more easy and agreeable.[15]

In approaching the analysis of progress, they adopted a thoughtful or
philosophical stance: that is, they attempted to order and systematise
all history by reducing it to a few general principles which were inferred
from a mass of observed facts. They were helped in their approach by
their belief in the uniformity of human nature in all periods, countries
and social circumstances.[16] Such facets of human nature as contradictory yet complementary as selfishness and 'fellow feeling' were
stressed in the kind of psychology employed by the philosophers.
Adam Smith's *Theory of Moral Sentiments,* a vital work of the Scottish
Enlightenment, particularly emphasised not only the selfishness but
also the capacity and drive for sympathy in man that led him to associate and form social bonds with others. Sources of control in society
were established precisely to curb the worst aspects of human nature,
and individuals also imposed restraints upon their behaviour.

Montesquieu, the French *philosophe,* was a most important
influence in the generation of the social philosophy of the Scottish
Enlightenment. The philosophers, as has been indicated by an earlier
quotation, never hid their debt to and regard of him.[17] Hume was
probably the first to appreciate the significance of the *Esprit des Lois*
when he read the work in Italy in 1748. Subsequently he received a
copy from the author who had read Hume's own *Essays Moral and
Political* in their third edition published in the same year. Like Montesquieu's book, Hune's essays were concerned with historical causation
and the relationship between the circumstances of a society and its
institutions. Then Hume saw translated parts of the *Esprit des Lois*
through the printing presses in Edinburgh in 1749 and, from the
1750s on, the approach of Montesquieu exerted a powerful influence
on the central, shared intellectual concern of the *literati*, the philosophical history of society.

Montesquieu shared with the Scots a belief in the uniformity of
human nature in all times and places, but differed from them first by

his essentially static conception of society, since he was not concerned with changes which took place through time. He also emphasised the importance of such environmental factors as climate and soil in determining the government, laws and other social institutions of different countries. Different forms of government such as republics, monarchies and despotisms were explained by physical causes: 'different climates produce different wants, different wants different styles of life, different styles of life different laws. Institutions like slavery, or polygamy, or parliamentary government arise in response to climatic requirements'.[18] The Scots were also concerned with explaining the relationship between the institutions of societies and their circumstances, but their approach was dynamic and historical, and by and large they believed that the form of economy dictated the nature and form of social institutions.

For the Scots, the passage from rudeness to refinement invariably went through several temporal phases: they were supreme practitioners of philosophic history which was concerned with progress, in the sense of movement, from one state to another. No qualitative judgement was implied by the *literati's* concept of progress: it did not necessarily imply betterment. Indeed barbarism was not a stage that had been left behind, but was a state that could be imminent and recurrent. Consider Millar's giving Scotland after the departure of the Crown as an instance of retardation, and also Ferguson on the Roman Republic, where at times he is reminiscent of Hobbes, rather than rejecting him:

The military and political virtues, which had been exerted in forming this empire, having finished their course, a general relaxation ensued, under which, the very forms that were necessary for its preservation were in process of time neglected. As the spirit which gave rise to those forms was gradually spent, human nature fell into a retrograde motion, which the virtues of individuals could not suspend, and men, in the application of their faculties even to the most ordinary purposes of life, suffered a slow and insensible, but almost continual decline.[19]

The outstanding explanation both of philosophic history and its accompanying approach of theoretical or conjectural history was given by Dugald Stewart in his panegyric of Adam Smith, originally read to the Royal Society of Edinburgh in 1793. Stewart himself belonged to the second generation of *literati*, but is more renowned for his talents as a teacher and populariser than as an original thinker.[20] His ability to popularise complex topics is seen well in the following series of quotations:

> When, in such a period of society as that in which we live, we compare our intellectual acquirements, our opinions, manners, and institutions, with those which prevail among rude tribes, it cannot fail to occur to us as an interesting question, by what gradual steps the transition has been made from the first simple efforts of uncultivated nature, to a state of things so wonderfully artificial and complicated.

The philosophic history of the Scottish Enlightenment set out to answer those questions scientifically—how society as a whole had developed, how particular facets of social existence had changed over time. However, as Stewart continued, the historical data for answering the questions were rarely available since in the primitive state of society, for example, steps to progress are taken before men think of recording them. The absence of crucial data, therefore, gives Scottish philosophical history or natural history (as in Hume's *Natural History of Religion*) or *histoire raisonée* (as it was called by some French exponents) its theoretical or conjectural character:

> In this want of direct evidence, we are under a necessity of supplying the place of fact by conjecture; and when we are unable to ascertain how many men have actually conducted themselves upon particular occasions, of considering in what manner they are likely to have proceeded, from the principles of their nature, and the circumstances of their external situation.

Theoretical history could be applied to diverse aspects of human knowledge and endeavour—from pure and mixed mathematical science, in which the gradual progress of philosophical speculation could be demonstrated in the natural succession of inventions and discoveries, to government, national and municipal. In the philosophical study of government laws are considered as arising from the circumstances of society and attempts made 'to account, from the changes in the condition of mankind, which take place in the different stages of their progress, for the corresponding alterations which their institutions undergo'.[21]

Dugald Stewart, this time in his *Dissertation exhibiting the progress of Metaphysical, Ethical, and Political Philosophy since the Revival of Letters in Europe,* believed that the main value of philosophic studies was in its cultivation of generalisation:

> . . . accustoming those who pursue them to regard events, less in relation to their own immediate and partial concerns, than to the general interests of the human race; and thus rendering them at once happier in themselves, and more likely to be extensively useful in the discharge of their social duties.

Furthermore, Stewart is found saying in his account of Smith:

> In most cases, it is of more importance to ascertain the progress that is most simple, than the progress which is most agreeable to fact; for, paradoxical as the proposition may appear, it is certainly true, that the real progress is not always the most natural. It may have been determined by particular accidents, which are not likely again to occur, and which cannot be considered as forming any part of that general provision which nature has made for the improvement of the race.[22]

A basic characteristic of philosophic history was the all-inclusive nature of its concerns. Hume considered the totality of civilisation to be the province of the historian, not merely politics.[23] Nonetheless, civilisation was to Hume and other philosophers dependent on a political notion, namely liberty. Liberty can here be defined as the opportunity to exist in a state of law and order and thus benefit from the 'civilised' pleasures of a 'civilised' environment without fear of plunder or anarchy. Civilisation also implied conditions which made liberty possible, such as economic progress.[24] Ferguson made the point often in his *Essays on the History of Civil Society* where he distinguished between civilisation and civil society. The actual conventions which safeguard property, for example, and order (law was such a social convention) could be termed civil society; the order civil society called forth could be termed civilisation because in a state of order man's finer aspirations could be fostered, nurtured and realised. Economic progress or the fine arts were such aspirations as could only emerge in a civilised state.

The philosophic history of the Scottish Enlightenment was necessarily integrated, since all that men did in societies, from the holding of property to the painting of pictures, was necessarily connected with the civil establishment of society—to paraphrase Hume's words, wars, treaties, and successions were not enough; history was useless and unintelligible without equal consideration being given to 'manners, finance, arms, trade, learning'. The philosophers remained consistent when they approached knowledge itself as a unity. Knowledge was no more compartmentalised into disciplines than human activities were seen by them as unrelated and diverse social arrangements. Just as all facets of society bore on society, so all fields of knowledge bore on the unity of knowledge. Such a view of knowledge was not peculiar to eighteenth-century Scotland but was a feature of the pre-specialist mind that was commonplace certainly before the nineteenth century and which was arguably rendered redundant by the work of the Enlightenment itself. In his *Dissertations*, Dugald Stewart quoted with obvious approbation Hume's views on the unity of knowledge, as expressed in his *Treatise of Human Nature*, simply because all knowledge bore on human nature.[26]

III

For the purpose of this analysis it has been necessary to stress how the philosophers saw all facets of society as bearing on each other, how they saw society as integrated, and how they believed in the unity of knowledge, because there now follows an examination of specific features of life in societies on which they commented. The feature that most of them saw as the factor which determined almost everything else in society was economics. In the words of William Robertson, 'In every inquiry concerning the operations of men when united together in society, the first object of attention should be their mode of subsistence. Accordingly as that varies, their laws and policy must be different.' Adam Smith's and John Millar's diagnoses of man's nature driving him on to improved material conditions have already been mentioned, and Smith's own emphasis on economic determinism is well known. In his *Wealth of Nations*, for example, when writing of the relationship between the developments of commerce in towns and the improvement of a country, Smith averred that:

Commerce and manufactures gradually introduced order and good government, and with them, the liberty and security of individuals, among the inhabitants of the country, who had lived before almost in a continual state of war with their neighbours, and of servile dependency upon their superiors.[27]

Robertson, seven years earlier, had made a similar point about the wide social effects of economic developments, when he wrote of the freedom of medieval cities in his *History of Charles V*. He went on in the same work to indicate how economic development underlay not only domestic matters (such as taxation, representation and justice) but also foreign relations.[28]

Hume's views on the matter were expressed at their pithiest in his essay 'Of Refinement in the Arts':

> [An] advantage of industry and of refinements in the mechanical arts is that they commonly produce some refinements in the liberal; nor can one be carried to perfection, without being accompanied, in some degree, with the other. The same age, which produces great philosophers and politicians, renowned generals and poets, usually abounds with skilful weavers and ship-carpenters. We cannot reasonably expect, that a piece of woollen cloth will be brought to perfection in a nation, which is ignorant of astronomy, or where ethics are neglected.

Luxury also bolsters the middle classes, the bedrock of opposition to tyranny of all kinds.[29] Smith and Millar echoed Hume's sentiments,[30] and essential to Adam Ferguson's analysis of society was that central economic concept, property. The possession of property is what distinguishes savage and barbarous societies from those that are refined.[31]

The views of the two lawyers among the philosophers considered here also displayed a primacy for matters economic in social arrangements. Millar believed that man's prime concern was to obtain subsistence and then more comfortable living:

> [Man's] first efforts are naturally calculated to increase the means of subsistence, by catching or ensnaring wild animals, or by gathering the spontaneous fruits of the earth; and the experience, acquired in the exercise of these employments, is apt, successively, to point out the methods of taming and rearing cattle, and of cultivating the ground. According as men have been successful in these great improvements, and find less difficulty in the attainment of bare necessities, their prospects are gradually enlarged, their appetites and desires are more and more awakened and called forth in pursuit of the several conveniences of life; and the various branches of manufacture, together with commerce, its inseparable attendant, and with science and literature, the natural offspring of ease and

affluence are introduced, and brought to maturity. By such gradual advances in rendering their situation more comfortable, the most important alterations are produced in the state and conditions of a people: their numbers are increased; the connections of society are extended; and men, being less oppressed with their own wants, are more at liberty to cultivate the feelings of humanity; property, the great source of distinction among individuals, is established; and the various rights of mankind, arising from their multiplied connections, are recognised and protected: the laws of a country are thereby rendered numerous; and a more complex form of government becomes necessary, for distribution justice, and for preventing the disorders which proceed from the jarring interests and passions of a large and opulent community.

Millar proceeded to give examples of the social effects of economic development such as the rise, perpetuity and heredity of class distinctions.[32] Millar entitled a part of his *An Historical View of the English Government*, 'The Effects of Commerce and Manufactures, and of Opulence and Civilization, upon the Morals of a People'. His economic interpretation of society and history might also be seen in another excerpt from the *Historical View*, remarking on England in Tudor and Stuart times:

While the tradesmen, manufacturers, and merchants of England, were thus rapidly increasing in number, and advancing to such comfortable situations, many individuals in those classes were, by successful industry in the more lucrative branches of trade, and by a rigid and persevering economy, the natural effect of their habits, enabled them to acquire splendid fortunes, and to reflect a degree of lustre upon the profession to which they belonged. In this, as in all other cases, property became the source of consideration and respect: and, in proportion as the trading part of the nation became opulent they obtained more weight in the community.[33]

So, too, Lord Kames gave equal emphasis and primacy to the economic drive in man and society—what he called man's 'remarkable propensity for appropriation'. Closely connected with the idea of 'appropriation' is the 'mode of subsistence' which prevailed in any society at any point in time. Like other *literati* here considered, Kames laid much emphasis in, for example, his *Historical Law Tracts* (1758) on the economic basis of a society and its consequent dictation of social, political and even foreign arrangements. In one of his *Sketches of the History of Man* (1774), for example, Kames wrote 'Without private property there would be no industry, and without industry, men would remain savages forever'.[34]

A second most important shared feature in the writing of the Scottish *literati* was that historical approach which, not surprisingly, saw the history of man as divided into four economic phases, one progressing from another. The four phases, the primitive, the pastoral, the agrarian and the commercial, while shaped by their economic characteristics, were also to be seen consequently as cultural periods of man's past. Of the philosophers considered in this chapter, only Ferguson did not accept the analysis of the history of society into the four divisions. At best he saw three stages: one where property is unknown, a second where it is known but not embodied in law and a third, refinement, where property is a principal distinction. His views as recorded in his *History of Civil Society*:

> Of the nations who dwell in those, or any other of the less cultivated parts of the earth, some intrust their subsistence chiefly to hunting, fishing ot the natural produce of the soil. They have little attention to property, and scarcely any beginnings of subordination or government. Others having possessed themselves of herds, and depending for their provision on pasture, know what it is to be poor and rich. They know the relations of patron and client, of servant and master, and suffer themselves to be classed according to their measures of wealth. This distinction must create a material difference of character, and may furnish two separate heads, under which to consider the history of mankind in their rudest state; that of the savage, who is not yet acquainted with property; and that of the barbarian, to whom it is, although not ascertained by laws, a principal object of care and desire.[35]

Ferguson is, however, the exception. Hume, Smith, Kames, Robertson and Millar had much to say about the four stages and what pressures existed within the first three to cause their progress on to a subsequent peak of development. Kames wrote that progressive changes in the order mentioned may be traced in all societies. Smith stressed and elaborated the analysis:

> The four stages of society are hunting, pasturage, farming, and com-

merce. If a number of persons were shipwrecked on a desert island
their first sustenance would be from the fruits which the soil naturally produced, and the wild beasts which they could kill. As these
could not at all times be sufficient, they came at last to tame some
of the wild beasts that they might always have them at hand. In
process of time even these would not be sufficient; and as they saw
the earth naturally produce considerable quantities of vegetables
of its own accords, they would think of cultivating it so that it
might produce more of them. Hence agriculture, which requires
a good deal of refinement before it could become the prevailing
employment of a country . . . The age of commerce naturally
succeeds that of agriculture. As man could not confine themselves
to one species of labour, they would naturally exchange the
surplus of their own commodity for that of another of which they
stood in need.[36]

Lecturing later, Millar showed the analysis necessarily led into such
other fundamental and interconnected aspects of society as property
and government:

The first object of mankind is to procure subsistence, to obtain
the necessaries, comforts and conveniences of life. Their next aim
is to defend their persons and their acquisitions against the attacks
of one another. It is evident, therefore, that the more inconsiderable
the possessions of any people, their political regulation will be the
more simple. And the more opulent a nation becomes, its government ought to be the more complicated. Property is at the same
time the principal source of authority; so that the opulence of a
people not only makes them in need of much regulation, but enables
them to establish it. By tracing the progress of wealth we may thus
expect to discover the progress of government. [Millar then proceeds
to establish four successive states of society:(1) Mere savages,
'people who live by hunting and fishing and by gathering the spon-
taneous fruits of the earth'; (2) Shepherds; (3) Husbandmen; and
(4) Commercial peoples.] [37]

Hume treated of the four same stages in his *Political Discourses,* as
did Kames in *Historical Law-Tracts.* [38] All elaborated in their various
works that matter of central importance to the *literati,* namely that in
each economic stage society necessarily makes particular arrangements
suited to the priorities and values of the time. For example, Adam

Smith, throughout his works, illustrated the close connections between the prevailing economy and the forms of government and social rank that subsisted within society at the time.[39] In the hunting stage, communities would be small and based on the family, and private property would arise (such as cattle) and there would then be a stimulus to the establishment of government to protect it, government necessarily being the creature of the propertied members of society to secure themselves against the propertyless poor. Property would also introduce distinctions in society between man and man, which did not exist in the primitive stage where all were equal in their poverty. The *literati* showed a considerable acquaintance with past history, classical authors, forgotten peoples (ancient Egyptians) and even surprising living examples of stages long past to eighteenth-century Europeans (the North American Indian) in illustrating their theories about the rise and development of institutions and relationships in society.

Forces existed within a given stage which would cause the transition to the next one. One such force which the *literati* delineated and which was seen in earlier quotations was man's own efforts to improve his conditions, and, given that basic human drive, one improvement led to others. Man's own nature and desires were not easily satisfied and were in themselves sufficient to account for progress. There were, however, other factors too, such as the notion of the heterogeneity of ends, that in attempting to secure one objective, man can set precedents then lay the basis of a second and unintended end.[40] The domestication of animals and their accumulation, to take specific examples, both contributed to the transition from the primitive stage to the pastoral. In the words of Smith:

> The appropriation of herds and flocks which introduced an inequality of fortune, was that which first gave rise to regular government. Till there be property there can be no government, and the very end of which is to secure wealth, and to defend the rich from the poor. In this age of shepherds, if one man possessed 500 oxen, and another had none at all, unless there were some government to secure them to him, he would not be allowed to possess them. This inequality of fortune, making a distinction between the rich and the poor, gave the former much influence over the latter, for they who had no flocks or herds must have depended on those who had them, because they could not now gain a subsistence from hunting, as the rich had made the game, now become tame, their own property.[41]

Kames suggested, it will be recalled, that once private property appeared it became a stimulus to hard work.[42]

The agrarian stage arises out of tillage, leads to settlement, and consequently confers particular importance on land. Property is still the arbiter of arrangements and conditions in society but, since the important form of property is now the different commodity of land, it causes different social developments. For example, feudalism was readily explicable when land was the basis of subsistence. Smith, when writing of the landowner in the agrarian economy, argued:

> He is at all times . . . surrounded with a multitude of retainers and dependants, who, having no equivalent to give in return for their maintenance, but being fed entirely by his bounty, must obey him, for the same reason that soldiers must obey the prince who pays them.

Similarly, there were factors at work within the agrarian stage which caused the emergence of the commercial. Consider two interacting matters for example: Smith shows in the *Wealth of Nations* that as subsistence precedes any development in society such as conveniences or luxury, the cultivation and improvement of land which permits subsistence must precede towns, which 'furnish only the means of conveniency and luxury'. Towns arose from surplus rural produce. He continued shortly afterwards to note how the cultivation of land required the activities of certain artificers—smiths, carpenters, wheelwrights, ploughwrights, masons, bricklayers, tanners, shoemakers, tailors. These artificers also frequently need one another and as, unlike the farmer, they do not have to reside in one locality, the artificers tend to congregate in the neighbourhood of each other, thus forming a town. They are then joined by those butchers, brewers, bakers and others necessary to supply the artificers' needs.[43] Thus two developments in agrarian society, the surplus and the spawning of artificers, together contributed to the formation of towns and cities, the centres of activity in the commercial stage.

David Hume put forward a similar analysis in his essay 'Of Money'. He noted how exchange is unknown in primitive society and only arises when men begin to refine their enjoyments. They are not always living at home nor content with the produce of their neighbourhood, more exchange takes place and products are cheaper in a refined society.[44] Smith, Ferguson and Millar pointed to a further contributory factor within the agrarian stage which could foster the commercial, namely the cultivation of 'the arts'. For Smith, the arts arose out of improving and multiplying the materials needed for man's necessities. Ferguson considered art natural to man, a basic skill that he learned to refine.[45] Hume considered the increasing refinement of the arts to be a reinforcement of man's natural inclination to be sociable:

> Enriched with science, and possessed of a fund of conversation . . . [T]hey flock into cities; love to receive and communicate knowledge; to show their wit or their breeding; their taste in conversation or living, in clothes or furniture . . . Particular clubs and societies are everywhere formed: Both sexes meet in an easy and sociable manner: and the tempers of men, as well as their behaviour, refine apace.[46]

These circumstances having come to prevail, the whole basis of the subsistence of the labouring part of the population changed. Trades, professions and independent labour arose.[47]

IV

It can now be seen more clearly that once the *literati* had delineated the forces at work in a given stage of history, certain features of society and certain questions would necessarily interest them, so that they would wish to explore and elaborate them further. This chapter will conclude by giving attention to some of those features and questions, namely property, government, justice and law, language and the division of labour. The significance of property has already been indicated as a stimulus to settlement, to the establishment of government and to the framing of law. It is necessary now to summarise the ubiquitous effects of property in the working of a society and in the working out of its history. Property was the arbiter of so much in social arrangements, namely government (and implicitly law), division into rich and poor, subordination of poor to rich, a hierarchy of economic groups, the fact that the prevailing group will be those with wealth, the power of property to perpetuate from one generation to another ruling dynasties, power, prestige and inheritance.[48] Kames' historical law tract on 'Property' is an important contribution to the Scottish Enlightenment's concern for the matter.[49] It will be recalled too how, for Adam Ferguson, acquaintance or otherwise with property was his yardstick for dividing a savage or barbarous society from a refined one. Property was that fundamental.

Authority and subordination, therefore, derived from property. Property and wealth were not the only sources of them, however; in that part of his *Wealth of Nations* entitled 'Of the Expense of Justice', Smith pointed to four causes of superiority—personal qualities (which are disputable), age, fortune (greatest in the primitive stage when inequality was at its most stark) and birth. But of these four fortune and birth were the most effective in the later stages of the history of society and, of course, they were closely linked to each other. Millar had written likewise in 1771, when he first published *The Origin of the Distinction of Ranks*.[50]

The philosophers give many examples of 'property in action', as it were, in different stages of society's progress and from many actual historical instances. For example, Smith showed how primogeniture could arise; when land was only thought good for subsistence, it was equally divided upon a father's death (as in Roman times). But when property came to men as more than mere subsistence and a means of power and protection, then it was inherited, undivided, by one heir.[51] Elsewhere, Smith noted how powerful landowners thus became: in France, before the introduction of feudal law, they had extensive authority and jurisdiction that necessarily flowed from their property holdings; property owners were the law makers and, naturally enough, framed law in their own interests.[52] Related to the situation thereafter was the dictum that William Robertson followed in the pursuing of his history. For him 'it becomes an object of importance to trace the progress of feudal property; for upon discovering in what state property was at any particular period, we may determine with precision what was the degree of power possessed by the king or by the nobility at that juncture'.[53] Prior to that stage, in the hunting era, when nations are strangers to the idea of property, people are so independent that government has little authority. Where the idea of private property is incomplete, and no criminal jurisdiction is established, there is hardly any function of internal government to exercise.[54] In short, property leads to government and to the framing of law by property-holders and law is consequently framed in their own interest.[55]

The possession of property was not static, and progress could so alter the personnel who actually held that form of property which was so influential at a particular stage in history that thoroughgoing social repercussions could result. Consider, for example, David Hume, writing about that favourite chestnut of the historians, the rising middle-class. In his essay on luxury, already quoted in other contexts,

Hume said that in the era of commerce and industry those hitherto
subservient members of society discover an independence, even a power
base for themselves. The land becomes 'property' cultivated by erst-
while peasants and tradesmen and merchants acquire property. The
result is to 'draw authority and consideration to that middling rank of
men, who are the best and firmest base of public liberty'. They neither
wish to be subservient nor to tyrannise—'They covet equal laws, which
may secure their property, and preserve them from monarchical, as
well as aristocratical tyranny.' Hume then proceeded to give a specific
example drawn from the English House of Commons: 'The lower house
is the support of our popular government; . . . it owed its chief influence
and consideration to the increase of commerce, which threw such a
balance of property into the hands of the commons.'[56]

To appreciate the full significance of what Hume was saying it is
necessary to consider a passage from his *History* concerning the reign of
James I. He practised a policy designed to maintain royal authority but
it was a policy which in fact ran completely counter to that of any
other prince who had set out to consolidate his power. Previous arbitrary governments had been concerned to keep the nobility at court
where they would incur heavy expenditure in indulging the pleasures
there and so reduce their fortune. Furthermore they would be sub-
ordinated to ministers by being close to them and their absence from
their provincial power bases would weaken their authority. James, not
having the means to support a splendid court, dispersed the nobility.
He did so too because he thought the proximity to each other would
enable them to realise their joint strength and their presence at court
would encourage them to pry into matters of state. However, the result
of his policy was to enable the nobility to amass great wealth at home;
at home they dispensed much hospitality and thus augmented their
influence. The court lost all power over them because the nobility
consolidated their property, totally altering the course of English
government in less than forty years. Royal authority waned when
aristocratic property waxed.

A further shift of political power occurred in the reign also as a
result of the dissipation of property. Progress in luxury and the arts,
which in earlier reigns than that of James had led to the barons' dissipation of wealth, continued in his reign to ruin smaller landed proprietors and men of rank, who sought to ape their superiors by the indulg-
ence in luxuries. The consequent vacuum was filled by the rise to wealth,
substance and consequently political power of those who could afford
fashionable expenses, but who had to pay some care and attention to

their domestic economy, and of the gentry whose only expense was country hospitality since no taxes were levied, no wars waged, no court attendance required nor election expenses necessary. Hence, in Hume's words 'Could human nature ever reach happiness, the condition of the English gentry, under so mild and benign a prince, might merit that appellation.'[57] Millar, more theoretically, proposed the same idea: families of ancient wealth would, with the progress of luxury and refinement, be reduced to poverty, since, having no experience of business, they could not maintain their wealth and yet, wishing to emulate their peers in elegance, they would spend all they had. The beneficiary would be 'the frugal and industrious merchant' who has been successful in trade and wishes to purchase that rank which is bestowed by property ownership. (Somewhat cyclically he too becomes the victim of extravagance in time.) Furthermore, with the demise of an ancient and formerly substantial family there was destroyed that tradition of dependence which is built up over time so that the *nouveau riche* must buy personal services which his predecessor had by tradition. The consequences of all this were to introduce 'a democratical government'.[58]

The consideration just given to property has (because of the primacy given by the philosophers first to the mode of subsistence and consequently to property) already touched on such social consequences of property and subsistence as government, law and justice. However, these matters too, since they were of some importance to the writers' work, are themselves in need of some elaboration. Kames wrote in his *Historical Law Tracts* that government arose to protect property.[59] Kames is important among the *literati* in the matter of government because it was his profession as a lawyer which prompted his thoughts on the subject. Hume, in his essay 'Of the Origin of Government', remarked that not only was man naturally inclined to form societies but he also naturally progresses further to establish political society, in order to administer justice, which in its turn brings peace, safety, and mutual intercourse. Government had ultimately no other object or purpose but the distribution of justice. And he had capped that with a comment in his essay 'Of the First Principles of Government' saying that those who possessed a large sphere of property could easily stretch their authority, and bring the balance of power to coincide with that of property.[60]

The powers of Government were, as expressed by Smith, heavily concentrated on justice and laws.[61] The philosophers, illustrating their general intellectual debt to Montesquieu, agreed that the form government took varied in time and place. Nonetheless, in emerging at all, government was satisfying a law of nature that all men were fitted for different places in a social hierarchy.[62] Likewise Robertson believed that 'It is only in societies which time and the institution of regular government have moulded into form, that we find such an orderly arrangement of men into different ranks, [as in ancient Mexico] and such nice attention paid to their various rights.'[63] For Kames, government was an art, one that had improved over time and should be subject to further improvement. He had much to say about the size and form of governments depending on geography, economy, population and similar factors.[64] Millar echoed, in his *Historical View of the English Government,* much of what others had said; government was an absolute necessity if disorders in human society were to be avoided, and law was entirely subordinate to the nature of government.

When justice and law were themselves specifically considered by the *literati* it was clear that they had a central part to play in the social philosophy of the Scottish Enlightenment. They were the forces of cohesion and discipline in a society.[65] It is clear that for Kames law was designed to ensure a peaceful society and justice consisted of orderly relations among members of society, balancing the claims of the individual with those of the society as a whole. As with his views on government and indeed reflecting the dynamic approach in his writing, Kames believed that law was not static.[66] Millar thought likewise for he wrote that 'the people are gradually led, by experience and observation, to introduce particular statutes or laws, in order to correct or ascertain their practice for the future'.[67]

The non-legal *literati* viewed law little differently as when Smith averred that justice, being an object of law, was the 'security from injury' and 'the foundation of civil government', and as when Ferguson, seen in the twentieth century as a pioneer of sociology, devoted some considerable space to that topic.[68] Elsewhere, when discussing the kind of law formed in free states, Ferguson made it clear that in such states the wisest law that was framed was esentially a compromise of interests. Only then could liberty be maintained. As lucre was the great motive in one man injuring another, so law principally referred to property, and was concerned with making property secure. Only by being sure of having his property and position safe, and by being restrained from committing crimes, said Ferguson, could a man regard himself as free.[69]

Liberty was not the only consequence of law in society. William Robertson showed, by reference to the regularising of feudal law before

the end of the twelfth century, to the enlarging and methodising of
Canon Law and the ordering, in the light of Roman jurisprudence,
of different social customs of various European provinces and king-
doms, a multiplicity of changes on society that law could occasion:

> They gave rise to a distinction of professions; and the obliged men
> to cultivate different talents, and to aim at different accomplish-
> ments in order to qualify themselves for the various departments and
> functions which became necessary in society. Among uncivilised
> nations there is but one profession honourable, that of arms.[70]

This analysis of Robertson's relates closely to the important idea in the
thought of the Scottish Enlightenment, namely the division of labour,
to which attention will shortly be given. Nonetheless it graphically
demonstrates, for present purposes, the close interconnections in the
social analysis: settled society depends on property, property gives
rise to government, government to law, law to freedom and to sophisticated accomplishments by man.

Language was clearly an important attribute of social man, simply
because there could be no society without it. On the practical level,
the social institutions of the Scottish Enlightenment, which form the
framework of this study, were highly dependent on social intercourse
and so, in a sense, the philosophers both practised and were intimately
involved in sociality. Secondly, it is clear that the study of language
and disquisitions upon it relate closely to an important area of eighteenth-century Scottish thought which it has not been the task of
this chapter to consider, namely philosophy of the mind. Language
was an index of intelligence and reflected human mentality, knowledge, memory, imagination, sensibility. The history of society and
of the human mind were linked, and in any work which could devote
itself solely to the ideas and thought of the Scottish Enlightenment,
it would be both interesting and necessary to examine the interconnections closely.[71]

Thirdly, and partially related to these words of Robertson, it must
be borne in mind that Dugald Stewart, when defining conjectural
history, referred to Adam Smith's *Considerations Concerning the
first Formation of Language, and the Different Genius of original and
compounded Languages* as a particularly fine specimen of the *genre*.
Rather than limiting the conception of the *literati's* historical writing
to economic changes, it is useful to see other facets of it as displayed
by Smith's work. For example:

> Let any one consider within himself . . . what he means by the word
> *three*, which signifies neither three shillings, nor three pence, nor
> three men, nor three horses, but three in general; and he will easily
> satisfy himself that a word, which denotes so very metaphysical
> an abstraction, could not be either a very obvious or a very early
> invention.[72]

Throughout the dissertation, Smith was concerned to show how particular situations, (e.g. savagery) would prompt men to name objects,
and how subsequent development would cause them to develop various
qualifying words for objects already known, new objects and novel
situations. Particular kinds of words would come at particular points
of time—some nouns and verbs before adjectives and prepositions.
Other *literati* concerned with language included Ferguson, Kames and
a fellow judge, James Burnet, Lord Monboddo.[73] Both judges' views
(Kames' in his *Sketches of the History of Man* and Monboddo's in
Of the Origin and Progress of Language) were at least in part connected
with idiosyncrasies pertaining to the two men. The first where Kames
'reconciles' reason and revelation by explaining the multiplicity of
languages in the world by reference to the Tower of Babel and by
postulating several separate creations of human beings: the second
where Monboddo contended that orang-utangs were primitive man,
and man lost his tail as he acquired intelligence and, along with
intelligence, language.

The final matter to be considered here is the division of labour,
the analysis of which was most fully given by Smith but he was not
the only author to comment on it. It is important to note when beginning consideration of this topic that the Enlightenment was not simply
concerned with the past, with analysing historical development. They
were as much concerned with learning useful lessons for the present
and future. One of Smith's objects, for example. in writing *Wealth
of Nations* was in showing how a society that has reached the fourth
stage of development, actually functions. Smith, Ferguson and Millar
with their different approaches and given the wider purposes of their
major works, commented on the division of labour—Smith and
Millar as economic and social analysts, Ferguson writing of its fragment-
ing the personality in an industrial society.[74] In the examination of
the division of labour, concentration will be on Smith and Ferguson,
with occasional references to Millar and Robertson.

Since individuals in a society require a means of subsistence and
since society as a whole needs finance for its public services, Smith is

concerned to show that the way labour is organised will facilitate
the wealth of nations. That is how he comes to treat of the division
of labour, for it is by dividing the labouring processes up into many
stages that the most advanced economy organises its industry and thus
makes itself and its members opulent. In Robertson's words (used
identically in his *History of America* and his *Disquisitions on Ancient
India*) 'In proportion as refinement spreads, the distinction of profession increases, and they branch out into more numerous and minute
subdivisions.'[75] Millar, too, writing of justice, noted how, for example,
law suits are rare in the stages of poverty and rudeness and in subsequent stages before that of opulence the sovereign and nobility can
act as judges. The opulent state, however, gives rise to numerous law
suits and judges, holding court regularly, are required by society:

> Thus the exercise of jurisdiction becomes a separate employment,
> and is committed to an order of men, who require a particular
> education to qualify them for the duties of their office, and who,
> in return for their services, must therefore be enabled to earn a
> livelihood by their profession.[76]

Smith's exposition of the division of labour was first given in his
Lectures in the early 1760s and published in almost identical wording
in the *Wealth of Nations* in 1776. In the second chapter of that work
he explains how the division of labour comes about; it arises from that
propensity in human nature and peculiar to human nature, to barter,
to truck and to exchange. Man always has need for other men but he
can scarcely hope to interest other men in him purely from benevolence.
Hence bargains are struck, and exchange for goods and services is made
between different specialists, for reasons of self-love, not benevolence.
The disposition of man to treaty leads to the division of labour. By
indulging in the exercise, a man appreciates that he can live sufficiently well by specialising in one task rather than undertaking both a
craft and foraging for provisions. The examples Smith gives include that
of a person adept at making bows and arrows in the primitive or pastoral stage of history. He exchanges what he makes for cattle or venison
till he sees that he can, by exchange, get more cattle and venison than
if he went to catch them himself. So he specialises as an armourer.
In this context Smith gives many other examples—smith, brazier,
tanner, dresser. A precondition of the division of labour would also
be the accumulation of stock—hence the initiator of the division of
labour is unlikely to be a poor man.

In the third chapter of the *Wealth of Nations*, Smith is concerned to show how the process of the division of labour is limited by the extent of the market. In a small market, one man's surplus produce may exceed the need he has for ther men's labour. In towns, division of labour is likely to be more common than in country areas where in scattered villages every farmer must be butcher, baker and brewer. Improvements in water-transport, because they enlarge the market, are, therefore, great stimuli to the division of labour.

It is now appropriate to notice Smith's opening chapter, which is concerned with the effects of the division of labour, the chapter which contains the celebrated example of pin manufacture. In that example Smith writes of the almost eighteen operations required in the process, undertaken by say ten men and producing 48,000 pins a day, whereas if only one of those men had tried to make pins independently, he could not have made twenty, perhaps not even one a day. The division of labour, in other words, massively increased production, and as it worked for pin manufacture so it equally well applied to other areas of manufacture. A consequence of this was the separation of different trades and employments: the greater the degree of refinement in a country, the greater the degree of separation of trades. Agriculture still does not subdivide the employments so greatly as manufacture and this may explain why agricultural production does not keep pace with manufactured production.

The division of labour occasions increased production by the same number of workers because of three factors; the increased dexterity of an individual workman concentrating on fewer processes; the saving of time by concentrating on one task and the introduction of labour-saving devices. In the case of the third factor, Smith maintained that the division of labour itself prompted the invention of machines as workmen thought of labour-saving devices to aid them in the single task they now had to perform. The final consequence was the 'universal opulence which extends itself to the lowest ranks of the people'.[77]

Adam Ferguson did not account for the rise of the division of labour other than by stating in his *History of Civil Society* that there would be no great progress in the arts of life unless it was introduced. He noted too the unequal division of the means of subsistence which assigned different work to different men, and a sense of utility led to further subdivisions. The advantages of the system that Ferguson saw were much the same as Smith's—more perfect work arising from a single preoccupation, more profits for the manufacturer from 'economic' use of his work force, more perfect produce for the consumer. On further examination of Ferguson's analysis it can be seen that he gives less place to self-interest because of his particular view of man as a community being. It led him into a most pessimistic view of the division of labour, which led to alienation and the soul destruction of individuals in a refined society. 'Where shall we find the talents which are fit to act with men in a collective body, if we break that body into parts, and confine the observation of each to a separate track?.'

That almost plaintive cry is the cue for Ferguson's constant criticisms of a society where the division of labour prevails. In considering his critique, it must be borne in mind that he was himself a former army chaplain and in the forefront of the campaign for a Scottish militia. He is absorbed with matters of defence and virtú. As a result of the division of labour , says Ferguson, tradesmen knowing of nothing but their own trade, may in fact contribute to the prosperity of their nation without knowing anything of human affairs, and without consciously making patriotism their object. Soldiers, statesmen and public servants have their work rigidly compartmentalised—they become cogs in a machine.

With individuals left to their own skills and callings of which others are ignorant, 'society is made to consist of parts, of which none is animated with the spirit of society itself'. At least savage societies are patriotic: refined societies no longer apprehend common ties, are languid and may even decay. The more the separation of professions takes place, as in China, the less strong in reality is the state because the fewer people there are able to defend the country physically from an enemy. 'By having separated the arts of the clothier and the tanner, we are the better supplied with shoes and with cloth. But to separate the arts which form the citizen and the statesman, the arts of policy and war, is an attempt to dismember the human character, and to destroy those very arts we mean to improve.' In short, the division of labour may be good for business and for comfort, but it can destroy the state and, worse, 'dismember the human character'.[78]

Smith had not been blind to the evil effects of the division of labour.[79] He did not, however, focus entirely on the same matters as Ferguson, nor did he approach the disadvantages he discerned in the same spirit. In Book Five of the *Wealth of Nations* Smith accepts, in a passage that might have been written after seeing Chaplin's 'Modern Times', that the division of labour, by confining many people to the performance of only one or two operations, can render man 'as stupid and ignorant as it is possible for a human character to become'. Rational conversations, generous, noble or tender sentiments, judge-

ments on his country's interests, capacity for defending his country—
all become impossible to him. Such drawbacks were not evident in the
societies of hunters, shepherds or husbandmen, where varied occupations stimulated man to exert body and mind—'Invention is kept alive,
and the mind is not suffered to fall into that drowsy stupidity, which,
in a civilised society, seems to benumb the understanding of almost
all the inferior ranks of people.' Smith, in common with Ferguson,
bemoaned the lack of interest in and acquaintance with the nation's
affairs that comes with the division of labour, as also the decline of
the martial spirit and ability. He was aware, too, that the lack of
varied occupations in a civilised state meant that men missed the
benefits available to them formerly of '[exercising] their minds in
endless comparisons and combinations, and [rendering] their under-
standings, in an extraordinary degree, both acute and comprehensive'. That led Smith on to his views on education, which was the
means he proposed for the government to combat the alienation and
atomisation implicit in the division of labour. But, as he noted in his
Lectures on Justice, education is precisely what can be lost in a rich and
commercial nation. With trades reduced to very simple operations,
children can be employed at a tender age. Once at work, boys tend to
throw over parental authority and indulge in riot and debauchery.
And a final drawback Smith perceived was that after the division of
labour took place. first the cultivation of land fell to be done by the
'meanest rank' while the highest order undertook military service;
then when arts and commerce became really lucrative, the defence of
the state became the meanest occupation.[80]

John Millar, following Smith, considered that the separation of
different trades and professions might improve arts and sciences but it
worsened the personal qualities of those engaged in them. Millar went
on to recommend that attention be given to educational institutions.
for the lower orders—not just the well-to-do—and he commended the
Scottish parish school system.[81]

In the discussion of the division of labour can be seen in a microcosm the approach and the content of the *literati* to the philosophy of
society. The historical approach is evident, the emphasis on solidarity,
on economic determinism, and yet the essential utility of their studies
also becomes evident as they prognosticate for the future and suggest
plans to preserve the values of the past in the new commercial
atmosphere.

V

The significance and the achievement of the social philosophy (as here considered) of the Scottish Enlightenment can be seen in a number of important ways. First, it has a significance for its own age: the writings of the philosophers reflect the preoccupations of their time, whether on the provincial level of Scotsmen, aware in a sense that their own country was coming through from the dark ages of barbarism to the stage of refinement and interested in the mechanisms of development and its results. Millar wrote of Scotland in his *Historical View* as a rude nation. On a smiliar level they were aware of their close proximity not only in geographic but now political and economic terms to an advanced neighbour and the stimulus to 'natural development' that the relationship in England would provide, and the effect it would have on traditional Scottish life and institutions. On a different, and arguably higher level, the social thought seen here is an example of European Enlightenment thought on man's environment. It is different, as others have noted before, because it sought to analyse and explain constructively contemporary social arrangements. There was no political or religious iconoclasm. And in providing a comprehensible analysis it demonstrated the confidence of the age to control human affairs, for if their mechanisms were understood, there was some point in prescribing for the future. A second significance arises from the notion of prescription. The thought was highly Whig in tendency. They were clearly preoccupied with progress and with the gradual diffusion through time of political liberty to classes of society hitherto considered beyond the political pale. As individuals they were often very close to specific reform movements, pressing at the time for parliamentary reform or 'justice' for the American colonists. In the case of John Millar and Dugald Stewart there were even suspicions that they were Jacobins. In short, the work of the Enlightenment gave an intellectual ballast to Whiggery in the late-eighteenth century that was to prove invaluable. That contribution leads on to a third significance of the social thought of the *literati*—their ultimate contribution to the industrial age which followed them. Many of the ideas they aired, whether they be to do with the numbing intellectual effects of the division of labour and the provision of working-class education, or the necessity for concerting the institutions of society with the circumstances of society, or with property and developing notions of property and, consequently, giving power to owners of other than real property—

these and other thoughts, when conceived largely in the abstract but transmitted through educational and other institutions of the Scottish Enlightenment, such as journals, contributed to the evolution of rather than revolution in early Victorian industrial society.[82]

There is a further way in which the significance of the social thought of the Scottish Enlightenment can be seen and that is in intellectual terms—first, in its contribution to the modern development of the social sciences, and second in its contribution to Marxist thought,[83] its stimulus to economic thought in the early nineteenth century and, linked perhaps to both of these, its contribution to the evolution and concept of the bourgeoisie, their place in a capitalist economy and their political ideas and aspirations (political recognition and free trade, for example). There has been much writing in recent years on the contribution of the Scottish Enlightenment to the social sciences.[84] The philosophers believed in the unity of knowledge and how different facets of human existence were necessarily interrelated and even inseparable. In writing of life in societies, they each necessarily slanted their approach towards their special interest be it moral, psychological, sociological, legal or economic. The importance of each of these facets was such that they were subsequently separated to make for ease of elaboration and study, thus destroying the unity of knowledge so passionately believed in by the Scottish exponents of the philosophic method. Nonetheless, their philosophy had laid the basis.

The philosophers were concerned with social man. In their own lives they drew on and contributed to those social institutions through which this study is examining the Scottish Enlightenment. In various manifestations, they were social men in practice. Unshackled by the division of labour, they never forsook that unity of life and knowledge for which subsequent generations have yearned.

Notes

1.   Dugald Stewart, 'Dissertation: exhibiting the progress of metaphysical ethical and political philosophy since the revival of letters in Europe', *Collected Works*, ed. Sir William Hamilton, 11 vols. (Edinburgh, 1854-60), II (1854), pp. 69-70.

2.   See, for example, William Robertson, *History of Scotland,* 3 vols. (London, 1817), III, pp. 190-200 and John Millar, *An Historical View of the English Government from the Settlement of the Saxons in Britain to the Revolution in 1688,* 4 vols. (London, 1803), III, pp. 84-94. Subsequently *H.V.*

3.   David Hume (1711-76) studied at Edinburgh University and, in 1725 or 1726-34 studied the Law. His celebrated *Treatise of Human Nature* was

published in 1738 after his first visit to France although it was well
advanced before the visit. His *Essays Moral and Political* were published
in 1742; 1745-6 held a tutorship; 1746 accompanied General James
St Clair in an attack on France and then as his ADC to Vienna and Turin.
Published *Enquiry concerning Human Understanding* in 1748. Moved to
Edinburgh in 1752 and also published *Political Discourses* and his
Enquiry concerning Principles of Morals. Began writing *History of England,*
first volume of which was published in 1754, the second volume in 1756
and further volumes to 1761. Also published *Natural History of Religion*
in 1759; 1763 went to Paris, became first, Secretary to the Embassy and in
1765, Chargé d'Affaires; 1767-9 Under-Secretary of State in Northern
Department. Returned to Edinburgh. *Dialogues* published posthumously
in 1779. For further details see E. C. Mossner, *The Life of David Hume,*
(London, Nelson, 1954). An interesting and recent work which places
Hume and his work in its Scottish context is Giancarlo Carabelli,
*Hume e la retorica dell'ideologia: Uno Studio dei 'Dialoghi sulla religione
naturale',* La Nuova Italia Editrice (Firenze, 1972).

4.   See Anthony Quinton, 'The Neglect of Victorian Philosophy', *Victorian
        Studies,* I (1957-8), pp. 245-54; Gladys Bryson, *Man and Society: The
        Scottish Enquiry of the Eighteenth Century* (Princeton University Press,
        1945), p. 3 and George E. Davie, *The Democratic Intellect: Scotland and
        her Universities in the Nineteenth Century,* 2nd ed. (Edinburgh U.P.,
        1964), *passim.* The Hume Reid debate is more appropriately considered
        in an account of eighteenth-century Scottish mental philosophy. Briefly,
        though, Hume pushed the sensationalism of Locke and the idealism of
        Berkeley to their ultimate conclusion, scepticism, leaving sensation as the
        only reality in the universe. Common sense philosophy was an inadequate
        attempt to reply to Hume, asserting that such considerations as matter,
        reality, God, values were held to be objects of common belief or sense,
        which everyone of whatever intelligence accepted as real. Reid's reply to
        Hume was more satisfactory even though it still posed problems. In the
        words of Dr George Davie, summarising Reid: 'it is inherent in the nature
        of the belief in an external world or in the mathematical ideals to envisage
        facts not contained in the sum of the various elementary experiences
        involved in the genesis of . . . items of the common sense, and this
        peçuliar and fundamental fact of self transcendance is held by Reid and
        most Scottish philosophers to be an ultimate irrational mystery'. (G. E.
        Davie, *The Democratic Intellect: Scotland and her Universities in the
        Nineteenth Century,* 2nd ed. (Edinburgh U.P., 1964), p. 275.) See also
        Franco Restaino, *Scetticismo e Senso Sommune: la filosofia scozzese
        da Hume e Reid,* Biblioteca di Cultura Moderna Laterza, 1974.

5.   Adam Smith (1723-1790) studied under Francis Hutcheson at Glasgow
        and at Balliol College, Oxford. In 1748 lectured on Rhetoric in Edinburgh,
        1751-2 Professor of Logic, and 1752-63 Professor of Moral Philosophy at
        Glasgow. Author of *The Theory of Moral Sentiments* (1759) and *An
        Inquiry into the Nature and Causes of the Wealth of Nations* (1776).
        1764 travelled widely in France when tutor to Duke of Buccleuch. 1777-90
        resided in Edinburgh as a Commissioner of Customs. His *Essays on Phil-
        osophical Subjects* (1795) were publish posthumously.

6.   A biography of Robertson has been given above. Adam Ferguson (1723-
        1816) was born on the Highland Line in Logierait, Perthshire. M. A. St
        Andrews 1742, entered ministry and was Chaplain to the Black Watch
        1745-54, seeing front line service at the Battle of Fontenoy. Resigned
        from the ministry in 1754; succeeded Hume as Keeper of the Advocates'

Library 1757; tutor to the sons of the Earls of Bute and Warwick 1757-9.
Professor of Natural Philosophy, 1759, of Moral Philosophy 1764 and
of Mathematics 1785 at Edinburgh, but he was effectively retired in 1785.
Married Joseph Black's neice. In 1778 was Secretary to the futile Carlisle
Commission sent to negotiate with the rebellious Americans. His works
included *An Essay on the History of Civil Society* (1767); *Institutes of
Moral Philosophy* (1772); *History of the Progress and Termination of the
Roman Republic* (1783) and *Principles of Moral and Political Science*
(1792). John Millar (1735-1801) studied at Glasgow 1746-52 including
a short period under Adam Smith. Spent some time in Edinburgh
qualifying for the Bar in 1760 and becoming intimate with Kames. Kames
and Smith secured for him the Chair of Civil Law at Glasgow in 1761,
which he held till his death forty years later. Well known as a disseminator
of Whig views in his lectures on Public Law on the Principles of Government, especially in the politically sensitive era of the American and French
Wars. His main works were the *Origin of the Distinction of Ranks* (1771)
and *Historical View of the English Government* (1786). Subsequently
O.D.R., and H.V.

7.   Millar, *H.V.*, II, pp. 429-430n.
8.   Adam Smith 'An Enquiry after Philosophy and Theology', *Edinburgh
     Review*, No. 2 (1756) pp. 3-12.
9.   Adam Ferguson, *Principles of Moral and Political Science*, 2 vols. (Edin-
     burgh, 1792), II, p. 198. Subsequently *P.M.P.S.*
10. Adam Ferguson, *An Essay on the History of Civil Society*, 1767, ed.
     Duncan Forbes (Edinburgh U.P. 1966), pp. 16 and 4. Subsequently *H.C.S.*
11. *The Philosophical Works of David Hume*, ed. T.H. Green and T. H. Grose,
     4 vols. (London, 1874-5), II, p. 259.
12. Bryson, p. 153. Francis Hutcheson (1694-1746) has been noted previously
     as the influential teacher of Glasgow-trained Moderates. He was one of the
     main bridges between Shaftesbury, Newton, Locke and the writers of the
     heyday of the Scottish Enlightenment. Sometimes called the Father of
     the Scottish Enlightenment, because of his influence on later thinkers,
     especially Hume and Smith. His major work, published posthumously in
     1755, was *System of Moral Philosophy*.
13. Ferguson, *P.M.P.S.*, I, p. 199; see also II, pp. 31-2 and Henry Home, Lord
     Kames, *Sketches of the History of Man*, 3 vols. (Edinburgh, 1807), II,
     pp. 30 and 40, 35. Subsequently, *Sketches*.
14. Quoted from the *Theory of Moral Sentiments* by Andrew Skinner in the
     introduction to his edition of *Wealth of Nations* (Pelican, 1970), p. 23.
     See also p. 30 and Adam Smith, *Lectures on Justice, Police, Revenue
     and Arms*, ed. Edwin Cannan, (Oxford, Clarendon Press, 1896), p. 158 and
     pp. 160-1.
15. John Millar, 'The Origin of the Distinction of Ranks', (subsequently *O.D.R.*)
     in William C. Lehmann, *John Millar of Glasgow 1735-1801; His Life and
     Thought and his contribution to Sociological Analysis* (Cambridge U.P.,
     1960), p. 218. See also Ferguson, *P.M.P.S.*, II, pp. 122-3.
16. see Andrew Skinner, 'Economics and History—the Scottish Enlightenment',
     Scottish Journal of Political Economy, XII (1965), p. 5, quoting from
     Hume's *Inquiry concerning Human Understanding*.
17. See also Ferguson, *H.C.S.*, p. 65.
18. Peter Gay, *The Enlightenment: an Interpretation*, 2 vols. (New York
     Alfred A. Knopf, 1966 and 1969), II, p. 329. But see Kames, *Sketches*,
     I, p. 59, and Millar, *H.V.*, IV, p. 210 noted that the colder a country, the
     more its propensity to drunkenness.

19. Millar, *H.V.*, III, pp. 84-6 and Adam Ferguson, *The History of the Progress and Termination of the Roman Republic* (London, 1825), pp. 468-9. Subsequently *P.T.R.R.*

20. Dugald Stewart (1753-1828) was the son of an Edinburgh University Professor of Mathematics, Matthew Stewart. Educated at Edinburgh High School and the Universities of Edinburgh and Glasgow. He became attached to Thomas Reid's common sense philosophy whilst at Glasgow. Taught Greek, Mathematics, Natural and Moral Philosophy at Edinburgh, whose Chair of Moral Philosophy he held from 1785-1810. His *Collected Works* run to eleven volumes, and include biography, political economy and moral philosophy. He boarded and taught many well-known students, mostly Whigs, and received patronage from that political quarter. Moved in intellectual circles both on the Continent and in England. Suspected of 'Jacobinism' in heyday of the Terror. He is best described in Cockburn's *Memorials*.

21. Stewart, *Works*, X (1858), pp. 33-5 of 'Account of the Life and Writings of Adam Smith'. For another explanation of conjectural history see Henry Home, Lord Kames, *Historical Law Tracts*, 4th ed. (Edinburgh, 1792) pp. 25-6. Subsequently *H.L.T.*

22. Stewart, *Works*, I, p. 520 and X, p. 37; see also *The Works of Wm. Robertson, D.D.*, 8 vols. (Oxford, 1825), III, p. 10.

23. David Hume, *The History of Great Britain: The Reigns of James I and Charles I*, ed. Duncan Forbes (Pelican Classics, 1970), p. 219.

24. *Ibid.*, p. 15.

25. See Ferguson, *H.C.S.*, pp. 156, 81, 122, and also Robertson, III, p. 16

26. Stewart, *Works*, I, pp. 433-4.

27. Smith, *Wealth of Nations*, p. 508.

28. William Robertson, *Works*, 12 vols. (London, 1812) IV, pp. 42-3; *Works*, 8 vols. (Oxford, 1825), III, pp. 69-70, and *Works* (London, 1812), IV, p. 97;

29. David Hume, *Essays, Moral, Political and Literary*, ed. T. H. Green and T. H. Grose. 2 vols. (London, Longmans Green, 1875), I. p. 301. See also p. 306

30. Smith, *Wealth of Nations*, ed. Skinner, p. 508 and Millar, *H.V.*, I, p. 4

31. Ferguson, *H.C.S.*, pp. 125, 11-12 and 82.

32. Millar, *O.D.R.*, pp. 176 and 204.

33. Millar, *H.V.*, III, p. 103.

34. Ian Simpson Ross, *Lord Kames and the Scotland of his day* (Oxford, Clarendon Press, 1972), pp. 209, 210, 338; and W. C. Lehmann, *Henry Home, Lord Kames and the Scottish Enlightenment* (Martinus Nijhoff, The Hague, 1971), pp. 184, 256, 261. See *Sketches*, I, p. 97.

35. Ferguson, *H.C.S.*, pp. 81-2.

36. Kames, *H.L.T.*, p. 56; and Smith, *Lectures on Justice*, pp. 107-8.

37. Quoted from 'Lectures on Government', in Lehmann, *John Millar*, p. 125n. Millar expressed similar views in *O,D,R.*, see, for example, at the top and bottom of p. 176.

38. David Hume, *Political Discourses* (London, 1908), pp. 3-4 and Kames, *H.L.T.*, p. 56n.

39. Andrew Skinner's rewarding introduction to the *Wealth of Nations*, Pelican edition, deals with this at some length, esp. pp. 32-43.

40. See Ferguson, *H.C.S.*, p. 122.

41. Smith, *Lectures on Justice*, p. 15.

42. Kames, *Sketches*, I, p. 97.

43. Smith, *Wealth of Nations* (Pelican ed.), pp. 480-1.

44.   Hume, *Essays*, I, pp. 317-8.
45.   Smith, *Lectures on Police &c.*, p. 160; Ferguson, *H.C.S.*, pp. 167-8.
46.   Hume, *Essays*, I, pp. 301-2.
47.   Millar, *O.D.R.*, pp. 285, 289, 290.
48.   Millar, *O.D.R.*, pp. 176; *H.V.*, I, p. 127 and *O.D.R.*, p. 204.
49.   Kames, *H.L.T.*, pp. 88-156 and it is discussed briefly in Ross, pp. 210-1.
50.   Adam Smith, *Works*, 5 vols. (Edinburgh 1811-12), IV, pp. 72-81. The quotation is from p. 77, and Millar, *O.D.R.*, o, 250.
51.   Smith, *Wealth of Nations* (Pelican ed.), pp. 484-5.
52.   *Ibid.*, pp. 511 and 493.
53.   Robertson, *Works*, (1812 ed.), IV, pp. 265-6.
54.   Robertson, *Works*, (1825 ed.), VI, pp. 311, 313, 372.
55.   See also Millar, *H.V.*, I, pp. 3, 76-7 and 358, and Ferguson, *P.T.R.R.*, pp. 3 and 28.
56.   Hume, *Essays*, I, pp. 306-7. For the wider significance of Hume's views in the context of Whig historiography, see Duncan Forbes' introduction to the Pelican edition of *The History of Great Britain*, pp. 39-43.
57.   Hume, *History of Great Britain* (Pelican ed.), pp. 229-30.
58.   Millar, *O.D.R.*, pp. 291-2.
59.   Kames, *Historical Law Tracts*, p. 57n.
60.   Hume, *Essays*, I, pp. 112, 113-14.
61.   Smith, *Lectures on Justice*, p. 17.
62.   See Ferguson, *H.C.S.*, pp. 62 and 63.
63.   Robertson, *Works* (1825 ed.), VII, p. 259.
64.   Lehmann, *Kames*, pp. 257-261. The quotation, given on p. 257, is taken from *Essays upon Several Subjects Concerning British Antiquities*, p. 196.
65.   See Millar, *H.V.*, IV, pp. 267, 293-4, 286.
66.   Henry Home, Lord Kames, *Principles of Equity*, 2 vols. (Edinburgh, 1778), I, p. 8.
67   Millar, *O.D.R.*, p. 257.
68.   Smith, *Lectures on Police, Justice, &c.*, p. 3, and Ferguson, *P.M.P.S.*, I, p. 302.
69.   Ferguson, *H.C.S.*, pp. 128, 155-6, 263-4.
70.   Robertson, *Works* (1812 ed.), IV, pp. 79-80.
71.   See Ferguson, *P.M.P.S.*, I, p. 269 and Robertson, *Works* (1825 ed.), VI, p. 259
72.   Smith, 'Considerations concerning the first Formation of Language', *Works*, V, p. 26.
73.   Monboddo (1714-99) maintained a rivalry with Kames throughout their public lives both as writers and judges. See Kames on language in *Sketches*. I, pp. 60-5.
74.   Smith and Ferguson quarrelled over an issue of purported plagiarism— Smith accusing Ferguson of the 'crime' and Ferguson in turn accusing Smith of lifting his celebrated example of pin-manufacture to illustrate the division of labour, from a French source, which was probably the *Encyclopédie*. See R. Hamowy, 'Adam Smith, Adam Ferguson, and the Division of Labour', *Economica*, XXXV (1968), pp. 249-59.
75.   Robertson, *Works* (1825 ed.), VII, p. 256 and VIII, p. 277.
76.   Millar, *O.D.R.*, p. 287.
77.   Smith, *Wealth of Nations* (Pelican ed.), pp. 118-19; *Lectures on Justice*, p. 222; *Wealth of Nations* (Pelican ed.), pp. 122, 109-10, 112, 115.
78.   Ferguson, *H.C.S.*, pp. 29, xxxv-xxxvi, 180, 181-3, 218-19, 226-7, 230.
79.   See E.G. West, 'Adam Smith's Two Views on the Division of Labour', *Economica*, XXXI (1964), pp. 23-32.

80.   Smith, *Works*, IV, pp. 182-4, and *Lectures on Justice &c.*, pp. 256-7, 260-1.
81.   Millar, *O.D.R.*, pp. 381-2. He compared England and Scotland as countries where the division of labour had gone to different extents in *H.V.*, III, pp. 89-91. See also *H.V.*, pp. 141-61.
82.   I intend to follow the current study with one on the evolution of Victorian society, showing how the body of ideas generated by the Scottish Enlightenment, interacted with Benthamite, Evangelical, Unitarian and other social ideas in the early-nineteenth century, to provide the ruling class with coherent solutions to the political and social problems of the age.
83.   As might be expected from the excerpts quoted, Marx quoted Ferguson most favourably in his *Poverty of Philosophy*, and even Smith has been regarded as a precursor of Marx. But see E. G. West,˙The Political Economy of Alienation', *Oxford Economic Papers*, XXi (1969), pp. 1-23. See also R. L. Meek, 'The Scottish Contribution to Marxist Sociology', *Democracy and the Labour Movement*, ed. John Saville (London, 1954), pp. 84-102.
84.   Sociologists have been in the van of those digging up their ancestors—see Professor D. G. MacRae's essay on Adam Ferguson cited above, and A. Swingewood, 'Origins of Sociology:the case of the Scottish Enlightenment', *British Journal of Sociology*, XXI (1970), pp. 164-80 and *The Scottish Enlightenment and the Rise of Social Theory*, Ph.D. Dissertation (University of London, 1968).

6 UNIVERSITIES: MEDICINE AND SCIENCE[1]

Introduction

The Scottish Enlightenment centred even more in the universities than on the Church or the Law, not least because professors predominated among the intellectuals. It was within the universities that much new thought was either adopted or fashioned. Furthermore, the concern that was shown, from the mid-eighteenth to early nineteenth centuries, for effective teaching in a wide range of disciplines was an achievement in itself of the Scottish Enlightenment, since it displayed a concern for the importance of education in society that harmonised with the social philosophy of the age. The interaction of both facets, original thought and effective education, are the concern here.

The Scottish universities of King's and Marischal College, Aberdeen, Edinburgh, Glasgow and St Andrews were an intimate part of the European, and latterly the European Protestant university scene. The European traditions and links continued throughout the eighteenth century and the Age of Enlightenment. Whereas in other spheres of Scottish life, the economy, agriculture, the Church, the Law, English influences could be seen to hasten 'improvement', it was Dutch influences, and sometimes French and German, which bore on the universities. The Scottish universities were not of a uniform distinction in the Age of Enlightenment. They experienced different fortunes economically, academically and in terms of student numbers. Indeed, by the end of the Scottish Enlightenment, they were being investigated by a Royal Commission of Inquiry (1826 and 1830).

Of the distinctive institutions of Scottish society in the age of the Enlightenment, the Presbyterian Kirk, Marischal College, Aberdeen, and the University of Edinburgh dated from the Reformation; the other universities went back further in Scottish history to the fifteenth century. The universities exemplify that the the Scottish Enlightenment flourished through those reinvigorated, traditional institutions of Scottish society in which a concern for philosophic knowledge, was shown. Seventeenth-century developments in the universities, as in the Church and the Law, when coupled with other impetus to improvement generally in Scotland in the early-eighteenth century, provided the basis for a distinguished intellectual movement later in the same century.

One thinker, himself a Glasgow professor for some forty years of the Scottish Enlightenment, accounted for the part played by the Scottish universities in the Enlightenment. John Millar, in his *Historical View of the English Government,* saw the period between the union of the Crowns and the union of the Parliaments as seminal: deprived of that stimulus to trade and manufactures which the presence of their own nobility and gentry had provided, and discouraged by the lowland Scottish tongue being regarded as merely a corruption of English 'The people of Scotland . . . were directed into the road of general science. Despairing of reputation, either as poets, or fine writers, they advanced by degrees in those branches of learning and philosophy, which had diffused themselves over the rest of Europe.' The pursuit of these intellectual matters was facilitated by two factors, physical and mental. The physical factor was the energy required to overthrow Roman Catholicism at the Reformation, and the mental factor was the accompanying moulding of the mind so that it was disposed to the spirit of inquiry. For Millar the Roman Catholic religion was deeply superstitious, opposition to it requiring, therefore, much reason. So the Scots were inclined to inquire, and to accept nothing without examination. Consequently:

> The energy requisite for the accomplishment of the reformation, and the impluse which that event gave to the minds of men, continued after the new system was established; and produced a boldness and activity, not only on examining religious opinions, which were of great extent, but in the general investigation of truth.

This activity and vigour of mind was backed up by education. As Francis Jeffrey put it in his review of Millar's book, the educational institutions of Scotland were the effect not the cause of a general desire for information. According to Millar, the Scottish universities broadened their courses to match the changes which took place in society. Furthermore, Scotland was in a 'rude' state between 1603 and 1707: in the terms of the social and historical theory of the Scottish Enlightenment, the members of a society in the period before the commercial era, with its accompanying division of labour, are more intelligent than the narrow-minded and ignorant commercial peoples. Hence, in the pre-commercial economy, and with the stimulus given by the Reformation to education and educational institutions, a great number of Scots had the time to be instructed and to go through a regular course of education at schools and universities. As a result the learned professions

became very prevalent in Scotland. Millar's analysis is compelling.
It clearly emphasised the importance of the Reformation, the seventeenth century and the universities to the Scottish Enlightenment.
It also showed the social theory of the movement in practice as the
institutions of society, in this case, the universities, adapted to the
changing circumstances of the Scots.[2]

John Knox's *Book of Discipline,* the manifesto of that revolution in
Scottish society which constituted the Reformation, laid great stress on
a national scheme for education. Education was to be the means of
leading children away from sin, and to the ways of godliness. Thus,
schools were of immense importance in the social theology of the
godly commonwealth. Educational provision was to be national;
ultimately every parish had to have a school. Upon the universities,
therefore, devolved the highly important tasks of training the candidates for the vital and ideally numerous positions of schoolmaster. As
important as schoolmasters were, of course, ministers, and it was the
task of the universities to train them, too. A slightly older responsibility placed on the universities, although it was not carried out until
much later, was embodied in an edict of James I and an Act of
Parliament of James IV, which laid down that the eldest sons of all
barons and freeholders should be taught law.[3] Hence well before the
Age of Enlightenment, the Scottish universities were established as
part of the European scene, basically concentrating on philosophy but
were also charged with the crucial social and professional tasks of in-
structing in the law and training ministers and schoolmasters. From at
least the sixteenth century, therefore, the Scottish universities were a
mixture of the purely academic and the socially relevant or professional.

The character of the Scottish universities was essential to the part
they played in the Scottish Enlightenment. They were always involved
in society and responded to the forces at work in society; at the same
time they gave an important place to philosophy in their curricula.
By the Act of Security which accompanied the Treaty of Union, it was
declared that the Scottish universities should continue forever. The
involvement with society nonetheless meant that when narrow minds
prevailed, when purges were common and when political and theological strife were the rule, as during and after the Reformation which
had bad as well as good effects, the universities could not expect to
escape. Similarly, in improving times the conditions could exist for the
Scottish universities to develop and be centres of enlightenment.

The following examination falls into two parts, which are broadly
described as 'institutional' and 'intellectual'. The first part discusses the

improvements which took place prior to the heyday of the Scottish Enlightenment, and which were the basis for it, the character of Scottish university education and features of it which impinged on the Scottish Enlightenment, and various miscellaneous social and economic factors which operated on the Scottish universities at the time. The second part centres on the more secular age that accompanied the Scottish Enlightenment, the reflection of that secularisation within the universities, the increase in the number of academic disciplines that grew out of older established subjects and the evident concern for effective teaching. Medicine and geology, which were particular fields of endeavour in the Scottish Enlightenment, will be considered in this part as examples both of general trends and of the achievements of the age.

I: Institutional

(i)

The background to the relationship between the Scottish Enlightenment and the Scottish universities consists in the improvements which were made in society at large and in various distinct features of the institutions, especially from the late-seventeenth century. One such improvement was the concern that had been shown for religious reasons, throughout the seventeenth century, for parish schools, schools which led on to the national network of universities. As early as 1616 an act was passed in Privy Council commanding the establishment of a school in every parish. Seventeen years later the act was strengthened by the Scottish Parliament's decree of 1633 that the local heritors should be held liable, through taxation, to pay for the schools and masters. Yet a third act in 1646 obliged the heritors to pay for the school. The measures had different effects all over Scotland, the Highlands being particularly deficient in comparison with the Lowlands. However by 1696 sixty-one out of sixty-five parishes in West, Mid and East Lothian, fifty-seven out of sixty Fife parishes, forty-two out of forty-four Angus parishes had all complied, as had most of the north-east, and more than half those parishes in Ayr had schools by 1660.[4] All the earlier legislation and provisions were merely reinforced by the act of 1696 for settling schools: every parish was to have a school, whose master's salary was payable by the heritors. In short, if the universities were to recruit students, then a necessary prerequisite, an adequate parish school system, was in existence by the beginning of the eighteenth century.[5]

The universities to which the Scottish pupils moved on were themselves undergoing several improvements in the seventeenth and early-eighteenth centuries, improvements that in themselves prepared the ground for the Enlightenment. For example, the philosophy syllabus, which had from late medieval times concentrated on Aristotle, refurbished its traditional concern for dialectic and the inculcation of accurate, precise and logical habits of thought. The improvements were, until the eighteenth century, confined within Aristotleianism: nonetheless, during the Westminster Assembly of 1643 and other theological debates up to 1688, there was a number of able examples of the kind of scholars that could be produced by the application of Aristotelian dialectic to theology. Aristotelian metaphysics also manifested themselves in various theological formulae adopted by the Kirk. Various religious pressures placed on the universities in the turbulent seventeenth century led to attempts in 1647 to produce a common curriculum in Arts. The civil war interrupted the enterprise, but by 1695, the universities were agreed on new books from which the regents would teach. They were given to Scottish Commissioners of Parliament in 1697 and published in 1701. Within the limited system of regenting, which restricted the pursuit of knowledge, the period prior to the writing and acceptance of Locke's *Essay on Human Understanding* was not totally barren nor preoccupied with political and religious matters.[6]

Two other examples of improvements prior to the Enlightenment were the early acceptance of the work of Sir Isaac Newton and the foundations that were laid for medicine and medical education in Edinburgh. Newtonianism entered the Scottish universities through particular individuals who were familiar with Newton and his research. James Gregory was appointed the first Regius Professor of Mathematics at St Andrews in 1668: he was a contemporary of Newton, anticipated some of his work, and introduced what is now called the Newtonian method into his teaching, as is indicated by St Andrews' graduation theses. Gregory himself, however, did not find St Andrews congenial to his new work and approach: an original mind that sought to operate in a university system that, in the mid-seventeenth century, still taught by means of regents expounding set and ancient texts would naturally feel constricted. Gregory moved to Edinburgh where he again became professor of mathematics in 1674.

James Gregory's nephew, David, succeeded his uncle at Edinburgh in 1683 and made Edinburgh the first European university where the *Principia* was publicly taught. As the second Gregory grew infirm he was provided with a successor, largely through Newton's own influence and liberality. This was Colin McLaurin, the most distinguished Scottish Newtonian of his age, who had been professor of Mathematics at Marischal College, Aberdeen since 1717, and who was appointed in November 1725. In writing McLaurin a testimonial, Newton had remarked that he regarded McLaurin's prospects at Edinburgh gladly 'not only because you are my friend, but principally because of your abilities, you being acquainted as well with the new improvements of mathematics, as with the former state of thise sciences'. Newton also wrote to the Lord Provost of Edinburgh offering to pay £20 a year to McLaurin until Gregory should actually die and thus free the salary.[7]

Newton was appreciated not only in the sciences. Since natural science was part of common culture *literati* in social and moral science also adopted his approaches later in the eighteenth century. Newton had taken further and sanctified the lessons urged on men of science by Francis Bacon (1561-1626) who was equally popular and influential among the *literati*. The quotation from Millar describing Adam Smith as the Newton and Montesquieu as the Bacon of social philosophy will be recalled. By Millar's time, the *literati* felt they had achieved their task. Smith saw himself applying the methods of Newtonian science to the study of morals in his *Theory of Moral Sentiments*. His essay 'On the History of Astronomy' gave further evidence of his Newtonianism as did his defence of Newton in the second and last number of the first *Edinburgh Review*.[8] Hume's *Treatise of Human Nature* was advertised as 'An Attempt to introduce the experimental method of Reasoning into Moral Subjects' and in it he wrote:"Tis evident, that all the sciences have a relation, greater or less, to human nature; and that however, wide any of them may seem to run from it, they still return back by one passage or another.' The lessons of Newton were incorporated into a range of university courses.

The foundations that were laid for medicine and medical education in Edinburgh owed much to Sir Robert Sibbald, Archibald Pitcairne and Sir Andrew Balfour.[9] They were instrumental in founding the Edinburgh Botanical Garden in 1670 and the Edinburgh Royal College of Physicians by 1681 and in the appointment of Edinburgh's first three professors of medicine in 1685. Botany was fundamental to the practice of physicians and apothecaries. Sibbald and Balfour organised the Edinburgh physicians and the surgeon-apothecaries into supporting the establishment of two Physic Gardens. Six years after their foundation James Sutherland (1638-1705) was made first Professor of Botany and in 1699 Botanist-Royal. He published an impressive first catalogue of the Gardens in 1682-83. With Sutherland's appointment some slight provision was made for the teaching of medicine. The provision was amplified first by the triumph of Pitcairne, Sibbald and others over the vested interests of the universities, town councils, universities and bishops, when the Edinburgh Royal College of Physicians was established by letters patent, and secondly, by the appointment of Pitcairne, Sibbald and a Dr James Halket to the first three chairs of Medicine in Edinburgh. The foundation of the College of Physicians made possible from 1699 the publication of a pharmacopoeia whose formulae were binding on Edinburgh apothecaries. No regular curriculum for medical study was yet established despite the professorial appointments, since lectures were given only periodically. From 1697, systematic anatomical instruction began to be given in the Surgeons' Hall, Edinburgh, which was opened that year.[10]

In Glasgow, a Faculty of Physicians and Surgeons had been founded in 1599. It examined and licensed surgeons and had a monopoly of the examination of the qualifications of physicians to practise in the west of Scotland. The dominating influence of the Faculty in the area led to the emphasis in the early-eighteenth century on medical and surgical practices. In time, the Faculty's power became a stranglehold on the university, since it believed that the strictly professional activities of the physicians and surgeons had no complementary activity in the educational functions of Glasgow University. In Edinburgh, by the 1720s, lines of demarcation were clearly drawn between the various medical groups. The Royal College of Surgeons primarily lectured on and demonstrated anatomy; the Royal College of Physicians examined and licensed practitioners; both defined and protected their members' privileges and established professional standards. The University carried out medical education and awarded degrees, but had no monopoly as the Colleges offered lectures and awarded diplomas and other qualifications. Easy relationships were fostered by the professors being members of one of the Royal Colleges and by the large numbers of students flocking to Edinburgh in the late-eighteenth and early-nineteenth centuries. The pressure on classroom and other facilities and professorial time indicated that there were more than enough students to be shared round. Extra-mural lectures in the basic medical subject of anatomy were particularly common.

Dutch influence was also important in early medical developments and more generally in the universities after 1688. Leyden offered the most complete and effective medical education in the late-seventeenth and early-eighteenth centuries. Its leading medical professor was Hermann Boerhaave (1668-1738) who was distinguished for research and teaching of a high order and who applied Newtonianism to medicine in his clinical and research work. He was particularly influential through his teaching of aspiring doctors from all over Europe and America.[11] One such aspirant was the first Alexander Monro (1697-1767) who had studied, *inter alia,* at Leyden, who in 1722 became the first professor of Anatomy in Edinburgh and who effectively built up the Edinburgh medical school to its eminence in the Age of Enlightenment.

It was not only Dutch influence that affected the development of the Edinburgh medical school. Politics also had a crucial part to play with the Revolution of 1688 and the settlement of William of Orange on the throne. One of the strongest influences at William's court, not least when it came to dealing with Scotland, was William Carstares, a Scottish Presbyterian minister and a royal chaplain, who had spent his exile in Holland. Carstares used his political talents for dealing with some general problems in Scotland in the post-Revolution period, but in particular, he was central to improvement in two of the Scottish universities, Glasgow and Edinburgh. In November 1690, the Crown appointed Carstares' brother-in-law, William Dunlop, as principal of Glasgow University, not least for having disclosed full details of a conspiracy against William that had been revealed to him. Dunlop then tried to use his family entrée to the Court to persuade the Crown of Glasgow's pressing financial needs in terms of debts, repairs to buildings, the suppression of chairs, the inability to found new chairs, the lack of apparatus for science subjects and the deficient library. Some money was forthcoming in the 1690s to the Scottish universities, though enough neither for Glasgow's needs nor Edinburgh's desires. One grant of 1693 which the Crown made to Glasgow had not been requested: it was to maintain a professor of theology from abroad and to provide ten divinity bursaries. Carstares urged on Dunlop the virtues of Dutch professors in particular, not least because they were able and would please the King.[12] His own time in Holland and a desire to toady to his master had convinced Carstares how Scottish universities might be modelled on such institutions as Utrecht (where he himself had studied) and Leyden. In 1703 the Whig, Presbyterian and family grip tightened when Carstares himself was appointed principal of Edinburgh University. His familiarity with the corridors of power brought more grants to Edinburgh from Queen Anne after his appointment, although Edinburgh was by no means the only Scottish

university to benefit from her bounty. He did not temper his desire
to model Edinburgh on Dutch lines: he could point to Leyden's influence on the development of medical and theological education by the
early-eighteenth century.

The first major improvement of the eighteenth century was the
abolition of regenting, first in Edinburgh in 1708, then at Glasgow in
1727 and at St Andrews in 1747. Except at Glasgow, a regent took the
same class through such subjects as logic, pneumatology, moral and
natural philosophy during the students' entire career of three or more
years, teaching them by means of approved books and by supervising
disputations. In subjects which did not have chairs until those years,
the change of system freed teachers from the expounding of set books,
left them free to speculate and facilitated the original writing of the
Scottish Enlightenment. In time, too, philosophy, for example, could
give birth to new disciplines such as political economy, as well as permit
the separate treatment of logic. Dugald Stewart likened the process to
Smith's discussion of the division of labour in industry, which increased
production:

> Different individuals are led, partly by original temparement, partly
> by early education, to betake themselves to different studies; and
> hence arise those infinitely diversified capacities of mind, which we
> commonly call diversities of *genius*. These diversities of genius, in
> consequence of the connexions and affinities among the various
> branches of human knowledge, are all subsequent one to another;
> and when the productions to which they give birth are, by means of
> the press, contributed to a common stock, all the varieties of intel-
> lect, natural and acquired, among men are combined together into
> one vast engine, operating with a force daily accumulating, on the
> moral and political destiny of mankind.[13]

The extent of specialisation after the abolition of regenting can, however
be exaggerated: professors moved from chair to chair within the sciences
and between the sciences and moral philosophy. Thomas Reid, Dugald
Stewart and Adam Ferguson all taught mathematics and/or natural
philosophy before making their reputations in moral philosophy chairs.[14]
The interrelated state of knowledge at the time gave professors
intellectual manoeuvrability.

That Edinburgh and Glasgow should have been the first universities
to abolish regenting appears to have given them a lead in the pursuit
of learning that they never lost in the Age of Enlightenment. They

founded more chairs and it was within their precincts that around 1745 the main advances were made in mental, moral and natural knowledge. Not that Aberdeen should be discounted simply because her colleges abolished regenting last of all: time and again Aberdeen gave an important lead or an important response, as, for example, in its inspired appointments of various Gregories, McLaurin, George Turnbull and Thomas Reid. The abolition of regenting did not necessarily mean that the horizons were broadened immediately, not least because the first professors were former regents and some were too set in their ways.

By the mid-eighteenth century, another improvement could be seen in the increasing number of students matriculating in the universities, a rise which reached its peak between 1778 and 1827. The one exception appears to have been St Andrews. In the early decades of the seventeenth century, St Andrews had been the ecclesiastical capital of Scotland with its archiepiscopal seat, and was in consequence the chief educational centre. Knox and Andrew Melville had always insisted on the close connection between and education and work of ministers and schoolmasters. Then, certainly after 1689, the fortunes of St Andrews plummeted: first, the archbishopric, and all it brought to St Andrews, was finally abolished; secondly, St Andrews as a city declined in relative importance. The consequences of the first can be best appreciated from a table which shows that while St Andrews was the university of 39.5 per cent of established church ministers between 1601 and 1650, only 25 per cent of the ministers went to the University between 1651 and 1700, 17.5 per cent between 1701 and 1750 and 15.5 per cent between 1750 and 1800.[15] The decline of St Andrews generally was a consequence of the rise and development in the early-eighteenth century of what were to become the major urban centres of Scotland's modern history. The new commercial stage of society, and subsequently industrial, through which Scotland was to pass gave little importance to a small port on the east coast, especially as Glasgow was opening up trade to the west, to the Americas, where the future appeared to lie. The English traveller and naturalist Thomas Pennant visited St Andrews in 1772, and found that its manufactures had been reduced to one, that of golf balls. 'The trade is commonly fatal to the artists', noted Pennant, 'for the balls are made by stuffing a great quantity of feathers into a leathern case, by help of an iron rod, with a wooden handle, pressed against the breast, which seldom fails to bring on a consumption.'[16]

During the eighteenth century, Edinburgh's population rose from about 40,000 to 70,000; Glasgow from 15,000 to nearly 80,000 and New Aberdeen (on which Old Aberdeen could draw) from 10,000 to

30,000. Aberdeen, being more distant from the central lowland belt which was so active in the eighteenth century, could thrive and develop as a provincial capital in the north-east and also for the Highlands. St Andrews, with a population that stabilised around 4,000 for the century could not for economic, geographical, or social reasons hope to rival the other Scottish towns that supported universities. It was even suggested at the end of the seventeenth century that the university should move to Perth. The stagnation of student numbers and the chronic financial position of the university itself meant that it could scarcely maintain existing professors and buildings let alone finance new chairs and facilities.

The other universities tell a different story from St Andrews. First, improvement can be seen in the numbers of students attending: Edinburgh had 400 in the late seventeenth century, 1,300 a century later and 2,300 by 1824. Glasgow had 250 students in 1696, 400 in 1702, rising to 1,240 by 1824. Aberdeen had 50 students at King's in 1776, rising to 156 in 1812 and 236 by 1824, and the 207 at Marischal in 1776 rose to nearly 500 by 1824. St Andrews had about 150 in 1730. Twenty-five enrolled for the first time in 1777 and 68 in 1824.[17] In the eighteenth century there was an increasing influx of non-Scottish students to the universities. For the English and Irish, only Anglicans could attend the universities of Oxford, Cambridge and Trinity, Dublin. Hence numbers of dissenters came especially to Glasgow and Edinburgh universities, numbers that increased either as the universities themselves began to offer more attractive courses, such as in medicine (the provision of medical education in Ireland was, in particular, in a disputatious state), or as the dissenting academies in England diminished in number from the mid-eighteenth century in the face of doctrinal difficulties, restriction of activities and tests. With the effective closing of the Continent in the aftermath of the French Revolution, yet another group appeared in the Scottish universities, the sons of the aristocracy and gentry for whom the hitherto 'educational' experience of the Grand Tour was prohibited. Edinburgh and, to a lesser extent, Glasgow became the alternative. Young Scots of almost schoolboy age from limited backgrounds were not the only students who came to take their places in the improving and ultimately enlightened universities of Scotland.

Along with the abolition of regenting and the increase in numbers, another development that testified to improvement was the creation of new chairs and lectureships. Most of the new chairs were to be found at Edinburgh. The abolition of regenting in 1708 established chairs in

Latin, Greek, Logic and Metaphysics, Moral Philosophy and Natural
Philosophy. Chairs of Divinity were already in existence. Chairs of
medicine had been founded in 1685, that of Mathematics in 1674
and that of Botany in 1676. Seven others were established between
the Union of the Parliaments and 1726. Four of these were in Law,
Public Law (1707), Civil Law (1710), Universal History (1719) and
Scots Law (1722). The other three chairs were in medicine or allied
to it, Anatomy (1705), Midwifery (1726) and Chemistry (1713).
There was a second spate of creating chairs at Edinburgh from 1760-90
and further medical professorships were established between 1803-
1807. They were Rhetoric and Belles Lettres (1760), History (1767),
Materia Medica (1768), Surgery (1777), Astronomy (1786) and Agriculture (1790); and then Clinical Surgery (1803), Military Surgery
(1806) and Medical Jurisprudence (1807). The significance of the
development of medicine in the University of Edinburgh can be
gauged from the foundation of eleven medical chairs between 1685 and
1807. In the opinion of Thomas Reid it was easier to innovate intellectually in medicine. He wrote that his Glasgow medical colleagues
were less hidebound.[18]

A similar pattern, though not on the same scale, was evident at
Glasgow. A chair of medicine was founded in 1713, to which was
added first a lectureship in anatomy that in about 1720 was raised
to a chair. In 1713 was founded too, a chair of law; 1747 was the
year when William Cullen seriously started Glasgow medicine and when
was established that lectureship in Chemistry in which Joseph Black
was first to make his reputation; in 1760 was established a chair of
Practical Anatomy; in 1765 a lectureship in Materia Medica; in 1790 a
lectureship in Midwifery; and in 1807 a Regius chair of Natural History.
In 1815 the Crown established two Regius chairs, of Surgery and of
Midwifery, and in 1817 and 1818 two more, of Botany and Chemistry.
These last five Regius chairs brought problems as well as an increase
in the College's academic offerings. Two different species of professor
now existed, college professors and university (the Regius) professors.
Those who were merely university professors were excluded from such
functions as electing professors, sharing in the management of university
funds, which Court of Session judgements in 1771 and 1772 placed
firmly in the hands of the college professors, nor could they take part
in examining candidates for medical degrees. It was an absurdity that
at the time of the 1826 Commission the professors of Surgery, Midwifery, Chemistry, Natural History and Botany could not examine the
medical candidates nor have a say in the disbursement of funds on

which their subjects, if taught effectively, would make heavy claims.
The professor of Chemistry in 1827, Thomas Thomson, felt keenly
that his position was such that he could not establish practical
chemistry at Glasgow as he wished, because of the expense. The University Principal at the time jealously guarded the restrictive practices
of the college professors.[19]

Marischal too established a chair of medicine in 1700, but King's
had always had from its foundation a regent called a 'mediciner', because
in medieval times physic was considered a branch of scholarship, and
because lairds and clergy coming to the college would be likely to
have to assume the function of a doctor in remote districts. As time
wore on, the seriousness with which the mediciner took his task varied
from occupant to occupant. St Andrews appointed its first Chandos
Professor of Medicine in 1722 but the appointment could achieve
little without other academic support.

Improvement can finally be seen in the concern for apparatus and
for facilities, especially in medicine. Examples are the Royal Infirmaries
of Edinburgh and Glasgow. The idea of establishing a hospital linked
to a medical school in Edinburgh dated from the end of the seventeenth century. Just as they had seen the importance of a Physick
Garden, so did Balfour and Sibbald set in train moves to erect or hire
suitable accommodation for a hospital. The first rented property that
constituted the Edinburgh Informary opened in August 1729. The
purpose-built Royal Infirmary was opened twelve years later, and made
possible the provision of clinical lectures as part of the medical curriculum from about 1746. Clinical teaching had been a feature of the
Leyden medical syllabus. Glasgow University Medical School did not
offer clinical lectures: by 1733, a hospital was maintained by the Town
Council, the Kirk and the various traders' and merchants' associations,
but it was served by the Faculty of Physicians and Surgeons, and not
the University. From the time when the new Glasgow Royal Infirmary
was opened in 1794 private clinical teaching was available to matriculated students of the University, but they had to pay fees to members
of the Faculty over and above the fees they paid to professors. The
professors sought access to the Infirmary and the allocation of two
wards where observations of patients and instruction of students might
take place. The University interpreted the Faculty's lectures as an under-
hand attempt to make the University recognise their lectures as part of
the University medical curriculum and as a step to establishing a Royal
College in Glasgow. The Faculty in its turn felt that to introduce the
professors to the Infirmary would ultimately give the University undue

weight there, and would discourage the best practitioners in Glasgow from practising in the hospital because the clinical lecturers would always appropriate the most interesting cases. The Faculty wielded superior political power in the matter, always securing a majority of the managers to support their monopoly and exclude the University. The University's contrary argument was that any hospital in a university town should be subservient to the medical school of the university.

The Faculty withheld recognition of Glasgow University medical degrees, and yet recognised those licenses awarded by the College of Surgeons of London, Dublin and Edinburgh, notwithstanding that it was these three Colleges and Glasgow University whose qualifications were considered equal for ships' surgeons. The Faculty stood its ground firmly in maintaining its monopoly to license surgeons in Glasgow and the four counties around, and prosecuted a number of those licensed by the University. The University took the Faculty to law over the matter. In its turn the University did not wish to recognise such lectures as were given by the Faculty members, nor did it wish to put up its own Professor of Surgery for election because a surgeon was elected to the Infirmary for no more than two years, and thus would be barred from giving regular lectures. The advantages of a professor undertaking clinical lectures in Surgery were spelled out to the Royal Commission as being the ability of a professor of surgery to show in practice what he taught in theory and the delivery of lectures by a specialist teacher and not by someone whose main task was other than teaching. But clinical lectures could not be given by university professors without offending the Faculty of Physicians and Surgeons who appointed all the surgeons in the Infirmary.

Glasgow was not slow to institute a Physick or Botanical Garden, also regarded at the time as fundamental to medical science. Indeed Lord Kames was of the view that a spacious garden was as essential to a college as good professors.[21] It was in 1704 that the Glasgow Physick Garden was first established and provision made for the teaching of botany. Marischal, Aberdeen, also endeavoured, after 1726 to introduce Anatomy along with a major extension of classes in Experimental or Natural Philosophy, all of which required 200 guineas worth of apparatus, but did not succeed.[22]

The Edinburgh Town Council which patronised so generously the University and its medical school, through chairs, botanic gardens, infirmaries, buildings, laboratories and apparatus, was composed of merchants and tradesmen who may have lost much by the reduced status of their city following 1707, and who would look kindly on a set of schemes designed to stimulate the local economy. Lord Provost Drummond was prominent in the development of the New Town, the making of the medical school and the building of the Infirmary. The development of a medical school as part of a prestigious university would attract outsiders as Leyden had done so successfully, and keep Scottish students (and their money) at home.[23] Creech's letters indicated the Town Council's success.

(ii)

The established character of Scottish university education and various features of its operation impinged on the Scottish Enlightenment. The Arts degree was fundamental to the entire philosophical objective of education in the Scottish universities. A general philosophical approach was being projected largely to a young teenage group of students, with the result that it could well either pass over their heads or in fewer cases serve as a most valuable preliminary to a specialist training. Teaching was largely by means of the lecture, the predominant method in the European universities, which could either be a thoroughly fine but empty performance that stirred the immature and inexperienced young auditors, or an opportunity that was used more pedagogically. Students paid a fee to each professor whose class they wished to take, in return for which a class ticket would be issued. The class fee system was a stimulus to any professor who might be inclined to treat his class as gullible and his post as a sinecure. To earn income he had to retain popularity or demonstrate utility or be intellectually distinguished. For the student, intellectual predilection or economic circumstances might mean he would wish only to take an individual class or two. Indeed by the heyday of the Scottish Enlightenment graduation in Arts was rare since the degree was little regarded, did not lead to promotion, and did not have the obvious utility of qualifications in divinity, law and medicine. Even in those subjects, however, graduation was achieved in a piecemeal fashion, by picking up courses one or two at a time, with studies being interrupted by adverse personal economic circumstances or by war, when partly trained doctors went off to battle, to return afterwards on half-pay to complete their degrees.

The youth of Scottish Arts students, has necessarily called into question the character of the Scottish universities as little more than high schools. Most of the students in the first classes, namely those of Latin and Greek, were about fourteen or fifteen. If a student did graduate it was commonly at the age of 19. To take three celebrated

examples from different periods in the course of a century, Colin
McLaurin graduated at the age of 15 from Glasgow, Dugald Stewart
completed formal studies at Edinburgh aged 17 and was carrying out
professorial duties at 19 and Henry Brougham, the future Lord Chancellor, was presenting, at the age of 18, optical experiments before the
Royal Society of London that he had worked out no less than three
years earlier as an Edinburgh student.[24] These three men are not the
only examples that could have been given but clearly most Scottish
students were not of like ability. Yet it was not peculiar to the Scottish universities to have mere schoolboys in the student body.
Jeremy Bentham, the Utilitarian philosopher, went to Queen's College,
Oxford aged 13 and Edward Gibbon, the historian, to Magdalen aged 14.
Even if only the first few pages of the first volume of *Alumni Oxonien-
ses* are examined, ten sixteen-year-olds, one aged fourteen and two
aged thirteen can be found. This is not exhaustive evidence nor is it
suggested that youngsters were at Oxford in the same numbers as in
the Scottish universities. Nonetheless it does indicate that the character
of the Scottish institutions as universities cannot be impugned on the
ground of student age. For most of the eighteenth century, the Scottish
universities were having to make good, in their first two classes of
Latin and Greek, the deficiencies of the schools. Rev. Sir Harry
Moncrieff, leader of the Evangelical party in the Kirk, told the 1826
Commission that he was not so worried about the High School of
Edinburgh but about the country schools, where Latin and Greek
were not always taught and where standards were less high. Others,
including professors, echoed his views.[25] It was felt by some witnesses
that if the Scottish school system was universally adequate, then
fifteen would be a suitable age for entry and for benefiting from the
Logic, Moral and Natural Philosophy, Mathematics and even Rhetoric
classes which contributed to the Arts curriculum, and whose standards
were higher than the first classes in Latin and Greek. Nonetheless,
the youth of the student body, even when leavened by older and more
mature Irishmen, English dissenters, gentry and aristocracy, cannot
be forgotten when consideration is given to the teaching that had to
be addressed to them.

The class fee system both furthered and hindered the development
of knowledge. Two of the philosophers rehearsed the arguments for
the system, Adam Smith in the *Wealth of Nations* and Thomas Reid
in his statistical account of Glasgow University. For Smith:

In every profession, the exertion of the greater part of those who exercise it, is always in proportion to the necessity they are under of making that exertion. This necessity is greatest with those to whom the emoluments of their profession are the only source from which they expect their fortune, or even their ordinary revenue and subsistence. In order to acquire this fortune, or even to get this subsistence, they must, in the course of a year, execute a certain quantity of work of a known value; and, where the competition is free, the rivalship of competitors, who are all endeavouring to jostle one another out of employment, obliges every man to endeavour to execute his work with a certain degree of exactness.

While Smith did not deny that the prosecution of great objects could equally be a stimulus to mere exertion, he believed that the greatest exertions were prompted by rivalry and emulation. Hence the class fee system necessitated application by a university professor and the other stimuli of reputation, affection and gratitude could be gained at the same time. The means of gaining regard and subsistence coincided. In the English universities, on the other hand, where salary constituted the only permitted income, the professor's interest was directly in opposition to his duty. And Smith continued:

It is the interest of every man to live as much at his ease as he can; and if his emoluments are to be precisely the same, whether he does or does not perform some very laborious duty, it is certainly his interest . . . either to neglect it altogether, or, if he is subject to some authority which will not suffer him to do this, to perform it in as careless and slovenly a manner as that authority will permit.

Oxford's authority consisted of teachers who were all in the same easy position; it was in each person's interest there to be very indulgent to one another and make common cause. There the greater part of the public professors had given up altogether even the pretence of teaching.

Thomas Reid, writing some fifteen years later, thought likewise, making virtually identical criticisms of the English universities. He commended particularly Glasgow and the Scottish universities for the class fee system because under it:

There is likely to grow up with [the professors] . . . a habitual liking to their objects and occupations, and that interest and zeal in the discharge of their duty, which are most likely to call forth the activity and industry of their pupils.

Reid hastened to argue, nonetheless, that he did not believe that the class fee should be the sole means of professorial emolument because otherwise, one man might try to teach too many subjects and be a jack of all trades.[26]

Class fees were increased by a guinea in 1812 so that it was reported to the 1826 Commission that at Edinburgh the basic Arts courses, Latin, Greek, and Logic, all had fees of three guineas; the professors of Rhetoric, Mathematics, Moral and Natural Philosophy charged four guineas. Of the professional courses, most in Divinity were free, most in Law and Medicine cost four guineas though the clinical class, Military Surgery, and Medical Jurisprudence cost only three. Over and above these fees, were small class dues, ranging between 15 and 25p, which went to pay door-keepers, janitors who prevented noise and interruption during lectures, and to meet the cost of apparatus, glass and like material required in some of the science and medical classes. At Glasgow the fees were also raised by a guinea from 1816 so that by 1826 the Divinity students were exempted and most other classes charged three guineas. The small dues amounted to nearly 18p to pay the man who provided the fire, the bell-ringer and the scavenger. St Andrews had a very distinctive system: the students were classified socially, primars being sons of noblemen, secondars being Gentlemen Commoners and ternars 'those of the common ranks of life'. From time immemorial the primars paid fees of six guineas per class, secondars three guineas, ternars a guinea and a half. Only two primars matriculated between 1776 and 1826; secondars scarcely amounted to a third of the students and most students at St Andrews were ternars, a term so broad as to be meaningless. Some of the small dues went to a student requiring financial help in his education. He assumed the post of class Luminator, furnishing lights and fires and being allowed to attend the class free. Divinity students at St Mary's College, St Andrews, paid no fees. Fees at King's College, Aberdeen, varied from three guineas for Greek, Mathematics, Natural Philosophy, Logic and Moral Philosophy, to one and a half guineas for Chemistry and Natural History, to 50p for the first Latin class. Three guineas appears to have been the standard fee at Marischal.[27] The issuing of class tickets was a flexible process, at the discretion of each professor. It was common for professors to issue cut-price or *gratis* tickets if students were poor, returning for a second time, were well-known or recommended to him, or were in particular categories, such as surgeons returning on half-pay from the wars after 1815. Class tickets were also sold by booksellers.

The professors who benefited most from the system were those whose classes were, by degree regulations, compulsory (for example, Moral Philosophy in Arts) or whose courses were fundamental to a particular professional qualification (for example, Anatomy in Medicine) In some cases, and in defiance of Smithian human psychology, the very subject professed by a man could bring him in a regular income because of the students' necessity to enrol for it. However, there were clearly cases in optional subjects where professors would have to establish a reputation for distinction or flamboyance or entertainment to increase their enrolment. Smith was correct when he emphasised the need for exertion, but that exertion need not be directed towards scholarship or teaching.Thomas Charles Hope, Edinburgh's professor of Chemistry for forty-four years after 1799, exemplifies the point.[28] In his time chemistry was becoming a popular subject because it was so spect-acular. One colleague of Hope's sensitive to the relatively small size of his classes compared to those of the chemistry professor, com-plained that 'All this is very mortifying—the taste of hard study being evidently on the decline—the glare of chemistry obscures everything else.'[29] Hope spent most of his time perfecting his experimental techniques for purposes of demonstrations, rather than engaging in research. He aimed to maintain the numbers of well over 500 students that attended his official university classes and also to attract others to attend extra-mural lectures. The Faculty of Advocates, for example, prevailed upon him in 1800 to lay on a summer course. In 1826 he had a rather more surprising audience. In Henry Cockburn's words:

The fashionable place here now is the College, where Dr Thomas Charles Hope lectures to ladies on Chemistry. He receives 300 of them by a back window, which he has converted into a door. Each of them brings a beau, and the ladies declare that there never was anything so delightful as these chemical flirtations. The Doctor is in absolute extacy with his audience of veils and feathers, and can't leave the Affinities, The only thing that inwardly corrodes him, is that in an evil moment, when he did not expect to draw £200, he published that he was to give the fees to found a Chemical prize, and that he can't now retract, though the said fees amount to about £700. Horrible—I wish some of his experiments would blow him up. Each female student would get a bit of him.[30]

Hope's income from regular class fees came to about £2,000 per academic session. With his career set in a popular, exciting subject, he had little need to pursue his earlier promising research career.

The class fee system could obstruct the progress of learning by dis-couraging professors from supporting the creation of new chairs, which might encroach on their territory and thus draw off students from their classes, or from supporting the extension of the number of compulsory courses by including subjects hitherto optional, which would spread the number of students more thinly. Such new chairs and curricula revisions as there were, therefore, were established in the face of a system that bolstered vested interests and set it in the face of innovation. On the other hand professors were interested in education as well as guineas. For example, Robert Jameson, Edinburgh's professor of natural history, was asked by the 1826 Commission about meteor-ology being included not only in his course, but also those of the pro-fessors of chemistry and Natural Philosophy. Jameson considered the situation advantageous to the student who would thus have several views of the same material.[31]

The best statement of the educational objectives of the Scottish Arts course is to be found in the work of Dr George Davie.[32] They must also be appreciated in the context of philosophical generalising in the delineation and analysis of history. The Scottish universities professed to believe in a general higher education which might sub-sequently be followed by a specialist higher education or a profes-sional course. As in Continental universities, that general course was largely philosophic and there was no premature specialisation. Philosophy was to be the basis on which subsequent specialisation might be built, 'the general should take precedence over the particular and the whole over the parts'.[33] The similarity with the predominant social philosophy of the Scottish Enlightenment is readily apparent. In Dugald Stewart's words:

> It is from this tendency of philosophical studies to cultivate
> habits of *generalisation*, that their chief utility arises:
> accustoming those who pursue them to regard events, less
> in relation to their own immediate and partial concerns, than to
> the general interests of the human race; and thus rendering them
> at once happier in themselves, and more likely to be extensively
> useful in the discharge of their social duties.[34]

The Scottish university system was at least intellectually democratic because those who were unable to go on to higher levels of learning had at least the rudiments of knowledge and education to permit them to exercise their critical judgement on a common-sense level. Consequently, the Scots believed that educational democracy was the precondition of material advance. In Dr Davie's view, Smith and Reid stressed the dangers of over specialisation which threatened communication within the strata of society.[35]

Francis Jeffrey, one of those educated in the Scottish university system during the Enlightenment, a founder, with others, of the *Edinburgh Review* in 1802 and later Lord Advocate, accepted an obvious criticism of this general and democratic education when he gave evidence to the 1826 Commission, but he pointed up the major advantage, that relatively superficial knowledge which a student might acquire might later be broadened by deeper study, and that all study was pleasurable and broadened the mind and experience.

The contemporary spokesman for the Scottish system was George Jardine, Professor of Logic at Glasgow from 1774 to 1827, whose book, while published late in the Enlightenment, must be considered central to the philosophical and educational concerns of the movement. It was entitled *Outlines of Philosophical Education* and appeared in two editions in 1818 and 1825. It covered the two facets of importance to the present analysis, what was taught and how it was taught. While Jardine was the professor who most fully explained the educational thinking and practice of his age, he was not its only practitioner, and Glasgow was not the only university where it was implemented. Jardine's objectives went beyond the mere communication of knowledge and were also to foster intellectual habits of thinking, judging, reasoning and communicating. His book fell into two parts, the first concerned with the teaching matter, the second with teaching methods. His lectures, he confessed, were unoriginal but suited to youths just beginning philosophy. The art of learning was taught first by reference to the students' own minds and then more advanced matter such as logic, the syllogism and similar subject matter could be considered. Jardine moved on, thereafter, to taste, the sources and effects of grandeur, beauty and novelty, an analysis of the powers of taste, and the examination of examples of composition. Such, in brief, was a general philosophical course in action.[37] Teaching methods in Arts included the lecture, catechetics, essays and other exercises, and prizes and like stimuli designed to encourage hard study. The lecture was a feature common to universities in the mainstream of the European tradition. Thomas Reid believed that universities which did not give lectures encouraged superficiality of knowledge in specialist areas and discouraged zeal for new thinking. Consequently, the name of *scholar* was restricted merely to someone proficient in Greek and Latin. On the other hand, where lectures prevailed, a professor would be obliged (not least by pecuniary interest) to keep up with his subject as well as be familiar with traditional authorities, and his teaching should suit the purposes and promote the best interests of his students.[38] In short, the lecture served to show students a trained mind at work, dealing with complex material, treating of it systematically, communicating the state of knowledge in the field and communicating an enthusiasm for the subject to the novices and less experienced. The success of the lecture could depend on the receptivity of the students, therefore, their age, outlook and disposition. All were likely to be quite mixed in the Scottish university classrooms in the Age of the Enlightenment.

It was Jardine, John Millar and others too who supplemented the lecture with catechising. Catechising would take place in a supplementary hour and involved questioning students about the lecture given earlier and becoming involved in arguments with them over its subject matter. Debates were held and questions asked around the class and subsequently written class essays set for which prizes would be awarded for the year's work, largely paid for by the professor himself, though sometimes he might be granted an allowance from the Town Council.[39] It was also common for professors to talk privately with students after class or at some other time, during which difficulties might be elucidated. In his written evidence to the 1826 Commission, sent from his death-bed, Jardine explained and justified his system of teaching in detail; he believed catechising required much preparation and was best conducted by a teacher of long experience since the questions had to be suited to all the different kinds of student. Since there was no set order for asking students questions, all would have to think of the answer before the professor actually alighted on a particular individual. Jardine considered the size of the class no handicap, rather the bigger the class the more the competition and talent available. The exercise grew more difficult as the year went on, being based on the lectures until the student grasped the arts of lucidity, systematic thinking and clear expression. Essays were read out and criticised publicly by the professor before the students' fellows. Later in the course the exercises were more original pieces of work in which the student judged and reasoned for himself. Towards the end of the course was set a more elaborate essay, chosen by the student himself and written in prose or verse. The student had longer to complete it and it was appraised differently. The professor chose up to a dozen of the best students who then covered those topics with which the professors had no time to deal. Their work and essays were read out

and sometimes the students themselves were given the tasks of critic-
ising.[40]

Francis Jeffrey thought highly of the system. If lectures were the
sole means of instruction, a professor had no means of knowing how
well his teaching was coming across or of knowing if any part of his
instructions needed further elaboration. Consequently, if lectures
alone were employed, the professor would not know the qualifications
of a student to move on to further study; nor would any spirit of
emulation enliven the class. Jeffrey spoke of the particular talents a
professor needed and exemplified them by referring to Millar's great
gifts and the advantage of his small class.[41]

(iii)

Effective university teaching was an identifiable concern and prime
achievement of the Scottish Enlightenment. Yet it depended on
students, why they went to university, their social origins and the
costs they would incur, and it depended too on the recruitment of and
economic prospects for professors.

To comprehend the reasons why students went to university in
eighteenth-century Scotland it may be sufficient to recall the limited
number of occupations available in a pre-industrial and predominantly
agricultural society, that attendance at college might qualify a man
for such posts as were available, such as that of schoolmaster, and
that the college session always began when the harvest was in and
winter under way, and ended with the coming of spring. A second
general reason for going to university was the desire to improve one-
self both mentally and socially. There was nothing new about using
some time at a university for these purposes, but the degree to which
it was seen during the Scottish Enlightenment was greater than formerly. The distinctiveness of a Scottish university education was
manifested by all sections of society. Aristocrats could express it
negatively; Lord John Russell wrote abortively to his father, the Duke
of Bedford, after his Grand Tour in 1809 'the thing I should most
dislike, and . . . least profit by, would be an endeavour to acquire
Scotch knowledge in a Scotch town. Political economy may surely
be studied in England.' The sons of manufacturers and merchants,
such as the Pottery family of Wedgwoods and the brothers, Francis and
Leonard Horner, to take but scant examples and humble Scots were
also to be found in a Scottish student body. The number of divinity
students at Glasgow per year averaged over 180 in the twelve years
prior to the 1826 Commission, despite the number of vacancies every

year amounting only to about 30, and the basic salary to £150. Yet to the impecunious the ministry represented security in the pre-industrial age. As a Glasgow minister commented of the Divinity students, a better station in life was the goal of many. He told the Commission again, when they took evidence in Edinburgh, that Edinburgh was preferred by Divinity students to Glasgow because it was a better field for employment. The Glasgow professor of Divinity was clearly worried by the same trend, despite his opening disclaimer:

> a great deal of good is done by the struggles of men of genius coming forward in every class, and in every rank. I do think it is a matter of desire, that clergymen should be taken from the middling classes of society, for there are many disadvantages attending the struggles of poverty; and it is impossible to suppose that there is not something of the original vulgarity which will often attach both to the sentiments and feelings of the man.

The middle group of manufacturers and merchants in particular showed a desire for college education for their sons which, for various reasons, had not been available to them. In some respects they viewed the curriculum as useful for their heirs and in Glasgow manufacturers casually attended university classes themselves.[42] Social improvements and, ultimately, economic improvement through patronage, was also to be had at college by association with the aristocracy. This was most commonly attained through the provision of tutorships with noble or well-to-do families. There was scarcely anyone among the thinkers who did not at some time take on a tutorship as did McLaurin with Lord Polwarth's son, Adam Smith with the Duke of Buccleuch, and Millar with Lord Kames. Ramsay of Ochtertyre explained that the 'improving' nature of the position as it was regarded early in the eighteenth century was due to the opportunity it offered for serious and elegant conversation.[43]

Citizens of the university towns audited the classes that particularly interested them or which developed a reputation. Dugald Stewart's lectures were even known to be attended by his fellow professors as well as outsiders and Thomas Thomson, who lectured both in Glasgow and Edinburgh, commented to the 1826 Commission, when asked if any manufacturers attended his chemistry class that some did, though fewer in Glasgow than in Edinburgh. An analysis was made some years ago of 'The Origins and Occupations of Glasgow Students 1740-1839'[45] based on the Glasgow matriculation albums, which showed that Glasgow

drew over 40 per cent of its students from industrial and commercial
backgrounds, nearly 17 per cent from tenant farming, and nearly 13
per cent from the nobility and landed families. Furthermore, 32.4
per cent of the commercial class of students were said to come from the
skilled artisan and craftsman class within Glasgow itself. The difficulties with the analysis are that Glasgow, then as now, was *sui generis*
in terms of student origins and no meaningful translation of the figures
could be made for a generalisation for the Scottish universities as a
whole. Secondly, and more important, the albums used Latin words
to describe a student's parental occupation which are ambiguous or
vague, *artifex, operarius* and *opifex*. Consequently, the historian must
resort to less quantifiable evidence, for showing that in the Universities
as a whole, the attendance of impecunious and humble students was by
no means unknown, and reached sufficient proportions for most witnesses to the 1826 Committee who were asked about the matter to
question the value of lengthening the Scottish university session, simply
on that account.

In their report, the Commissioners made a point of remarking that
what was peculiarly beneficial was the character of the Scottish universities as institutions where the humble could receive the highest
education in science and philosophy and the higher classes could also
be enlightened. The costs of attending the Scottish universities in the
mid-1820s were given to the 1826 Commission but several witnesses
remarked that they were little different, except for the rise in class
fees, from the late eighteenth century. The figures nonetheless are
only an indication of costs that prevailed for the entire duration of
the Enlightenment.[46] Glasgow's Principal reckoned that the average
cost of a session for the poorer class of students, not including class
fees, would have been £20 with £15 creating a struggle. The poorest
of his students were those who resided in Glasgow. A student estimated
differently: Glasgow expenses came to £25 for a student of middling
class in a single room (sharing cost £4 less); a humble student could
manage with £16 or £17 including all fees, his room, books but not
clothes. At St Andrews a secondar paid £2.60 for his gown, porter's
fees, matriculation and the Library, and a ternar £1.60. Class fees
varied for secondars from £3.25 in Logic to £9.65 in Mathematics, or
£1.60 in Logic for ternars to £6.45 in maths, all including the professor's fee, books and the contribution to the luminator. One witness
calculated that St Andrews too would cost £15 a year, but that included fees. A room could be had for the twenty-six to twenty-seven
week session for £4. At King's, Aberdeen, class fees were three guineas

each, a student's costs in his second year would be £10 but they would be only £5.75 in his third year, including fees to all professors and the charges for servants, books and fires. At Marischal too, fees varied from year to year, amounting in the four successive sessions to £4.85, £7.05, £6.05 and £3.90; the maximum that fees, dues and books would total was just over £30. Another witness quoted an Aberdeen student in 1820 who kept all his expenses down to £16: his lodging cost £1.20, fees four to five guineas, his gown two guineas and the rest went on maintenance for the session. In Edinburgh a room appears to have cost from 35p to 42p a week or all expenses less class fees from 35p to 50p. Estimates of outgoings less class fees varied from £10 in the opinion of a former Librarian, to £12-£15 for a Divinity student. It was said that an Edinburgh room cost some 8p a week more than Glasgow.[47]

Various comments were passed on the poor students. For example, it was stated that Edinburgh was more expensive because students were temped to spend more on theatres, exhibitions and the like; clothing cost more there and the wear on shoes in particular was heavy. On the other hand, others noted that Edinburgh had in its student body poorer young men even than Aberdeen, because the Divinity students especially considered Edinburgh a more fruitful hunting ground for tutorships; or again that expenses in the four towns were much the same or that Edinburgh was the cheapest to live in. To substantiate the last claim the example was given of one young man who in 1827 was living on 35p for rent and fire (£8.10 a session) plus £4.50 a session for maintenance: he 'imported' a little butter and cheese occasionally from the country but otherwise his diet, which was quoted, was bought in the city: porridge and milk for breakfast; for lunch broth and meat on three days, bread and milk on the other days, sometimes potatoes and herrings. He had tea in the afternoon but no supper. Another student dined merely on potatoes and a little butter; yet a third wore no stockings, only gaiters; others allowed themselves no candles but studied by firelight. Professor Forbes, King's College, Aberdeen's professor of Humanity, was one of the many opponents of a longer session because of the dire effects it would have on the poorer students; he told the following tale to the Commission whereby a young Highland student was found spitting blood in his lodgings and when questioned said he was living solely on cornmeal. His landlady said he was not short of money, merely that he spent most of it on books, paying her less than £5 for food, fuel, candles and lodgings for a whole session. The Irish students were said to be the

poorest and little distinction was drawn between Highlanders and Lowlanders. An argument was also advanced that those who had the greatest
difficulty in eking out the circumstances were those who, prior to study,
were used to well-fed, agricultural jobs, rather than those coming
straight from school.[48] The traveller, Edward Topham, wrote of Scottish
students in 1775:

> The miserable holes which some of them inhabit, their abstemious-
> ness and parsimony, their constant attendance to study, their in-
> defatigable industry, even border on romance. They seem to look
> on learning as a diversion, and when once they have roused her from
> her abstruse and concealed haunts, never quit her footsteps, till
> they have pursued her to the covert.[49]

The nation's system of bursaries could reduce fees and other costs to
students. At the time of the Commission Edinburgh offered 80, 3 worth
£100, and 51 of less than £15 each. Glasgow had 71, 1 of £50 and 31
less than £10. Of St Andrew's 72, 49 did not exceed £10 and a quarter
of the students were bursars; King's had 134 bursaries for 356 students,
55 less than £10 in value and Marischal, rather similar, had 106 bursaries
for 371 students, 83 worth less than £10.[50] Such were the economic
facts of life for students in the era of the Scottish Enlightenment.
Scottish democracy was not merely intellectual but neither did the
universities encompass everyone in society. On the other hand for all
its imperfections, in no other European country was it more possible
for the son of an urban manual labourer to hear the prelections of an
Adam Smith. Nonetheless, the state of society outside the universities
made it difficult for any great use to be made of the educational
opportunities that existed in Smith's day.

It is evident that as a result of ther enquiries, the 1826 Commission
felt that the financial provision made for professors was derisory and,
consequently, some of the universities were finding it hard to make
suitable appointments.[51] By the end of the Enlightenment, employment
opportunities for outstanding Scottish university alumni, who formerly
would have stayed to take up chairs, had increased and they were not
staying in Scotland. Even better pay might not have kept them since
their horizons were now expanded to posts in journalism or seats as
MPs that would have been unthinkable in the mid-eighteenth century.[52]

The basic revenues of professors stemmed from a salary and from
the class fees. Again the somewhat late document of the 1826 Commission must be used to indicate the levels of salary which prevailed during

the Enlightenment. The Commission considered the Edinburgh Professors' revenues 'ample': the Logic professor had a salary of just over £52 met both by the Crown and the College; the Moral Philosophy professor's was just over £102, mostly met by the College; the salary of the Mathematics chair was just over £148, Natural Philosophy £52, Natural History £100 (a Regius chair), Anatomy £50, Botany nearly £128, and Clinical Surgery, Military Surgery and Medical Jurisprudence all £100. The chairs of Chemistry, Materia Medica, Theory of Physic, Practice of Physic, Midwifery and Clinical Medicine all had no salaries attached to them. Glasgow salaries were noticeably greater and details of all the increases made throughout the eighteenth century, six between 1777 and 1817, were given: if certain chairs only are selected, the salaries derived in Moral Philosophy was just over £286, Natural Philosophy just over £291, Logic just over £289, Mathematics £292, Medicine £270 and Anatomy £250. The Regius Professors' salaries were much less, Natural History earning £100, Botany £150, and Surgery, Midwifery and Chemistry all £50. Some Glasgow professors received payments in grain: at King's College, Aberdeen professors received payments in meal. The professor of Medicine there received just over £201 and others in the region of £168-£172. At Marischal, the Mathematics professor earned just over £198 from various sources including grants and bequests, and others in Arts just over £184. Medicine and Chemistry had much less lucrative salaries, £46 and £73 respectively. Finally at St Andrews, where costs of living increases had been granted in, for example, 1769, 1779 and 1784, the chairs of Logic, Moral Philosophy, and Natural Philosophy derived salaries of £254, Mathematics £245 and Medicine £234.[53]

Some observations are required, not least because the Commissioners' view that Edinburgh revenues were ample seems at odds with the figures. This is because the lower salaries at Edinburgh were more than compensated for by the greater number of students, sufficient even to remunerate almost lavishly the professor of Chemistry, who had no salary. It has been shown in tabular form, by means of three arbitrarily chosen years and with no allowance for such matters as *gratis* class tickets, just how lucrative an Edinburgh chair could be and selections from the table are instructive (on the following page). Such a table makes it all the more clear why chairs drew of talent from the Kirk, where normal stipends even in 1810 were £150. It also demonstrates why professors of the eminence of Joseph Black and William Cullen were tempted to forsake Glasgow for Edinburgh.

Edinburgh was highly lucrative compared with other universities

EDINBURGH PROFESSORIAL INCOMES

	Salary (to nearest pound)	Class fees (in guineas)	Class Size			Emolument (guineas)		
			1794-1795	1796-1797	1798-1799	1794-1795	1796-1797	1798-1799
Logic	52	2	87	87	79	174	174	158
Moral Philosophy	102	3	116	95	100	348	285	300
Natural Philosophy	52	3	93	81	85	279	243	255
Natural History	100	3	c.50	c.50	c.50	c.150	c.150	c.150
Botany	128	3	78	93	97	234	279	291
Institutes of Medicine	0	3	80	97	68	240	291	204
Practice of Medicine	0	3	225	227	232	675	681	696
Anatomy	50	3	307	326	274	921	978	822
Chemistry	0	3	225	253	262	675	759	786
Midwifery	0	3	79	126	144	237	378	432
Materia Medica	0	3	58	66	95	174	198	285

even if the salaries and class fees are disregarded. As Edinburgh was the capital, the professors there were consulted about scientific aspects pf public works: John Leslie and Robert Jameson reported, for example, on reservoirs to be constructed on the Water of Leith. Edinburgh's flourishing publishing trade in the Enlightenment and the activities of a bookseller-cum-literary agent like William Creech interacted well with the professors' interests and enabled them to profit much from their text-books and research monographs. Yet a third source of income not entirely missing from the other university towns, was the housing by professors of the sons of the aristocracy and gentry, from whom they exacted often exorbitant lodging fees. The most exaggerated example was Dugald Stewart: his class emoluments have already been indicated. He earned vast sums from his writing, £1,600 for his *Dissertation* alone whereas John Playfair earned £500 for his. A later editor of the *Encyclopaedia Britannica,* Macvey Napier, was required to give evidence in a court case of 1844 when Stewart's son sued the publishers A. & C. Black for publishing the *Dissertation* on the grounds that the copyright lay with the family, during which he remarked of the £1,600 that no such sum had ever been paid before for a single piece of serious literature. Napier also revealed that he himself had negotiated the sale of two other books of Stewart's, for which the professor had received £200 each. The admiration of the Whigs for Stewart brought him furthermore the sinecure of the writership of the *Edinburgh Gazette* and a salary of £300 a year. Yet he charged the Palmerston family £400 a year for each of their sons, including the future prime minister, as lodging fees.[55] Dugald Stewart was a very wealthy man and several of his colleagues would almost have matched him. Such could be the emoluments of the Scottish Enlightenment.

To be a professor was, therefore, highly desirable from many viewpoints; it was intellectually satisfying, financially rewarding and one of the few professions that there were in the age of the Scottish Enlightenment. Consequently, the method of appointment was of some importance: there were effectively three methods of appointment to a Scottish university chair, politics, patronage and nepotism. There is more than ample documentary evidence in the Scottish Records Office for all three methods in the papers of Henry Dundas, the great Scottish political manager in the late-eighteenth and early-nineteenth centuries, who received myriads of requests for places including university chairs. Studies of particular contributory stories to the Scottish Enlightenment have pointed up the facets of politics and patronage. Consider, for example, the analysis of Robertson's appointment as Edinburgh's principal where the Earl of Bute is shown to disregard political claims and to alienate his supporters and dependents, remarkable in eighteenth century politics, in the appointment of Leechman to the principalship of Glasgow. On the other hand, the article shows the sheer power and influence of the lawyer Andrew Fletcher, Lord Milton (1692-1766) the domestic political manager of first the Duke of Argyll and then Bute, in disposing of places far beyond straight government appointments. As the minister, Thomas Somerville, wrote in his autobiography, Provost Drummond always consulted Lord Milton (the Duke of Argyll's agent) before promoting anyone. Since Drummond was anxious to stimulate the city's economy by promoting the university's welfare, there was a close connection between patronage, central and municipal politics, operated locally by lawyers, and university appointments. Church politics too, Moderates *versus* Evangelicals, also had some part to play prior to 1770 or so.[56]

A second example of manoeuvres to obtain an Edinburgh chair appears in the account of the founding of the Royal Society. There the positions at stake were the chair of Natural History and the monopoly of the subject in the City, and the competition was between Rev. John Walker and William Smellie, the first translator of Buffon. Both men became embroiled in at least two controversies that were raging, Whig *versus* Tory and the clash of Enlightenment culture with antiquarian culture that was embodied in the opposition to each other of the Royal Society and the Society of Antiquaries. Smellie backed the Whigs and the Antiquaries through his patron the Earl of Buchan and lost, because the era of political instability in the 1770s and the deep-rooted power base of the Dundas interest worked against him.[57] There are other and later examples of politics interfering in the appointments of a professor of moral philosophy in 1820 and of botany the following year.[58] Finally, the words of Thomas Thomson to the 1826 Commission might be noted, commenting on the power of college professors at Glasgow and St Andrews to elect any new professors. Both universities were riven with general, as opposed to institutional, political factions, and the politics of the country distracted professors from their duties.[59]

Nepotism and the establishment of dynasties were also rife in the universities of the Scottish Enlightenment. The Gregories were one dynasty; Robert Simson was appointed to the Glasgow Mathematics chair through his uncle, the professor of Divinity; and the Monros, Matthew and Dugald Stewart, Francis and James Home, the Andrew Duncans, all testify to the fact that once a chair was in the hands of a family, it was difficult to prise it away if a close relative should wish to succeed. A professor could effectively dictate the succession by appointing the relative as his assistant. The extraordinary result of politics, patronage, nepotism and dynasties was that they worked. Personal connexions often ensured an adequate system of professorial appointments, that provided the Scottish Enlightenment by and large with a group and succession of distinguished teachers and scholars. It is a remarkable testimony to eighteenth-century ways that patronage could ensure so much distinction. Nonetheless, the system did have drawbacks that manifested themselves in what has been called the pre-bureaucratic structure of the Scottish universities.[60] The proprietary approach to a chair and its subject area caused resistance to the foundation of new and much needed professorships, the regarding of apparatus as belonging to a given science professor rather than to his chair or a vested interest centering on the text-books a professor wrote. A letter of John Leslie's commenting on the appointment of William Wallace as his successor in the chair of Mathematics in 1819 is a case in point, since Wallace was apparently going to alter Leslie's syllabus:

I have received a long letter from Wallace which gives me a great
deal of pain. Indeed, I regret I ever quitted the Mathematical Chair,
where everything was going on in the train I wished. Now it seems
we are to relapse to the state it was twenty years ago. Wallace may
fancy that I contemplate the diminished sale of my text books—but
this scarcely enters my mind. What I shudder to think of is the total
demolition of all my schemes of improvement.

The letter was written to Archibald Constable, Leslie's publisher.61

II: Intellectual

(i)

The concerns of the Scottish Enlightenment that manifested themselves
in the universities were dictated by the secularisation that was taking
place generally in society at an accelerating pace throughout the eighteenth century. By secularisation is meant that the leaders of Scottish
society were more concerned in the eighteenth century with economic
growth, agricultural improvement and other worldly affairs than with
the religious and ecclesiastical preoccupations which had dominated
seventeenth-century Scottish social history. The Moderates reflected
the change. They were concerned with reconciling the Church with
worldly realities which would have been unthinkable to seventeenth-
century ecclesiastical leaders. In the universities secularisation was made
evident in the declining provision that was made for Divinity in relation
to other disciplines, and in the lack of any original work of theology
among the *corpus* of Scottish Enlightenment thought. On the contrary,
the universities concentrated increasingly on mundane matters such as
medicine, and among the leading original treatises of the age produced
by professors were books on political economy and the sciences.
Medical education became more important than the education of
ministers. The ills of the world were to be resolved in life rather than
compensated for in the hereafter.

Secondly, the improvements in the Scottish universities that were
implemented from the late seventeenth century facilitated the Enlightenment of the mid- to late-eighteenth century. The philosophical cast
of the Arts curriculum interacted with the writings on social philosophy
of the intellectuals, so that new disciplines emerged from existing
subjects, such as political economy from moral philosophy. The development of medicine and medical education boosted subjects previously
considered merely as ancillary to medicine, such as chemistry. The

interest in natural history and botany, and the more general social
and economic concern for agriculture, were also reflected in the provision made for those subjects in the universities. The pursuit of specialised areas of knowledge led to those new ideas and discoveries that
constituted the Enlightenment. The new ideas and discoveries emerged
from institutions that traditionally had a utilitarian purpose in society
such as the training of ministers or schoolmasters. In the eighteenth
century the universities were also training men for new professions,
especially medicine. Consequently, the Enlightenment, professional
training and education all came to be linked.

Thirdly, a concern for effective higher education was a feature and
an achievement of the Scottish Enlightenment because many writers of
distinction were professors, whose work can only be fully appreciated if
it is seen in the light of their desire to inform. Their lectures were
often either original and distinguished works, the basis of their books,
or the media through which they made use of the intellectual legacies
of Bacon, Locke, Newton and others. The Scottish universities in the
Enlightenment employed professors in a wide range of disciplines,
from philosophy to natural history and the whole panoply of medical
subjects, who dedicated themselves to the art of teaching. The concern
was not universal but it was sufficiently widespread to be considered
a preoccupation, and it contributed to the part played by the Scottish
universities in generating and disseminating the Enlightenment.

A significant barometer of secularisation in the universities was the
place of Divinity within them. At Edinburgh, for example, the number
of Divinity chairs remained static while the number of medical chairs
increased and then exceeded them. Only two of the new chairs and
lectureships established at Glasgow and Marischal in the eighteenth
century related to Divinity. The chair of Ecclesiastical History was
founded at Edinburgh in 1694 but not filled until 1702; at Glasgow the
chairs of Oriental Languages and Ecclesiastical History, founded in 1709
and 1716, were not filled for five years. This state of affairs was remarkable in view of the social and religious tasks laid on the universities by
John Knox. In 1831 the Royal Commissioners could say, speaking of
all the institutions that they were not ecclesiastical in character, but
offered a general education. In so far as Divinity was simply one of the
subjects taught, the universities were technically subject to inspection
of the religious opinions taught.[62]

Three other instances taken from the beginning, middle and towards
the end of the Enlightenment illustrate the secularisation of the universities. First, the abolition of regenting introduced as professors to the

universities lay intellectuals whose power base lay in their ability as philosophers and teachers rather than in their status as Kirk ministers. Colin McLaurin (1698-1746) was a case in point: his research ability and reputation earned him the Edinburgh Mathematics chair. They even compensated for his dereliction of teaching duties at Aberdeen when he had sought more money as tutor to Lord Polwarth's son, between 1722 and 1725. Secondly, there was the Principalship of Edinburgh University from 1762-93 of William Robertson, the Moderate leader and Moderator of the General Assembly. It has already been seen how Robertson brought the leadership of the Kirk into tune with the new currents of thought and the new social and economic climate. His presidency of the Scottish metropolitan university in what were among the most illustrious decades of the Scottish Enlightenment made it possible for Edinburgh to capitalise on the earlier groundwork, secure the services of the outstanding Scottish professors of their day, expand the College building and facilities and thrive materially as it had never previously done. Yet, despite being a clergyman, Principal Robertson showed great vigour in putting 'scholarship before preaching',[63] and it was under him that the religious tests previously applied to new professors were abandoned.

The appointment of Robertson to the Principalship was itself a highly secular, political affair which only involved the Church because of the power struggle in which the Moderates were engaged in the early 1760s. The cause of good letters and of Moderation, the secular and the sacred, intertwined. His inaugural oration was entitled 'The advantages to be derived from the study of the Stoic philosophy', which in the view of one student of Robertson illustrated his belief that liberal education in the modern age should draw on cultures other than Christian, and that education should inculcate, in true stoic fashion, the moral duty man has to society.[64] Christian aspirations being framed in secular language and receiving pagan, intellectual support. Once he was Principal, he reorganised the library into a general and a medical branch and improved its financial basis. He endeavoured to raise better salaries for the foundation professors and funds for various buildings such as the natural history museum. He secured a major building programme for the University which included a new anatomy theatre in 1764, a new chemistry classroom and laboratory in 1782 and finally the building of a new College, now confusingly called Old College, in the early 1790s.[65] Material considerations were his concern.

The third instance of secularisation was Leslie's Case in 1805.[66] In that year, a new professor of Mathematics required to be appointed at

Edinburgh. John Leslie (1766-1832) was put forward, a young man
who had recently completed some distinguished work on heat for
which he was awarded unanimously by the Royal Society of London
the £60 gold and silver Rumford Medals in 1806. He had, therefore,
excellent academic qualifications but he was anti-clerical and ultra-
Whig. By 1805, the Moderate party was of a different ilk and operating
in very different circumstances from those prevailing when Robertson
retired in 1780. They were keen to secure the chair for one of their
number, Rev. Thomas MacKnight, a methematician of some attainment who might have been, if the other candidate had been less strong,
a worthy appointee. The Tory Moderates had long had a feud against
Leslie and used to full polemical advantage a footnote in his treatise
on heat which appeared to view favourably Hume's theory of causation. A general party and ecclesiastical political battle ensued in which
one of the Moderates' weapons was the revival of the ancient right
whereby the Town Council of Edinburgh might only elect professors
cum avisamento eorum ministrorum, with the approval of the Edinburgh
presbytery. An ancient right of *veto* was resurrected. One of Leslie's
supporters' arguments was that for MacKnight to hold the chair alongside his charge in the City would be pluralism. MacKnight himself
was prepared to surrender his charge, but the Moderate leaders made a
condition of his keeping it. Ultimately the Town Council elected
Leslie and the matter went before the General Assembly to be won
for Leslie by only 96 votes to 84. As Dr Ian Clark has shown there
were four fundamental issues at stake: first, the ancient right of the
ministry to supervise education; second, the right of Edinburgh ministers to advise the Town Council on filling academic posts; third,
pluralism, the propriety of clergymen holding livings and academic
posts; and finally, the nature and tendency of Hume's philosophy and
the relationship of natural and revealed religion. All four issues were
ultimately settled in favour of the secular interest.

Just as Scottish society itself had left behind the predominantly
ecclesiastical concerns of the sixteenth and seventeenth centuries and
was meeting the secular, economic and social challenges and opportunities of the eighteenth and early-nineteenth centuries, so too were the
universities adapting to changing circumstances.

(ii)

Various improvements in the universities in the late-seventeenth and
early-eighteenth centuries encouraged the development of knowledge
in the Scottish Enlightenment. Virtually no arts, scientific or medical

subject remained untouched as will subsequently be shown. The adaptation to a professorial system coincided with the Scottish interest and
concern for the thought of Locke, Newton and others. The tenure of
the Glasgow Moral Philosophy chair first by Gershom Carmichael (1672-
1729) and then Francis Hutcheson is instructive here. Carmichael had
been a regent for over thirty years before he became a professor in
1727 and so was proficient in the ways of regenting, the dictation from
set books and the limits of Cartesian knowledge and approaches. Yet
he made the necessary adaptation to the new age. In his early writings
he leaned heavily on the approaches of Grotius and Pufendorf (whom
he edited) when he equated the object of jurisprudence with moral
philosophy. In his final work, *Synopsis of Natural Theology*, he
rejected Descartes and indicated his awareness of the Newtonian
experimental method. Hutcheson was a student of Carmichael who
used the legacy well, and pioneered the work so central later in the
Enlightenment of Smith, Reid and Ferguson. His *Inquiry into the
Origin of our Ideas of Beauty and Virtue* (1725) was one of the
earliest modern treatises on aesthetics. It was he who began the break-
away from Latin as the lecture medium in the belief that Latin was the
vehicle of conveying ancient and received knowledge, and as a dead
language not the medium through which new knowledge might be
pursued. He also advanced philosophical knowledge beyond Locke.[67]

John Stevenson, professor of Logic at Edinburgh 1730-1775, was
the first actually to introduce Locke into a Scottish university curriculum. It is known from Alexander Carlyle that Stevenson was very
much a transitional figure since his teaching method was much akin to
that of the regents yet the books he actually used included modern
works, including Locke.[68] Locke's influence was clearly an important
part of the early to mid-eighteenth century's preparation for the Enlightenment, and Dugald Stewart, in his usual perspicacious way, was
able to detect the value of Lockean thought when combined with the
teaching function of the university system.[69] Since Locke's time,
wrote Stewart, there had been a general improvement in the conduct
of education:

in our universities . . . what a change has been gradually
accomplished since the beginning the eighteenth century! The
Studies of Ontology, of Pneumatology, and of Dialectics, have
been supplanted by that of the Human Mind, conducted with more
or less success, on the plan of Locke's *Essay;* and in a few seats of
learning, by the studies of Bacon's *Method of Inquiry* of the Prin-

ciples of Philosophical criticism, and of the Elements of Political Economy. In all this an approach has been made, or attempted, to what Locke so earnestly recommended to parents, 'that their children's time should be spent in acquiring what may be useful to them when they come to be men'.

Earlier Stewart had recognised that in Scotland, the prevailing spirit of the enquiry favoured the diffusion of Lockean philosophy. Locke's way had been prepared in Scotland by the acceptance already of Grotius' *De Jure Belli et Pacis* , which was the best introduction that had yet appeared to the study of moral science. Grotius had come into Scotland because of the connection with the Dutch universities and through his having been edited in 1724 by Carmichael. Stewart pointed to the effects of the embracing of Locke: he singled out Locke's encouragement of free-ranging human reason. This had in itself ensured progress by substituting understanding for abstraction, and directing the mind to the major concerns of human existence.[70]

George Turnbull (1698-1748), professor of philosophy at Marischal College, Aberdeen for six years until after 1721, was the first to suggest that Newtonianism could be applied to the moral sciences. He was among the pioneers of commonsense philosophy, which made itself evident in the work of his student, Thomas Reid, who fathered the school. Turnbull's main philosophic work was *The Principles of Moral Philosophy*, which he published in 1740.[71]

Advances in knowledge led to specialisation. Political Economy developed out of Moral Philosophy to become one of the new sciences to emerge from the Scottish Enlightenment. Adam Smith was the first to teach the subject in his moral philosophy lectures at Glasgow, which ultimately led to the Edinburgh newspaper, the *Caledonian Mercury* saying in their obituary of him that he had converted his chair to one of trade and finance. As one of his successors in the Glasgow chair expressed it more accurately to the Commissioners:

The duties and relations of man, as a moral agent, are so closely connected with those that belong to him as a member of a political or civil society, that it is natural enough to give both [Political Economy and Moral Philosophy] to one teacher.[72]

Dugald Stewart, who was a most effective intermediary of Enlightenment thought to subsequent generations, became the most noted teacher of Smithian political economy in the Scottish Enlightenment.

He first began a separate course on the subject, the first, in 1800 and continued until he effectively retired from teaching in 1808. An average of 49 students attended.[73] He believed that the right implementation of the principles of Political Economy would promote human happiness by consolidating the connection between individual, national and international prosperity. The subject was necessarily broader for Stewart than earlier writers like Sir James Steuart and Quesnay had implied; Political economy

> may be extended to all those speculations which have for their object the happiness and improvement of Political Society, or, in other words, which have for their object the great and ultimate *ends* from which Political regulations derive all their value; and to which *Wealth* and *Population* themselves are to be regarded as only subordinate and instrumental.

He was also concerned to define the occasions and limits of state interference, saying that as long as a man observed the law, he could pursue his interest, employ his capital and foster competition.[74] Colin McLaurin (1698-1846) and Robert Simson (1687-1768) specialised with distinction in mathematics early in the eighteenth century. Simson, who held the chair at Glasgow from 1711 to 1761, concentrated on ancient geometry, notably the work of Euclid, Pappus and Appolonius. The Glasgow senate minutes recorded on his retirement that he 'was the first to discover and understand in its full extent the Analytical Geometry of the ancients after it had been lost for so many ages, and after it had been entirely mistaken or despaired of by the best modern mathematicians, as is evident from the writings of some of the greatest among them [including Newton]'.[75] Before the 1730s, ancient geometry was a mysterious science, for while some extent of the scope of the ancients' discoveries was known, the method whereby they had carried out their investigations was not. It was Simson who, building on the work of earlier mathematicians such as Halley, resolved the mysteries. It was the porisms of Euclid which particularly occupied Simson.[76] In the words of an eighteenth-century historian of science, these 'formed the most intricate and paradoxical subject in the history of ancient mathematics'. The sense of three books of porisms which Euclid wrote was conveyed by Pappus but time had ravaged his sense. Simson directed himself to the task of reconstruction without a diagram to help him or even the form of the propositions. Such was his achievement—'the second invention of Porisms, to which more genius was perhaps required than to the first discovery of them'.[77] McLaurin's abilities were manifested young, by the age of sixteen he had already invented many of the propositions subsequently published in his *Geometrica Organica, Sive Descriptio Linearum Curvarum Universalis* (1720). His graduation thesis was on the power of gravity and he was professor at Marischal at the age of nineteen after withstanding some competition. Between 1722 and 1725 he wrote his essay on the percussion of bodies for which he was awarded the prize of the Royal Academy of Science in 1724.

McLaurin was the man chosen by Newton's family to write an account of his work, and in the first ten pages provided a clear exposition of Newtonianism as he saw it and as he sought to institutionalise it through his teaching of mathematics in two Scottish universities. Natural philosophy, the search for causes in and a description of the operation of the universe, was subordinate to natural religion or natural theology, the argument for God based on design, and moral philosophy. Hence method in pursuing natural philosophy was of great importance, because the wrong method, leading to false inquiries, could lead to atheism and other dangerous results. Supposition was no substitute for inquiry, for 'learning from observation and experience the true constitution of things'. Newton saw that it was necessary to watch nature itself, and to experiment with it. By the use of analysis, synthesis and a fine sense of judgment as to when to experiment and when to cease experimenting, he gave shape to what he called 'experimental philosophy'.[78] McLaurin's own importance at the time during which he was teaching and writing was to bolster and elaborate that Newtonianism which others in science and medicine had already introduced.

John Leslie was a successor to McLaurin in the Edinburgh Mathematics chair, and a natural philosopher of some accomplishment in the Enlightenment. A brief account of his work indicates how the physical sciences maintained a high standard of originality in the Scottish Enlightenment even fifty years after McLaurin and Simson had died. Leslie was a geometer like Simson and so was in the mainstream of eighteenth-century Scottish mathematics. He endeavoured to illustrate the strictness and beauty of ancient Greek geometry, which Simson had revealed, while at the same time connecting it with modern discoveries. It has been argued that geometrical reasoning prevailed because it was reinforced by common sense philosophy which required sensory referents rather than the imaginary ones of algebra.[79] Leslie showed how Euclid could be modernised. From the late-eighteenth century he was also undertaking pioneer research work in meteorology

conducting experiments on such problems as the power of rarified
air to dissolve humidity and why clouds should be lower in cold
climates. He published a book in 1814 on weather prediction for
farmers,[80] and a year earlier had appeared his *A Short Account of
Experiments and Instruments, depending on the Relations of Air to
Heat and Moisture.* It was here he described the various meteorol-
ogical instruments he had invented, the Differential Thermometer,
Photometer, Hygrometer, Hygroscope and Atmometer. Later he
invented the Ethrioscope to measure the impressions of cold transmitted from the higher atmospheres. Leslie also undertook private research work into artificial refrigeration, freezing not only water but
mercury in June 1810, and he went to demonstrate his achievement
to the London Royal Society the following year. He even received a
request from the authoress and traveller Lady Maria Callcott who
wrote:

> A relation of mine who is very anxious to eat cool butter at his
> breakfast has begged me to write to you and ask where your
> apparatus for cooling, or rather ice-making is to be had, and at
> what cost. If you will be so good as to let me know these part-
> iculars I will transmit them to him.

In 1825 a purchaser from India solicited the 'mode of making ice' and
so Leslie transcribed long and elaborate 'Instructions for the Forming,
Keeping and Transporting of Ice in Warm Climates'. His other research
was into electricity, magnetism, the elasticity of water and the poss-
ibility of a steamboat. Leslie could report on the flattery of eminent
Parisian scientists in 1814: 'I find that Edinburgh stands high here as
the *centre des Sciences exactes*.'[81]

The establishment of medicine in Scotland as an academic discipline
and the provision of various facilities permitted medical science to play
a part in the intellectual achievements of the Enlightenment. The first
Monro who began the regular teaching of anatomy and surgery in the
1720s wrote some fifty medical treatises.[82] His anatomical preparations were of a high order and osteology was another field in which he
worked. His book on the subject considered the relations, articulations,
covering, attachments, blood and nerve supply, and uses of all the
bones of the body and he wrote further treatises on particular aspects,
such as the skull, dislocation of the jaw, the caries of bones (which
covered all bone diseases) and the knee joints. He worked, too, on
lymphatics and neurology and made vital contributions to the then

elementary knowledge of embryology and the nutrition of foetuses in
the womb. Among other medical topics into which he undertook
research were aneurysms, tumours, ulcers, hernias, gallstones, smallpox
and comparative anatomy. He had a penchant for the dissection of
unusual cases which included the eye, the ovary, the spermatic vessels
and the scrotum and the duodenum. He founded the Edinburgh Medical
Society in the 1730s and all but one of the professors contributed accounts of interesting patients with whom they had dealt in the Infirmary
to six volumes of *Medical Essays and Observations, revised and published
by a Society in Edinburgh*, published between 1731 and 1738. The
Essays received international notice and acclaim.[83] A colleague of
Monro's was Robert Whytt, professor of the Institutes of Medicine
1747-66, whose research included important contributions to the
knowledge of reflex actions, hysteria and tuberculous meningitis.
The second Alexander Monro (1733-1817) continued with greater
distinction his father's research in medical science. His MD thesis was
on the testis but he also wrote papers on nervous physiology with
which his study of nervous anatomy was bound up. He showed how
the function of the sinuses was to bear increased pressure caused by
sudden neck movements, so as to prevent the rupture of the small
veins of the brain. He showed how the lateral ventricles of the brain
communicated with each other (called the foramen of Monro) and with
the third ventricle. He emphasised the importance of nerves to the
operation of the muscles and conducted his most important research
into bursae, discovering thirty-three in each superior and thirty-seven
in each inferior extremity. He also undertook comparative anatomical
studies of man and fishes.

The MD thesis, a requirement of the Edinburgh degree, several
times laid the groundwork for the later original research of scientific
literati of the Scottish Enlightenment, both those who stayed in
university work and those who made their mark in other spheres.
Joseph Black is an example of the first category with his discovery of
carbon dioxide (or 'fixed air' as it was called); John Conolly (MD 1821
with a theses on the insane and melancholy mind) was later a noted
psychiatrist and James Cowles Prichard (MD 1808 with a dissertation
on the varieties of the human race) was a prominent ethnologist; they
constitute examples of the second category.

Medical advances stimulated the development of subjects that had,
hitherto, been considered ancillary. The prime example was chemistry.
The work of William Cullen (1710-90) and Joseph Black (1728-99)
contributed to chemistry being viewed as a science in its own right.

Cullen first lectured at Glasgow on chemistry, botany and materia
medica before becoming professor of Medicine in 1751. Black became
professor of Anatomy in 1756 at Glasgow and then of Medicine and
Chemistry from 1757. It was to the detriment of the Glasgow medical
school that Cullen forsook it for Edinburgh in 1755 because it was
developing so slowly, and he was followed eleven years later by Black.
Cullen had studied under the first Monro, Black studied under Cullen.
Black was related to Adam Ferguson and with James Hutton was one
of Adam Smith's executors. Cullen was David Hume's physician. They
were, therefore, personally and intellectually at the centre of the
Scottish Enlightenment. Cullen showed that chemistry was not to be
confined to medicine by showing its importance to natural philosophy
and to such utilitarian matters as fertilisation in agriculture, mining,
brewing, vinegar manufacture, bleaching and the manufacture of
alkalies. He conducted experiments on the cold produced by the evap-
oration of a variety of fluids.

In medicine he generalised the phenomena of disease, and his originality lay in his concentrating on body solids and giving little attention
to prevailing views on body fluids. He divided the body's solids into
two kinds, simple and vital. Simple solids were the same in a living body
as in a corpse, had fewer functions than vital solids and were, therefore, susceptible to less disease. Vital solids were fundamental to the
nervous system and disappeared upon death, yet changes in them accounted for nearly all the body's dysfunctioning. He based his pathology
on the nervous system, saying that most important in its operation was
the animal power or energy of the brain, including the spinal column.
The animal power or energy acted on the vital solids and when it worked
well there was health; when it worked poorly there was illness. Consequently, if energy was so crucial it was necessary to know what influences
prevailed over it: Cullen divided those influences into physical and
mental. The physical influences, heat, cold, effluvia, acted on the body;
the mental influences acted on the brain, will, emotions, appetites,
propensities, habit and imitation. Fever, for example, in Cullen's
pathology was explained not by the state of the blood but by the
diminution of brain energy caused by physical or mental influences
and could be countered by increasing the action of the heart which
would restore the energy of the brain. He derived some fame from his
Nosology (1769), a pamphlet designed to classify diseases by symptoms.
While it simplified matters in his own day it rapidly became neglected,
not least on account of advances made in the knowledge and number
of diseases.[84]

Black was led into his investigation of alkaline substances through medicine. For his MD thesis he originally wanted to test the efficacy of limewater in dissolving urinary calculi, an area of research that interested Cullen, Whytt and Charles Alston (1683-1760), the professor of botany. Since Whytt and Alston disagreed with one another, and since Black did not wish to offend either man, he set out to examine other absorbent earths than limewater in his search for a powerful agent to crush stones in the bladder so that the fragments could be removed through the urethra. He chose *magnesia alba*, then used as a mild purgative, and discovered that it had unexpected properties when it was strongly heated and changed into *magnesia usta*. He subsequently discovered that *magnesia alba* lost air when combined with acids, whereas *magnesia usta* lost air when it was heated, and before it combined with acids. That air was carbon dioxide or as Black called it, 'fixed air'. The thesis was, therefore, more chemical than medical though Black attempted to give it medical respectability by dealing with gastric acidity in the first part of the dissertation and devoted the second part to his experiments on *magnesia alba*.

Cullen stimulated Black to his discoveries concerning heat when they were professor and student at Glasgow in the early 1750s. The first explanation Black offered concerned latent heat, namely heat lying concealed and not detectable even by a thermometer, that caused melting of ice and vaporisation of water. Latent heat had first been observed by Fahrenheit and recorded in Boerhaave's *Elementa Chemiae*, which Cullen and Black recommended to their students in translation. Black first conducted his experiments on the problem in 1760. Crucial to his experiments was the distinction he drew between quantity of heat and temperature, a distinction that was not original to Black but he was the first to make systematic use of it. Temperature could be measured by a thermometer but quantity of heat was more difficult to assess. To resolve the problem Black used the dynamic method of Newton which had been used in 1701 to estimate temperatures beyond the reach of a linseed oil thermometer. Black dilated on Newton's experiments in his lectures, and in his own experiments used Newton's law of cooling. Black required, therefore, to relate the time required to heat or cool water to a given temperature to the amount of heat transferred. He undertook his experiments on freezing in December 1761 and on vaporisation about a year later.

Black's second discovery, specific heat, was that different substances have different heat capacities. Again Fahrenheit through Boerhaave's text-book gave Black the initial clue to the problem: when he had mixed equal quantities of mercury and water at different temperatures, the mercury exerted far less effect in heating or cooling the mixture than did the water. Thus did Black realise that mercury had a smaller store of heat than an equal amount of water at the same temperature; consequently, he deduced that the capacity of bodies to store up heat did not vary with their bulk or density. Thirdly, Black purveyed the doctrine of chemical affinity, where again he owed much to Cullen and, further back, to Newton's *Opticks*. He noted that chemical reactions resulted from the differential or 'elective' attraction of chemical individuals for one another. Simple elective attractions are produced by heat and double elective attractions chiefly take place in solution.[85]

The discoveries of Cullen and Black, which are among the outstanding achievements of the Scottish Enlightenment, demonstrate the powerful effects which earlier improvements had on Scottish intellectual life. They demonstrate the use made of Newton's pioneering work and of Boerhaave's broad approach to medicine and associated sciences. They demonstrate, too, how specialisation led chemistry away from being regarded merely as an aid to medicine, but as a theoretical and utilitarian discipline in its own right.

Natural history and geology in particular were also part of the intellectual interests of the Scottish Enlightenment that were facilitated by earlier improvements, and made evident in the universities by the provision of chairs and courses. Scotland's awareness of natural history and geology was another example of her contact with Continental thought and interests. Geology had been in vogue not least for the utilitarian needs of the mining industry but also because of an intellectual interest in the science that had been evident from the seventeenth century. Four approaches were evident before the Scottish Enlightenment and which contribute to an appreciation of eighteenth-century Scottish work in natural history and geology. First, the systematic analysis of strata and minerals in localities all over Europe was undertaken. Secondly, precedents were set for discarding the biblical authority for the Flood as a force in determining the earth's surface, notably by Italian geologists. Thirdly, travelling to further the cause of geology and mineralogical cartography became more popular and common. Finally, there was the writing of George-Louis Leclerc de Buffon whose multi-volume *Natural History* began to appear by the mid-eighteenth century and was both a stimulus and an indication of contemporary interest. In the study itself Buffon necessarily touched on many subjects which fascinated the eighteenth-century *literati*, theories

of the earth, social and animal organisation, social and animal propensities, the relationship of food and climate to race. It is under-
standable how in the wake of Buffon and when philosophical history
was in vogue natural history would be a desirable addition to Scottish
university education as well as a pursuit that was often of more consuming general interest outside the universities. Buffon's *Epochs of Nature*
(1778) proposed successive and ceaseless revolutions in the history
of the earth, a theory later to be taken up by the Scottish *literatus*,
James Hutton. Controversy was endemic to the subject, since, for
example, one set of mountains in one area could illustrate a totally
different theory from another set in another area.

Intellectual interest in natural history was preceded and supported
by economic developments within Scotland, such as agricultural
improvement and surveys of the Highlands and islands carried out by
the Board of Trustees for the Encouragement of Fisheries, Arts and
Manufactures, the Board of Commissioners for the Annexed Estates
and the Society for the Propagation of Christian Knowledge. Even
prior to that, concern for natural history and topography had been
shown by Sibbald's *Scotia Illustra*, his geographical work, and by
Sibbald and Balfour's foundation of the botanical garden.

Likewise the rise of Scottish geology was an outgrowth of the same
or similar improvements: intellectually, the sciences, such as chemistry,
on which geology was based had to be developed. The expansion of the
Scottish coal-mining industry from the end of the sixteenth century,
the various concerns of Archibald Cochrane, ninth Earl of Dundonald
(1749-1831), which included the sale of ammonia to the sal-ammoniac
manufacturers of Edinburgh and of whom James Hutton was the
principal, and the development of land were also potent forces. It has
been shown, too, that in the Royal Society of Edinburgh between 1783
and 1820 earth sciences were of immense interest and of the members
who were particularly active 43 per cent were landowners. It has been
contended that their concern was a manifestation of the desire to
identify their cultural activities as far as possible with their primary
activity in society, and to patronise what was apprehended as materially useful. Earlier, in the age of improvement to about 1780, the
scheme initiated in the 1740s by the Edinburgh Philosophical Society
whereby landowners who wanted free and expert assays of ores,
minerals and soils could submit samples to the Secretary, the then
Edinburgh professor of Chemistry, was potentially of benefit both to
science and to the landowner's pocket.[86]

In the 1780s, the most influential geological theory was that of

Abraham Gottlob Werner, of the School of Mines at Freiberg in Saxony, which had been founded in 1765. He started from the premise that originally the whole world was covered by sea. The first stage thereafter saw the crystallisation of primitive rocks out of water which was generally chemically laden. The same chemical solution caused the second stage of transition strata (slates, shale) while the third stage saw the recession of the waters. In the fourth stage, climatic turbulence led to such new strata as clay, sand and pebbles. Finally, after the waters had totally receded from the present continental areas, volcanic activity followed the disappearance of water. The whole process took place in stages. Werner published little, but his personal influence, exercised through his students, was immense. It lingered well into the nineteenth century not only through Robert Jameson, the professor of natural history at Edinburgh, 1804-54, but through the work of two rather more celebrated former students, Leopold von Buch (1774-1852) and Alexander Humboldt (1769-1859).

In Edinburgh, James Hutton, who like Hume was not part of the formal institutions on which the Enlightenment was based but who was active in clubs and societies, communicated an alternative 'Theory of the Earth' to the Royal Society in 1785.[87] Hutton was not in the mainstream of Scottish geological activity but he was a major *literatus* of the Enlightenment.[88] Hutton's theory was divided into four parts, two of which were devoted to the origin of rocks, the third showed that present land areas of the world were composed of rock strata which had consolidated over the ages under the sea and the fourth demonstrated that older continents and islands, now disintegrated, provided the materials which composed the more recent land areas. Hutton thought that the events of past geological ages could best be interpreted by a careful examination of present conditions and processes. There were two categories of rocks: the first was classified as volcanic-magmatic, that is lava, pumice, granite; the second was sedimentary, that is all others including rocks usually thought primary, such as schist. In past ages, said Hutton, there had always been a similar distribution of land and sea to the present, though different continents and seas had been in different places. Some continents were always being denuded, and some new continents were always forming. Heat transformed the situation by making new islands and continents from solid rock converted from the loose sedimentary material, and by raising the new consolidations above sea level. Heat pushed up the rock strata which had amassed under the ocean; for volcanoes had a part in raising continents to the surface. Once this

first force, heat, had been delineated, Hutton then went on to the
second of his forces, water, which went to work on land surfaces.
Atmospheric weathering, chemical decomposition, and the effects of
sun and of rivers denuded the earth, wore it away so that particles once
more fell to the bottom of the sea, where the agency of heat would once
again cause them to consolidate, and rise to form new continents. It
was a cyclical, continuous and timeless process. As John Playfair wrote:
'in the economy of the world, we see no mark, either of a beginning or
an end' and the word economy is significant for Hutton was dealing
with the economy of nature, as Smith had dealt with the economy of
society.[89] Hutton was not concerned with origins but with the mechanics of operation, yet his opponents continually assailed him on the
matter of origins.

Hutton differed from Werner's disciples not only in rejecting the
biblical Flood and Mosaic chronology (which Werner himself did not
accept), with the consequence that his theory required aeons of time,
which was not a novel 'heresy' but he differed from Werner much
more distinctively in the cyclical process, in the dual forces of heat
and water which worked in equilibrium to construct and to destroy.
Hutton was unoriginal in a sense because his concentration on heat
clearly owed much to the work, help and advice of his close friend,
Joseph Black. Without the theory of latent heat no new dimension
could have been brought to the subject of rock formation, no alternative to the action of water could have been suggested. Here was one
idea of the Scottish Enlightenment emerging from another. Equally
important is the fact that Hutton published an important work of
moral philosophy in 1794, *An Investigation of the Principles of Knowledge and the Progress of Reason from Sense to Science and Philosophy*, without some understanding of which no just appraisal can be
made of the totality of his work as a *literatus*.

In *An Investigation* Hutton displayed commonplace eighteenth-
century natural theology:

> man, from the brute state in which he is born, ascends, first, in
> the order of knowledge to intellect; secondly, in the order of
> intellect to wisdom, by reading the will of God, the wisdom of the
> Creator in the nature of the creature; and lastly, in the order to
> wisdom to know God, in loving or studying wisdom, for its own
> sake, which is philosophy, or the perfection of the human mind.[90]

He was also intimating that his prime object in pursuing natural philosophy was to strive towards the perfection of the human mind through the attainment of wisdom. God was a precondition of wisdom and, consequently, the universe must be ordered because wisdom/God are ordered. Wisdom consisted in relating pieces of knowledge possessed and was hence an ordering process. The extent to which man saw order in the universe was the extent to which he was wise. If the 'Theory of the Earth' is seen against this background then it can be viewed not as a work of a mere observer of rocks, but a demonstration of the progress of the human mind, achieved through an exposition of the order of the natural world.

Once Hutton is seen as a moral philosopher he can be related to other *literati* of the Scottish Enlightenment. The social philosophers were concerned too with the natural order, but as manifested in society. Hutton was more of a mental philosopher, to use an old-fashioned term: while his fellow philosophers saw happiness in an understanding of the natural order in society, Hutton saw it in an understanding of order in the mind, the attainment of wisdom. By exposing the order of the external world in his 'Theory of the Earth' he showed that the human mind had reached a degree of order in itself. He shared the conjectural method with his fellow philosophers and a third common factor was his preoccupation with Man. The form of order he detected in the Earth showed that the world was in equilibrium, harmonious, continuously life supporting and, therefore, designed for the benefit of Man. Hutton's idea that 'This earth, like the body of an animal, is wasted at the same time as it is repaired' was a commonplace to theism long before his time and was shared with David Hume. In his *Dialogues concerning Natural Religion*, Hume, speaking through Philo, said that the universe:

> bears a great resemblance to an animal or organised body, and seems actuated with a like principle of life and motion. A continual circulation of matter in which it produces no disorder: a continual waste in every part is incessantly repaired; the closest sympathy is perceived throughout the entire system: and each part of member in performing its proper offices, operates both to its own preservation and to that of the whole. The world, therefore, I infer, is an animal; and the Deity is the SOUL of the world, actuating it, and actuated by it.

Philo went on to say that every part of the globe was continuously for many ages entirely covered with water:

And though order were supposed inseparable from matter, and
inherent in it; yet may matter be susceptible of many and greater
revolutions, through the endless periods of eternal duration. The
incessant changes, to which every part of it is subject, seem to intimat
some such general transformations; tho' at the same time it is observ-
able, that all the changes and corruptions of which we have every had
experience, are but passages from one state of order to another;
nor can matter ever rest in total deformity and confusion . . . I
esteem [no system of nature] more plausible than that which
ascribes an inherent principle of order to the world; though attended
with great and continual revolutions and alterations . . . Chance
has no place, on any hypothesis, sceptical or religious. Every thing
is surely governed by steady, inviolable laws.

Thus Hutton can be placed yet more firmly in the context of Scottish
Enlightenment thought.[91]

Hutton, however, diverged from the *literati* as well as concerting
with them. While Bacon, Locke and Newton were important intellectual
influences on all the thinkers of the Scottish Enlightenment, Hutton,
it may be suggested, shared ideas with Descartes, demodé in his time.
The common ideas, it must be admitted, were also commonplace in
the seventeenth and early eighteenth centuries. As Descartes deduced
the universe and order from God, so did Hutton. There is no mention
in Hutton, as with Smith, of an 'invisible hand'. Hutton spent time in
Paris and Leyden studying the human body and his MD thesis was concerned with the circulation of the blood. He must be seen too, as a
doctor as well as a geologist and philosopher. Descartes' opinion that
heat had a central part to play in the circulation of the blood bears a
correspondence to Hutton's theory: first 'blood vapours' entered the
lungs, where the softness of the flesh and 'the air of respiration' caused
these vapours to be 'thickened and reconverted into blood'; this blood
then circulated till it re-entered the heart, which 'containes in its pores
one of those fires without light'; and these inflated and dilated the
blood which vapourised again, so that a circular process was continually
in motion.[92] In both men's theories a diffusion of substance, rock to
particles, blood to vapours, consolidation or coalescence of the diffused substance, and elevation or inflation caused by central heat,
all appeared. The difference between Hutton attributing consolidation
to heat and Descartes attributing coalescence to 'the air of respiration'
can be explained by Black's intermediate discovery of latent heat.
So Hutton may have learned as much from Paris and Leyden as from

Edinburgh: all came together to enable him to formulate a geological theory set in the context of the moral philosophy of his age. Therein lies his originality.

Hutton diverged, too, from some other thinkers in his optimism which was part of his refusal to concern himself with theological matters. Ferguson, it will be recalled, for example, saw savagery as an ever-recurrent prospect. If religious orthodoxy was adhered to, sin corrupted everything; even the earth would decay. Hutton, on the other hand, portrayed a dynamic and self-perpetuating earth, untrammelled by biblical chronology. He opposed the ethos of the Kirk, which may be a partial explanation for the opposition to his theory which arose. In the last decades of the Scottish Enlightenment, Edinburgh became a battle field for rival geological theories. Hutton's full significance was never appreciated in his own time.

(iii)

The pursuit of knowledge in a number of fields was matched by a concern to disseminate that knowledge through university courses. Teaching excellence was an attribute of some thinkers and it is significant that many professors ceased to produce original research, especially in science, once they assumed the duties of a chair. Subsequent exemplification is taken from Glasgow and Edinburgh and also from the latter part of the Enlightenment, the 1760s to the 1820s, because the intellectual, material and academic base for effective teaching was stronger than it had been earlier. The examples are admittedly the best, but they were neither alone in their proficiency, nor was every Scottish professor endowed with ability in education.

The student of autobiographies and memoirs of those who studied in the era of the Scottish Enlightenment cannot fail to become familiar with the plethora of eulogies heaped on their professors. Dugald Stewart's encomia are the most remarkable of all: many will know Henry Cockburn's 'To me his lectures were like the opening of the heavens' and 'there was eloquence in his very spitting', Stewart's slight tendency to asthma made him often clear his throat whilst lecturing.[93] It is important to appraise these testimonies with care, not necessarily discounting them on grounds of nostalgia, or of being written in old age or even as the impressions of immature youth for whom eloquent professors were idols. The sheer weight of approbation is such that there was clearly an art to being a Scottish professor, which some mastered particularly well with memorable results.

Francis Jeffrey complimented John Millar, professor of law, both on his learning and on his ability to teach according to the abilities of each member of his class.[94] In the *Edinburgh Review* of 1803 and 1806, Jeffrey gave further and extensive consideration to Millar in two articles devoted to his *Historical View* and *Origin of the Distinction of Ranks*. Jeffrey and his contemporaries bear out the reputation that Millar's classroom had for being one of the two nurseries of early nineteenth-century Whiggery, the other classroom being Dugald Stewart's. As Jeffrey noted in the first of the reviews, Millar's books contained the substance of his lectures from which his students probably derived their earliest impressions of politics. Millar's success as a teacher appears to have stemmed as much from the particular use he made of the lecture system and a commitment to his students as from the actual content of his lectures. Jeffrey thought, quite wrongly as it subsequently appeared, that Millar's reputation would be greater among those who knew or studied under him than among those who read his work, not least because his writing style was nothing like that of his lecturing.

> The constant alacrity and vigour of his understanding, the clearness and familiarity of his illustrations, and the great variety of his arguments and topics of discussion, together with something unusually animated and impressive in his tones and expressions, gave an interest and spirit to his living language, that can scarcely be traced in his writings.

The vivacity and familiarity of Millar's lecturing style contrasted with the solemnity found in a pulpit and eloquence where the style rather than the substance impressed the auditors. He was informal, clear, simple, light, argumentative and capable of conveying highly intellectual matter most palatably. He was, for Jeffrey, the embodiment of the English conception of a Scottish philosopher:

> with little or no deference to the authority of great names, and not very apt to be startled at conclusions that seem to run counter to received opinions or existing institutions; acute, sagacious, and systematical; irreverent towards classical literature; rather indefatigable in argument, than patient in investigation; vigilant in the observation of facts, but not so strong in their number, as skilful in their application.

Millar united the thought of the Scottish Enlightenment of which he was so prominent an exponent with the philosophical education that underlay the university system. He also managed to convey that thought and philosophical approach by using effectively another fundamental feature of the university system, the lecture. Jeffrey said of Millar that 'everything [law, morality, government, language, the arts, sciences, manners] arose spontaneously from the situation of the society' and he taught that all 'diversified appearances of human manners and institutions could be referred to 'one simple principle, and [could be seen] as necessary links in the great chain which connects civilized with barbarous society'. Millar also practised the catechetical method of teaching. He made himself available after his lectures, so as to learn which parts had not been understood, to debate with students and consolidate informal relationships. The informality spilled over into his home where he both entertained students, encouraged further philosophical debate, and cultivated friendships.[95]

Dugald Stewart at Edinburgh, contrasts with Millar. The education of many effective early nineteenth-century Whigs was in their hands, yet in so many ways Stewart differed from his Glasgow counterpart. A vast array of testimonies has been left as to his eloquence as a lecturer: 'I have heard Pitt and Fox deliver some of their most admired speeches; but I have never heard anything so eloquent as some of the lectures of Professor Stewart', wrote James Mill, Bentham's aide, in 1821.[96] Cockburn's impressions have already been given and others, including some in verse, sonnet and ode form could be quoted.[97] He taught Moral Philosophy and so it might well have been that some of the subjects of his prelections, such as sensibility and taste, required and were suited to eloquence. On the other hand, Jeffrey's dismissal of the 'eloquent' lecturer might be recalled, in which he criticised the tendency to put manner before matter.[98] When the eulogies are considered, Jeffrey's words might well be said to describe Dugald Stewart. Many of his auditors, furthermore, were at an impressionable age and too inexperienced of life to have formed views unique to themselves. Until 1790, he used notes, but thereafter he read his lectures, largely because the changed political climate laid him open to charges of being a Jacobin. Yet ironically Millar was more of a republican. Stewart used the lecture system apparently to his students' great delight, but in a very different way from Millar.

Millar, while a disciple of Adam Amith, nonetheless had original contributions to make to the *corpus* of Scottish Enlightenment thought. Stewart's great strength lay in his ability to popularise and transmit the work of the previous generation of *literati* and to encourage philosophical generalising. His explanations of theoretical history, of political economy and of philosophical generalising itself remain outstanding as does his exposition of Thomas Reid's common sense philosophy. The very ability to transmit, to interpret to others the philosophy of the Scottish Enlightenment, was most suited to his work as a professor and he excelled in the task. On the other hand Stewart, with three times the number of students that Millar had, did not employ the catechetical or essay methods of teaching. It is known, too, that with a few rather prominent exceptions he did not really come to know his students as well as Millar, nor feel able to write personal testimonies. He appears, though, to have kept in touch with his prominent students, many of whom distinguished themselves in various public careers whereas Millar apparently tended to decline familiarity with his influential students. Consequently, Stewart was the one who received a sinecure from the Whigs in 1806.

The two men professed different subjects and that may account too for distinctions that can be made between them. However, it can be argued that as a professor of moral philosophy who bridged the eighteenth and nineteenth centuries, Dugald Stewart played a valuable part in a crucial transitional period. He emphasised as a writer the Enlightenment's interests in man and society and in other worldly concerns such as political economy. On the other hand he espoused Reid's common sense philosophy which tempered any tendency he might have had to make a thoroughgoing rejection of old values. The students he taught were witnessing the questioning of traditional certainties and the collapse of political and social establishments. His professorship coincided not only with debates over religious belief but with the Industrial and French Revolutions. Stewart effectively equipped his students with responses to the new age: classical economics, moral seriousness and virtue, industry and sensibility. One of his objectives in teaching political economy was 'to enlighten those who are destined for the functions of government, and to enlighten public opinion in respect of their conduct'. Stewart's views were echoed by Jardine who recommended, in his *Outlines of Philosophical Education,* that, among other subjects, political economy should be taught, since it was so vital to public business and would enable young men of rank to carry out their duties.[99] Through some able students in Stewart's political economy classes were the doctrines of the subject put into practice, albeit in modified ways, in the early nineteenth century.

In mathematics and natural philosophy, John Playfair (1748-1819) was an able populariser.[100] He put considerable effort into text-books which testified to his and other professors' commitment to pedagogy. The text-books were original and expressed technical matters in everyday speech. They aimed to democratise the sciences.[101] Playfair's text-book for his Natural Philosophy class was entitled *Outlines of Natural Philosophy* (1814) and was projected in three volumes. The first dealt with Dynamics, Mechanics, Hydrostatics, Aerostatics and Pneumatics, the second with Astronomy, while the third, which was never completed, was to have embraced Optics, Electricity and Magnetism. In both his chairs Playfair specialised in making known the work of Continental mathematicians and natural philosophers. He incorporated their discoveries into the Edinburgh curriculum, thus illustrating the development of science since Newton, and also how Leibnitz's calculus and algebraic method could, in certain circumstances, be seen as simpler that Newton's more geometrical approach. Indeed, Playfair's distinct contribution could be said to have been in disseminating continental work in Algebra as seen in Leonard Euler's application of algebra to trigonometry, which was used especially in physical astronomy and, consequently, improved on Newton. Euler was not the only Continental scientist whose work received Playfair's attention both as professor and publicist: Lagrange's calculus of variations, D'Alembert's mechanical principle, Clairaut and Leplace were all familiar to him. Playfair's specialisation can be seen not in original work, therefore, but in his exemplifying what advantages a professorial system could bring by contrast to the old regenting system, although mathematics had been a chair at Edinburgh since 1674. Rather than merely take students through received, traditional and, therefore, static knowledge, he endeavoured to ensure their awareness of the current developments in the areas he taught.[102] He also set in train the arrangements for the building of an astronomical observatory to make possible further specialised research work, but the whole history of observatories in Edinburgh up to 1830 is a story of incompetence.

In medicine and chemistry, earlier improvements in medical education received some bolstering before the middle of the eighteenth century. The medical essays which were produced by Monro I and his colleagues in the 1730s attracted attention and numbers to the burgeoning Edinburgh medical school. In 1748, official sanction was first given to John Rutherford, professor of medicine 1724-47 and trained at Leyden, to inaugurate clinical medical lectures. His method and objective were stated thus:

I shall examine every Patient capable of appearing before you, that no circumstances may escape you, and proceed in the following manner: 1st, Give you a history of the disease. 2ndly, Enquire into the Cause. 3rdly, Give you my Opinion of how it will terminate. 4thly, lay down the indications of cure yt arise, and if any new Symptoms happen acquaint you them, that you may see how I vary my prescriptions. And 5thly, Point out the different Method of Cure. If at any time you find me deceived in giving my Judgement, you'll be so good as to excuse me, for neither do I pretend to be, nor is the Art of Physic infallible, what you can in Justice expect from me, is some accurate observations and Remarks upon Diseases.[103]

Charles Alston, professor of Botany at Edinburgh from 1738 to 1761, developed the teaching of materia medica and extended the range of the botanical garden. Various professors took an interest in the Glasgow botanical garden throughout the eighteenth and early nineteenth centuries, stocking it with plants, erecting a conservatory and using it for teaching prior to the establishment of the chair of Botany in 1818.

By the time of the 1826 Commission, and following a revision in 1824, Edinburgh University's medical curriculum was as follows:[104]

BRANCHES OF EDUCATION

Preliminary

Latin	Required
Greek	
Mathematics	Required
Modern Languages	
Natural Philosophy	

Professional

Anatomy	
Surgery	Six Months
Chemistry	Six Months
Materia Medica	Six Months
Practical Chemistry and Pharmacy	
Theory of Medicine	Six Months
Practice of Medicine	Six Months
Midwifery	Six Months
Clinical Medicine	Six Months

Clinical Surgery	
Practical Anatomy	
Natural History	Two for
Legal Medicine	Three Months
Military Surgery	
Botany	Three Months
TOTAL	
Three Months' Courses	Three
Six Months' Courses	Seven
Hospital	Two Six Months
	in different years

Lectures were as significant to medicine, according to one witness who
appeared before the 1826 Commission, as they had been to the subjects
of Stewart and Millar. The witness, like Jeffrey, distinguished between
the content of lectures and the influence which could be wielded by
the adroit use of personal qualities by the lecturer:

> The lectures of the late Dr Monro, Dr Black, Dr Cullen and Dr
> Gregory, and others, were taken in short hand, and numberless
> copies written verbatim as they were delivered: but no one ever
> ventured to read them to a class, although they confessedly
> contained an immense mass of valuable information. If the
> attempt had been made it would have proved abortive. The
> value of these lectures resided in their authors, themselves masters
> of their arts, who, by their genius and talents and industry, and
> scientific discoveries and zeal, acquired a mastery over the
> minds of the pupils, which elicited whatever zeal, and enthusiasm
> and talents they possessed, and thus riveted in their minds what
> was propounded to them.[105]

Cullen was apparently not merely a clear lecturer but took every
opportunity to come to know his students in the way later advocated
by Jardine and Millar.[106] His reputation as a teacher lies not merely
in his skill at imparting information but on a number of innovations
which he introduced. He was not the first to apply any of the innovations but never before had one man employed them all. He lectured
in English, from his own notes rather than a set text, illustrated his
points by simple demonstrations and encouraged students to undertake laboratory work. Black was also lucid and gently impressive as

was intimated by the editor of his lectures, writing to Black's nephew
during his work on the task:

> I see that your excellent Uncle made it his great Aim to be completely
> understood by the most illiterate of his hearers—and for this reason
> he avoids on all occasions all refined or abstruse reasonings, all
> subtile philosophical disquisition . . . Satisfied with the clearness and
> justness of his conception of any point, he could put it in the same
> simple form and make it clear to the apprehension of his hearers
> without any abstruse reasoning—he never attempted to please their
> fancies with a fine theory which promised the explanation of every-
> thing, and he knew that his own discoveries gave him sufficient
> authority in all matters of controversy.[107]

In materia medica, Andrew Duncan junior employed increasingly
practical methods of demonstration, brought together a considerable
pharmaceutical apparatus and a notable collection of materia medica,
including the only collection of Indian materia medica in Europe, and
alimentaria. A museum of materia medica was established where he
exhibited all his material to his students, and which was designed to
excite the students and impart information. The specimens were
so laid out that the lecture was not interrupted and students came down
afterwards to examine, taste, smell and otherwise come to know them.[10]

Midwifery was another subject where successive professors saw the
importance of practical experience: Thomas Young, who was professor
from 1756-80, first established a special Lying-In Ward at the Royal
Informary; in the time of his successor, Alexander Hamilton, professor 1780-1800, the ward was too small; provision could be made for
only six patients at a time and those pupils anxious to see much
practice were allowed to accompany him to private deliveries. In
February 1792, a Lying-In Hospital was established independently not
only for expectant mothers but also to give students practical opportunities to study obstetrics. James Hamilton succeeded his father in 1800
and had extended the service to women in their own homes by 1824.
The objects of his Lying-In Institution for delivering Poor Married
Women at their Own Houses were:

> to afford every requisite attendance, either by a Medical Gentleman,
> or a Midwife, (as circumstances may require) to Poor Married
> women lying-in at their own habitations; to furnish them with the
> necessary Medicines; to supply the most needy of them with the

temporary use of Child-bed Linen, Flannels, Blankets, &c., and with and other addition to the means of comfort and health that may be essentially necessary. At present, there is not any Public Institution of the same kind established in this City, embracing such manifold advantages to the Industrious Poor at such a period of anxiety, when all the evils of Poverty are felt in an accumulated degree.

The hospital was supported by subscription. Hamilton had a museum of his own costing £1,200 and he gave private classes to Edinburgh midwives.[109] At Glasgow, John Towers, who was appointed annually between 1790 and 1815 to lecture on midwifery prior to being appointed to the Chair, established a Lying-In Hospital, principally at his own expense, for teaching as much as for medical purposes. His son, who succeeded him, received various subventions from the Town, students and the Trades' House to meet some of the expenses but nothing from the University.[110]

Clinical courses were the centrepiece of Edinburgh University's commitment to medical education. They had been implemented at Padua during the Renaissance, then at Utrecht in the 1630s. From thence clinical teaching was adopted at Leyden and it came to Edinburgh in the early years of the Infirmary. It fitted in with the educational objectives embraced by the Scottish universities, that is to illustrate general truths from special cases. Four professors taught the courses in rotation, and at the time of the 1826 Commission they were the professors of the practice of medicine, botany, materia medica and the institutes of medicine, a subject that combined physiology, anatomy and a little chemistry. Each professor had charge of the clinical wards for three months, every second year. Duncan junior spoke of the advantages of the rota system as giving students the opportunity of seeing a variety of practice and thus be led to think for themselves:

Almost every practitioner, even the most skilful and experienced, gets into a kind of routine practice, and in less than three months that practice is known to all the students, so that they look merely to a repetition of the same thing; whereas almost every two practitioners have a different routine practice.

His view was supported by the professor of Medical Jurisprudence, Robert Christison, who thought Edinburgh graduates remarkably free from the trammels of authority because of the variety of practice they saw.[111]

Andrew Duncan junior left invaluable and minute accounts of the conduct of the clinical medicine course in his evidence to the 1826 Commission and in his book, *Reports of the Practice in the Clinical Wards of the Royal Infirmary of Edinburgh*. Duncan modelled himself on Boerhaave's clinical lectures. In two weekly lectures he showed how to examine patients and the nature of the questions to be put to them to permit a diagnosis. He visited the hospital at noon and observed cases or dead bodies, with the assistance of two advanced students, called clerks, selected by himself. He had the right of selecting any of the patients in the hospital waiting room who had already been examined by an ordinary physician. (Ordinary physicians were not university professors but had charge of the wards and conducted the daily business of the Infirmary.) The clerks then drew up a very accurate account of the cases selected on the basis of a schedule laid down by the professor. The professor then criticised the account and might call for revision. In urgent cases, the professor would call again in the evening, or during the night. The next step was to report publicly in English, and prescribe in Latin, by the bedside of each individual patient. Before dictating the report, however, 'it is the business of the physician to examine the patient; and this is an art of considerable difficulty, which is only to be acquired by experience'. He then gave the results of the examination which all the students wrote down in case-books, where they had already noted the admission of the patient. This was done daily as long as the patient remained in their care. In the case of death, any changes were noted, and the body was dissected before all the students in the hospital to show the causes of death. When relatives permitted, the most important morbid parts were also brought into the classroom and chemical experiments might be performed—for example, in the case of diabetes the specific gravity of the urine was ascertained.[112]

In his *Reports* Duncan added that in the concluding lecture of each clinical course he summarised the occurrences that had taken place while he was in charge. While he recognised the primary function of hospitals as the restoration of health, he also saw them as necessarily giving practitioners personal experience and the pupils much valuable instruction. However, Duncan emphasised the collection and accumulation of a store of professional information on the history of the disease, which could not be acquired even in the most extensive private practice. Hence, he gathered hospital reports which he published in 1818, with the aim of informing both the profession and the public.[113]

The reputation of one celebrated professor who took his turn in the rota of clinical medical lectures belies some of the claims Edinburgh made for the system. James Gregory was professor of the Practice of Medicine between 1790 and 1821 and the distinguished surgeon, Sir Astley Cooper, testified to his effectiveness in dilating on the clinical reports and extracting the maximum amount of useful information from them.[114] Gregory's popularity was such, though, that the number of students grew too great for the proper conduct of his class, hence some students took the part of 'repeaters' and in loud voices repeated his dictation. After Gregory's time the clinical wards were enlarged, but still it would have been better to have had more than one professor teaching clinical medicine in any three month period.[115]

Clinical Surgery, taught privately from 1786 and an established chair from 1803, was not taught on a rota basis and the 1826 Commission recommended that it be left in the care of one man for the same reasons as had been argued before them in Glasgow for the establishment there of a clinical professor, namely that clinical lecturing in surgery should be undertaken by one man who made it his business rather than an assortment of individuals who might be good surgeons but poor teachers.[116]

The commitment to education which imbued the Edinburgh medical school was made evident in various facilities which the professors established, such as lying-in wards, hospitals and institutions, and anatomical, materia medica and midwifery museums. Other kinds of facility which combined education with medical care were the City's dispensaries, and other forms of medical institution. Andrew Duncan senior, for example, professor of the Institutes of Medicine 1790-1819, advocated the building of the mental hospital that bears his name in 1792, although it was not built until 1807. He anticipated Philippe Pinel's *Traité Medico-Philosophique sur l'alienation mental* by nine years. Duncan was active in linking medical education to the early public health movement in Scotland, when he founded the Old Town Dispensary in 1776 primarily as a medical teaching centre which would provide different opportunities from the Infirmary.

In 1815 was founded the New Town Dispensary to the great bitterness of Andrew Duncan senior.[117] Its objects were to give relief to the sick and diseased poor, to provide domiciliary attendance to pregnant women and to give free vaccination to children. The founders saw the value of their institution in the expensive and overcrowded hospitals. They set out to provide for seven groups of people: those with slight complaints which might grow dangerous if neglected; those among the

labouring classes who needed remedies while continuing work; those
needing hospital treatment but whose circumstances either made it
necessary for them to remain at home or meant that they could not be
separated from their families, especially the mothers of young
children; the chronic sick and incurables; the children of the poor and
the aged poor. The Old Town Dispensary was open only twice a week,
it was not sufficient for Edinburgh's needs, and its doctors made no
official domiciliary calls.[118] There was nothing unique in themselves
about Edinburgh's dispensaries and other facilities. Their distinction
lay in the educational purpose which underlay them. Students worked
alongside their professors and were introduced to unfashionable
practice.

One way of assessing Edinburgh's medical education is to form an
impression of the subsequent careers of those who studied in Edinburgh
during the Enlightenment. The evidence is scanty and inevitably the only
students to be traced are those who acquired a reputation. It is known,
however, that one-third of all doctors in the Army, Navy and East
India Company service were educated at Edinburgh, where they, by and
large, filled the middle ranks on entry.[119] Ninety-two students from
the period 1790-1826 have been traced from a variety of Victorian
reference works, histories of public health, biographies and similar
sources but all were prominent alumni. Six rose to high rank in the
Army or Navy medical service, 32 became medical teachers at
institutions other than Edinburgh (Edinburgh professors were excluded
from the analysis), 15 were connected in some way with mental health,
16 with public health, 12 were medical scientists including one who
also specialised in mental health, and a further 12 became physicians or
surgeons to the Queen or held leading positions in the London Royal
Colleges or other posts of fashionable status.[120] Others who can be
traced made careers in sciences auxiliary to medicine such as botany
and natural history. The sample is extremely small, not allowing for the
third in the services, and it must be assumed that the rest became
absorbed all over Britain as country physicians, apothecaries and in other
unknown tasks. That many former medical students became apothecaries is known because all the Scottish universities complained to the
1826 Commission about the deleterious effects on their alumni of the
Apothecaries Act of 1815. In the selected period 2,309 men graduated
and thousands more would have taken courses.

The increasing importance attached to practical field work in natural
history can be seen by comparing the place given to it in their respect-
ive courses by two professors of the subject at Edinburgh. Edinburgh

was not unique in teaching natural history: Berlin and Padua were but two instances of Continental universities where it was taught, though it was more commonly attached to mining schools. John Walker, the second occupant of the chair from 1779-1804, exhorted his students in 1781:

> The objects of nature themselves must be sedulously examined in their native state, the fields and mountains must be traversed, the woods and waters must be explored, the ocean must be fathomed and its shores scrutinised by everyone that would become proficient in natural knowledge.[121]

Nonetheless Walker never took his classes to the field; he urged them to keep journals of their own private excursions and he showed them specimens in his laboratory but he did not conduct field excursions as part of his formal teaching.[122] His successor, Robert Jameson, who was professor for fifty years from 1804, made field excursions an important part of his course. They would take place in the country roundabout Edinburgh or as far afield as the Western Isles. On them he would show students how to carry out investigations into natural history; how to examine mineral appearances; and he would point out any interesting animals they saw or any atmospheric phenomena which might occur. He also explained the nature of springs, lakes and similar features which occurred on the walks.[123]

Robert Jameson's teaching of natural history appears to have been thorough, effective and professional. He was a controversial figure in the closing two decades of the Scottish Enlightenment, espousing geological doctrines of his former teacher, Werner, in a city and university which had powerful Huttonian interests, and because of his proprietary attitude to the Keepership of the Natural History Museum.[124] His course covered 'General and Particular Details and Views of Meteorology, Hydrography, Mineralogy, Geology, Botany and Zoology'. [125] In his consideration of water, he discussed its importance both to man and to nature; in geology, he treated of the earth's composition, structure and formation; and he dealt with botanical matters that impinged on other departments of natural history. In zoology, he discussed man before vertebrate and invertebrate animals, and gave lectures on the philosophy of zoology. He concluded the course with lectures on such matters as the collecting, preserving, transporting and arranging of objects of natural history. He listed 273 different lecture topics in his syllabus; when asked if he completed the entire course of lectures on one session, Jameson replied that sometimes he did, and sometimes he divided the material between the winter and summer sessions. Nonetheless, his course must have been superficial, at least in some sessions.

He taught by means of five methods which might have gone some way to counter the superficiality; he lectured and demonstrated objects of natural history; he conversed with his students one hour before the lecture and also after it; he met those attending his course three times a week, often six days a week, in the Museum.[126] They grew in numbers from about 50 in 1807-8 to 200 between 1825 and 1830. At the meetings he inquired as to his students' progress and proposed exercises which included writing descriptions of objects of natural history with which they were previously unacquainted, descriptions being in Jameson's view 'a principal object in the study' and capable of stimulating learning through correction. Lastly, Jameson undertook the field excursions as part of the class's activity and his teaching. The excursions were specifically designed to correct any mistaken impressions formed in the classroom, and to prepare students for travelling and for the active and accurate pursuit of natural history. In their report, the Commissioners remarked, on the basis largely of what Jameson had told them rather than independent enquiry, that most of Jameson's students went on these expeditions and despite their number there was no confusion but a good deal of pleasure and satisfaction was derived from them.[127] One anonymous member of the class testified that during the excursions, which took place on a Saturday morning Jameson made the personal acquaintance of anyone who joined in, student or amateur, which led in time to a proliferation of friendships and consequently a voluminous correspondence and even the sending of specimens to the Museum, all of which furthered knowledge of natural history.[128] Walker and Jameson were the culmination in the Enlightenment of the tradition of Scottish geology established by Sibbald and others in the late-seventeenth century.

Jameson was helped by the current vogue. He responded by creating the opportunity to go on expeditions, which would be preferable to junior students to staying in a stuffy classroom. Nonetheless, there was a great variety of occupations among those who attended the course over and above the students, presumably because it was useful to them, surveyors, civil and army engineers, silversmiths, jewellers and farmers. Furthermore, seven of Jameson's students in the first twenty years of his professorship became professors themselves at Edinburgh, London, Aberdeen, Cork and Geneva. Two became officials of the London Geological Society and many, too numerous to detail here, made contributions of varying importance to geology, ornithology and mineralogy in the nineteenth century. Four became significant explorers in the Arctic and Africa.[129]

Conclusion

The chapter has surveyed the Universities of Scotland over a long period from the seventeenth to the nineteenth centuries. Naturally there were changes over time and the Universities were required to operate in different political, social and economic climates. Certain different periods can be delineated: the age of improvement that led to enlightenment, from the 1680s to 1745; the period of high Enlightenment from then until 1790 although that is not a clear terminal date in some fields such as science and medicine, and the decline of the Scottish Enlightenment as it merged into the first industrial society especially from 1815. Certain other trends are discernible, that of contact with such English and Dutch influences and ideas that the Universities could use in the early-eighteenth century, the accommodation to new knowledge in the mid- to late-eighteenth century and the new atmosphere engendered by the French Revolution and Terror, leading to wartime. Politics were never far below the surface, though not the dominating force in the universities of the Scottish Enlightenment: the politics of patriotism not rebellion from 1689-1745 and of Toryism from 1789. That the intervening years should have been the heyday of the Enlightenment is not mere coincidence.

The dominant concern throughout, however, was the provision of education: to start with there were the duties laid on the Universities by Knox that developed in a secular climate to absorb other professional courses. The content and methods of the Universities, and the personnel in them and economic forces working on them might change over two hundred years, but the objective did not. In the course of development and improvement, the intellectual and educational enterprises in the universities were raised to a level of distinction that became a prime feature of the Scottish Enlightenment.

Notes

1.   At various points throughout this chapter reference is made to an invaluable source, *Evidence, Oral and Documentary taken and received by*

the Commissioners appointed by his majesty George IV, July 23rd,
1826; and re-appointed by his majesty William IV, October 12th, 1830,
for Visiting the Universities of Scotland, 4 vols. (London, 1837). Vol I
University of Edinburgh; Vol. II University of Glasgow; Vol. III University
of St Andrews; Vol. IV University of Aberdeen. These volumes will subsequently be referred to as Edinburgh Evidence, Glasgow Evidence, St
Andrews Evidence and Aberdeen Evidence in the rest of the book. The
Commissioners' findings were published in Report made to his majesty by
a Royal Commission of Inquiry into the State of the Universities of Scotland (House of Commons, 7 October 1831) and hereafter referred to as
Report. Edinburgh's is by far the fullest volume of evidence and, consequently, is quoted more often than others.

2. John Millar, An Historical View of the English Government from the
    Settlement of the Saxons in Britain to the Revolution in 1688, 4 vols.
    (London, 1803), III, pp. 87, 88, 134; Francis Jeffrey, 'Millar's View of the
    English Government', Edinburgh Review, (October, 1803), p. 166; Millar,
    Historical View, pp. 88, 91-2.

3. John Clive, 'The Social Background of the Scottish Renaissance', Scotland
    in the Age of Improvement, ed. N. T. Phillipson and Rosalind Mitchison
    (Edinburgh U.P., 1970), p. 229.

4. T. C. Smout, A History of the Scottish People 1560-1830 (Collins/Fontana,
    1972), pp. 82 and 424.

5. Edinburgh Evidence 234] – [239 gave a list of presbyteries in whose
    parishes there were established schoolmasters who had spent up to four
    years at university, with comments on the list. Most of the schoolmasters
    had spent four years, and only 241 out of 1,147 parishes had school-
    masters who had not spent some time at a university.

6. John Veitch, 'Philosophy in the Scottish Universities', Mind, old series,
    II (1877), pp. 86-91;

7. Henry W. Meikle, Some Aspects of Later Seventeenth Century Scotland,
    (Glasgow, 1947), pp. 18-19. 25-9, Ronald G. Cant, The University of St
    Andrews: A Short History (Scottish Academic Press, Edinburgh and
    London, 1970), pp. 74-5; Clive, p. 232 and Colin McLaurin, 'An Account
    of the Life and Writings of the Author', An Account of Sir Isaac Newton's
    Philosophical Discoveries (London, 1748), pp. iv-v.

8. T.D. Campbell, Adam Smith's Science of Morals (Allen and Unwin, London
    1971); Adam Smith, 'An Enquiry after Philosophy and Theology', Edin-
    burgh Review (March, 1756), pp. 3-12 and Peter Gay, The Enlightenment:
    An Interpretation, 2 vols. (Knopf, New York, 1966 and 1969), II, pp.
    165-6.

9. Sir Robert Sibbald (1641-1722) was Charles II's physician. He studied
    first Divinity at Edinburgh and then medicine at Leyden. He was first
    Geographer Royal for Scotland and wrote numerous books on antiquities,
    local and natural history, including Scotia Illustra and a bibliography of
    Scottish writers and historical manuscripts. Archibald Pitcairne (1652-1713)
    set out to study law, and went to Paris where, in fact, he studied medicine
    and graduated MD of Rheims. David Gregory interested him in mathematics
    which he applied to medicine. He became one of the founders of the
    iatro-mechanical or iatro-mathematical school of thought, which explained
    all bodily activities, including those of the nervous system and digestion,
    as mere mechanical processes. Balfour's dates were 1630-94.

10. Meikle, pp. 29-33; J. D. Comrie, History of Scottish Medicine to 1860,
    (London, 1927), pp. 97 and 183-92.

11. Gay, II, pp. 18 and 135.

12.   quoted in Hugh Trevor-Roper, 'The Scottish Enlightenment', *Studies on Voltaire and the Eighteenth Century*, cviii (1967), p. 1648.

13.   Dugald Stewart, 'Dissertation: exhibiting the progress of metaphysical, ethical, and political philosophy since the revival of letters in Europe', *Collected Works*, ed. Sir William Hamilton, 11 vols. (Edinburgh, 1854-60), I, pp. 504-5.

14.   J. R. R. Christie, 'The Origins and Development of the Scottish Scientific Community, 1680-1768', *History of Science*, XII (1974), p. 127.

15.   R. N. Smart, 'Some Observations on the Provinces of the Scottish Universities, 1560-1850', *The Scottish Tradition: essays in honour of Ronald Gordon Cant*, ed. G. W. S. Barrow (Scottish Academic Press, Edinburgh, 1974), p. 94.

16.   Thomas Pennant, *A Tour in Scotland, 1772*, Part II (London, 1790), p. 198.

17.   These figures are culled from Smout, p. 449, Cant's history of St Andrews, p. 85 and from evidence presented to the Royal Commission of 1826 on the Scottish Universities.

18.   Thomas Reid, 'A Statistical Account of the University of Glasgow', *The Works of Thomas Reid, D.D.*, 2 vols. (Edinburgh, 1880), II, p. 736.

19.   Glasgow Evidence, pp. 205-11, 537-9. See the important article on the subject, J. B. Morrell, 'Thomas Thomson: Professor of Chemistry and University Reformer', *The British Journal for the History of Science* (1969), pp. 244-65.

20.   Glasgow Evidence, pp. 25-6, 127-8, 138, 193-4, 213.

21.   quoted in Harold R. Fletcher and William H. Brown, *The Royal Botanic Garden Edinburgh 1670-1970* (Edinburgh, HMSO, 1970), p.v.

22.   R. S. Rait, *The Universities of Aberdeen: A History* (Aberdeen, 1895) pp. 295-6.

23.   Steven Shapin, 'The Audience for Science in Eighteenth Century Edinburgh', *History of Science*, XII (1974), p. 97 and Christie, pp. 126-8. Christie quotes from a Town Council minute of 1713: 'through the want of professors of physick and chymistry in this Kingdom the youth who have applyed themselves to study have been necessitat to travel and remain abroad a considerable time for their education to the great prejudice of the nation by the necessary charges occasioned thereby'.

24.   G. N. Cantor, 'Henry Brougham and the Scottish Methodological Tradition', *Studies in the History and Philosophy of Science*, II (1971), p. 83.

25.   Edinburgh Evidence, p. 364. See also, for example, *ibid.*, pp. 304-5, 380 and Glasgow Evidence, p. 23.

26.   Adam Smith, *An Inquiry into the Nature and Causes of the Wealth of Nations*, ed. Edwin Cannan, 2 vols., 5th ed., (London, Methuen, 1930), pp. 249-51 and Reid, p. 733.

27.   Edinburgh Evidence, pp. [51-[67; Glasgow Evidence, pp. 35 and 312; St Andrews Evidence, pp. 35, 292, 377; Aberdeen Evidence, pp. 185, 249-50.

28.   On T. C. Hope, see J. B. Morrell, 'Practical Chemistry in the University of Edinburgh, 1899-1843', *Ambix*, XVI (1969), pp. 66-80. Jack Morrell's many articles have done most to open up the history of science in the Scottish Enlightenment and to cause other scholars to see it in its cultural and social context. On the class fee system, see his 'Science and Scottish University Reform: Edinburgh in 1826', *British Journal for the History of Science*, VI (1972), pp. 39-56.

29.   John Leslie to James Brown, advocate, 25 December 1813. E[dinburgh] U[niversity] L[ibrary] MS Dc.2.57, Letter 196a. Leslie was then professor

of Mathematics.

30.   *Letters chiefly connected with the Affairs of Scotland from Henry Cock-burn . . . to Thomas Francis Kennedy, M.P.,* (Edinburgh, 1874), pp. 137-8. In 1781, the professor of Natural Philosophy separated the class where experiments were shown from the 'tedious or difficult' lecture. *(Caledonian Mercury,* 3 November 1781.)

31.   Edinburgh Evidence, p. 145.

32.   G. E. Davie, *The Democratic Intellect: Scotland and her Universities in the Nineteenth Century,* 2nd ed. (Edinburgh U.P., 1964) and 'The Social Significance of the Scottish Philosophy of Common Sense', *The Dow Lecture* (University of Dundee, 30 November 1972), published 1973.

33.   Davie, *Democratic Intellect,* p. 4.

34.   Stewart, 'Dissertation', *Works,* I, p. 520.

35.   Davie, *Dow Lecture,* pp. 7 and 11.

36.   Edinburgh Evidence, p. 393.

37.   George Jardine, *Outlines of Philosophical Education illustrated by the Method of teaching the Logic Class in the University of Glasgow,* 2nd ed., (Glasgow, 1825), pp. v-viii and Jardine's written evidence to the 1826 Commission, Glasgow Evidence, pp. 513-5.

38.   Reid, *Works,* II, p. 734.

39.   An account of Jardine's teaching is given by a former student in Edinburgh Evidence, p. 174.

40.   Glasgow Evidence, p. 514.

41.   Edinburgh Evidence, pp. 390-2.

42.   Spencer Walpole, *The Life of Lord John Russell,* 2 vols. (London, 1891), I, p. 45; Report, p. 251; Glasgow Evidence, p. 222; Edinburgh Evidence, p. 574; Glasgow Evidence, p. 62; I am grateful to Desmond Brogan for pointing out to me the references to working class Divinity students at Glasgow. The Horner brothers referred to were sons of a Glasgow linen merchant, who studied at Edinburgh in the late-eighteenth century and early-nineteenth century; Francis became an MP and a currency expert before his early death; Leonard was active in many ventures, including the Edinburgh School of Arts (now Heriot-Watt University), London University and the Geological Society of London.

43.   *Scotland and Scotsmen in the Eighteenth Century, from the MSS of John Ramsay, Esq. of Ochtertyre,* ed. Alexander Allardyce, 2 vols. (Edinburgh and London, 1888), I, p. 226, n.2.

44.   Glasgow Evidence, p. 204.

45.   W. M. Mather 'The Origins and Occupations of Glasgow Students 1740-1839', *Past and Present* (1966), pp. 74-94.

46.   There is some secondary evidence for about 1737 and 1777 in W. R. Scott, *Adam Smith as Student and Professor* (Glasgow, 1937), pp. 28-30.

47.   Glasgow Evidence, pp. 167 and 222; Edinburgh Evidence, p. 589; St Andrews Evidence, pp. 292-3; Edinburgh Evidence, p. 572; Aberdeen Evidence, pp. 185-6, 249 and 251; Edinburgh Evidence, pp. 598-9, 572, 584, 586 and 565.

48.   Edinburgh Evidence, pp. 572 and 598-9; Aberdeen Evidence, p. 14 and Edinburgh Evidence, p. 549.

49.   Edward Topham, *Letters from Edinburgh,* (London, 1776), pp. 208-9.

50.   L. J. Saunders, *Scottish Democracy 1815-1840: The Social and Intellectual Background* (Oliver and Boyd, Edinburgh, 1950), p. 361.

51.   Report, p. 69.

52. Adam Smith made the point in the *Wealth of Nations* that the Church and Universities of a country competed for the able minds. Where church benefices were moderate, a chair was preferable, and where church benefices were considerable, then the universities would be bereft of *literati*. Scotland seems to have been an example of the first situation. Smith, II, pp. 295-6.

53. Report, pp. 193, 110-111, 229-33, 312-15, 347-8 and 392-3.

54. compiled from Edinburgh Evidence, p. [51-64] and 130] by J. B. Morrell 'The University of Edinburgh in the late Eighteenth Century: Its Scientific Eminence and Academic Structure', *Isis*, LXII (1970), p. 165.

55. Thomas Constable, *Archibald Constable and his Literary Correspondents*, 3 vols. (Edinburgh, 1873), II, pp. 318-19; British Museum, Add. Mss. 34630, ff. 19-21; Stewart, *Works*, X, p. lxxix and Brian Connell, *Portrait of a Whig Peer; compiled from the papers of the second Viscount Palmerston 1739-1802* (London, 1957), p. 431.

56. Jeremy J. Cater, 'The Making of Principal Robertson in 1762: Politics and the University of Edinburgh in the second half of the eighteenth century', *Scottish Historical Review*, XLIX (1970), pp. 62-3, 67-71 (with the quotation from Somerville on p. 69), 72 and 75-80.

57. Steven Shapin, 'Property, Patronage and the Politics of Science: the Founding of the Royal Society of Edinburgh', *The British Journal for the History of Science*, VII (1974), pp. 11-20.

58. Morrell, 'Science and Scottish University Reform', pp. 43-4.

59. Glasgow Evidence, p. 152.

60. Morrell on 'Science and Scottish University Reform'.

61. National Library of Scotland, MS. 331, f. 150.

62. Report, p. 8.

63. D. B. Horn, *A Short History of the University at Edinburgh 1556-1889* (Edinburgh U.P., 1967), p. 76.

64. Cater, pp. 84 and 78n.

65. For a brief account of Robertson's tenure of office, see Horn, pp. 76-90.

66. Accounts of Leslie's case include Henry Cockburn, *Memorials of his Time* (Edinburgh, 1856), pp. 200-11; Francis Horner, 'Professor Stewart's Statement of Facts', *Edinburgh Review*, VII (1805-6), pp. 113-4; Ian D. L. Clark, 'The Leslie Controversy' 1805', *Records of the Scottish Church History Society*, XIV (1963), pp. 179-97 and Ian D. L. Clark, *Moderatism and the Moderate Party in the Church of Scotland 1752-1805*, PhD dissertation (University of Cambridge, 1964), pp. 318-52 and 411-15. See also J. B. Morrell 'The Leslie Affair: Careers, Kirk and Politics in Edinburgh in 1805', *Scottish Historical Review* (April, 1975). I am grateful to the author for giving me a preview. Leslie's expenses in attending St Andrews had been paid by the Earl of Kinnoull on condition he became a minister. He devoted himself to science on his patron's death and first maintained himself by tutoring in Scotland (Adam Smith's nephew), Virginia (the Randolphs) and England (the Wedgwoods). He was professor first of Mathematics 1805-19 at Edinburgh, and then of Natural Philosophy from 1819 until his death. He was made a Knight of the Order of the Guelphs in 1831, along with other noted scientists such as John Herschel, Charles Babbage, James Ivory and David Brewster.

67. Veitch, p. 209 and James McCosh, *The Scottish Philosophy* (London, 1875), pp. 36-42.

68. Alexander Carlyle, *Anecdotes and Characters of the Times*, ed. James Kinsley (London, O.U.P., 1973), p. 22 and Veitch, p. 216.

69. 'Dugald Stewart presents no original facets of thought for the modern

reader. His service to us to-day is that of a man thoroughly versed in the knowledge of his time, able to interpret to us not only the regularities, but many of the vagaries of his contemporaries.' (Gladys Bryson, *Man and Society: The Scottish Inquiry of the Eighteenth Century* (Princeton, New Jersey, 1945), p. 261, n. 20.)

70. Stewart, *Works*, I, pp. 479, 216, 223 and 475.
71. Veitch, pp. 212-13 and McCosh, pp. 95-106.
72. *Caledonian Mercury*, 9 August 1790 and Glasgow Evidence, p. 103.
73. Edinburgh Evidence, p. 79.
74. Stewart, *Works*, IX, p. 348 and VIII, p. 10.
75. Quoted in James Coutts, *A History of the University of Glasgow*, (Glasgow, 1909), p. 226.
76. A porism was a corollary or a proposition intermediate between a problem and a theorem.
77. John Playfair, 'Biographical Account of . . . Matthew Stewart', *Works*, ed. J. G. Playfair, 4 vols. (Edinburgh, 1822), pp. 4-6.
78. McLaurin, pp. 1-10 *passim*.
79. Richard Olson, 'Scottish Philosophy and Mathematics 1750-1830', *Journal of the History of Ideas*, XXXII (1971), p. 30.
80. With the lengthy title, *Remarks, for a series of years, on Barometrical Scales, showing they are inadequate to predict the Weather: the results of these observations exhibited and corrected upon a new and enlarged plan; as also, an improvement proposed on the Rain Gage; with a few hints of the effects on the weather by the different directions of the Wind. Principally intended for the use of the farmer.*
81. Anand C. Chitnis, *The Edinburgh Professoriate 1790-1826 and the University's Contribution to Nineteenth Century British Society*, Ph.D. dissertation (University of Edinburgh, 1968), pp. 159-63. The quotations are from E.U.L. Mss. Phot. 1144/1, f. 28 and Phot. 114/2, f. 88. The ice-making instructions are in the latter ms. ff. 119-36. The French assessment of Edinburgh is to be found in B.M. Add. Mss. 34611, f. 100.
82. They are listed in a useful article, S. William Simon, 'The Influence of the three Monros on the Practice of Medicine and Surgery', *Annals of Medical History*, IX (1927), p. 265.
83. Shapin, 'Property, Patronage, and the Politics of Science', pp. 6-7.
84. *Dictionary of Scientific Biography;* M. P. Crosland, 'The Use of Diagrams as Chemical "Equations" in the Lecture Notes of William Cullen and Joseph Black', *Annals of Science*, XV (1959), pp. 75-90 and H. T. Buckle, *Introduction to the History of Civilization in England*, new and revised ed. (Routledge, London, 1904), pp. 864-72.
85. *Dictionary of Scientific Biography*.
86. Shapin, 'The Audience for Science', pp. 105-8 and 102-3.
87. James Hutton (1726-97) went to the University of Edinburgh aged 14 and studied under McLaurin and Stevenson and subsequently entered the medical faculty. He studied, too, in Paris and took his medical degree in Leyden in 1749 with a thesis entitled *De Sanguine et Circulatione in Microcosmo*. In 1750, having inherited a farm in Berwickshire, he settled to agriculture, taking to the study of it and moving, in 1752, to Norfolk to prosecute his studies further. In the course of his agricultural work, he developed an interest in geology and mineralogy. He travelled on the Continent before settling back in Berwickshire. Meanwhile, he lived on the profits of the manufacture of sal-ammoniac, into which business he had gone. He indulged in further chemical experiments and was a close friend

of Black. He travelled widely in Britain, took an interest in Scottish improvement plans and settled in Edinburgh in 1768. From then on, he was active in the Philosophical Society and in the Royal Society of Edinburgh to which he read several papers. Apart from his geological writings he also published *An Investigation of the Principles of Knowledge, and of the Progress of Reason from Sense to Science and Philosophy*, in 1794. He worked on a treatise on agriculture before his death, but it was published posthumously.

88. I owe much, in the following discussion, to a seminar given by Dr Roy Porter, Churchill College, Cambridge, to the Seminar on Scottish Cultural History in the Eighteenth Century, Institute for Advanced Studies in the Humanities, University of Edinburgh, 8 March 1974, and to some detailed comments he made on an earlier draft of this section. Dr Porter's work is accessible in *The Making of the Science of Geology in Britain, 1660-1815*, Ph.D. dissertation, (University of Cambridge, 1974) chapters VI and VII. I also owe much to a brilliant undergraduate essay submitted by John S. Shaw to my Scotland and the Enlightenment course at the University of Stirling, Spring 1974, which was on the topic 'Relate James Hutton's "Theory of the Earth" to the social and intellectual environment in which it was received.'

89. John Playfair, 'Illustrations of the Huttonian Theory', *Works*, I, p. 131.

90. James Hutton, *An Investigation of the Principles of Knowledge*, 3 vols. (Edinburgh, 1794), II, pp. 113-14.

91. Gordon L. Davies, *The Earth in Decay: A History of British Geomorphology 1578-1878* (Macdonald Technical and Scientific, London, 1969) p. 174 and David Hume, *Dialogues concerning Natural Religion*, 2nd ed., (London, 1779), pp. 115 and 124-5.

92. René Descartes, *Treatise of Man, (1664)*, ed. T. S. Hall (Harvard U.P., Cambridge, Mass., 1972), pp. 9-11.

93. Cockburn, *Memorials*, pp. 26 and 25.

94. Edinburgh Evidence, p. 392.

95. Jeffrey, 'Millar's *View*', pp. 155 and 159; Francis Jeffrey, 'Craig's Life of Millar', *Edinburgh Review*, IX (1806), pp. 86-7; 'Millar's *View*', pp. 156 and 157; Jardine, p. 465; and 'Craig's Life', pp. 88-9.

96. *Selections from the Correspondence of the Late Macvey Napier*, (London, 1877), p. 30.

97. See Chitnis, pp. 42-6 and 48-9.

98. Jeffrey, 'Craig's Life', p. 86.

99. Stewart, *Works*, VIII, p. 17 and Jardine, pp. x-xi.

100. Playfair studied at St Andrews, became a minister and held the livings of Liff and Benvie 1773-82. He then tutored for three years before becoming professor first of Mathematics 1785-1805, and then of Natural Philosophy 1805-19, at the University of Edinburgh. He wrote on an immense variety of topics especially in the *Edinburgh Review*; was a virulent Whig, prominent Huttonian in the geological debate, Secretary of the Royal Society of Edinburgh and thus a figure who was ubiquituous in the late Enlightenment scene.

101. Davie, *Dow Lecture*, p. 12.

102. Chitnis, pp. 125-6. 127 and 134-6.

103. quoted in Horn, p. 56.

104. Edinburgh Evidence, p. 450.

105. *Ibid.*, p. 447.

106. John Thomson, *An Account of the Life, Lectures and Writings of William Cullen, M.D.*, 2 vols. (Edinburgh, 1832 and 1859), I, pp. 122-35.

107.   *Partners in Science: Letters of James Watt and Joseph Black,* ed. Eric Robinson and Douglas McKie (Constable, London, 1970), pp. 348-9.

108.   Edinburgh Evidence, p. 222.

109.   James Hamilton, *Edinburgh Lying-In Institution for delivering Poor Married Women at their own Houses* (Edinburgh, 1824), p. 6 and Edinburgh Evidence, p. 316.

110.   Glasgow Evidence, pp. 200-1.

111.   Edinburgh Evidence, pp. 200, 224 and 293.

112.   *Ibid.,* pp. 223-4.

113.   Andrew Duncan junior, *Reports of the Practice in the Clinical Wards of The Royal Infirmary of Edinburgh* (Edinburgh, 1818), pp. vi, 1-3.

114.   *Report from the Select Committee on Medical Education with the Minutes of Evidence and Appendix,* 2 vols. (1834), II, p. 87.

115.   Edinburgh Evidence, pp. 25 and 280.

116.   Report, p. 148.

117.   Henry Cockburn, *Memorials of his Time,* new ed. (London, 1909), pp. 272-3 on the 'civic war' occasioned by the foundation.

118.   *Statement regarding the New Town Dispensary by the Medical Gentlemen Conducting that Institution* (Edinburgh, 1816), pp. 1, 7, 13-17.

119.   Edinburgh Evidence, pp. 528 and 535.

120.   This analysis is discussed in full in Chitnis, pp. 256-71.

121.   John Walker, *Lectures on Geology: including Hydrography, Mineralogy, and Meterology with an introduction to Biology,* ed. Harold W. Scott (Chicago, 1966), p. vii.

122.   Chitnis, p. 195n.

123.   Edinburgh Evidence, p. 141.

124   Anand C. Chitnis, 'The University of Edinburgh's Natural History Museum and the Huttonian-Wernerian Debate', *Annals of Science,* XXVI (1970), pp. 85-94.

125.   The ensuing details are based on *Syllabus of Lectures in Natural History* (Edinburgh, 1821), a pamphlet to be found among the Edinburgh University MSS. Gen. 615.

126.   The Museum itself is discussed in the next chapter.

127.   Edinburgh Evidence, p. 141 and Report, p. 138.

128.   'Biography of the late Professor Jameson', *The Monthly Journal of Medical Science,* XVIII (January-June, 1854), p. 574.

129.   For details see Chitnis, *Edinburgh Professoriate,* pp. 209-11.

7 NEW INSTITUTIONS AND THE SCOTTISH ENLIGHTENMENT

I

Hitherto, the origins and development of the Scottish Enlightenment have been studied through institutions fundamental to Scottish life and history long before the eighteenth century. They made it possible for the movement to be under way by the middle of that century. The Enlightenment, however, gave birth to institutions of its own, that were obviously not of the same kind as the Kirk, Law and Universities, some of which lasted only as long as the movement which fathered them. Others, under different guises and even in different locations from their original ones, still survive. Like so much else, the new institutions that appeared in the era of the Scottish Enlightenment often developed in the wake of the improving spirit that was evident from the late-seventeenth and early-eighteenth centuries. Hence, of the new Scottish institutions which arose, some were merely concerned with improvement and not enlightenment and are consequently not of concern here; others were central to the concerns of the Scottish Enlightenment, and yet others gave evidence of both improvement and enlightenment so that it is difficult to draw a precise line between them. The bodies referred to and the concern of subsequent discussion were various learned societies such as the Royal Society of Edinburgh, the Newtonian Club, the Aberdeen Philosophical Society and various student societies: the sociable clubs that by catering both for specialist groups like physicians (for example, the Aesculapian) or for polymathic *literati* such as the Oyster Club, fostered the intimacy of the *literati*, so central to the achievements of the Scottish Enlightenment; then there were periodical ventures such as the *Encyclopaedia Britannica* and the *Edinburgh Review*; and museums and the botanical gardens whose development was so essential to the scientists of the day, since so much of their work necessarily had to take place in them.

Scottish eighteenth-century clubs and societies have been covered as a whole in three works of Davis McElroy.[1] Steven Shapin's *The Royal Society of Edinburgh: A Study of the social context of Hanoverian science* has been completed more recently and has concentrated specifically on a society which was part of the Enlightenment rather than the bigger phenomenon of general cultural and economic

195

improvement.[2] There are important distinctions to be made: some
societies were formed out of a concern for the pursuit of knowledge;
others, usually founded earlier. were devoted to improvement whether
of agriculture, the economy, English composition and speaking, or
various other matters. Societies also developed from educational
stimuli when students, exposed to ideas or exercises such as debates
in the classroom, took them up outside. To that extent certain significant and successful student societies arose from the distinctive Scottish
university education. Then again clubs (here distinguished from societies
by their essentially convivial nature rather than seriousness of purpose)
promoted the social life and, consequently, furthered the intellectual
interaction of the *literati* or specific professional groups. The societies
that can specifically be seen as part of the Enlightenment will first be
discussed here, then the *literati's* social clubs and, finally, the student
societies and societies that relate to the Scottish Enlightenment's
achievements in higher education. The clubs and societies that thrived
in Edinburgh will necessarily predominate, but the capital was by no
means unique and the number of its organisations does not in itself
testify to their quality. It is clear, for example, that the Aberdeen
Philosophical Society was of a high order. In general it can be said that
clubs and societies of the Scottish Enlightenment institutionalised the
informal acquaintance of people of different expertise and, in so doing,
furthered the movement of which they were a part. It is not enough
to explain the clubs and societies away as simply a pre-industrial
recreation or extra-curricular activities, not least because they were
foundations of the eighteenth century, and do not appear to have been
foreshadowed in seventeenth-century Scotland, like so much else that
preceded the achievements and expression of the Scottish Enlightenment.

　　The major societies of international standing among which the
Royal Society of Edinburgh was to become numbered did arise in the
seventeenth century, however, elsewhere in Europe. The first, which
carried in its name the concern for experiment, was Florence's
Academia del Cimento, founded in 1651, although it can be argued
that the Royal Society of London, while not chartered until 1662, was
meeting during the Civil War at Oxford as early as 1645. Bacon's
advocacy of the experimental method, that was later to be boosted
and sanctified by Newton, appears to have been a powerful influence at
the time, not least because in the *Nova Atlantis* he had sketched out the
plan of a society devoted to scientific experiment. Bacon's spirit
was also at work in the *Academia Naturae Cursorum* (1652) in Germany

and Paris and Bologna respectively housed the Royal Academy of Sciences (1666) and the Institute of Bologna. In a survey of such institutions which formed part of his *Dissertation on Mathematical and Physical Science*, John Playfair considered that the societies were of particular virtue to scientists who were not closet philosophers but men required to examine nature with their own eyes, and be present in the work-shop of the mechanic, or the laboratory of the chemist. Scientists, he said, being fewer in number and separated, were less apt to come together, and, unlike *literati* in the arts, less likely to find others who readily appreciated their work. Consequently, associating with men of like interests was a necessary stimulus to their exertions, and facilitated the collection of facts which, with true Baconian devotion, they were all, in individual ways, busy accumulating. Similarly the proceedings or transactions of such associations made possible the combined public-ation of papers that singly would constitute too great an expense, and which together were of greater interest and convenience for the reader. (Playfair added, doubtless bearing in mind his own pet project in Edinburgh, that scientific or philosophical societies throughout history were frequently accompanied by the establishment of an astronomical observatory, since observation should be carried out throughout many generations, from the same place, albeit by different men, to permit the accumulation of data on the past, present and future conditions of the heavens).[3] Playfair's historical analysis was to prove largely correct for the Royal Society of Edinburgh, with which he was associated as secretary for many years, since it began with a literary and scientific section, and in a relatively short time the literary section died out.

The first society which can be seen as part of the Scottish Enlight-enment began in about 1716 and so was certainly not contemporaneous with, and in many cases anticipated, 'improving' societies concerned with manners, agriculture and the like (the Society of Improvers in the Knowledge of Agriculture in Scotland was, to take an instance, not founded until 1723). The Society was named after the tavern, Ranken's, where it met in Edinburgh, and its members included the then principal of Edinburgh University, William Wishart, and Colin McLaurin, George Turnbull, John Stevenson and Robert Wallace, who have all figured in this history. The object of the society was 'mutual improvement by liberal conversation and rational inquiry', and at its meetings criticism of new books was aired and an essay read in a given subject followed by opinions on the paper by other members—a common format for the organisations of the era. Its significance for the Enlightenment lies in two related fields, first its early espousal of the philosophy of George

Berkeley (1685-1753) which denied the existence of matter and said that material objects only existed through being perceived; and second, its instrumentality, consequently, in disseminating the liberty of thought and speculation and concern for reason that was so essential if eighteenth-century Scottish philosophy were to thrive. David Hume was an Edinburgh student while his professor was a Rankenian and corresponding with Berkeley: since Hume subsequently pushed Berkeley to his logical conclusion it seems more than plausible that the Rankenian Club indirectly contributed to his later work. Likewise Turnbull went on to lecture at Aberdeen in the late 1720s, where Thomas Reid heard him, and McLaurin dealt in his courses with Berkeley's views on physics and mathematics from 1730.[4]

The second society of significance for the Enlightenment, both in itself and in its being an antecedent for the Royal Society of Edinburgh, was the Medical Society of Edinburgh, founded in 1731 by the Edinburgh medical professors led by the first Alexander Monro. Its object was to improve medical knowledge, which it undertook primarily for reasons that Playfair well explained in his *Dissertation*, by publishing the accounts of interesting cases observed in the Edinburgh Royal Infirmary. The work of the society devolved almost entirely on Monro and consisted simply in producing *Medical essays and observations, revised and published by a Society in Edinburgh*, of which first volumes were published between 1733 and 1744, another in 1771 and various French, German and other translations were also made. The publication of the essays first attracted recognition to the then embryonic Edinburgh Medical School, but, unlike the School, the Society was dependent on one man, Monro. When he was taken ill his colleague in the Mathematics chair, Colin McLaurin, whose appointment to Edinburgh had permitted the distinction of the University in a scientific field other than medicine, proposed in 1736-7 the broadening of the Society to take in all sorts of physics, together with the antiquities of the country. The development was not entirely novel, because one section of the *Essays* had originally been concerned with meteorology. The greater degree of expansion, and McLaurin's intention to recruit into the society's ranks professors other than medical and *literati* from the City, did mean the coming together in the new Philosophical Society, as it was called, of professional men (professors, lawyers, ministers) and the landed gentry, since one-third of the membership were required to be 'Gentlemen who do not make Philosophy or Physick their particular Profession'. McLaurin's scheme for broadening an existing Society and building on its foundations appears to have taken its roots in the proposal of a broad section of townsfolk interested in philosophic matters to form a society in 1737. McLaurin enabled them to realise their hopes by fusing them with the declining Medical Society and forming, as a result, the Philosophical Society. The Society lasted till 1783, numbered the most distinguished *literati* amongst its members (such as McLaurin, Black, Hume, Hutton, Smith, Cullen, Stewart) and its three volumes of essays contained important and original papers by some of their number, although publication and the Society's fortunes were both affected seriously by the '45 and McLaurin's death.[5] It will shortly be seen that the Philosophical Society in its turn led to the Royal Society of Edinburgh.

Glasgow's earliest manifestation of the Enlightenment as far as societies were concerned came in 1743 when the Provost, Andrew Cochrane, recognising the interation of matters fundamental to the economic well-being of his city and of intellectual developments, founded the Political Economy Club. It met weekly, its membership was drawn largely from the city merchants, though Adam Smith was a member from 1751, and its object was 'to Enquire into the Nature and principles of Trade in all its Branches, and to Communicate their Knowledge and Views on that subject to each other'. Smith evidently found the club invaluable to him in collecting material for the *Wealth of Nations*, and Robert Foulis, the Glasgow printer, found himself having to reprint various classic treaties on economics, so significant was the interest awakened. Practical matters such as the consequences of paper money were discussed as also more philosophic matters, such as when Smith spoke in 1755 on natural liberty in industrial affairs.[6] The Glasgow Literary Society held its first meeting in 1752 and was composed largely of professors though Hume and non-professorial Glasgow citizens did belong. Meetings were weekly, papers read and criticised, and accounts of new books given. Cullen, Smith (on what was ultimately his *Essay on Language* and on Hume's essays on Commerce) and Dugald Stewart all read papers, and Black's discovery of latent heat was made known to the Society too.[7] Thus the two crucial and identifiable groups in Glasgow, merchants and professors, each had a forum that was predominantly their own but in which they interacted with each other.

The Aberdeen Philosophical Society, known affectionately as the Wise Club, was organised in 1758, lasted for fifteen years and numbered among its members all those who so predominated in the intellectual life of the north-east, including George Campbell (principal of Marischal 1759-96 and author of the *Philosophy of Rhetoric* and a dissertation in reply to Hume on the subject of miracles), Thomas

Reid, James Beattie (author of another response to Hume, *Essay on Truth*, which gained for him a £200 pension from George III), the Moderate professor of Divinity in both Aberdeen colleges and author of essays on taste and genius, Alexander Gerard, and David Skene, an Aberdeen physician who established the study of natural history in the north-east. The Society indicates the increasing secularisation of the age, in that it grew out of a theological club of which most of the ministers had been members and which broke up when they were appointed to their first charges. Meetings of the new society took place in a tavern, and port, punch and porter as well as more solid comestibles were provided for the members. The subject matter was to be rigidly philosophical, not grammatical, historical or philological. By philosophy was meant:

> Every Principle of Science which may be deduced by Just and Lawfull Induction from the Phaenomena either of the human Mind or of the material World; All Observations and Experiments that may furnish Materials for such Induction; the Examination of False Schemes of Philosophy and false Methods of Philosophising. the Subserviency of Philosophy to Arts, the Principles they borrow from it and the Means of carrying them out to their Perfection.

a statement that was described more than a century later as the motto of Reid's subsequent works. The later writings of the members received their first airing in the Aberdeen Philosophical Society: Reid spoke on the philosophy of the mind in general, and on perception by sight in particular, in 1758; in 1760 he was analysing the senses particularly that of touch. Gerard read a series of papers on genius, on the effect of the passions on the association of our ideas, on the operations of the mind that formed or did not form ideas, on the difference between common sense and reason, and many other subjects. Other questions discussed included the effects of enthusiasm and superstition on the human mind, freedom of action, attitudes to morals, plants that enrich the soil, the origin of blacks, civil liberty, and the refraction of light and reflection. Political economy was also pursued, as in 1761 when the best expedients for preventing the rise of servants' wages were discussed, and among the matters that necessarily arose in the discussion were supply and demand, and the fact that the rise of manufactures and agricultural improvement was diminishing the number of servants. Measures to increase the birth rate were another topic that interested the Aberdeen *literati* and they proposed that a tax be levied on the unmarried and that the unmarried should work more.[8]

The remaining intellectual societies to be discussed here were all in Edinburgh, the Glasgow Philosophical Society, for example, not really coming into its own until the 1830s.[9] Four years prior to the founding of the Aberdeen Philosophical Society in 1754, the Select Society had been inaugurated by Allan Ramsay, the artist. The Society met in the Advocates Library, weekly during the summer and winter sessions of the Court of Session. It brought together in its membership leading Moderate clergy (Robert Wallace, John Jardine, John Home, Hugh Blair, Alexander Carlyle), *literati* and university men (Robertson, Hume, Ferguson, Cullen, Smith), and a large number of advocates including Monboddo, Kames and Wedderburn, the lay Moderate. Provost Drummond also belonged to complete the charmed circle, for here was the Edinburgh Enlightenment acting together in a microcosm. The objectives were the pursuit of philosophical inquiry and the improvement of members in the art of speaking; one of the incidental results was said by Dugald Stewart to have been that up until the foundation of the Select Society, the clergy of the Kirk had always been considered inferior to the members of the other learned professions in knowledge and liberality. A question was debated at each meeting and a different member presided. The actual concerns of the Society included, to an important degree, improvement, in arts (such as printing), sciences, manufactures, agriculture, and in the reading and speaking of the English language in Scotland. The improving activities of the Society are to be distinguished from its concern with topics more appropriate to the Enlightenment proper. Matters which were debated included various aspects of political economy, and *vide* Montesquieu, whether the difference of national characters was due to different climates, or to moral and political causes. A topic that was rejected in 1754 when, it will be remembered, the times were particularly hard for anything that smacked of liberalism let alone libertarianism, was one proposed by Wedderburn—whether the law of Queen Joan of Naples, allowing licensed brothels, would be advantageous to a nation. The Select, if no account is taken of its 'improving' concerns, appears to have thrived for only a few years after its foundation, and gradually so declined that by the 1760s it was totally lacking in vigour, and it seems to have died in 1763.[10] The history of the Select Society parallels the brief life of the first *Edinburgh Review* and similarly indicates that, despite the galaxy of talent and the interests represented, the 1750s may yet have been too early a stage in development for the corporate expression of high Enlightenment to have been made manifest.

More than twenty years after the foundation of the Select Society, in 1778, a group of members of the Philosophical Society formed the Newtonian Club as a society within a society. The vast majority of its members were Edinburgh professors and in view of developments in the University in the eighteenth century, the name given to the club was not surprising. It is not known precisely what activities if any the members undertook.[11] Its secretary was William Smellie, a man who was perpetually on the fringes of the Scottish Enlightenment, without ever attaining a position central in its concerns either by his occupation or by his writing. Smellie figures in his usual marginal way not only in the Newtonian Club but in the evolution of the Royal Society of Edinburgh from out of the Philsophical Society, and in the foundation of the *Encyclopaedia Britannica*. He was born in 1740 and died in 1795 and spent most of his life as a 'learned printer': he had begun his apprenticeship at the age of twelve in the Edinburgh University printers; he was able to attend classes and since the university printers' guaranteed market lay in the printing of text-books, including the classics, it was not surprising that Smellie produced an edition of Terence in 1757, for which he was awarded a prize from the Philosophical Society. His next work was in opposition to Linnaeus' doctrine on the sexes of plants. He worked on the study while being a corrector of the Press for another firm of printers, while collecting material for the *Scots Magazine* and while devising a scheme, which marked him out as an industrial conciliator, for the payment of journeymen printers, whereby they were paid according to the number of letters, of different size types, laid in a certain space. While in employment at the second firm of printers, Smellie became known to Kames, and he went on to found his own printing business in 1765 with the financial backing of two Edinburgh professors. In 1768 he was associated with the *Encyclopaedia Britannica*, and he was now sufficiently well known by the *literati* (almost certainly because of the necessity for them to work closely with their printers) for Kames to stand security for £300 in his business ventures, and for Smith to give him the run of his library (Smith wrote to Smellie that he was a 'beau' in nothing but his books, and Smellie, indeed, agreed that they were either 'elegantly' or 'superbly' bound). In the 1770s, Smellie became printer to Edinburgh University, secretary to the Newtonian Club, was translating Buffon into English, substituting for the professor of Botany and attempting to make a career at the hub of the Enlightenment by using his contacts to secure for himself in 1778 the Edinburgh chair of Natural History. In the early 1780s, he went into partnership with William Creech.

Smellie's being in the Scottish Enlightenment but not of it leads to the consideration of the establishment of the Royal Society of Edinburgh in 1783. Smellie was the unsuccessful contestant for the chair that John Walker succeeded to in 1779, but as Walker was more or less confined to his clerical duties at Moffat, Smellie's new patron, the eleventh Earl of Buchan, decided to use him as a means of establishing a Society of Antiquaries (and by its antiquarian nature, anti-Enlightenment), under the auspices of which natural history would be treated as a means of involving the Society with a science subject that was considered to be within the pale of Enlightenment culture. Smellie was used first through his being made keeper of a rival museum to the University's (whose keepership he had lost along with the chair), and secondly, through the idea of his lecturing on natural history in the Antiquaries' Society. A collision course was consequently set between the centre of Edinburgh Enlightenment culture, with its claim to teach natural history and to foster the distinction of its own natural history museum, and the anti-Enlightenment Society of Antiquaries led by Buchan, who proposed a rival set of lectures and museum.[12]

Walker proposed a plan in March 1782 whereby professors, advocates, nobles and members of the Philosophical and Antiquarian societies should form the Royal Society of Edinburgh to advance learning and useful knowledge. In effect it was a take-over bid for the Antiquaries, certainly an attempt to curb any threat they posed to Walker's professorial monopoly, and to marshal the forces in Edinburgh society disposed to the concerns of the Enlightenment. The full force of political machinations was unleashed with Buchan and the university professors each trying to obtain a royal charter. Shapin had described the steps that ultimately embroiled the entire issue in national politics as well as local rivalries.[13] In the end both groups were chartered, although the Antiquaries were markedly less active in the bulk of the remaining period of Enlightenment. The Philosophical Society was duly subsumed and, as Shapin has shown, a threat to upset the highly prized institutional stability and agreeable intercourse of the Enlightenment was removed. It was felt, too, that the public recognition that a charter conferred on the Antiquaries would have been a blow to the intellectual distinction of the other bodies central to the Enlightenment in Edinburgh, the University, the Faculty of Advocates and the Philosophical Society.

The objects of the Society were expressed by the two branches, physical and literary, into which it was divided, but the literary branch appears to have lasted only some fifteen years. The physical class covered

mathematics, natural philosophy, chemistry, medicine, natural history
and matters relating to the improvement of arts and manufactures.
The literary class embraced literature, philology, history, antiquities
and speculative philosophy. The general tenor of the papers put the
Society into the 'enlightened' rather than the improving class (although
improvement was within its purview) and there was also the practice,
in imitation of foreign academies, of compiling biographies of eminent
members who died, of which Dugald Stewart's of Smith, Robertson
and Reid are the best known. Like the Select Society thirty years
previously, the Royal Society embraced all those people essential to
the prosecution of the Enlightenment, but this time with far
greater success—Edinburgh University professors, professors from other
Scottish universities, the whole panoply of lawyers, eminent ministers,
doctors and surgeons, and the aristocracy and gentry who were so
crucial to the patronage of the movement. To take one year's office
bearers as an instance, in 1792, the President was the Duke of Buccleuch
the Vice-Presidents included the political manager of Scotland, Henry
Dundas, and the Secretary was the then Edinburgh professor of Natural
Philosophy, John Robison. The counsellors from the physical class
included James Gregory and Dugald Stewart, and the presidents Black,
Hutton, Monro *secundus*; the counsellors from the literary class
numbered Adam Ferguson and the advocate, Henry MacKenzie, and
the presidents William Robertson and Hugh Blair. The secretaries of
the classes included Playfair and Walker (physical) and the Edinburgh
professor of Greek, Andrew Dalzel (literary).[14]

The Society became a forum in which significant scientific achievements of the Scottish Enlightenment were made known: one of the
most important was Hutton's 'Theory of the Earth' in 1783, another
was T. C. Hope's discovery of strontianites, first made public in 1793.
A third scientific communication ironically undercut the earlier scientific work of Joseph Black: Sir James Hall of Douglass (1761-1832)
who had been a student of Black's in 1781-2, visited the celebrated
French chemist, Antoine Lavoisier, in 1786 and became converted
to his 'new chemistry'. Prior to Lavoisier, chemists followed the
phlogiston theory of Stahl, which said that combustible bodies were
compounds, one of the constituents of which was a substance called
phlogiston. During combustion, phlogiston escaped and the other
constituents remained behind. Lavoisier showed that phlogiston was,
in fact, imaginary, and that combustion, far from being a decomposition was a combination of the combustible material with oxygen.
It can, therefore, be seen why, since Black was so concerned with

heat, Lavoisier's new chemistry should have troubled him in his senility. Hall not only converted Black's successor, T. C. Hope, to Lavoisierian chemistry, but he also boldly entered the haunt of Black and his close friends, the Royal Society, and read a paper entitled 'Lavoisier's New Theory of Chemistry' in 1788.[15] (Hall also became an ardent Huttonian and tested the theory by stimulating the accumulation and action of heat in his laboratory. Indeed, the Royal Society was regarded as a Huttonian-orientated group.) Most of the *literati* of the late-eighteenth century and early-nineteenth century read original papers to the Royal Society and made its *Transactions* invaluable collections of scientific, medical and other papers.[16] The Society manifested the research side, especially in natural knowledge, of the Scottish Enlightenment in Edinburgh, and fostered the co-operative and independent intellectual work of Hutton, Walker, Black, Hall and others.

The last intellectual society was the Wernerian Natural History Society, founded in 1808 by Robert Jameson, partly as a reaction to the Huttonian character of the Royal Society (in 1808 the Royal Society sought and received a new charter which effectively put its property of collections into the hands of the University) and also to pursue geology, mineralogy, botany and zoology. The Society was obviously named after Werner and met in the University's Natural History Museum. The members included Thomas MacKnight, Leslie's unsuccessful opponent for the Mathematics chair in 1805, and the anatomist, John Barclay, and the Society published eight volumes of memoirs up to 1838, although its vigour declined from 1823. Its existence testifies to the concern for earth science in eighteenth-century Scotland which could be expressed in the 'improving' sphere of agriculture on one level, or in 'enlightenment' on a higher level as in the debates that took place in various Edinburgh forums over the rival merits of the theories of Hutton and Werner.[17] The Wernerian Society itself was not immune: in 1819 a letter was read to the society from Ami Boué, a French professor and former student of Jameson, who suggested that there was a similarity between the volcanic rocks of Auvergne and Vivarais and those of Scotland. Jameson hotly denied the suggestion at the next meeting, insisting that Arthur's Seat, in Holyrood Park, Edinburgh, which was an extinct volcano, was of aqueous origin.[18]

Of the four general sociable and convivial clubs that were related to the Scottish Enlightenment, three were in Edinburgh and one in Glasgow. Simson's Club in Glasgow was the first in time, centred on the Glasgow professor of mathematics and existed before the Glasgow

Literary Society was founded in 1752, although once the Literary Society was founded, Simson's Club became its recreational section. The meetings took place over dinner in the village of Anderston on a Saturday afternoon and on Friday nights at a tavern near the College where whist, conversation and the singing of Grecian odes occupied the members. The members included leading Glasgow *literati* such as Cullen and Smith.

Edinburgh's three general social clubs were the Poker, the Oyster and the Friday. The Poker Club lasted from 1762 to 1784 and was founded to promote the establishment of a Scottish militia. The significance of its objectives has to be seen in the light of the social philosophy of the men of letters: it will be recalled that it was believed that as society grew more refined and as the division of labour became more ingrained, so would patriotism dwindle. The militia question, therefore, relates centrally to an intellectual 'doctrine' of the philosophers. The club was named by Adam Ferguson, who had seen active service as a chaplain in the '45 and who felt particularly strongly about the threatened loss of the martial spirit. The membership was drawn from the old Select Club and so once again embraced those groups central to the Scottish Enlightenment—authors, Moderate ministers, lawyers, landed gentry. Individual members included not only Ferguson but Carlyle (the club's effective historian), Hume, Robertson, Smith, Blair, Jardine, Black, Robison, Henry Dundas, the Duke of Buccleuch and the Earl of Haddington. Over the years the club met in a succession of taverns and its significance was discerned by Carlyle as improving manners, countering the pedantry of scholars and broadening the gentry's views.[19]

The Oyster Club was established by the three close friends, Smith, Black and Hutton, and others joined them including Adam Ferguson, Robert Adam, the architect, Hugh Blair, Cullen, Sir James Hall, Henry MacKenzie, Playfair, Robertson and Stewart. The Club first met at a stabler's inn in the Grassmarket, but as attendance at its meetings were much sought after, the meeting-place was often changed. In his biography of Hutton, read to the Royal Society, Playfair wrote of the original members and their club, as informal and amusing despite their great learning. The Club, dependent as it was on Smith, Black and Hutton, died with them.[20]

The last convivial club, the Friday, belonged to a different generation since it was founded in 1803 by those who had been educated by the distinguished teachers of the Scottish Enlightenment, Stewart, Millar, Playfair. Their students, led by the writer Walter Scott, determined to meet once a week for social intercourse and gather about them 'every one in the city who combined literary taste with social instincts'. The original membership included Sir James Hall, Stewart, Playfair and Henry MacKenzie of the older generation, and Henry Brougham, the maverick politician who ultimately became Lord Chancellor, Francis Horner, Francis Jeffrey and Henry Cockburn. It was Cockburn who wrote an account of the Club in 1827; its objectives were social and no contentious political or religious issues were allowed to creep in, although its general creed was Whiggism. Secondly, he wrote of procedures: a somewhat dangerous but very pleasant punch concocted by Brougham was drunk, made of rum, sugar, lemons, marmalade, calves-foot jelly and much water, 'a sort of warm shrub'. Later it was iced and the marmalade and jelly omitted. Suppers gave way to dinners, claret replaced the punch, and patriotism told against French and German wines, but despite the Club's adherence to good taste 'I don't think it was till the Peace of 1814 that, the Continent being opened, we soared above prejudice, and ate and drunk everything that was rare and dear.'[21]

Specialist groups also founded convivial clubs of their own, notably the doctors. The Harveian Society was founded in 1752 to commemmorate Harvey's discovery of the circulation of the blood (a dinner was held on Harvey's birthday, 12 April), to promote friendship among the medical profession and to stimulate the Edinburgh medical students to experimental inquiry. A prize was awarded for the best essay on a subject announced by the Society. Its members were fellows of the two Edinburgh Royal Colleges and active or retired medical officers in the public services. It was founded by Andrew Duncan senior, who went on to found the Aesculapian Club in 1773, which met in a tavern first for suppers and from 1810 for gargantuan dinners, every quarter. Again members had to be fellows of one of the two Edinburgh Royal Colleges and they spent their time laying numerous bets on marriages, legal and theological questions, gold matches and the like. There were occasional gymnastic and athletic competitions between members. An intention to promote medical research died out soon after the award, in 1777, of a prize medal to the uncle of Charles Darwin, the scientist. Members included Alexander Hamilton, the second Monro, T. C. Hope, Andrew Duncan junior, Barclay and Robert Graham, the botanist.[22]

Finally the clubs and societies founded by students on the basis of the education they received in certain classrooms must be examined. The Speculative Society, founded in Edinburgh in 1764 is a case in

point, for while it avowedly was established to improve literary composition and public speaking, it had many topics suggested by lectures
pursued further under its aegis. Its meetings took the form followed
by virtually all the student groups—a paper was read and discussed,
and a debate then took place on another subject. The range of topics
covered was history, politics, legislation and general literature, and it
is known that Dugald Stewart read an essay on dreaming to the Society
in the 1770s, the first philosophical work he wrote. During his time
as a professor, the students discussed various questions that could have
been prompted by his political economy lectures, whether MPs should
be bound to follow their constituents' instructions, the abolition of
the slave trade, the desirability or otherwise of owning territory in the
East Indies, the diffusion of knowledge among the lower orders, whether
the Union was dusadvantageous to Scotland.[23] Members could continue
to belong after they had left University and the society numbered among
them many who distinguished themselves in literature, public life,
politics and medicine in the nineteenth century.

The other Edinburgh student societies can be classified in a more
specialised manner as medical, scientific and legal. The Medical Society
was first in evidence in 1734, three years after the professorial medical
society and avowedly in imitation of it. It originally met in student
lodgings and then in taverns where the members read a dissertation on
some medical topic, rabies, gonorrhea and epilepsy being among the
first. By 1737 the Society was more firmly established: since professional improvement and the need to prepare themselves for graduation
were of prime importance, members performed exercises similar to
those prescribed by the universities. Discourses and discussions of a
disease or other medical question constituted the business of the
Society. By 1763, a meeting room was provided in the Royal
Infirmary and members began to collect a library of books. The
Library eventually grew to such a size that a whole building was
required for the housing of it and for the carrying out of the Society's
other business which now took place not only in meetings, but in a
museum and in a chemistry laboratory. The building was completed in
1776 and, indeed, the Philosophical Society had the use of a room in
it. By 1778, and forestalling the Royal Society by some years, the
Society was chartered as the Royal Medical Society.

The Royal Medical Society was closely connected with the medical
school of Edinburgh by its publication of the best MD dissertations
submitted for graduation. An annual prize essay was also sponsored
to encourage experimental inquiries on questions connected with

medicine. As far as the discussions were concerned, they could include such matters as catarrh, in 1790-1, but the author of that paper, also in the same year, debated the question which was absorbing so many Edinburgh forums of the day, the agents employed by nature in consolidating the strata of the globe. Medical questions, therefore, did not monopolise the members' attention: Robert Jameson continued the Huttonian-Wernerian debate further by asking in 1796 if the Huttonian Theory of the Earth was consistent with fact; in 1810, Henry Holland, subsequently a physician to Queen Victoria, made 'An Inquiry into the Nature and Origins of Passions in their Relation to the Intellect and Bodily Economy of Man'; Richard Bright, who later discovered Bright's disease, spoke on gangrene in 1813 and in the same year, Marshall Hall, who was later distinguished for his researches on the nervous system, especially the reflex action, was to be found speaking 'On the Dispensive and Refractive Powers of the Human Eye and on some Motions of the Iris'.

The Royal Medical Society became embroiled not only in disputes over scientific theories that were nothing to do with medicine but also, of course, with those that were intimately involved with it. The most notorious row was that over the medical system of John Brown (1735-88) a former secretary of William Cullen, whose Brunonian Theory attributed disease processes to a state of too great or too little excitability of the tissues. He consequently recommended stimulation of excitability by, for example, alcohol, or soothing remedies if excitability was too great. It was a simple theory, that required little knowledge of medicine and that had strong and popular appeal. When Sir James Mackintosh, the future Whig MP and judge in India, came to Edinburgh in 1784, he found the controversy raging between the different approaches of Cullen and Brown, and he became a partisan of the Brunonians in the Royal Medical Society. Brown's theory illustrated the dangers of that generalising which was so central to Scottish philosophy in the Enlightenment, since, to quote Mackintosh, Brown could 'generalise plausibly, without knowing facts enough to disturb him by their importunate demands for explanations, which he could never have given'. Mackintosh continued the theme by pointing out how 'The metaphysical character of his age and nation gave a symmetry and simplicity to his speculations unknown to former theories of medicine.' His theory captivated Mackintosh and other young students of medicine at the time because it was simple, facile, easily appreciated and supposedly infallible. It attracted students because it gave them the 'pleasures of revolt' against the establishment, their professors. As Mackintosh himself felt in his later reflections, 'I was speculative, lazy, and factious, and predisposed to Brunonianism by all these circumstances.' The Royal Medical Society passionately debated the rival merits of the prevailing and Brunonian system 'with as much factious violence as if our subjects had been the rights of a people, or the fate of an empire'. Nonetheless, Mackintosh ultimately had no doubts that the liveliness of the Society was due to the able teaching then available in the Edinburgh Faculty of Medicine.[24]

The student scientific societies were quite numerous and also ephemeral, and it is important to distinguish between those that related to the Enlightenment and those like, for example, the American Physical Society, which was founded to provide an occasional home atmosphere for American medical students in Edinburgh. In 1788 the Royal Physical Society received its charter and by 1813 it had absorbed a number of small student societies concerned with science, medicine and general philosophical topics. At best it is possible to discern, reflected in the interests of the societies founded, the scientific interests of the Enlightenment itself, chemistry and natural history predominating. In 1800, for example, a chemistry society was founded to permit students the opportunities for practical experiment that were not provided in the formal chemistry classes by T. C. Hope. The student Natural History Society, which was also interested in chemistry, was founded in 1782, collected twelve volumes of papers and received much encouragement from interested professors.[25] Two groups formed by legal students were the Juridicial Society (1773) and the Logical Society (1793). The Juridicial had intellectual and social purposes, discoursing on institutes of law, arguing hypothetical cases and questions of law. A legal library was also established and a valuable collection of styles used in legal documents by eminent lawyers was made and published in 1786. The Logical was not so rigorously devoted to law, debating more general topics as well, but with the onset of the French Revolution, and the consequent curb on free political discussion, it merged in 1797 with the Juridicial.[26]

Glasgow students never received the same encouragement from the university authorities as, for example, Principal Robertson gave in Edinburgh. Free intellectual discussion was suspect on religious grounds and professors also much opposed students meeting in taverns. Clubs and societies appeared spasmodically in the 1740s, 1770s and 1790s but cannot be said to have been part of the Scottish Enlightenment.[27]

II

Two of the new institutions of the Scottish Enlightenment were in periodical form and, as such, of a different character from the societies of the age. They were the *Encyclopaedia Britannica* (1768) and the second *Edinburgh Review* (1802).[28] The *Britannica* commenced as a not particularly enlightened venture, in that certainly its first edition was a scissors and paste affair, and there was a court case involving the second edition in which plagiarism was alleged.[29] When the *Britannica* began it was by no means the first work of its type even in the eighteenth century. Chambers' *Cyclopaedia* was published in 1728 and the noted French *Encyclopédie* in 1750. There was a positive rash of encyclopaedias advertised in Edinburgh from the 1790s: William Henry Hall's *New Royal Encyclopaedia*, the *English Encyclopaedia*, the *New Encyclopaedia* which may have been identical with the *Encyclopaedia Perthensis*, and the *Encyclopaedia Metropolitana*. The proliferation itself reveals much about the age's concern for knowledge as a means, if not necessarily of enlightenment, then of improvement. It is hard now to believe that to the eighteenth century the *Britannica* was not unusual, despite its claims to be based on a new system of composition, the distinct treatises being compiled from the writings of the best modern authors. It is a distinctive venture now to historians because it still survives and unlike most of its contemporaries fell into the hands of a succession of successful publishers, the relevant man in the Scottish Enlightenment being, from 1804, Archibald Constable, and the *Britannica* became for the leading contributors, a welcome source of additional income. Consider, for example, a letter from the professor of Mathematics, John Leslie, to a friend in St Andrews in 1812, concerning the dissertations by himself, Dugald Stewart and John Playfair to be published as a supplement to the fifth edition:

> What think you of this trio of stalking horses to Constable.
> Could you have imagined that Stewart who looks with such
> contempt on writers for reviews and Encyclopaedias would have
> lent his name? It was for the benefit of Constable's family he says—
> but more probably as a douceur to the purchase of the II vol. of
> the Phil[osophy] of the H[uman] Mind. Constable talks of very
> liberal terms.

The writers were, if Leslie is to be believed, highly dependent on publishers; consequently it is as well to contrast Leslie's letter with one of Constable's:

> I need not tell you that Mr Stewart's name stood in the first rank
> of the philosophers of the day, and it required the high premium
> of payment, my own intimate connexion and friendship with him,
> and a negotiation conducted with some address, to accomplish the
> important end in view. He had never contributed to any work of
> the kind, nor was his name to be found as a literary man, except
> in the title-pages of his own books, and perhaps to an article or two
> in the Royal Society Transactions of Edinburgh.

The supplement's editor wrote that the £1,000 paid to Stewart for the
Dissertation was the equivalent of the value of the copyright of the
entire work.[30]

In its early years, however, the *Britannica* did not have the prestige
it was later to acquire. Smellie, the marginal man, was central to the
production of the first edition in three volumes, published in fort-
nightly parts. The advertisements were even reduced to basing the
Britannica's reputation on the quality of its engravings, which was
not surprising since one of the two founders, Andrew Bell, was an
engraver and the other, Colin Macfarquhar, was a printer. There is no
evidence that the *Britannica* was a notable feature of the scene in the
heyday of the Scottish Enlightenment. Nonetheless, as successive
editions appeared, the work clearly became more popular and profitable: the number of copies of the first edition is unknown, 1,500 were
made of the second edition (1777-84) and 10,000 of the third (1787-
97). Many practices were employed to promote sales such as inspection
copies and the part exchanging of an old edition upon the purchase of
a new one. The *Britannica* was also remaindered every so often. However
from about 1797 philosophers, or those from a similar intellectual
level as they, began to be involved with the *Britannica,* writing for
editions subsequent to that date and for supplements that were
published to those editions. Their involvement increased with Constable's
involvement with the business, since he was one of the thinkers' main
publishers. The first professor to contribute was John Robison, professor of Natural Philosophy at Edinburgh 1774-1805, who wrote for
the third edition and its supplement. The first time a clutch of
philosophers became involved was with the supplement to the fifth
edition in 1812, when Stewart and Playfair wrote the *Dissertations*
which have been quoted in this study and for which they were paid
such princely sums. From then on, the *Britannica* sought to have its

articles written by the leading authorities of the day, but it is likely that the inspiration to do so was competition from like works and Constable's own connections, rather than any other particular factor inherent in the late years of the Scottish Enlightenment.

The Edinburgh Review, on the other hand, was intimately connected with the Scottish Enlightenment, reflected its concerns and indicated how the generation that followed the heyday of the movement and/or was educated under its aegis, modified its ideas in the new circumstances created by the French and Industrial Revolutions. As Cockburn wrote of the turn of the nineteenth century:

> Grown-up people talked at this time of nothing but the French Revolution, and its supposed consequences; younger men of good education were immersed in chemistry and political economy; the lower orders seemed to take no particular concern in anything.[31]

The *Review* developed out of a student society founded in 1797 which lasted three years, called the Academy of Physics.[32] Both the Academy and the *Review* had the same people as their moving spirits, including Henry Brougham, Francis Horner and Francis Jeffrey; both were prompted by similar causes and shared the same concerns. The young Whigs desired to engage in scientific activity that was precluded in Edinburgh classrooms and societies, and their sense of exclusion led to the creation of separate forums where they could indulge their interests. Once established the Academy concerned itself with precisely those scientific and philosophic matters which had preoccupied the philosophers — heat, geology, liberty, property, labour, different human societies, ancient and modern. The *Review* concerned itself with the same matters through an alternative medium of book reviews, which were as much concerned with discoursing at length on the reviewer's opinions, as considering an actual work. The parallel with the Academy is undoubted when Brougham is found writing that the Academy was as much concerned with examining the opinions of others as with undertaking new enquiries.[33] Francis Jeffrey's critical ability could well have been fostered by taking Jardine's Logic Class at Glasgow and indulging in the criticism of exercises that was so central to it.[34]

The Edinburgh Review was founded some two years after the demise of the Academy of Physics and the story of its origin and early years has been chronicled by Professor John Clive.[35] It is clear that the *Review* was part of the Scottish Enlightenment, albeit in one of its last phases, because it was inspired by the concerns of the philosophers,

which were duly reflected in its pages. To that extent, the *Review*
looked back to the eighteenth century. On the other hand, it had a mind
of its own and duly espoused nineteenth-century causes which it saw
as fields for putting the thought of the Enlightenment in practice.
More independently yet, the *Review* criticised and modified the
views of the earlier authors in the light of circumstances that prevailed
in the early-nineteenth century, and in the age that was coming to
terms with the aftermath of the French and the Industrial Revolutions.
To this extent did the *Review* belong to the evolving Victorian age.
By analysing articles written by those educated by the main teaching
philosophers of the Scottish Enlightenment within the first twenty
years or so of the *Review's* life, it is possible to see the reflections,
the carrying through of the Enlightenment and the modification or
criticisms of it. The subjects for analysis are higher or adult education
(which was so marked an achievement of the Scottish Enlightenment);
science especially the work of Hutton and its repercussions; and conjectural history, politics and political economy which were all so
enmeshed one with the other.[36]

There are three aspects which can be considered of the
Edinburgh Review's early concern for higher or adult education: first,
the modification of Scottish philosophical education in what was
regarded as a more utilitarian age; second, John Playfair's strictures on
Oxford and Cambridge in the first decade of the nineteenth century
and, finally, the causes of London University and Mechanics'
Institutes in the 1820s. Francis Jeffrey began to question the re-thinking
of the relevance of a philosophical education in two articles in 1804 and
1810, which respectively considered two works by Dugald Stewart,
his life of Reid and his *Philosophical Essays*.[37] He was writing when
the threshold of the new age had already been crossed, and the philosophers themselves would have been the last people to regard their
writings as fixed, sacrosanct and immune to modification in the light
of changed circumstances. The essence of Jeffrey's argument in both
articles was that philosophy of the mind, a most important preoccupation of the Scottish Enlightenment, was, in fact, a useless
concern compared with experimental philosophy. Implicit in his
argument was the demotion of philosophy of the mind in any 'modern'
educational scheme of things. After the appearance of Jeffrey's first
attack, Stewart had a chance to reply in his *Philosophical Essays*
which, in their turn, were duly answered in the *Review*.

Stewart and Jeffrey agreed on the importance of the Baconian
method, the importance of experiment, observation, the collection of

facts, as a means of acquiring knowledge, since 'knowledge is power'. Bacon, like Newton, was a central intellectual influence on the Scottish Enlightenment, and so it was likely that Stewart and Jeffrey as products of the Enlightenment should attend devotedly to him. But they differed as to the universal application of Bacon: Jeffrey made a distinction between substances capable of being subjected to experiment (those actually within man's power and with which he could tamper) and those which might merely be observed, like the mind, which was beyond reach. He was sceptical of that tenet crucial to the social philosophy of the Scottish Enlightenment, namely that the experimental method could as well be applied to the science of mind as to the science of matter. No great benefit was to be gained from such abstract study. The improvements that had been made on the basis of the approaches of Bacon and Newton were in areas which man could actually handle and on which he could experiment (such as gravity). On the other hand, there was no direct utility to be gained even from the most accurate observation of occurrences beyond human control, and observation itself was an art that was not susceptible of improvement. Man merely required to be vigilant and attentive, and

> though a talent for methodical arrangement may facilitate to others the study of the facts that have been collected, it does not appear how our knowledge of these facts can be increased by any new method of describing them.

Consequently, and central to Jeffrey's argument:

> Facts that we are unable to modify or direct, in short, can only be the objects of observation; and observation can only inform us that they exist, and that their succession appears to be governed by certain general laws.

In proper experimental philosophy, on the other hand, every acquisition of knowledge was of necessity an increase of power, whereas in observational philosophy it was merely satisfying curiosity. Causes might be ascertained in experimental philosophy, whereas they remained conjectures in matters of observation, as defined by Jeffrey.

The philosophy and, therefore, the phenomena of the human mind were matters of observation alone, said Jeffrey—'We cannot decompose our perceptions in a crucible, nor divide our sensations with a prism.' Nor could thoughts and emotions be produced artificially in a laboratory.

Furthermore nothing new could be discovered by metaphysical analysis in the same sense that a chemist discovers a new earth or a new metal. Metaphysics was solely an observational science and Baconian induction had no place in it:

> A groom, who never heard of the association of ideas, feeds the young war-horse to the sound of a drum; and the unphilosophical artists that tame elephants and train dancing dogs, proceed upon the same obvious and admitted principle.

As a result, Jeffrey did not consider the metaphysician to be considered on a par with the chemist or natural philosopher, but he was like a 'grammarian who arranges into technical order the words of a language which is spoken familiarly by all his readers; or of the artist who exhibits to them a correct map of a district with every part of which they were previously acquainted'. Systematisation might lead to lucidity and precision but not to an increase of information, and the chief value of metaphysics lay in the exercise it afforded to the mental faculties and to the pleasure derived from intellectual exertion.[38]

Between 1804 and 1810, Stewart formulated a reply which appeared in the second part of the Preliminary Dissertation to his *Philosophical Essays,* which Jeffrey duly reviewed in the *Edinburgh Review.* The essence of Stewart's reply was that the distinction between experiment and observation was of little importance to the argument because experiments were merely phenomena being observed. Naturally Jeffrey could still not accept Stewart's point:

> Substances which are in our power, are the objects of experiment; those which are not in our power, of observation only.

Experiments elucidated as no amount of observation could, whereas observation did not illustrate anything that was not in the power of everybody to perceive. Mental faculties were incapable of analysis and contained nothing that was not already known, even if not formulated into words. Such experiments as Stewart alluded to referred to matter not mind, as in his analogy between the physiologist and the metaphysician:

> the business of anatomy is to lay open, with the knife, the secrets of that internal structure, which would never otherwise be apparent to the keenest eye; while the metaphysical inquirer can disclose

nothing of which all his pupils are not previously aware.

Stewart also pointed to astronomy as an observational science which had added to human power. Jeffrey duly noted, however, that observation alone had not been responsible since experiments with small pieces of matter on the laws of projectile motion had been employed. Furthermore, astronomical knowledge did not give power over the stars but over the earth and ocean, since knowledge of the stars aided navigation. Knowledge of the mind, on the other hand, gave no new power over either the mind itself nor any other substance. Experiment implied power: he who discovered the identity of lighting and electricity gave a power to man that the observer of the periodic immersions and emersions of the satellites of Jupiter clearly did not. Man still had no control over the satellites of Jupiter. Jeffrey distinguished, too, between social and mental philosophy: the observation of varieties of mankind and philosophy of the mind were pursued in completely opposing ways by students, the one by social intercourse and travel, and the other by solitary reflection. More important, philosophy of the mind was concerned with what was common to human consciousness not what distinguished men from one another.

Stewart took particular trouble to refute Jeffrey's views on the prunciple of association, saying that it was useful to evolve general theorems from laws of nature that were already familiar to the generality of man, even if they were not formulated in words. Jeffrey, in his second article, denied the utility yet again, on the grounds that the discovery and statement of general laws did not make possible the employment of them to areas other than those in which they already operated. And Jeffrey emphasised his attack on the utility and practical importance of mental philosophy (while nevery denying its dignity, interest and capacity to exalt the human faculties) by noting that the advances in human comfort and intelligence were due, not to the increased knowledge of our mental constitution, but to an increase in political freedom, reformed Christianity, printing and the mechanical arts.[39] Hence can be seen in the pages of the *Edinburgh Review* a significant debate, and a modification of a central concern of the Scottish Enlightenment in the early industrial age. Utility in the shape of practical sciences and education, was seen by the younger generation as having a more important place in society than the mental philosophy which had been so all consuming in the heyday of Hume and Reid.

The Scottish Universities' opinion of English higher education has

already been seen. Despite the Stewart-Jeffrey debate confidence was
still high in the 1808-10 period when a series of articles in the *Edinburgh Review* by, among others, John Playfair, attacked the English
Universities. The shafts appear to have struck home, for that great
nineteenth-century influence on university education, John Henry
Newman, (wrongly) regarded the *Review* as 'the organ of the University
of Edinburgh' and the University as 'the party of the North and of
progress'.[40] On the other hand, by the early-nineteenth century, both
the English Universities were in the throes of reform, which may have owed
nothing to the *Review* articles. The articles were on Pierre Simon La
Place's *Traité de Mécanique Céleste*, the Oxford edition of Strabo,
Richard Lovell Edgworth's *Professional Education,* a reply to replies
on the earlier attacks, entitled 'Calumnies against Oxford', and an
article on Robert Woodhouse's Trigonometry.[41] The arguments
ranged from Sydney Smith, one of the *Review's* founders and later
Canon of St Paul's, saying that Oxford students were confined 'to the
safe and elegant imbecility of classical learning' because the ecclesiastical tutors were afraid of their turning sceptical, to Playfair also
blaming Oxford for still considering Aristotle as infallible and
mistaking the infancy of science for its maturity, and blaming Cambridge
for giving students portions of Newton to learn by rote so that they
could be questioned on him:

> invention finds no exercise; the student is confined within narrow
> limits; his curiosity is not roused; the spirit of discovery is not
> awakened

and

> Newton is taught there in the way least conducive to solid
> mathematical improvement.

The attack on the edition of Strabo (a work which described known
parts of the inhabited earth and stressed the geographer's need for
mathematical and scientific knowledge) was on the grounds that it
was obsolete by fifty years in its knowledge of Greek geography, and
the edition gave no evidence of being aware of German philology.
In general and briefly, the *Review* attacks reflected the concern for
effective university education that had been so marked a feature of
the Scottish Enlightenment in the mid- to late-eighteenth and early-
nineteenth centuries.

The third example of concern for education in the *Review* that stemmed from the work of the Scottish Enlightenment was manifested in the major campaign of support that was mounted in the mid-1820s for a university in London and for the provision of mechanics' institutes. The links with the Scottish Enlightenment can be seen in four ways: first, the new institutions would encourage the natural development of society rather than revolution (knowledge would enlighten and moderate); secondly; they would spread the new and useful knowledge that had emerged in the form of new disciplines during the Scottish Enlightenment, especially in science and political economy; thirdly, the University of London would provide for the first time in England, amongst a range of disciplines, professional education in medicine that had been commonplace in Scotland for more than a century; and, finally, the institutes would counter those ill-effects of the division of labour which Ferguson, Smith and Millar had pointed out. The first, second and last of these points are almost inseparable and are quite implicit in the *Review* articles.

It is important to see excerpts from *Review* articles alongside such writings from the height of the Scottish Enlightenment as were discussed in Chapter 5, and also others given here especially from one of the prime educators of the movement, Dugald Stewart. He had concluded, on the question of the natural development of society in an age of great upheavals, that:

> the perfection of political wisdom does not consist in an indiscriminate zeal against reformers, but in a gradual and prudent accommodation of established instutions to the varying opinions, manners and circumstances of mankind.

His sentiments echoed a common view of the thinkers of the Scottish Enlightenment. Furthermore Stewart had lectured on Political Economy because he believed that the subject was of great value to political society. Stewart's general aim in teaching political economy was to enlighten those destined to govern as well as public opinion. It was important to define the precise limits of the legislator and the areas in which selfish passions should be allowed to roam unchecked. He had been concerned not only with the rulers, but also with the ruled in these lectures, devoting some space to the education of the lower orders:

> Wherever the lower orders enjoy the benefits of education, they will be found to be comparatively sober and industrious; and, in

> many instances, the establishment of a small library in the neigh-
> bourhood of a manufactory, has been known to produce a
> sensible and rapid improvement in the morals of the work
> people. The cultivation of mind, too, which books communicate,
> naturally inspires that desire and hope of advancement, which,
> in all the classes of society, is the most steady and powerful
> motive to economy and industry.[42]

He advocated too a system of national instruction adapted especially
for the lower orders.

Consequently, it is here argued that there is a close connection
between Stewart both as a representative of the social thinking of the
Scottish Enlightenment and as the teacher of the influential early
reviewers, and between the articles subsequently written advocating
particular measures of adult and higher education. Consider, for
example, Brougham's argument in the *Review,* in November 1825,
that those working men who were encouraged to pursue knowledge
would:

> generally be the friends, and the effectual friends of improvement
> in all our institutions; but they will never be found to aid measures
> of rash and sudden innovation by which the peace of society is
> endangered. The possession of knowledge, . . . must produce the
> same effect upon the working classes that the possession of wealth
> does upon the rich; it gives them a direct *interest* in the peace and
> godd order of the community, and renders them solicitous to avoid
> whatever may disturb it.

A later article by John Ramsay M'Culloch, the most prolific writer on
political economy to emerge from Stewart's classroom, remarked that
industrial unrest might be expected to disappear the more the manufacturing population became intelligent. To aid this process, the working
class must be instructed in:

> the principles that must determine their condition in life. The poor
> ought to be taught, that they are in great measure the architects
> of their own fortune; that what others can do for them is trifling
> indeed, compared with what they can do for themselves. that they
> are infinitely more interested in the preservation of public tran-
> quillity than any other class of society; that mechanical inventions
> and discoveries are always supremely advantageous to them; and that

their real interests can only be effectually promoted by their displaying greater prudence and forethought. Such subjects ought to form a prominent part of every well digested system of public instruction. And if they were clearly explained, and enforced with that earnestness which their vast importance requires, we should have the best attainable security for the maintenance of the public tranquillity, and the well-being and comfort of the community.

It might be finally noted that the *Review* permitted Brougham to quote with approbation his own idea in founding the Society for the Diffusion of Useful Knowledge that political economy, when taught to working men, could prevent a social crisis if a commercial depression set in:

I can hardly imagine, for example, a greater service being rendered to the men, than expounding to them the true principles and mutual relations of population and wages; and both they and their masters will assuredly experience the effects of the prevailing ignorance upon such questions, as soon as any interruption shall happen in the commercial prosperity of the country, if indeed the present course of things, daily tending to lower wages as well as profits, and set the two classes in opposition to each other, shall not of itself bring on a crisis. The peace of the country, and the stability of the government, could not more effectually be secured than by the universal diffusion of this kind of knowledge.[43]

The mutual exchange of property and condition, which theoretically could have been a consequence of educating the lower orders, was scarcely in tune with the natural evolution of society. Hence, the *Review* espoused the cause of the University of London. As Brougham wrote:

When the working classes are becoming scientific, their Superiors ... to continue their betters, must learn a little more than they do now. Accordingly we expect most confidently the greatest increase in the education of the higher and middle classes, and the greatest improvement in their virtues, from the new Institution.

His views were echoed by Francis Jeffrey in another article.[44] The *Review* was important as a means of elucidating the problem of the division of labour for the first era to experience the problem on a large scale. Mechanics, after all, were the élite of the lower orders, and there were thousands of others who would suffer the numbing effects of what had been discerned by Smith, Ferguson and Millar. In general, the *Review* was fatalistic about the division of labour; it was a concomitant to the stage of society that had come to prevail. Nonetheless the *Review* advocated that concern and care be shown for the lower orders, in a sympathetic rather than patronising spirit.[45]

In the intellectual expression of the Scottish Enlightenment, science was regarded as part of general culture, and the scientific articles in the *Review,* which were quite numerous, continued the tradition in the nineteenth century. John Playfair undertook for the science of the age what Dugald Stewart had undertaken for the philosophy: he was thoroughly versed in the science of the Scottish Enlightenment, and his familiarity with the subject matter, and his didactic abilities, made him a most capable interpreter and disseminator of the scientific activity of the new era. His promulgation largely took place through the *Review's* pages, and he was its principal writer on scientific topics, penning sixty articles in fifteen years. His own Huttonianism, consequently, accounted for the partisanship of the *Review* as far as geology specifically was concerned, but he wrote also on mathematics, natural philosophy and non-scientific subjects too. Sometimes, as in his attacks on the two English Universities, he could combine his views on education with the valuable task of familiarising British readers with Continental scientific discoveries. The task became an especially important characteristic of the *Review* as was witnessed by his article in 1807 on Mechain and Delambre's famous work on the length of the arc of the earth's meridian. There he welcomed the metric system of weights and measures, and he was a proponent of the duodecimal rather than the decimal system of numbers. He urged Britain to follow the French, despite the war that subsisted between them, simply because it was mere prejudice not to recognise their scientific achievements.[46]

Perhaps his most celebrated review was that of La Place's *Traité de Mécanique Celeste,* in 1808. There he listed and discussed the principal mathematical improvements which had taken place on the Continent and which put Britain to shame: Descartes' application of algebra to trigonometry and its consequent utility for physical astronomy; D'Alembert's improvement in integral calculus and his discovery of the mechanical principle, Lagrange's calculus of variations. All these improvements enabled Newton's work in physical astronomy to be elaborated and completed, and the importance of algebra was crucial.

Yet the distinguished British mathematicians of the eighteenth century were all geometers and consequently could not be compared with their Continental brethren. He went on to say that a host of mathematical discoveries were not known in England until recent years, and many were incomprehensible to English mathematicians. (It has been argued that geometrical reasoning prevailed in Scotland because of the predominance of common sense philosophy necessitating sensory rather than imaginary referents.) Yet another of Playfair's reviews, in 1810, which both demonstrated his familiarity with French research and his desire to make it known in Britain, was that of *le Compte rendu par l'institut de France,* covering the years 1790-1809.[47] His numerous pro-Hutton geological articles, following his own book published in 1802 entitled *Illustrations of the Huttonian Theory,* included 'Werner on the formation of veins', 'Transactions of the Geological Society', 'Sir George Mackenzie's *Travels in Iceland*' (a work by a former student of Jameson whose training in observation was so successful that he became a Huttonian as a result of his field research); 'Lichtenstein's *Travels in Southern Africa*', 'Cuvier on the theory of the earth', 'Humboldt, *Researches*', 'Holland's *Travels into Albania etc*' and 'Baron de Zach, *The Attraction of Mountains*'.[48] The Huttonian-Wernerian debate found a powerful, frequent and active Huttonian advocate in the *Edinburgh Review* almost up until Playfair's death in 1819.

The third and final area of the *Review's* concerns which related to the Scottish Enlightenment, and which is considered here, are conjectural history, politics and political economy. That the *Review* had drunk at the wells of Scottish philosophical education and theoretical history can at least be seen from a brief excerpt from a letter Jeffrey wrote to Francis Horner *à propos* a contribution to the *Review:*

> there is a good part of [it] which I thought in considerable danger of being attacked and ridiculed, as a caricature of our Scotch manner of running everything up to elements, and explaining all sorts of occurrences by a theoretical history of society.[49]

The *Review* spanned the ages of Enlightenment and industrialisation. It embodied the approaches of the Scottish Enlightenment and yet was aware of the pressing issues of the early-nineteenth century. These characteristics became more confirmed when conjectural history, politics and political economy are considered. On the one hand, the *Review* believed as passionately in its own educational function as did the universities from which its founders had come. Whether the matters

were science or political economy, the object was to inform the readers
of the latest knowledge, to break down old prejudices and habits of
mind. On the other hand, the *Review* put its faith in the new *bourgeoisie,* the class at the hub of the commercial-cum-industrial society
which was now coming to prevail, and the class displayed all the moral
virtues of industry and, helped by the *Review,* culture and liberty.
The middling classes were to become the apostles of the new progress
and the bulwarks against the tyranny either of the aristocracy or the
mob.[50]

Conjectural history was a prime concern of the *Review* and the
space given to the reviewing of travel books indicated the interest that
could still be evinced for different societies in the world. The ambi-
valence evident in the writings of the Enlightenment on civilisation
and progress was also continued by the *Review:* civilisation and progress
distinguished a refined society from a rude one, but, on the other hand,
they brought such evils in their train as the division of labour and the
decline of patriotism. The *Review's* early life coincided with the repres-
ssive political atmosphere which followed the French Revolution.
The young Whigs, whose mouthpiece it was, were more aware than
the philosophers of practical problems to be faced, and of the necessity to present the case for reform at a difficult time. Nonetheless,
the French Revolution made the historical theory of the Scottish
Enlightenment more compelling for them. Jeffrey could, for example,
convey in the *Review* precisely that theory of the constitution that he
would have heard in Dugald Stewart's political economy lectures.
Both accepted royal and aristocratic patronage and influence in the
Commons since the balance of the Constitution was still maintained
within the single chamber of the Commons. Stewart had said:

the *three powers* which have been so long regarded as the disting-
uishing feature of the English plan of policy, *do* all exist in fact,
and all operate in a most effectual and important manner, but not
in the manner expressed in our laws, or in general supposed by our
speculative politicians. In consequence of the changes which time
has produced, they do not *now,* as formerly, operate separately
and ostensibly; but restraining and modifying each other's effects,
they operate in a manner not so palpable, though equally real, by
being blended together in the composition of the *House of
Commons;* an assembly which is no longer composed of men whose
habits and connexions can be supposed to attach them exclusively
to *the people,* but of men, some of whom, from their situation,

may be presumed to lean to the regal part of a government, others
to the aristocratical; while, on the important questions, the majority
may be expected to maintain the interests of the community at
large.[51]

Here, presumably, was a perfect instance of the prudent accommodation
of institutions to changing circumstances. The *Review* took a solid
middle line between aristocracy and democracy, and its contents
contributed to William Cobbett's scorn of 'Scotch feelosophy'. But if
the *Review* thus donned an eighteenth-century guise, its pleas to
implement timely reform before a French-type revolution occurred in
Britain were more 'modern'. That was the burden of the celebrated
review published in October 1808, 'Don Pedro Cevallos on the French
Usurpation of Spain', which provoked the establishment of a rival
Tory *Quarterly Review* as well as tainting the *Edinburgh Review*
as Jacobinical. The Tory Lockhart regarded 'Mr Jeffrey and the Edinburgh reviewers, as the legitimate progeny of the sceptical philosophers
of the last age.'[52] The *Review* displayed all its Whiggery when noting
that as society advanced and developed the consequential heightening
of public awareness and education was bound to agitate the people. If
a calamity akin to that in France were to be avoided, there would have
to be suitable adjustments made to the constitution.[53] The *Review*
duly reflected its origins and anticipated the future turn of British
politics.

The story is much the same with economics. The *Review* advocated
that political economy be taught both to working men and their employ-
ers because it was a useful educational and social discipline. It deeply
believed in the value of the science to the actual workings of society.
The *Review* harked back because it was Smithian, adhering to such
tenets as self-interest and free trade; on the other hand the *Review*
was required to pass opinion on current economic problems and on
contexts that Smith could not have visualised. The main writers on
economic matters were two former students of Stewart, who had had
Smith purveyed to them almost undiluted, Francis Horner and John
Ramsay M'Culloch. Both believed in the educational importance
of political economy because it facilitated national prosperity and the
welfare of the individual. Since economic problems came to the fore
simultaneously with the *Review's* concern for them, the *Review,*
consequently, became a significant organ of economic opinion on all
the important questions such as the monetary standard, (Horner
favoured cash payments), banking policy, taxation, the corn laws,

population, the poor laws, Ireland's economic condition and the East India Company monopoly. The alignment of the *Review* with the bourgeoisie was later emphasised under M'Culloch, who was an avowed Ricardian.[54] In its similarity of concerns and views, therefore, as well as in its origins, the *Review* was a new institution of the Scottish Enlightenment. It made possible the dissemination of its ideas into the new and different era that was early industrial society.

III

The last new institutions to be considered are the museums and the botanical gardens, which were but sensible developments if the lessons of Newton and Bacon were to be implemented. The museum and gardens belonged to universities and were amply used in the teaching process. Edinburgh had the most museums and a succession of botanical gardens from the late-seventeenth century to early-nineteenth century but Glasgow and Marischal, Aberdeen, did not lack them. Indeed it was the lavish provision in Edinburgh that, in the opinion of one witness to the 1826 Commission, prevented Marischal alumni in India, who already sent some articles of natural history to the north-eastern museum, from sending more. If the Aberdeen facilities could only match those of Edinburgh, then he was sure articles of interest would be forthcoming.[55]

The outstanding museum of the Scottish Enlightenment was the Natural History Museum of the University of Edinburgh. The University could also claim to have a collection of natural philosophy apparatus; a museum of anatomical preparations; a considerable collection of pharmaceutical apparatus and an extensive collection of materia medica and alimentaria which constituted the materia medica museum; a midwifery museum consisting of a collection of preparations and apparatus used in the teaching of the subject; and a small collection of surgical apparatus, instruments, models of machines for transporting sick and wounded and similar equipment used in the teaching of military surgery. There was a problem concerning the ownership of all these collections and small museums. It was unclear at the time of the Commission if they belonged to the chair, to the professor personally, to the University or even to the Town Council who sometimes contributed, albeit minimally, to their purchase and upkeep. Consequently, there were often difficulties if a professor died, and his successor might have to amass a new collection. The question of property underlies the pre-bureaucractic nature of the eighteenth-century Scottish University.

Nonetheless the widespread concern in medical or para-medical subjects, especially for visual aids, confirm the concern for effective teaching that was a hallmark of the Scottish Enlightenment. The museums could also be causes of expense and concern: the professor of anatomy testified that not only did the City provide annually twelve gallons of whisky for his museum but that it was full of other combustible materials which could easily lead to the destruction of the whole building.[56]

Glasgow University, in 1807, inherited the famed Hunterian Museum. William Hunter (1718-83) was one of two eminent medical brothers who, after a period as Cullen's assistant, had moved to London where he became a noted teacher and practitioner of medicine, midwifery and especially anatomy. He collected a remarkable museum and library consisting of books, prints, copperplates, drawings, pictures, medals and coins, anatomical preparations of every kind, fossils and ores, shells, corals, other marine productions, birds, insects, other preserved animals, dried plants and curiosities from the South Seas. He bequeathed them, their cabinets and cases to the University of Glasgow where he had studied, as well as £8,000 to erect a building for them, to maintain them and to provide lectures. The Museum was to be useful both to the students and public of Glasgow.[57] Following some terms in Hunter's will, the Museum arrived in Glasgow in 1807, late in the Enlightenment but coming at a time when the teaching of medicine and natural history were becoming established in the west of Scotland. In fact, the material that might have been useful to anatomy was decrepit, and while the articles of natural history were of greater value, students were unable to examine them minutely in the Museum, since they were allowed in only once per session.[58] Consequently, while the Museum itself testified to the interests and concerns of the Enlightenment, it was not harnessed to teaching as was the Edinburgh Natural History Museum.

The Edinburgh museum was built up in a proprietary way by the successive professors of natural history. The obscurity as to who owned collections could lead to professors positively rejecting the accumulations of their predecessors. John Walker, for example, on assuming the chair, wrote in 1780 of Robert Ramsay's Museum:

The greater part of it is mere rubbish, that can never be of any use. Some parts of it, particularly many birds and fishes ought to be immediately thrown out, being so over run with moths and other insects, that no animal preparations can be placed with safety in the room, till they are removed.[59]

Robert Jameson in his turn spoke of Walker's Museum thus:

> The speciment were of birds, serpents, minerals and dresses and
> weapons of savage nations. The birds were in so decayed a state,
> that I was forced very soon to throw them out, and thus the
> original collection was reduced to a few glasses of serpents, a small
> collection of minerals, and the arms and dresses already
> mentioned.[60]

Walker was responsible for bringing a new museum together: he urged
the Town Council to raise subscriptions for buying collections that were
for sale and to persuade Scotsmen to present objects.[61] Jameson made
a wider appeal: between 1804 and 1819, he enlisted the support of the
University authorities, the Town Council, the Commissioners for the
College Buildings and Lord Castlereagh in the fitting up of a museum
that was described to the 1826 Commission as 'probably the fourth
or fifth collection in Europe'. By the time of the Commission, those
articles of Natural History brought home by expeditions fitted out
at public expense, were deposited partly in the British Museum and
partly in the Museum in the University. Castlereagh agreed to ask
British Government servants abroad to send objects to the Museum:
'it will give me the truest satisfaction, if I shall be enabled to further
the views of the University . . . and the promote those particular
objects to which you point my attention', he wrote in 1807. Joseph
Planta, Castlereagh's secretary, was among those who sent items and he
addressed the package to his employer. Successful applications were
lodged with the Lords of the Treasury for Customs exemption on such
items as the Dufresne Collection in 1819.[62] This material, formerly
the possession of an assistant at the Jardins des Plantes in Paris, was
sold to the University of Edinburgh despite higher bids from the
Emperors of Austria and Russia.[63] Government co-operation went still
further: the Admiralty ordered Rear-Admiral Otway, stationed at
Leith, to send a vessel from Leith to Le Havre to bring over the Dufresne
Collection. The University expressed its gratitude to Castlereagh for securing objects of interest for the Museum from foreign dependencies
and for arranging special passage through Customs.[64]

Jameson was responsible for rebuilding the Museum to a distinctive
position in Britain and Europe. The University and Town Council had
co-operated by increasing the space available to the College Buildings to

house the purchases and donations. James Hutton's minerals, bequeathed to Joseph Black, and then entrusted to the Edinburgh Royal Society, were among the collections. In 1804, Jameson was provided with 'a very spacious and handsome museum'. The increase of material, especially after the appeal to Castlereagh, convinced the Commissioners for the College Buildings of the urgent need to expand the museum space so that storage, with its attendant risk of damage, would not be necessary. By 1820, there was a larger museum in the new College. In 1826, when the collection had doubled yet again, Jameson received further consideration from the Buildings' Commissioners. He ordered a suite of five rooms and envisaged his Museum equalling the distinguished museums of the world. By the time of his death in 1854, the Museum contained 40,000 specimens of rocks and minerals, geographically arranged; 10,000 specimens of fossils: 800 specimens of crania and skeletons; 8,000 birds; 900 fishes and reptiles; 900 invertebrate animals; many thousand speciments of insects; 300 specimens of insects, 300 specimens of recent shells and valuable collections of drawings, casts, models, geological and geographical maps, and instruments used in the surveying of countries.[65] It has been said that Jameson rebuilt the Museum upon assuming the Keepership and Chair of Natural History in succession to John Walker in 1804. One reason for the alleged deficiency of Walker's Museum was that his trustees removed his collection when he died.

The Museum can be seen as yet another example of the Town Council's willingness to enhance the intellectual distinction of its University, by generously providing facilities for the pursuit of natural history. The Museum was fully used for teaching purposes. Once Jameson was entrenched as its keeper, however, the Museum also became enmeshed in the Huttonian-Wernerian debate, in that it was brandished as a weapon by Jameson in the Wernerian cause. The extent to which he used his position for doctrinal ends was made abundantly clear when the 1826 Commission began to take its evidence. Jameson was convinced of the importance of such instruments as museums and field excursions in teaching his students and in furthering knowledge. Lectures were insufficient in themselves, there had to be first-hand contact with materials. This was his rationale for the efforts which made the Museum one of the leading five in Europe. Jameson was the leading Wernerian in Edinburgh. By 1804, the Huttonian school was being led by his colleague, John Playfair, who saw the issue clearly:

The theory of Dr. Hutton stands here precisely on the same footing
with the system of Copernicus; for there is no reason to suppose
that it was the purpose of revelation to furnish a standard of
geological any more than of astronomical science. It is admitted,
on all hands, that the Scriptures are not intended to resolve physical
questions, or to explain matters in no way related to the morality
of human actions; and if, in consequence of this principle, a considerable latitude of interpretation were not allowed, we should
continue at this moment to believe, that the earth is flat; that the
sun moves round the earth; and the circumference of a circle is no
more than three times its diameter. It is reasonable, therefore,
that we should extend to the geologist the same liberty of speculation
which the astronomer and mathematician are already in possession
of; and this may be done, by supposing that the chronology of
Moses relates only to the human race. This liberty is not more
necessary to Dr. Hutton than to other theorists.[66]

The Commission was flooded with complaints, notably from the Royal
Society of Edinburgh. Sir George Steuart Mackenzie (a distinguished
mineralogist), Samuel Hibbert (also a celebrated mineralogist and
antiquary) and Sir David Brewster (the natural philosopher, inventor
of the kaleidoscope and later Principal of the Universities of St Andrews
and Edinburgh. The substances of the complaints was that Jameson
restricted entry to the Museum and only exhibited in it materials and
collections which supported the Wernerian hypothesis.

Jameson told the Commission that he admitted applicants for entry
to the Museum only if they would do credit to the academic establishment, the University of Edinburgh, and this credit he assumed for
himself. When asked how the University's reputation would be involved,
he said that unscientific drawings and descriptions emanating from the
Museum would hazard the scientific character of the Keeper. Jameson,
therefore, at the time of the Commission, had the power to decide
what was of credit to science, and at his own discretion could exclude
scientists from one of the finest collections in Europe. As he was
heavily committed to the Wernerian thesis, the power was abused.
Jameson excluded men who by any acceptable standards were scientific
worthies.

In their petition to the Commission, signed by the President, Sir
Walter Scott, the Royal Society of Edinburgh claimed admission to
the Museum where Hutton's collection of minerals was housed. The
collection was designed to explain the principles of geology and to

illustrate the changes through which mineral substances went. The Society's charter forbade its making any collection or museum and so Hutton's minerals had been placed in the University's Museum. The Society sought a new charter in 1808 because of the inconvenience caused by having to refer to Jameson every time a visit to the minerals was intended. Under the terms of the 1808 charter, the old collections became University property, but members of the Royal Society were to be admitted to the Natural History Museum. However, in recent years the Keeper refused admittance to members. Sir David Brewster spoke, as a curator of the Huttonian Collection, of its value in illustrating Hutton's theory of the Earth. Other valuable articles belonging to the Society and housed in the Museum included a collection presented by Captain James Cook, from the South Sea Islands. It is clear that the Commissioners themselves dropped a bombshell when they announced that they had asked to see Hutton's minerals and had discovered that the collection had never been opened by Jameson—'It was shown to the Commissioners in boxes'.

Sir George Mackenzie told the Commission that he had brought back from his expedition to Iceland in 1810-11 a very large and intersting collection of valuable specimens. He divided them in two, giving one part to the Royal Society and the other to the College Museum. He had not had a chance to label the specimens at the time of the donation and Jameson had never since let him do so. His collection supported views other than those of Jameson. When asked if specimens in favour of the Huttonian system were generally or at all exhibited to the Public, Mackenzie replied that they were not. The only beneficiaries of the material exhibited in the Museum were Jameson's students and the members of the Wernerian Society which Jameson had founded.

Brewster voiced more complaints: the William Thomson of Palermo bequest was not exhibited. Further, he required specimens from the Museum to aid his research into mineralogy and its connection with optics, but had difficulty in obtaining the specimens. The horticulturalist, Robert Kay Greville, elaborated on Brewster's difficulties with Jameson: the two men were not on good terms and also edited rival journals. Yet, admission to the Museum was vital for Brewster if he was to illustrate his discoveries in crystallography. This was an example of Jameson's arbitrary refusal to admit certain people and his personal feelings were inhibiting scholarship.

Some of the complaints to the Commission were by men who had no personal axe to grind against Jameson and yet were disturbed by his policy. Indeed two of Jameson's former students were sufficiently

moved to give evidence. Henry Hulme-Cheek, President of the
Edinburgh Royal Medical Society, complained that he was unable to
see a skeleton in the Museum and that it was imperative that he do so
for a work on comparative anatomy. Along with William Ainsworth,
President of the Edinburgh Royal Physical Society, Cheek attacked
Jameson in 1830, in the pages of the *Edinburgh Journal of Natural
and Geographical Science* (which they jointly edited). They belaboured
him for the poor scholarship of the Wernerian Society and for taking
for his own use papers that ought to have formed part of the *Transactions*. Only Daniel Ellis, a horticulturalist, defended the professor
on the grounds that it was one of the Keeper's perquisites to have the
first claim on Museum materials for his own research and writing.
The judgement of the Royal Commission was that

> the whole arrangement is brought too much under the control of
> one individual who acts according to his own opinion and discretion.
> In the present case, his private interests interfere with the manage-
> ment of a great public institution.[67]

Although Jameson abused his position as Keeper in a partisan Wernerian
fashion, a distinction has to be drawn between his activities as Keeper
and Professor. Despite the 'exercise of his discretion', there is no
doubt that his course and museum were intensely valuable both in
prosecuting research in natural history and in the training of naturalists.
Despite the Wernerian curriculum, Huttonian mineralogists and natural
scientists emerged. If this educational aspect was one part of the
University's contribution to natural history in the period, it also had a
part in the realm of geological theory. The University was the battle-
ground for Huttonians and Wernerians and its importance was not
limited to British science and society. Similarly, if the Natural History
Museum had a place as a teaching instrument, it was also a weapon in
the intellectual dispute. In both respects it was an intimate institution
of the Scottish Enlightenment.

The Botanical Gardens in Edinburgh began in the late-seventeenth
century and were closely linked with the concern then beginning to be
shown for medical education in the City. Before the eighteenth century
began, there were three gardens, the Physick Garden, the Botanic Garden
and the King's Garden at Holyrood. James Sutherland, the first attendant and professor of botany, laid the foundations for the later work
that complemented advances in medicine, medical education and
botany itself. It was not until 1738 that both the personnel and the

circumstances were propitious for continuing his work when Charles Alston (1638-1760) became professor, participated in the medical curriculum and employed to full effect the lessons he learned under Boerhaave at Leyden. Indeed Boerhaave was one among many who sent him seeds to develop at the Garden. In his research, Alston attacked Linnaeus' sexual classification of plants since he denied that sex even existed in them. John Hope (1725-86) was appointed professor both of botany and materia medica in 1760, and was able to move the Garden to Leith Walk in 1763, where it occupied five acres. Atmospheric pollution as well as expansion had been among the reasons prompting the move, and with it came for the first time, a financial endowment from the Crown. The Garden was now clearly divided into medical and botanical sections. Unlike Alston, Hope was a Linnaean. He took great pains to use the Garden for teaching purposes by means of living material, by diagrams and by experiments. His keenness for teaching systematisation stemmed from his Linnaean views, he encouraged students to explore on their own the flora of Scotland, and he awarded an annual gold medal for the best student herbarium.

Like so many of the new institutions of the Scottish Enlightenment the Botanic Garden cannot be separated from the teaching of the subject with which it was associated. While Hope's successor was not as keen on the Garden, he had the initiative to secure from Kew the services of the foreman gardener there, William McNab, who arrived in Edinburgh in 1810. His task was not that of a teacher but he built up the collection, introduced numerous new plants and trees to Scotland, went on botanical expeditions with the students, and contributed to the founding of the Leith Walk Linnean Society. By the time Robert Graham (1786-1845) moved from the Glasgow chair to that of Edinburgh in 1820, the time had come for yet another move to a new site, since five acres no longer sufficed. The new site (the present one) was in Inverleith and extended over fourteen and a half acres. The move took two years and McNab was immersed in the task, incurring not a single loss, not even that of a yew tree which had grown in the first botanic garden and which survived the two transfers. The difference between Hope and Graham was similar to that between Walker and Jameson. Graham included in his curriculum field trips of over fifteen miles on Saturdays, and was not content merely to exhort. He had a large, light conservatory where students could see shrubs and flowers especially gathered for his lectures.[68] It was to be expected that Glasgow's Botanic Garden would lag behind that of Edinburgh, because medical and scientific education as a whole in Glasgow was behind. In 1813, the nucleus of the Garden was formed, and then established on an eight-acre site west of Sauchiehall Street. Graham was appointed to be the first professor in 1818.[69]

The new institutions of the Scottish Enlightenment both fostered and reflected the real intellectual developments of the age. Their manifest forms, from societies to periodicals and to museums, also bore witness to the versatility of the movement and to the co-operative social and critical spirit which characterised it.

Notes

1.   D. D. McElroy, *Scotland's Age of Improvement: A Survey of Eighteenth Century Literary Clubs and Societies* (Washington State U.P., 1969); D. D. McElroy, *A Century of Scottish Clubs, 1700-1800* (Edinburgh, 1969) in typescript in all the main Edinburgh libraries and D. D. McElroy, *The Literary Clubs and Societies of Eighteenth Century Scotland, and their influence on the literary productions of the period from 1700 to 1800*, Ph.D. dissertation, University of Edinburgh, 1952. References, given as 'McElroy p. . . . ', are to *Scotland's Age of Improvement*.

2.   Ph.D. dissertation (University of Pennsylvania, 1971).

3.   John Playfair, 'Dissertation; exhibiting a General View of the Progress of Mathematical and Physical Science since the Revival of Letters in Europe', *Works*, 4 vols. (Edinburgh, 1822), II, pp. 212-20.

4.   'Memoirs of Dr. Wallace of Edinburgh', *Scots Magazine*, XXXIII (1771), pp. 340-1 ; Dugald Stewart, *Collected Works*, I (1854), p. 351 and G. E. Davie, 'Berkeley's Impact on Scottish Philosophers', *Philosophy*, XL (1965), pp. 222-3.

5.   Colin McLaurin, 'An Account of the Life and Writings of the Author', *An Account of Sir Isaac Newton's Philosophical Discoveries* (London, 1748), p. vii; McElroy, pp. 27-30 and Steven Shapin, 'Property, Patronage, and the Politics of Science: the Founding of the Royal Society of Edinburgh', *British Journal for the History of Science*, VII (1974), pp. 6-11.

6.   Alexander Carlyle, *Anecdotes and Characters of the Times*, ed. James Kinsley (London, O.U.P. 1973), p. 38 and McElroy, pp. 30-1, 40-1.

7.   McElroy, pp. 40-4.

8.   James McCosh, *The Scottish Philosophy* (London 1875), p. 228; John Veitch, 'Philosophy in the Scottish Universities', *Mind*, old series, II (1877), p. 215 and Walter R. Humphries, 'The First Aberdeen Philosophical Society', *Transactions of the Aberdeen Philosophical Society*, V (1938), pp. 203-6, 218, 219-36.

9.   J. B. Morrell, 'Reflections on the History of Scottish Science', *History of Science*, XII (1974), pp. 89-91.

10.   Stewart, *Works*, X, pp. 203-7 and McElroy, pp. 48-67.

11.   McElroy, p. 78.

12.   Shapin, pp. 11-22.

13.   *Ibid.*, pp. 22-35.

14.   *Caledonian Mercury*, 29 November 1792.

15. Thomas Thomson, 'History and Present State of Chemical Science', *Edinburgh Review*, L (1829), pp. 264-5 and V. A. Eyles, 'The Evolution of a Chemist: Sir James Hall Bt., FRS., PRSE., of Dunglass, Haddington-shire (1761-1832), and his relations with Joseph Black, Antoine Lavoisier and other scientists of the period', *Annals of Science*, XIX (1963), pp. 154, 158-9, 172, 174-5.

16. See Appendix for a select list of papers which indicates the kind of matters that interested the Society and the original papers read to it.

17. Steven Shapin, 'The Audience for Science in Eighteenth Century Edinburgh' *History of Science*, XII (1974), p. 111 and C. P. Finlayson, 'Records of Scientific and Medical Societies preserved in the University library, Edinburgh, *The Bibliotheck*, I (1958), p. 19.

18. Jessie M. Sweet, 'The Wernerian Natural History Society in Edinburgh', *Freiberger Forschungshefte* (223 Mineralogie-Lagerstattenlehre Abraham Gottlob Werner Gedenkschrift aus Anlass der Wiederkehr series Torestages nach 150 Jahren am 30 Juni 1967) p. 215.

19. Carlyle, pp. 213-6 and the quotation is given in McElroy, p. 167.

20. Playfair, *Works*, IV, pp. 116-7 and McElroy, p. 169.

21. Harry A. Cockburn, 'An Account of the Friday Club, written by Lord Cockburn, together with notes on certain other Social Clubs in Edinburgh', *The Book of the Old Edinburgh Club*, III (Edinburgh, 1910), pp. 108-9, 112.

22. W. J. Stuart, *History of the Aesculapian Club*, Edinburgh, 1949, pp. 3, 11, 12-15, 28-9.

23. Edinburgh University Library Ms.Dc. 6. 11. folios 163-4.

24. McElroy, pp. 131-2; John Thomson, *An Account of the Life, Lectures and Writings of William Cullen, M.D.*, 2 vols. (Edinburgh, 1832-59), Annex to II, p. 12; *Dissertations by Eminent Members of the Royal Medical Society*, (Edinburgh, 1792), pp. 32-9, 40-63, 64-83, 84-94; J. D. Comrie, *History of Scottish Medicine*, 2 vols., 2nd ed. (London, 1932), I, p. 315; and *Memoirs of the Life of the Right Honourable Sir James Mackintosh*, ed. Robert James Mackintosh, 2 vols. (London, 1835), I, pp. 23, 24, 25, 26, 30.

25. Finlayson, p. 17.

26. McElroy, pp. 128-30.

27. *Ibid.*, pp. 120-3.

28. I would here acknowledge that Encyclopaedia Britannica International, at the instigation of the late Senator William Benton, and under the supervision of John Armitage Esq., financed a research project from 1968-1970 during which research on the origins and early history of the *Encyclopaedia Britannica* was undertaken.

29. *Caledonian Mercury*, 25 June 1785.

30. Edinburgh University Library, Ms. Dc. 2.57. Letter 195 and Thomas Constable *Archibald Constable and His Literary Correspondents*, 3 vols. (Edinburgh, 1873), II, pp. 319-20, British Museum, Add. Mss, 34360, folio 191 and 22.

31. Henry Cockburn, *Memorials of his Time* (Edinburgh, (1856), p. 45.

32. Dr Geoffrey Cantor of the University of Leeds has an article forthcoming in *Social Studies in Science* on the Academy.

33. *Correspondence Book of the Academy of Physics* Edinburgh, National Library of Scotland, Ms. 755, pp. 24-5. Letter dated 20 February 1798.

34. Francis Jeffrey (1773-1850) studied at the universities of Glasgow, Edinburgh and Oxford; a founder and editor of the *Edinburgh Review* he was an active lawyer, being Dean of the Faculty of Advocates in 1829 and Lord Advocate in 1830. As MP for Malton and for Edinburgh he was

one of the drafters of the muddled Scottish Reform Act of 1832. Regarded as one of the most able literary figures and critics of his age.

35.   John Clive, *Scotch Reviewers: The Edinburgh Review 1802-15* (London, Faber and Faber, 1957).

36.   I shall only cover these matters relatively briefly for the present purposes, since I consider it more appropriate to give education and politics greater consideration in my subsequent study on the evolution of Victorian society.

37.   My attention to the Stewart-Jeffrey debate was drawn by Dr G. E. Davie, especially in his 'The Social Significane of the Scottish Philosophy of Common Sense', *The Dow Lecture*, University of Dundee, 1973, pp. 14-16.

38.   Francis Jeffrey, 'Stewart's Life of Dr. Reid', *Edinburgh Review*, III (1804) pp. 273-7. The quotations are from pp. 274, 275, 276.

39.   Francis Jeffrey, 'Stewart's Philosophical Essays', *Edinburgh Review,* XVII (1810), pp. 173-86. The quotations are from pp. 175, 177 and 183.

40.   J. H. Newman, *Historical Sketches: the Rise and Progress of Universities* (London, 1872), pp. 181 and 182.

41.   *Edinburgh Review*, XI (1808), pp. 249-84; XIV (1809), pp. 429-41; XV (1809), pp. 40-53;XVI(1810),pp. 158-87 and XVII(1810–, pp. 122-35. Most were reprinted in Playfair's *Works.* The reviewers of Continental science had a part in a bigger story of science and society following the French Revolution: see J. B. Morrell, 'Professors Robison and Playfair, and the *Theophobia Gallica:* Natural Philosophy, Religion and Politics in Edinburgh 1789-1815', *Notes and Records of the Royal Society of London* XXVI (1971), pp. 43-63.

42.   Stewart, *Collected Works*, II (1954), pp. 229-30; VII (1855), pp. 10 and 17; IX (1856), pp. 346-7 and VII (1855), p. 330.

43   *Edinburgh Review*, XLIII (1825-6), p. 245; XLVI (1827), pp. 38 and 234-5.

44.   *Edinburgh Review*, XLII (1825), pp. 223 and 356; XLIII, p. 11.

45.   Clive, pp. 137-9.

46.   *The Works of John Playfair*, IV, p. 258. See also Morrell, pp. 56-9.

47.   Playfair, *Works*, IV, pp. 263-9, 321-3; Richard Olson, 'Scottish Philosophy and Mathematics 1750-1830', *Journal of the History of Ideas*, XXXII (1971), p. 30; Playfair, *Works*, pp. 333-79.

48.   *Edinburgh Review*, XVIII (1811), pp. 80-97; XIX (1811), pp. 207-29; XIX (1812), pp. 416-35; XXI (1813), pp. 50-72; XXII (1814), pp. 454-75; XXIV (1814), pp. 133-57; XXV (1815), pp. 455-85 and XXVI (1816) pp. 36-51.

49   Henry Cockburn, *Life of Lord Jeffrey with a selection from his correspondence*, 2 vols. (Edinburgh, 1852) II, p. 139.

50.   Clive, pp. 145-6, 179-80.

51.   Stewart, *Works*, IX, pp. 445-6; 'Cobbett's *Political Register*', *Edinburgh Review*, X (1807), pp. 386-421.

52   *Edinburgh Review*, XIII (1808), pp. 215-34; J. G. Lockhart, *Peter's Letters to his Kinsfolk,* 3 vols., 2nd ed. (Edinburgh, 1819), II, p. 128.

53.   See, for example, Jeffrey and Brougham's articles, respectively on 'Parliamentary Reform' and 'Leckie on the British Government', *Edinburgh Review*, XVII (1811), pp. 281-2 and XX (1812), pp. 331-2.

54.   F. W. Fetter, 'The Economic Articles in the Quarterly Review and their Authors, 1809-1852', *Journal of Political Economy*, LXVI (1958), p. 47 and F. W. Fetter, 'The Authorship of Economic Articles in the *Edinburgh Review* 1802-1847', *Journal of Political Economy*, LXI (1953), pp. 234 and 238.

55. Aberdeen evidence, p. 101.
56. Edinburgh evidence, pp. 168-9 and 274.
57. Glasgow evidence, p. 541.
58. Glasgow evidence, pp. 195-6 and Report, p. 284.
59. John Walker to Lord Provost and Town Council of Edinburgh,
     21 March 1780. McLeod's Bundle 16, Shelf 36, Bay C, Edinburgh City
     Chambers.
60. Edinburgh evidence, p. 167.
61. Letter, n.d. 1785, McLeod's Bundle 16, Shelf 36, Bay C, Edinburgh
     City Chambers.
62. Edinburgh evidence, p. 144, 145, 182], [183, and 182]-184] for an
     extensive list of objects secured with Government co-operation and
     exempted by the authorities from import duty.
63. Ibid., p. 146 [Edinburgh] College Minutes, vol. iii, p. 183, 187, 190
     list further purchases including the collection of the reputable traveller,
     naturalist and antiquarian, William Bullock.
64. Edinburgh evidence, p. 182 and College Minutes, vol. iii, p. 225, 19 May
     1820.
65. Edinburgh evidence, pp. 167-8 and 'Professor Jameson', *Gentleman's
     Magazine*, XLI (1854), p. 657.
66. John Playfair, 'Illustration of the Huttonian Theory', *Works*, I, p. 137.
67. Edinburgh evidence, p. 491; Report, p. 178; Edinburgh evidence, pp.
     178] [179-80] 558, 559, 618, 619, 620, 621, 626, 622-3, 627-9;
     Edinburgh Journal of Natural and Geographical Science II (1830), p.
     269; Edinburgh evidence, p. 571 and Report, p. 178.
68. Harold R. Fletcher and William H. Brown, *The Royal Botanic Garden
     Edinburgh 1670-1970* (Edinburgh, HMSO 1970), pp. 11-13, 40-3, 58-61,
     80-6, 103-12 and Charles Ransford, *Biographical sketch of the late
     Robert Graham* (Edinburgh, 1846), pp. 15, 19, 20.
69. Fletcher and Brown, pp. 96 and 103.

8 CONCLUSION AND INTERPRETIVE

By 1830, the Scottish Enlightenment was over. Its end was a gradual one, probably setting in from about 1780, but there were periodic revivals such as the theory of Hutton in the 1780s, the writings of John Millar and the foundation of the *Review*. However, from the mid-1820s the former relatively disinterested concern for knowledge no longer asserted itself. The death of the Scottish Enlightenment was caused by a growing malignancy in the institutions which had supported it, and through which it had been expressed. As the pillars or the infra-structure crumbled, so too inevitably did the superstructure.

There were two major changes of atmosphere from the 1780s, in which the Enlightenment was going to be required to operate but which slowly suffocated it. The first was the increasing party politic-isation of the traditional and new institutions, and the second was industrialisation. Both were to prove fatal. Politics had always pervaded Scottish society throughout the Enlightenment, from the triumph of the Whigs in 1688-9, to the collapse of the Jacobite '45, and also to the activities, on a local level, of such bodies as the Edinburgh Town Council. Political considerations were nothing new; nor were they ever far below the surface prior to the accession of George III. It is clear, however, that from then on the whole political atmosphere became charged: not because of the political activities of the monarch himself, which have traditionally been seen as the causes of the more lively and divided political scene in Britain in the late-eighteenth century. Rather it was the rise of a host and succession of controversial issues which caused a breakdown of the old way in which British politics had operated. Formerly politics rested on the basis of family ties, tradition and the stand taken in 1688. Over a considerable period of at least fifty years a system emerged, more recognisable to modern eyes, where politicians divided on grounds of principle or ideology. If it is remembered that the thirty last years of the eighteenth century saw successive governments having to tackle such problems as Wilkes, parliamentary reform and patronage, the American troubles and war, the East India Company monopoly, the French Revolution and consequent war, Roman Catholic emancipation and the Test Acts, the Irish question, income tax, all of which matters involved principle and not mere administration, then it can be seen how charged a political atmosphere existed nationally and internationally. No intellectual side of British life could hope to escape the repercussions, nor escape being affected by them.

The Scottish Enlightenment was no exception. Scotland as a political unit consisted of a number of crucial seats that together have been said to constitute a rotten political borough. As the Tories through Henry Dundas, following the equally adept management earlier of Argyll and Bute, cemented their hold on Scotland, so too did they seek to control other areas of Scottish life that were potential sources of Whig opposition, such as the Church, Legal System and Universities. Consequently, there could be grounds for such descriptions of the Moderates as 'the Dundas interest at prayer', or there arose bitter political struggles within the Faculty of Advocates for its Deanship, which was won by the Whig Henry Erskine in 1785, or manoeuvrings to secure the appointment of safe political candidates to vacant university chairs, or attempts to thwart the Whig Earl of Buchan from founding the rival Society of Antiquaries to the Royal Society of Edinburgh. The party politicisation became so much more marked after the French Revolution when the Law sported a clutch of reactionary judges hell-bent on suppressing Jacobins, when the ruling Moderates in the Kirk adhered to their old war-cry of order but for political not ecclesiastical reasons, and when university professors had to watch what they said in lectures for fear of being branded as revolutionaries and perverters of youth. The politics of the *Edinburgh Review* and the religious backlash to Hutton's theory in the aftermath of the French Revolution are perfectly consonant: politics and party principle were, by the early-nineteenth century, of consuming interest and importance, and were backed by the intellectual social theory of the earlier Scottish Enlightenment. Hutton was a victim of the fear which resulted from the destruction of so many of the old certainties, and it was but natural for many to resist his apparent questioning of the Bible.

Simultaneously, Britain was becoming the first industrial nation. Among the consequences for Scotland was the solution of a problem which had for at least two generations plagued her, and to which she had remained most sensitive, namely questions of union and assimilation. The industrial revolution was a British phenomenon, not merely an English one. It amalgamated the two countries in a way that no mere treaty could have done, and made such cities as Manchester and Glasgow more alike than the cities of Edinburgh and Glasgow. The

Scottish Enlightenment suffered as a result: while it had been in part a movement which had sought to make the most of English intellectual influences channelled through traditional Scottish institutions to make the union a success, it was itself snuffed out by a much more blunt and less subtle instrument working for union, namely industrialisation.

The horizons of talented Scots were broadened by industrialisation, not least through the unifying of the economy and the sharing of. social circumstances. A host of new careers was opened up, in journalism, administration, politics, professional science, medicine. Consequently, the young men who in former years would have succeeded to and been content with university chairs in Scotland, church livings and places in the Scottish legal system, and who would have spent their leisure time in co-operative intellectual pursuits, now commonly left Scotland for the lucrative and personally rewarding South, or remained in Scotland but in other, newer avocations. In other circumstances, for example, Francis Horner might well have succeeded to Dugald Stewart's chair of Moral Philosophy, or Francis Jeffrey to John Millar's chair of Law. However, the French wars brought aristocrats to Edinburgh who saw in Horner and others admirable candidates for their parliamentary seats, and Jeffrey, too, in the wider world of early nineteenth-century Britain, could find many fields in which to deploy his talents, and find satisfaction beyond that open to him in a chair, as a politician, literary critic and Dean of the Faculty of Advocates. In short, the natural successors of the *literati* did not take their places, and where those places were required to be filled, as with chairs, the calibre of the Scottish professoriate for a while declined, and when it rose again the Scottish Enlightenment had passed.

In the industrial age, too, as was demonstrated by the Jeffrey-Stewart debate in the pages of the *Edinburgh Review,* there seemed little place, in the view of the up and coming generation, for such pursuits as philosophy of the mind which had been so dominant a concern of the Enlightenment. The Scottish Enlightenment contributed to its own demise by 'the great multiplication' of the branches of study which had been a feature of the movement, and which, even by 1810, Jeffrey thought had contributed to the decline of philosophy.[1] The Scottish Enlightenment had little to say of a technical nature to an industrial society. Such Scottish technical contributors as did emerge from the eighteenth and early-nineteenth centuries (Watt and Telford to name but two) were not strictly part of the Scottish Enlightenment. The Scottish Enlightenment did, however, point out problems of an industrial society, such as alienation and the division of labour, and propose solutions, such as education. The movement also made distinctive contributions to the new age in the formulation of the discipline of economics as applied to commercial societies, and in laying down the foundations of systematic and professional medical education. The increasingly mechanised society that emerged from the eighteenth century, and to which non-technical areas the Scottish Enlightenment had contributed, found little place for a philosophical movement.

If increasing party politicisation and industrialisation made it progressively difficult for the Scottish Enlightenment to survive in any distinctive way, soo too did the removal, almost one by one, of the props which had supported it from its inception. The souring of the relationships between the Enlightenment and Scottish institutions had much to do with the two major causes of decline already delineated. Consider, first, the Kirk, which was left at the end of Chapter 3 with the Robertsonian Moderates duly managing affairs by 1780 but with Robertson himself in retirement from the Kirk and party leadership. Thereafter, the Moderates' outlook changed with civil circumstances. Robertson himself retired because he foresaw that with the rise of the Tory Dundas, his own association with the Whigs, Milton and Bute, could embroil the Church in secular politics. He anticipated the difficult times ahead.[2] There was thus removed from the Moderate leadership an influential and able manager. Prior to the French Revolution and wars the Moderates might well have been regarded as enlightened radicals: they led the agitation for a Scottish militia in the 1760s and 1770s; they led the campaign for ministers to be exempted from the window tax in the 1770s; they argued for burgh reform; they preached in the churches of the Edinburgh well-to-do on the moral obligations of the rich and powerful, and they condemned slavery and the slave-trade as early as 1755.

Under Principal George Hill of St Andrews, Robertson's successor as the Moderate leader, there was a wholesale change of approach. Whereas Robertson defended patronage on grounds of expediency, Hill took a tougher line emphasising that patronage was the law of the land. Whereas Robertson had argued for the co-operation of church and government because each needed the other, Hill, albeit operating in revolutionary times, cemented an alliance with Dundas. That alliance made the Scottish opposition to Dundas comprise not only the Whigs and proponents of reform, but also the Evangelicals. Leslie's Case in 1805 showed not only how far the Moderates had departed from Robertson's line of appointing the ablest of candidates to vacancies in livings or chairs, but how corrupted by power they had become. From being the radical critics of the 1750s the Moderates had become the establishment conservatives of the early 1800s, opposing, for example, the repeal of the Test Acts on the grounds that then was not the most appropriate time to consider such a move. The sympathy and close personal connections between the Moderates, the effective Church leadership, and the Scottish Enlightenment were sundered by 1805, when the last living philosophers, Stewart and Playfair, attacked the Kirk leaders over their attitude to Leslie. There was, by the nineteenth century, a great divide between Robertson's motto of *Vita sine literis mors est* or Carlyle's oft-quoted statement that clergy had by the 1760s written the best histories, the clearest delineation of human understanding, the best system of rhetoric, a tragedy deemed perfect, and the best treatise on agriculture, and the judgement of the writer, J. G. Lockhart in 1819, Lockhart noted the clergy's decline of interest in general literature.[3] Beyond the Enlightenment, the Moderate power complex ultimately led to the Disruption of 1843, the latest and greatest of secessions, secessions which had been conspicuous by their absence during the heyday of the Scottish Enlightenment. Harmony and integration, the social watchwords of the Robertsonian Moderates, were reversed by their successors and one pillar supporting the Scottish Enlightenment was, consequently, weakened.

The legal system was a second pillar whose support of the Scottish Enlightenment weakened. It is hard, however, to pinpoint a specific instance, such as was Leslie's Case in 1805 for the Kirk, when the Law can be said to be opposing the movement. Party politics, which had always been central to the interests of eighteenth-century Scottish lawyers, became more lively and ideological, and lawyers became even more involved with politics at the expense of other areas of Scottish life. Industrialisation too effected a change in the society in which Scots lawyers operated. It was no longer a Scotland that was experiencing agricultural improvement as had predominated in the early days and high period of the Scottish Enlightenment. Commercial law was developing and the balance of the economy was shifting west of the main legal centre in Scotland. In the eighteenth century the legal profession had been probably the one all-purpose entrée to a way of life that certainly in Edinburgh could hope to influence and mould a developing Scotland. But in time the centrality of the profession to Scottish life corrupted and narrowed it. As the Scottish legal system evolved so did it become more tied to self-generating professional concerns. As the Moderates' long tenure of power undermined their integrity and original ideas, so too, in time, did lawyers no longer play the literary and social part that had been common fifty and more years before 1820. Once again Lockhart in his satirical work, *Peter's Letters to his Kinsfolk* (1819), is a sharp contemporary observer of the situation. It became a way of life for advocates to seek mere office, of which there were many, and which they hoped to gain by virtue of blood or marriage or patronage. Consequently, the advocates were 'the chief community of loungers and talkers in Edinburgh'.[4]

A useful indication of the pretty pass to which reforming lawyers had come was the Reform Act (Scotland) of 1832, in the shaping of which Jeffrey and Cockburn had much to say. Muddled thinking, bad drafting, confusion and, more ironic yet, ignorance of Scots law, led to the creation of new abuses in the place of older ones which were abolished.[5] By the 1830s, it was perhaps unremarkable that youthful idealism had left those Whigs who had been nursed in the classrooms of Millar and Stewart, and who were tasting the responsibilities of power for the first time. They fell back on a gradualism strongly reminiscent of their teachers. Fifty or so years had passed and it was evident that new ideas to help solve the problems of the new society were not forthcoming from those who had emerged from the traditional avenue to Scottish public life, the Law. In the nineteenth century, the legal system was not so aware of or so connected with enlightenment and society. The French Revolution and the repression which followed it in Britain also gave to Scottish judges, in the 1790s, the opportunity to be so reactionary that they contrasted badly with those enlightened judges of a generation earlier. The most notorious was Robert Macqueen, Lord Braxfield, lord justice clerk, (1721-99) so viciously recalled by the Whig Cockburn in his *Memorials,* as the Jeffreys of Scotland:

Illiterate and without any taste for refined enjoyment, strength of understanding, which gave him power without cultivation, only encouraged him to a more contemptuous disdain of all natures less coarse than his own. Despising the growing improvement of manners, he shocked the feelings even of an age which, with more of the formality, had far less of the substance of decorum than our own.

His conduct as a criminal judge 'was a disgrace to the age'; he was cruel (not unlike Kames, however) and even was reported as saying 'Let them bring me prisoners, and I'll find them law.'[6] Consequently, the accuracy of the judgement of Lockhart, a bitter political opponent of Cockburn's, might be accepted, written in 1819:

> The uniform gravity of the Bench has communicated a suitable
> gravity to the Bar—the greater number of the practitioners at the
> Bar having, indeed, necessarily very much diminished the familiarity
> with which the Bench and the Bar were of old accustomed to treat
> each other; while the general change that has every where occurred in
> the mode of life, has almost entirely done away with that fashion of
> high conviviality in private, for which, of old, the members of the
> legal profession in this place were celebrated to a proverb. In short,
> it seems as if the business of all parties were now regarded in a much
> more serious point of view that formerly.[7]

In another work, Cockburn, writing in 1848, emphasised the importance
of the traditional institutions to the literature of the country. The Law
was for him 'the great field of our native practical talent' which had still
maintained literature in Scotland after the departure of the Crown and
Parliament. The paring down of Scottish judges implied that

> the profession most intimately connected with literature and public
> discussion must be narrowed and cooled into insignificance. The
> Church is now no high sphere: medicine has no connection with
> public life: our colleges are too poor to create for themselves the
> talent or learning which they cannot pay.[8]

In the nineteenth century, the third and last of the traditional pillars,
the Universities, were no longer providing able Scotsmen, by means of
chairs, with one of few intellectually rewarding and lucrative employments. Richer pickings were to be had in the South. Furthermore,
the Scottish university system was no longer unique. In 1828 there was
founded in London a university modelled on those of the North. It not
only drew off from the Scottish student body English dissenters,
but now provided an extended range of subjects including political
economy as in the Scottish Universities, it operated by the lecture
system and by that of class fees, students were not resident and they
could enrol for single courses. The professoriate, especially in medicine,
was drawn largely from Scotland. The foundation of the University
of London, supported by the *Edinburgh Review*, is another example of
the Scottish Enlightenment contributing to its own demise. The faith of
the movement in traditional Scottish higher education produced men
who wished to carry the message to others, and in founding a university
on the Scottish model, necessarily bled the home institutions of valuable

students and staff.

It is evident too that by the 1820s the Universities were facing many difficulties. The mammoth volumes of evidence to the 1826 Commission testify to some real problems that were being experienced, especially of a financial and administrative nature, and which had arisen not least from the growth experienced during the Scottish Enlightenment. But academic features were sharply questioned too, the shortness of the session, the lack of classics, especially as a preliminary to medicine, the lecture system, the proprietorial attitude of professors to institutions in their care or to their subjects. The days of pre-bureaucratic *laissez-faire* were clearly numbered, even if those of philosophical education were not. The Universities and their system were, in various other ways, manifestly not working as they had worked in the heyday of the Scottish Enlightenment. Consequently, they could no longer provide many spokes let alone be the hub of the movement.

The new institutions, too, illustrated how, by 1830 at the latest, the philosophical movement was over. It has already been seen that the literary class of the Royal Society of Edinburgh lasted a short time which, while not qualifying the scientific importance of the Society's work, did mean the loss of the broader philsoophic approach implicit in its origins. The *Edinburgh Review* lost Jeffrey in 1829: he and his fellow Edinburgh alumni grew out of their youthful idealism, and professors and *literati* who wrote for it died. By 1830, the period of transition between the Age of Enlightenment and the ages of industrialisation and of Victoria was over, and during the transition the *Review,* while it still maintained strong personal and intellectual connections with the Enlightenment, was a powerful agent. With the natural demise of those connections and in the course of its own development as a periodical, the *Review* became caught up in nineteenth-century concerns that looked beyond reforming Whig politics of the Liverpool era, Huttonian geology, political economy and mechanics' institutes. An offspring of the Scottish Enlightenment grew up and alone could not support a weak and dying parent. Symbolic of much else too, Constable, the Enlightenment's main publisher, went bankrupt early in 1826: the time was passed when sales of the works of philosophers, their text-books, the *Britannica* and *Review* were so great that they could mask indifferent business management.

In a sense, then, the Scottish Enlightenment was too successful, because it helped to create and develop circumstances and conditions in which it could no longer survive. In the end, the ultimate then known in improvement and political upheaval, economic growth and the after-

math of the French Revolution, swamped the Scottish Enlightenment.
Improvement and enlightenment had for well over a century co-existed
and enlightenment had 'taken off' from improvement. In the many ways
in which the Scottish Enlightenment had been expressed, there had
always been a thin dividing line between the two, that only the strictest
of definitions would permit of separating. Nonetheless (and here is
another story to be told) the Scottish Enlightenment was a lasting force
in the formation of the era that succeeded it, and with favourable
economic circumstances, it made possible the expression of a distict-
ive Scottish contribution to the United Kingdom, Europe and the wider
world, by exploiting institutions traditional to Scottish life and history.

II

The present study pretends to be the first of any length to account for,
and examine the social history of, the Enlightenment in Scotland.
However, the movement has not lacked interpreters over the years
and this study concludes by considering relationships between the
interpretation offered here and those of others. First, it is important
to bear in mind that politics have played a relatively small part in the
analysis offered here. It is not that they were very far from the surface
even prior to 1780; nor was the Scottish Enlightenment immune from
eighteenth-century 'management'. Nonetheless, Whiggery was an
accepted fact of life in the Scottish Enlightenment and it was even
stiffened by the intellectual or 'scientific' Whiggery of the philosophers.
It was not respectable to be Tory/Jacobite in the developing years of
the movement, nor in its heyday, and the Scottish establishment and
the authors were concerned to be accepted by the English. After about
1780, the party politics of the nations invaded the Scottish Enlightenment, and, as has been argued, did so to the overall detriment of
the movement.

Secondly, the current analysis has laid little emphasis on Scotland as
a province of England and on the part played in the Enlightenment by
the landed gentry and aristocracy, with their wings clipped and reduced
to the status of provincial grandees after 1707.[9] It cannot be denied
that many of the writers saw themselves as provincial to England,
looked to England as the standard of polite culture, and took pains
over the Scottishness of their speech. In any political or economic
sense, Scotland was clearly a province. However, in sheer intellectual
terms, in terms of the philosophy and science which prevailed in
Scotland, she was by no means inferior to England. In philosophic

and scientific terms she was a province, of if anywhere, the Continent of Europe. In Europe, the philosophers were not regarded as simply country cousins but as scholarly equals. Clearly, there was a tension between the political and intellectual environment in which the Scottish Enlightenment was required to thrive. Culturally, Scotland related to Europe in many ways, though politically she was being required to forge a new relationship with England. That the tension necessarily manifested itself in the Enlightenment does not detract from either Scottish philosophical and institutional superiority to England, or from the dialogue that took place during the Enlightenment with Europe rather than England. England's contributions came from Newton, Locke and Bacon, and it was the Scots and other Europeans who made the most of pioneering English work of the seventeenth century and earlier. The landed classes found in the Scottish Enlightenment a movement already well under way by 1707 and which, for their own reasons, they wanted to patronise. Their contribution, however, does not rank among the foremost reasons for the Enlightenment occurring in Scotland. The patrons were desirable but not necessary, and their desire to bestow patronage was matched by those of a very different social status, the burgesses of Edinburgh.

In terms of sheer wordage, the most substantial book which comprehended the Scottish Enlightenment was that of the nineteenth-century sociologist, Henry Thomas Buckle, whose *Introduction to the History of Civilisation in England* was first published between 1857 and 1861. The work contained a chapter entitled 'An Examination of the Scotch Intellect during the Eighteenth Century', in which Buckle attributed the Scottish Enlightenment to 'a reaction against that theological spirit which predominated during the seventeenth century'. He went on to elaborate his view by saying that the struggle against the Stuarts kept alive certain faculties in the Scots which, while devoted to practical ends in the seventeenth century, were redeployed in the peaceful conditions of the eighteenth century and became speculative, producing 'a literature which attempted to unsettle former opinions, and to disturb the ancient landmarks of the human mind'. That was the first explanation Buckle gave, and as will shortly be seen, his view clearly influenced the latest social history of Scotland, namely that by Professor Christopher Smout. Buckle was, of course, unaware of the developments in social and economic spheres in the seventeenth century which have been pointed out in this book, and which ultimately permitted the Enlightenment to develop. Buckle's own views made him see history through theocratic spectacles.

The second part of Buckle's explanation, relating to the nature of the Scottish Enlightenment, was particularly idiosyncratic: he fixed on two terms, deduction and induction, to which he ascribed his own definitions. Deduction was theory preceding experience and controlling it; particular principles are accepted without question and facts are forced to fit in with those principles. Induction was theory arising from experience; that facts would lead to the formulation of principles. Irrespective of the accuracy of these definitions or whether or not deduction and induction might be so arbitrarily opposed to each other, Buckle maintained that in his terms, religious belief was necessarily deductive, and such secular thought as was pitted against religious belief was necessarily inductive. One would, therefore, expect the thought of the Scottish Enlightenment to be inductive, but in fact it was all (in Buckleian terms) deductive. That it was so was the result of the clergy-ridden nature of Scotland and her history prior to the eighteenth century, and the consequent domination of the Scottish mind by deduction. Hence, to quote Buckle:

> The inductive or analytic spirit being thus unknown, and the deductive or synthetic spirit being along favoured, it happened that when, early in the eighteenth century, the circumstances already mentioned gave rise to a great intellectual movement, that movement, though new in its results, was not new in the method by which the results were obtained. A secular philosophy was indeed established, and the ablest men, instead of being theological, became scientific. But so completely had the theological plan occupied Scotland, that even philosophers were unable to escape from its method and . . . the inductive method excercised no influence over them. This most curious fact is the key to the history of Scotland in the eighteenth century, and explains many events which would otherwise appear incompatible with each other.

Buckle then proceeded to cover in some detail most if not all of the great Scottish men and ideas of the eighteenth century, Hutcheson, Adam Smith, Hume, Thomas Reid, Black, Leslie, Hutton, Watt, Cullen, Hunter. They and their work were all explained in terms of Buckle's own curious thesis and, while that may be amusing to-day, his lengthy treatment of individual contributions still remains as the only comprehensive discussion of the work of the Scottish Enlightenment. His is a valuable work for students to consult but the bases on which the whole chapter rests are questionable.[10]

The year 1967 brough forth two more very personal interpretations from Dr George Davie and Professor Hugh Trevor-Roper. It was the year that saw both the bicentenary of the New Town of Edinburgh and the holding of the second International Congress on the Enlightenment at St Andrews University, and it was in published proceedings commemmorating both events that Dr Davie and Professor Trevor-Roper offered their views. George Davie's view, also enshrined in his *Democratic Intellect: Scotland and her Universities in the Nineteenth Century* (Edinburgh University Press, 1961) may be described as that of the intellectual nationalist. In the article considered here, he made it quite clear that for him, the Enlightenment in Scotland saw the fusion of 'national with intellectual aims'.[11] Dr Davie has explained, most cogently, the relevance of the exploitation of the legal, ecclesiastical and educational institutions considered earlier. He has noted that the ideas of the Enlightenment were the common property of persons of the most varied backgrounds throughout Scotland; that the Scottish philosophical historical approach was a more vital alternative to French reductive empiricism as a vehicle for ideas on progress, and it also facilitated the ability to look beyond eighteenth-century limits. Scottish far-sightedness was stimulated by the crisis of national existence that followed the Treaty of Union, and by the fear of assimilation. Hence, Hutcheson, Hume, Smith, and Reid all emphasised the value of the native institutions, the use that could be made of them in the new conditions, and above all, the desire, successfully realised, to continue the distinctive tradition of Scottish philosophy, so different from the English and so much akin to that of the Continent. It is, therefore, to Dr Davie that must be attributed that interpretation which places so much influence on the coincidence of the Union with the two-way traffic in philosophy between Scotland and the Continent, after 1707, as a cause of the particular character of the Scottish Enlightenment. In the current study, Dr Davie's emphasis on the historical institutions has clearly been adhered to. It has questioned the Union as anything more than a catalyst, and what must also be queried is the degree of consciousness employed by the philosophers when they channelled their work through the native institutions. It seems to have been done not deliberately but because they were at hand. Furthermore, the writers attached a good deal of importance to their societies and clubs as vehicles of the Enlightenment.

Professor Trevor-Roper rejected as not entirely satisfactory both the Union of 1707 and the moral and mental discipline of the Kirk as causes of the Scottish Enlightenment. He sought to find more satisfying explanations through focussing on the Scottish philosophers' pre-occupation with the social behaviour of mankind which, in its turn, was due to the Scots' discovery of themselves in the years after 1680. In those years, the Scots not only suffered economic decline, but also resumed their broken contact with the rest of Europe. That resumption of contact was achieved not by the Church, 'but by its enemies and rivals: by its open enemies, the episcopalians and Jacobites; but its secret enemies, the "arminian" heretics within the fold; and—perhaps most important of all—by that body of men without whom no intellectual movement can bear fruit: the new class of educated laity'. The remainder of the Regius Professor's study is devoted to an elaboration of the argument and the specific contribution of the three groups, concluding (in direct opposition to Davie) that by the end of the eighteenth century, the process of assimilation was complete and Scottish feelings and habits had sunk 'into the past as the raw material of the new romanticism'.[12]

One of the philosophers, Dugald Stewart, had discerned that 'from time immemorial, a continued intercourse had been kept up between Scotland and the Continent'.[13] This contemporary analysis would seem to be nearer the mark: as has been indicated in the book, Protestant universities such as Leyden, Groningen and Utrecht were not as illiberal as Professor Trevor-Roper has suggested, especially in law and medicine, which were studied by many Scots. Furthermore, the findings of the springs of the Scottish Enlightenment among the rebels, the outlawed, almost the alternative society of the day, does not match up to the wealth of evidence that conventional Scottish society and institutions, because of their nature, their historical position, their being penetrated by the spirit of improvement and stimulated by post-Union challenges, account for the making of the Scottish Enlightenment. The emphasis too, consequently, on Aberdeen is exaggerated: of course the North-East shared in the approach to and the expression of the Scottish Enlightenment as has been shown, but Aberdeen was not exceptional. Scotland was not a closed society in social and economic matters in the seventeenth century: The Earl of Stair, for example, who in 1681 wrote the Institutions, was a regent at Glasgow as early as 1641 and in 1677 established the Snell Exhibitions to Balliol. Yet other seventeenth-century developments (Newtonianism and the concern for botany and medicine, for example) outside of Aberdeen have also been shown. It is important, indeed, not to confuse the Scottish with the Edinburgh Enlightenment: Aberdeen is important but not in the ways suggested by Professor Trevor-Roper.

This study has benefited immensely from the writings and lectures of the last two interpreters to be considered here, Professor Roy Campbell and Professor Christopher Smout.[14] If the institutional basis has been stimulated by the writings of Dr Davie, then the idea of enlightenment arising out of improvement, the second part of the book's approach, has equally owed much to the work of Professors Campbell and Smout. Both historians have been concerned in their writings to explain the much wider cultural and economic phenomena of eighteenth-century Scotland than simply the Scottish Enlightenment. The forces which produced Watt and Scott are also relevant to the Enlightenment and, while recognising that Campbell and Smout were painting on a bigger canvas, the appraisal of their work is limited to the concerns of the present study. There is much on which the two authors agree, the central point of disagreement being whether or not the Scottish Enlightenment is to be explained by the failure of Calvinism to achieve its religious objectives, and by the energy which it had generated being diverted to secular ends, or by the fact that theology actually paved the way for the Enlightenment, and the Enlightenment, rather than being a substitute for religious objectives, was a natural outgrowth of them. Professors Smout and Campbell concur as to the importance of theology in Scottish life but the question that is left to be debated is the suddenness of the change from purely religious to more secular concerns.

Professor Campbell does not believe that the indigenous quality of the Scottish interest in theology was as harmful as tradition has suggested:

Preoccupation with propositional theology was preoccupation with the supreme social science for those for whom the acceptance of secularism had not compelled theology's displacement in pre-eminence by sociology or psychology. The propositions of theology are as concerned with social transformation as are those of sociology, especially when, in the protestant tradition, they begin with the personal transformation of the individual. Scottish theologians at the height of their influence, were certainly never averse to political or social theory, so the theological concern may be interpreted as an early aspect of social engineering, as one which is perpetuated and given new clothing by the increasingly secular values of the eighteenth century.[15]

Consequently, the social scientific thought of the Scottish Enlightenment had its precursor in the particular form of Scottish Protestant theology and was an outgrowth of it. The theme was elaborated in the Balfour-Melville Memorial Lecture where Professor Campbell quoted psychologists who had said that the psychological characteristics of an innovational person are acquired and developed in a society motivated towards high achievement. The Scottish motive to achieve was based on the general influence of theology on Scottish thought and the influence of conscience, predestination and pietism. Adam Smith, for example, emphasising, with Calvin, conscience, held that conduct was controlled by the man within acting in ways approved by the man without, the impartial spectator. As far as the pietism was concerned, Calvinism was not limited to the spiritual life of the individual but spilt over into social action: Scottish theology encouraged social action. In short, secular and theological thought complemented each other in Scotland, and resulted in social stability. The mild reformism of the philosophers which accepted established property rights and social stability created an atmosphere in which individual qualities, encouraged by theological traditions, could flourish. After 1780 the clergy's concern to show themselves to be intellectual and progressive, and, therefore, following after the false gods of Smith and Malthus, caused disaster. So the moral was 'Set your hearts on his kingdom first, and on his righteousness, and all these other things will be given you as well.'[16]

Professor Smout is no less concerned with psychology. Like John Millar and Buckle he is also concerned with energy and its deployment. It will be recalled how Millar, in his *Historical View of the English Government,* had written:

> The energy requisite for the accomplishment of the reformation, and the impulse which that event gave to the minds of men, continued after the new system was established, and produced a boldness and activity, not only in examining religious opinions, which were of great extent, but in the general investigation of truth.[17]

Smout saw in the agricultural improvers, inventors and authors a 'singleminded drive . . . strangely reminiscent of the energy of the seventeenth century elders in the kirk when they set about imposing discipline on the congregation'. Hence he proposed that: 'Calvinism thus seems to be released as a psychological force for secular change just at the moment when it is losing its power as a religion: indeed, it could not be released any earlier because a systematic Calvinist religion is itself so all-consuming in its demands.' A further gloss on Professor Smout's view, presented later in his book, concluded:

> It is possible that the nation gained a particular stimulus from adopting in the seventeenth century an ideology with one over-riding and narrowly religious aim, and then, finding this int-rinsically impossible to achieve, from being catapulted into an eighteenth-century world where the legitimate objects of aspiration were suddenly felt to be wider and more diverse. The energy generated towards the achievement of the original objective was contained in the race for the new ones, and society for a time got the best of both worlds.[18]

Smout's psychological analysis depends on the frustration which results from the failure of old values to satisfy, thus abruptly, (and he uses the word catapult), causing a release into the secular opportunities available. It took place over a short period: in his paper on modernis-ation he suggests it could happen between childhood and adulthood, or when individuals moved from rigid country parishes to more secular-orientated urban ones. The volatility of eighteenth-century Scottish religious opinion would also have produced a stimulating transitional situation. The questions raised are ones of time, and whether or not religion helped to produce the Enlightenment, or whether a turning away from religion facilitated the movement. This social history, while recognising that much work is required to test both hypotheses (and, of course, the disappearance of the phenomenon and its unlikely re-appearance makes such testing problematic) inclines to the evolution, not sudden or abrupt causation of the Enlightenment, on the basis of many improvements and the theology established by the Reformation. Evolution has been a theme of preceding chapters. As far as theology and the Kirk are concerned, they did, as Smout and Campbell both pointed out, co-exist and religious fervour did not diminish as the secessions of the eighteenth century and the bitter Evangelical–Moderate debates exemplified. More telling is the social scientific character of Scottish theology; seventeenth-century religious aspirations were translated by eighteenth-century ministers and philo-sophers into secular language without altering the fundamental message. An awareness and easy acceptance of secular social sciences were created and were prominent in the thought of the Scottish Enlighten-ment. Recent studies on the positive connections between religion and science in seventeenth-century England would suggest that further research into the Scottish experience would confirm the view of origins of the Scottish Enlightenment offered here.[19]

In conclusion, while it has traditionally been regarded as unlikely that Scotland, of all countries in Europe, should be the centre of so much that was new, enlightened and progressive in the realm of ideas on society on the eve of industrialisation, it can be seen that there were stirrings of improvement and reform even before the eighteenth century began. Those stirrings were particularly evident in those Scottish social institutions that traditionally had shaped her life and history. The Treaty of Union acted as a catalyst, especially as the institutions of Church, Law and education were left intact, and so, in their improving state, could be used not only as repositories of distinctively national self-expression, but also as potent contributors to an age of enlightenment for which their pre-Union history had made them particularly suitable.

The institutions were operating in a society that was itself well able to support and countenance a movement such as the Scottish Enlightenment: it appreciated, pursued and invested in knowledge. In the post-Union situation, the problems of a backward society or a society considered such by the yardsticks of its new partner, would naturally be uppermost in the minds of that society's intellectuals and, hence, there might here be found a partial explanation for the preoccupation of the *literati* with the progress of society. This preoccupation, the Scottish view of theology as a social science, and the systematic thinking associated with the Law, all at work within a vital higher educational structure, created a potent and cogent body of thought for contemporary use and for transmission to subsequent generations.

Notes

1. Francis Jeffrey, 'Stewart's *Philosophical Essays*', *Edinburgh Review*, XVII (1810), pp. 168-9.
2. Ian D. L. Clark, *Moderatism and the Moderate Party in the Church of Scotland 1752-1805*, Ph.D. dissertation (University of Cambridge, 1964), pp. 406 and 115, and John Hill, *Account of the Life and Writings of Hugh Blair* (Edinburgh, 1807), p. 214.
3. J. G. Lockhart, *Peter's Letters to his Kinsfolk*, 3 vols. 2nd ed. (Edinburgh, 1819), I, p. 80. See also, for the contrast, *Autobiography of the Rev. Dr Alexander Carlyle*, 2nd ed. (Edinburgh, 1860), p. 561.
4. Lockhart, I, p. 210.

5. See W. Ferguson, 'The Reform Act (Scotland) of 1832: Intention and Effect', *Scottish Historical Review* (1966), pp. 105-14.
6. Henry Cockburn, *Memorials of his Time* (Edinburgh, 1856), pp. 114-16.
7. Lockhart, II, p. 116.
8. *Journal of Henry Cockburn, being a continuation of the Memorials of his Time 1831-1854*, 2 vols. (Edinburgh, 1874), II, pp. 229-30.
9. For this argument see, in part, John Clive and Bernard Bailyn, 'England's Cultural Provinces: Scotland and America', *William & Mary Quarterly*, XI (1954), pp. 200-13. The two most important recent expositions of the 'provincial' interpretation and of the interpretation that lays greater emphasis than I believe is warranted on the Treaty of Union are: Nicholas Phillipson, 'Towards a Definition of the Scottish Enlightenment', *City and Society in the 18th Century*, eds. P. Fritz and D. Williams (Toronto, 1973), pp. 125-47 and N. T. Phillipson, 'Culture and the Scottish Enlightenment', *The University in Society*, ed. Lawrence Stone, 2 vols. (Princeton U.P., 1975), II, pp. 407-48. The Edinburgh Town Council had started to develop alternative attractions, following the departure of the Court, before 1707, among which were the university medical school. As I argue in the study intellectual and institutional foundations for the Scottish Enlightenment pre-date the Treaty of Union which acted merely as a catalyst on an already developing situation.
10. H. T. Buckle, 'An Examination of the Scotch Intellect dueing the Eighteenth Century', *Introduction to the History of Civilization in England*, new and revised ed. by John M. Robertson (London, n.d.), pp. 792-902. The quotations are from pp. 792 and 797. The most recent edition of Buckle's work has been published as H. T. Buckle, *On Scotland and the Scotch Intellect*, ed. H. J. Hanham (Chicago University Press, 1970).
11. G. E. Davie, 'Hume, Reid and the Passion for Ideas', *Edinburgh in the Age of Reason* (Edinburgh U.P., 1967), pp. 23-39. The quotation is from p. 23.
12. Hugh Trevor-Roper, 'The Scottish Enlightenment', *Studies on Voltaire and the Eighteenth Century*, cviii (1967), pp. 1635-53. The quotations are from pp. 1643 and 1658. On Scotland and Europe see for interest, Giancarlo Carabelli, 'Hume, Scotland and Europe', *Scottish International*, VI (1973), pp. 24-7.
13. Dugald Stewart, 'Dissertation: exhibiting the Progress of Metaphysical, Ethical and Political Philosophy, since the Revival of Letters in Europe', *Collected Works of Dugald Stewart*, ed. Sir William Hamilton, 11 vols. Edinburgh, 1854-60, I (1854), p. 550.
14. I am considering in particular, R. H. Campbell, 'The Union and Economic Growth', *The Union of 1707: Its Impact on Scotland*, ed. T. I. Rae (Blackie, Glasgow, 1974), pp. 58-74 and R. H. Campbell, 'Theology and Economic Growth', unpublished Balfour-Melville Memorial Lecture, Historical Association in Scotland, 27 April 1974; T. C. Smout, *A History of the Scottish People 1560-1830* (Collins/Fontana, 1972) and I am grateful to Professor Smout for letting me see a lecture he gave in Leningrad in 1971, 'Problems of Modernization: Non-Economic Factors in Eighteenth-Century Scotland'; I also much appreciate Professor Campbell letting me use the text of his Balfour-Melville Memorial Lecture.
15. Campbell, 'The Union and Economic Growth', pp. 67-8.
16. Matt. VI, v. 33.
17. John Millar, *An Historical View of the English Government from the Settlement of the Saxons in Britain to the Revolution in 1688*, 4 vols. (London, 1803), III, p. 88.
18. Smout, *History*, pp. 92 and 482-3.

19.   See Charles Webster, *The Great Instauration: Science, Medicine and Reform, 1626-1660* (Duckworth, 1975) and John Redwood, *Reason, Ridicule and Religion: The Age of Enlightenment in England, 1660-1750* (Thames and Hudson, 1976).

APPENDIX

Some papers read by selected persons active in the social history of the Scottish Enlightenment to the Royal Society of Edinburgh 1783-1826. (compiled from *Index to the Transactions of the Royal Society of Edinburgh 1783-1888* (Edinburgh, 1890) pp. 27-44)

1783-1785

Physical Class:

John Walker, Experiments on the Motion of the Sap in Trees'.
James Hutton, 'The Theory of Rain'.
John Playfair, 'On the Causes which affect the Accuracy of Barometrical Measurements'.
John Playfair, communicated Rev. Thomas Fleming's 'Account of a remarkable Agitation of the Waters of Loch Tay'.
James Hutton, 'Theory of the Earth'.
John Robison, 'The Orbit and Motion of the *Georgium Sidus,* determined directly from Observations'.

Literary Class

Alexander Carlyle, communicated late William Collins' 'An Ode on the Popular Superstitions of the Highlands'.

1785-1789

Physical Class:

James Hutton, 'Of certain Natural Appearances of the Ground on the Hill of Arthur's Seat'.
John Robison, 'Observations on the Places of the Georgium Planet, made at Edinburgh with an Equatorial Instrument'.
James Hutton, 'Answers to the Objections of M. de Luc, with Regard to the Theory of Rain'.
John Robison, 'On the Motion of Light, as affected by Refracting and Reflecting Substances, which are also in Motion'.
John Playfair, 'Remarks on the Astronomy of the Brahmins'.
John Leslie, 'On the Resolution of Interminate Problems'.

Literary Class:

Alexander Fraser Tytler, 'An Account of Some Extraordinary Structures on the Tops of Hills in the Highlands; with Remarks on the Progress of the Arts among the Ancient Inhabitants of Scotland'.

James Beattie, 'Remarks on some Passages of the Sixth Book of the Eneid'.

Andrew Dalziel, 'On Certain Analogies observed by the Greeks in the Use of their Letters; and particularly of the Letter [Sigma]'.

James Gregory, 'Theory of the Moods of Verbs'.

1789-1793

Physical Class:

James Hutton, 'Observations on Granite'.

James Hutton, 'Of the Flexibility of the Brazilian Stone'.

Joseph Black, 'An Analysis of the Waters of Some Hot Springs in Iceland'.

John Playfair, 'Of the Origin and Investigation of Porisms'.

Alexander Monro, 'Description of a Human Male Monster'.

Alexander Monro, 'Experiments relating to Animal Electricity'.

Daniel Rutherford, 'A Description of an Improved Thermometer'.

Alexander Monro, 'Observations on the Muscles'.

1793-1797

Physical Class:

T. C. Hope, 'An Account of a Mineral from Strontian, and of a peculiar Species of Earth which it contains'.

John Playfair, 'Observations on the Trigonometrical Tables of the Brahmins'.

Literary Class:

Sir James Hall, 'Of the Origin and Principles of Gothic Architecture'.

Andrew Dalzel, 'M. Chevalier's Tableau de la Plaine de Troye illustrated and confirmed from the Observations of subsequent Travellers and others'.

[Literary class papers are not listed separately from at least 1797].

1799-1803

John Playfair, 'Investigation of Theorems relating to the Figure of the Earth'.

Sir James Hall, 'Experiments on Whinstone and Lava'.

Alexander Fraser Tytler, 'Remarks on a Mixed Species of Evidence in Matters of History: with an Examination of a New Historical Hypothesis, in the *Mémoires pour la Vie de Petrarque,* by the Abbé de Sade'.

T. C. Hope, 'Experiments on the Contraction of Water by Heat'.

1804-1811

Sir James Hall, 'Account of a Series of Experiments shewing the Effects of Compression in modifying the Action of Heat'.

John Playfair, 'Of the Solids of Greatest Attraction, or those which, among all the Solids that have certain Properties, Attract with the Greatest Force in a given Direction'.

Thomas Thomson, 'Chemical Analysis of a Black Sand, from the River Dee in Aberdeenshire; and of a Copper Ore, from Airthrey in Stirlingshire'.

John Playfair, 'On the Progress of Heat when communicated to Spherical Bodies from their Centres'.

Thomas Thomson, 'Experiments on Allanite, a New Mineral from Greenland'.

Thomas Thomson, 'A Chemical Analysis of Sodalite, a New Mineral from Greenland'.

1812-1815

Dugald Stewart, 'Some Account of a Boy Born Blind and Deaf, collected from Authentic Sources in Information; with a few Remarks and Comments'.

Sir James Hall, 'On the Vertical Position and Convolutions of certain Strata, and their Relation with Granite'.

Sir James Hall, 'On the Revolutions of the Earth's Surface', Parts I and II.

Sir George Mackenzie, 'An Account of Some Geological Facts observed in the Faroe Islands'.

1815-1818

Macvey Napier, 'Remarks, illustrative of the Scope and Influence of the Philosophical Writings of Lord Bacon'.

John Leslie, 'On certain Impressions of Cold transmitted from the Higher Atmosphere, with the Description of an Instrument adapted to measure them'.

1818-1823

John Playfair, 'Memoir relating to the Naval Tactics of the late

John Clerk, Esq., of Eldin; being a Fragment of an Intended Account of his life'.

1823-1826

Robert Knox, 'Observations on the Comparative Anatomy of the Eye'.

Sir George Mackenzie, 'On the Formation of Chalcedony'.

Sir George Mackenzie, 'Notice respecting the Vertebra of a Whale, found in a Bed of Bluish Clay, near Dingwall'.

Robert Knox, 'Inquiry into the Structure and Probable Functions of the Capsules forming the Canal of Petit, and of the Marsupium Nigrum, or the peculiar Vascular Tissue Araversing the Vitreous Humour in the Eyes of Birds, Reptiles, and Fishes'.

Sir James Hall, 'On the Consolidation of the Strata of the Earth'.

SELECT BIBLIOGRAPHY

CHAPTER 1. THE SCOTTISH ENLIGHTENMENT

Cole, A. V., 'Lord Lauderdale and his "Inquiry" ', *Scottish Journal of Political Economy*, III (1956), pp. 115-25.

Davie, George Elder, 'Anglophobe and Anglophil', *Scottish Journal of Political Economy*, XIV (1967), pp. 291-302.

Steuart, Sir James, *An Inquiry into the Principles of Political Economy*, ed. Andrew S. Skinner, Scottish Economic Society, 2 vols. Oliver and Boyd, Edinburgh and London, 1966.

CHAPTER 2. THE PRELUDE AND THE SETTING

Arnot, Hugo, *The History of Edinburgh*, Edinburgh and London, 1779.

Baird, William, 'George Drummond: An Eighteenth Century Lord Provost', *Book of the Old Edinburgh Club*, IV, Edinburgh, 1911.

Campbell, R. H., *Scotland since 1707: The Rise of an Industrial Society*, Blackwell, Oxford, 1965.

Chambers, Robert, *Traditions of Edinburgh*, 2 vols., Edinburgh, 1815.

Cockburn, Henry, *Memorials of his Time*, Edinburgh, 1856.

Cockburn, Henry, *Journal*, 2 vols., Edinburgh, 1874.

Creech, William, *Letters addressed to Sir John Sinclair, Bart., respecting the mode of living, arts, commerce, literature, manners, etc. of Edinburgh in 1763 and since that period*, Edinburgh, 1793.

Daiches, David, *The Paradox of Scottish Culture: The Eighteenth-Century Experience*, O.U.P., London, 1964.

Edinburgh in the Age of Reason, Edinburgh University Press, 1967.

Graham, H.G., *The Social Life of Scotland in the Eighteenth Century*, 2 vols., London, 1899.

Hume, David, *Letters*, ed. J. Y. T. Greig, 2 vols., Oxford, Clarendon Press, 1932.

Kaufman, Paul, 'A Unique Record of a People's Reading', *Libri*, XIV (1964-5), pp. 227-42.

Law, Alexander, 'Teachers in Edinburgh in the Eighteenth Century', *The Book of the Old Edinburgh Club*, XXXII, Edinburgh, 1966, pp. 108-57.

National Library of Scotland, Ms. 3464.

Phillipson, N. T., *The Scottish Whigs and the Reform of the Court of Session, 1785-1830*, Ph.D. dissertation, University of Cambridge, 1967.

Proposals for carrying on certain Public Works in the City of Edinburgh, Edinburgh, 1752.

Ramsay, John, *Scotland and Scotsmen in the Eighteenth Century, from the mss. of John Ramsay of Ochtertyre*, ed. Alexander Allardyce, 2 vols., Edinburgh and London, 1888.

Scots Magazine, XXII (1760), pp. 686-7.

Scott, Walter, *Provincial Antiquities and Picturesque Scenery of Scotland*, 2 vols., London, 1826.

Simond, Louis, *Journal of a Tour and Residence in Great Britain, during the years 1810 and 1811*, 2 vols., Edinburgh, 1815.

Sinclair, Sir John, *Analysis of the Statistical Account of Scotland*, 2 parts, Edinburgh, 1826.

Smout, T. C., *A History of the Scottish People 1560-1830*, Collins/Fontana, London, 1972.

Statistical Account of Scotland, 21 vols., Edinburgh, 1791-9.

Topham, E. C., *Letters from Edinburgh: Written in the Years 1774 and 1775*.

Watt, Ian, 'Publishers and Sinners: The Augustan View', *Studies in Bibliography*, XII (1959).

Wesley, John, *Journal*, 8 vols., London, 1938.

Withrington, Donald J., 'Lists of Schoolmasters teaching Latin, 1690', *Miscellany of the Scottish History Society*, X, T. & A. Constable, Edinburgh 1965.

Youngson, A. J., *The Making of Classical Edinburgh 1750-1840*, Edinburgh U.P. 1966.

CHAPTER 3. THE CHURCH

The Autobiography of Dr Alexander Carlyle of Inveresk, 1722-1805, ed. John Hill Burton, London and Edinburgh, 1970.

Clark, I. D. L., 'From Protest to Reaction: The Moderate Regime in the Church of Scotland 1752-1805', *Scotland in the Age of Improvement*, ed. N. T. Phillipson and R. Mitchison, Edinburgh U.P., 1970, pp. 200-24.

Clark, Ian D. L., *Moderatism and the Moderate Party of Scotland, 1752-1805*, Ph.D. dissertation, University of Cambridge, 1964.

Cockburn, Henry, *Memorials of his Time*, Edinburgh, 1856.

Cunningham, John, *The Church History of Scotland*, 2 vols., 2nd ed., Edinburgh, 1882.

Edinburgh Review, 1755-6.

Hume, David, *Letters*, ed. J. Y. T. Greig, 2 vols., Oxford, Clarendon Press, 1932.

Leighton, Robert, *The Whole Works of Robert Leighton, D.D.*, 2 vols., London, 1846.

Lockhart, J.G., *Peter's Letters to his Kinsfolk*, 3 vols., 2nd ed., Edinburgh, 1819.

Mackenzie, Henry, *An Account of the Life and Writings of John Home*, Edinburgh, 1822.

Mossner, Ernest Campbell, *The Life of David Hume*, Nelson, Edinburgh and London, 1954.

Ramsay, John, *Scotland and Scotsmen in the Eighteenth Century, from the mss. of John Ramsay of Ochtertyre*, ed. Alexander Allardyce, 2 vols., Edinburgh and London, 1888.

Ranken, Alexander, *The Importance of Religious Establishment*, Edinburgh, 1799.

'Reasons of Dissent from the Judgement and Resolution of the Commission, March 11th 1752, resolving to inflict no censure on the presbytery of Dunfermline for their disobedience in Relation to the Settlement of Inverkeithing', *Scots Magazine*, XIV (1752), pp. 191-7.

Ross, Ian Simpson, *Lord Kames and the Scotland of his Day*, Oxford, Clarendon Press, 1972.

The Scotch Preacher: or a Collection of Sermons by Some of the Most Eminent Clergymen of the Church of Scotland, 2 vols., Edinburgh, 1776.

The Scottish Pulpit: a Collection of Sermons by Eminent Clergymen of the Church of Scotland, ed. Robert Gillan, Edinburgh, 1823.

Scots Magazine, XVII (1755) and XLI (1770).

Scougal, Henry, *The Life of God in the Soul of Man*, Inter-Varsity Fellowship,

London, 1961.

Smith, Norah, 'Robert Wallace's "Of Venery" ', *Texas Studies in Literature and Language*, XV (1973), pp. 429-44.

Somerville, Thomas, *My Own Life and Times 1741-1814*, Edinburgh, 1861.

Statistical Account of Scotland, 21 vols., Edinburgh 1791-9.

Stewart, Dugald, *Account of the Life and Writings of William Robertson, D.D., F.R.S.E.*, London, 1801.

Topham, E. C., *Letters from Edinburgh: Written in the Years 1774 and 1775*, Dublin, 1776.

Wesley, John, *Journal*, 8 vols., London, 1938.

Witherspoon, John, *Ecclesiastical Characteristics: or the Arcana of Church Policy being an humble attempt to open up the Mystery of Moderation, wherein is shewn a plain and easy way of attaining to the Character of a Moderate Man, as at present in Repute in the Church of Scotland*, 2nd ed., Glasgow, 1754.

Withrington, Donald J., 'Non-Church-Going, *c. 1750-c. 1850*. A Preliminary Study', *Records of the Scottish Church History Society*, XVII (1970).

CHAPTER 4. THE LAW

Boswell, James, *A Letter to the People of Scotland on the alarming attempt to infringe the articles of the Union and to introduce a most pernicious innovation by diminishing the number of the Lords of Session*, London, 1785.

Caledonian Mercury.

Campbell, R. H., 'The Law and the Joint-Stock Company in Scotland', *Studies in Scottish Business History*, ed. Peter Payne, Cass, London, 1967.

Cockburn, Henry, *Journal*, 2 vols., Edinburgh, 1874.

Cockburn, Henry, *Life of Lord Jeffrey with a selection from his Correspondence*, 2 vols., Edinburgh, 1852

Cockburn, Henry, *Memorials of his Time*, Edinburgh, 1856.

Cockburn, Henry, 'Office of Lord Advocate of Scotland', *Edinburgh Review*, XXXIX (1823-4), pp. 363-92.

Ferguson, William, *Scotland: 1689 to the present*, Oliver & Boyd, Edinburgh & London, 1968.

Hanham, H. J., *Scottish Nationalism*, Faber, London, 1969.

Hume, David, *Letters*, ed. J. Y. T. Greig, 2 vols., Oxford, Clarendon Press, 1932.

An Introduction to Scottish Legal History, Stair Society, Edinburgh, 1958.

An Introductory Survey of the Sources and Literature of Scots Law, Stair Society, Edinburgh, 1936.

Lockhart, J. G., *Peter's Letters to his Kinsfolk*, 3 vols., 2nd ed., Edinburgh, 1819.

Meikle, H. W., *Some Aspects of Later Seventeenth Century Scotland*, Glasgow, 1947.

Millar, John, *An Historical View of the English Government from the Settlement of the Saxons in Britain to the Revolution in 1688*, 4 vols., London, 1803.

Phillipson, N. T., *The Scottish Whigs and the Reform of the Court of Session 1785-1830*, Ph.D. dissertation, University of Cambridge, 1967.

Ramsay, John, *Scotland and Scotsmen in the Eighteenth Century, from the mss. of John Ramsay of Ochtertyre*, ed. Alexander Allardyce, 2 vols., Edinburgh and London, 1888.

Robertson, William, *Works*, 8 vols., Oxford, 1825.

Ross, Ian Simpson, *Lord Kames and the Scotland of his Day*, Oxford, Clarendon Press, 1972.

Scott, Walter, *Provincial Antiquities and Picturesque Scenery of Scotland*, 2 vols., London, 1826.

Simpson, John M, 'Who Steered the Gravy Train?', *Scotland in the Age of Improvement*, ed. N. T. Phillipson and Rosalind Mitchison, Edinburgh U.P. 1970.

Smout, T. C., *A History of the Scottish People 1560-1830*, Collins/Fontana, London 1972.

Stein, Peter, 'Legal Thought in Eighteenth Century Scotland', *Juridicial Review*, 1957.

Stein, Peter, 'The Influence of Roman Law on the Law of Scotland', *The Juridicial Review*, 1963.

Stein, Peter, 'Law and Society in Eighteenth-Century Scottish Thought', *Scotland in the Age of Improvement*, ed. N. T. Phillipson and Rosalind Mitchison, Edinburgh U.P., 1970.

CHAPTER 5. THE STUDY OF SOCIAL MAN

Bryson, Gladys, *Man and Society: The Scottish Enquiry of the Eighteenth Century*, Princeton U.P., New Jersey, 1945.

Caledonian Mercury.

Carabelli, Giancarlo, *Hume e la retorica dell'ideologia: uno studio dei 'Dialoghi sulla Religione naturale'*, La Nuova Italia Editrice, Firenze, 1972.

Davie, George Elder, *The Democratic Intellect: Scotland and her Universities in the Nineteenth Century*, Edinburgh U.P., 2nd ed., 1964.

Ferguson, Adam, *An Essay on the History of Civil Society, 1767*, ed. Duncan Forbes, Edinburgh U.P., 1966.

Ferguson, Adam, *The History of the Progress and Termination of the Roman Republic*, London, 1825.

Ferguson, Adam, *Principles of Moral and Political Science*, 2 vols., Edinburgh, 1792.

Gay, Peter, *The Enlightenment: an Interpretation*, 2 vols., New York, Alfred A. Knopf, 1966 and 1969.

Hamowy, R., 'Adam Smith, Adam Ferguson, and the Division of Labour', *Economica*, XXXV (1968), pp. 249-59.

Home, Henry, Lord Kames, *Essays upon Several Subjects concerning British Antiquities*, Edinburgh, 1747.

Home, Henry, Lord Kames, *Historical Law Tracts*, 4th ed., Edinburgh, 1792.

Home, Henry, Lord Kames, *Principles of Equity*, 2 vols., Edinburgh, 1778.

Home, Henry, Lord Kames, *Sketches of the History of Man*, 3 vols., Edinburgh, 1807.

Hume, David, *Essays, Moral, Political, and Literary*, ed. T. H. Green & T. H. Grose, 2 vols., London, Longmans Green, 1875.

Hume, David, *The History of Great Britain: The Reigns of James I and Charles I*, ed. Duncan Forbes, Pelican Classics, 1970.

Hume, David, *Philosophical Works*, ed. T. H. Green and T. H. Grose, 4 vols., London, 1874-5.

Hume, David, *Political Discourses*, London, 1908.

Lehmann, W. C., *Henry Hume, Lord Kames and the Scottish Enlightenment: A Study in National Character and in the History of Ideas*, Martinus Nijhoff, The Hague, 1971.

MacRae, Donald G., 'Adam Ferguson 1723-1816', *The Founding Fathers of Social Science*, Pelican, 1969.

Meek, R. L., 'The Scottish Contribution to Marxist Sociology', *Democracy and the Labour Movement*, ed. John Saville, London, 1954, pp. 84-102.

Millar, John, *An Historical View of the English Government from the Settlement of the Saxons in Britain to the Revolution in 1688*, 4 vols., London, 1803.

Millar, John, 'The Origin of the Distinction of Ranks', in William C. Lehmann, *John Millar of Glasgow 1735-1801: his Life and Thoughts and his Contributions to Sociological Analysis*, Cambridge U.P., 1960.

Quinton, Anthony, 'The Neglect of Victorian Philosophy', *Victorian Studies*, I (1957-8), pp. 245-54.

Robertson, William, *History of Scotland*, 3 vols., London, 1817.

Robertson, William, *Works*, 12 vols., London 1812.

Robertson, William, *Works*, 8 vols., Oxford, 1825.

Ross, Ian Simpson, *Lord Kames and the Scotland of his Day*, Oxford, Clarendon Press, 1972.

Skinner, Andrew S., 'Adam Smith: Philosophy and Science', *Scottish Journal of Political Economy*, XIX (1972), pp. 307-19.

Skinner, Andrew S., 'Economics and History—The Scottish Enlightenment', *Scottish Journal of Political Economy*, XII (1965).

Smith, Adam, 'An Enquiry after Philosophy and Theology', *Edinburgh Review*, 1756, pp. 3-12.

Smith, Adam, *An Inquiry into the Nature and Causes of the Wealth of Nations*, ed. Andrew S. Skinner, Pelican, 1970.

Smith, Adam, *Lectures on Justice, Police, Revenue and Arms*, ed. Edwin Cannan, Oxford, Clarendon Press, 1896.

Smith, Adam, *Works*, 5 vols., Edinburgh, 1811-12.

Stein, Peter, 'Law and Society in Eighteenth-Century Scottish Thought', *Scotland in the Age of Improvement*, ed. N. T. Phillipson and Rosalind Mitchison, Edinburgh U.P., 1970.

Stewart, Dugald, *Collected Works of Dugald Stewart*, ed. Sir William Hamilton, 11 vols., Edinburgh, 1854-60.

Stewart, Dugald, 'Dissertation: exhibiting the progress of metaphysical, ethical and political philosophy since the revival of letters in Europe', *Collected Works*, ed. Sir William Hamilton, 11 vols., (1854-60), I (1854).

Swingewood, Alan, 'Origins of Sociology: the case of the Scottish Enlightenment', *British Journal of Sociology*, XXI (1970), pp. 164-80.

Swingewood, Alan, *The Scottish Enlightenment and the Rise of Social Theory*, Ph.D. dissertation, University of London, 1968.

West, E. G., 'Adam Smith's Two Views on the Division of Labour', *Economics*, XXXI (1964), pp. 23-32.

West, E. G., 'The Political Economy of Alienation', *Oxford Economic Papers*, XXI (1969), pp. 1-23.

CHAPTER 6. UNIVERSITIES: MEDICINE AND SCIENCE

Bell, John, *Letters on the Education of a Surgeon*, Edinburgh, 1810.

'Biography of the late Professor Jameson', *The Monthly Journal of Medical Science*, XVIII (January-June, 1854), pp. 572-5.

British Museum, Add. Mss. 34611, 34612, 34630.

Bryson, Gladys, *Man and Society: The Scottish Enquiry of the Eighteenth Century*, Princeton U.P., New Jersey, 1945.

Buckle, H. T., *Introduction to the History of Civilization in England*, new and revised ed., Routledge, London, 1904.

Caledonian Mercury.

Campbell, T. D., *Adam Smith's Science of Morals*, Allen and Unwin, London, 1971.

Cant, R. G., 'The Scottish Universities and Scottish Society in the Eighteenth Century', *Studies on Voltaire and the Eighteenth Century*, cviii (1967).

Cant, Ronald G., *The University of St. Andrews: A Short History*, Scottish Academic Press, Edinburgh and London, 1970.

Cantor, G. N., 'Henry Brougham and the Scottish Methodological Tradition', *Studies in the History and Philosophy of Science*, II (1971), pp. 69-89.

Carlyle, Alexander, *Anecdotes and Characters of the Times*, ed. James Kinsley, London, O.U.P., 1973.

Cater, Jeremy J., 'The Making of Principal Robertson in 1762: Politics and the University of Edinburgh in the second half of the eighteenth century', *Scottish Historical Review*, XLIX (1970), pp. 60-84.

Chitnis, Anand C., *The Edinburgh Professoriate 1790-1826 and the University's Contribution to Nineteenth Century British Society*, Ph.D. dissertation University of Edinburgh, 1968.

Chitnis, Anand C., 'The University of Edinburgh's Natural History Museum and the Huttonian-Wernerian Debate', *Annals of Science*, XXVI (1970), pp. 85-94.

Christie, John R. R., 'The Origins and Development of the Scottish Scientific Community, 1680-1760', *History of Science*, XII (1974), pp. 122-41.

Clark, Ian D. L., 'The Leslie Controversy, 1805', *Records of the Scottish Church History Society*, XIV (1963), pp. 179-97.

Clark, Ian D. L., *Moderatism and the Moderate Party in the Church of Scotland, 1752-1805*, Ph.D. dissertation, University of Cambridge, 1964.

Clive, John, 'The Social Background of the Scottish Renaissance', *Scotland in the Age of Improvement*, ed. N. T. Phillipson and Rosalind Mitchison, Edinburgh U.P., 1970, pp. 225-44.

Clow, Archibald and Nan L., 'Archibald Cochrane, 9th Earl of Dundonald (1749-1831)', *Chemistry and Industry* (10 June 1944), pp. 217-20.

Cockburn, Henry, *Letters chiefly connected with the Affairs of Scotland from Henry Cockburn . . . to Thomas Francis Kennedy, M.P.*, Edinburgh, 1874.

Cockburn, Henry, *Memorials of his Time*, Edinburgh, 1856.

Cockburn, Henry, *Memorials of his Time*, new ed., London, 1909.

Comrie, John D., *History of Scottish Medicine*, London, 1927.

Connell, Brian, *Portrait of a Whig Peer: compiled from the papers of the Second Viscount Palmerston, 1739-1802*, London, 1957.

Constable, Thomas, *Archibald Constable and his Literary Correspondents*. 3 vols., Edinburgh, 1873.

Coutts, James, *A History of the University of Glasgow*, Glasgow, 1909.

Crosland, Maurice P., 'The Use of Diagrams as Chemical "Equations" in the Lecture Notes of William Cullen and Joseph Black', *Annals of Science*, XV (1959), pp. 75-90.

Cullen, William, *Works*, 2 vols., Edinburgh, 1827.

Davie, George Elder, *The Democratic Intellect: Scotland and her Universities in the Nineteenth Century*, 2nd ed., Edinburgh U.P., 1964.

Davie, G. E., 'The Social Significance of the Scottish Philosophy of Common Sense', *The Dow Lecture*, University of Dundee, 30 November 1972. Published 1973.

Davies, Gordon L., *The Earth in Decay: A History of British Geomorphology 1578-1878*, Macdonald Technical and Scientific, London, 1969.

Descartes, René, *Treatise of Man* (1664), ed. T. S. Hall, Harvard U.P., Cambridge, Mass., 1972.

Donovan, A. L., *Philosophical Chemistry in the Scottish Enlightenment*, Edinburgh U.P., 1975.

Duncan, Andrew, junior, *Medical Education*, Edinburgh, 1827.

Duncan, Andrew, junior, *Reports of the Practice in the Clinical Wards of the Royal Infirmary of Edinburgh*, Edinburgh, 1818.

Edinburgh City Chambers Ms. College Commissioners' Papers 1816-26.

Edinburgh University Library, Ms. Dc.2.57 Phot. 1144/1, Phot. 1144/2.

*Evidence, Oral and Documentary taken and received by the Commissioners appointed by his majesty George IV, July 23rd, 1826; and re-appointed by his majesty William IV, October 12th, 1830; for visiting the Universities of Scotland.*Volume I: University of Edinburgh; Volume II: University of Glasgow; Volume III: University of St. Andrews; Volume IV: University of Abderdeen.

Fletcher, Harold R. and Brown, William H., *The Royal Botanic Garden Edinburgh, 1670-1970,* Edinburgh, HMSO 1970.

Gay, Peter, *The Enlightenment: an Interpretation,* 2 vols., New York, Alfred A. Knopf, 1966 and 1969.

Hamilton, James, *Edinburgh Lying-In Institution for delivering Poor Married Women at their own Houses,* Edinburgh, 1824.

Horn, David Bayne, *A Short HIstory of the University of Edinburgh 1556-1889,* Edinburgh U.P., 1967.

Horner, Francis, 'Professor Stewart's Statement of Facts', *Edinburgh Review,* VII (1805-6), pp. 113-14.

Hume, David, *Dialogues concerning Natural Religion,* 2nd ed., London 1779.

Hutton, James, *An Investigation of the Principles of Knowledge,* 3 vols., Edinburgh, 1794.

Jameson, Robert, *Syllabus of Lectures on Natural History,* Edinburgh, 1821.

Jardine, George, *Outlines of Philosophical Education illustrated by the Method of teaching the Logic Class in the University of Glasgow,* 2nd. ed., Glasgow, 1825.

Olson, Richard, *Scottish Philosophy and British Physics 1750-1880,* Princeton, New Jersey, 1975.

Olson, Richard, 'Scottish Philosophy and Mathematics 1750-1830', *Journal of the History of Ideas,* XXXII (1971), pp. 29-44.

Partners in Science: Letters of James Watt and Joseph Black, ed. Eric Robinson and Douglas McKie, Constable, London, 1970.

Pennant, Thomas, *A Tour in Scotland, 1772,* Part II, London, 1790.

Playfair, John, *The Works of John Playfair,* ed. J. G. Playfair, 4 vols., Edinburgh, 1822.

Porter, Roy, *The Making of the Science of Geology in Britain, 1660-1815,* Ph.D. dissertation, University of Cambridge, 1974.

Rae, John, *Life of Adam Smith* (1895), introd. Jacob Viner, Kelley reprint, New York, 1965.

Rait, R. S., *The Universities of Aberdeen: A History,* Aberdeen, 1895.

Ramsay, John, *Scotland and Scotsmen in the Eighteenth Century, from the mss. of John Ramsay of Ochtertyre,* ed. Alexander Allardyce, 2 vols., Edinburgh and London, 1888.

Reid, Thomas, 'A Statistical Account of the University of Glasgow', *The Works of Thomas Reid, D.D.,* 2 vols., Edinburgh, 1880, Vol. II.

Report from the Select Committee on Medical Education with the Minutes of Evidence and Appendix, 2 vols., 1834.

Report made to his majesty by a Royal Commission of Inquiry into the state of the Universities of Scotland, House of Commons, 7 October 1831.

Ritchie, James, 'Natural History and the Emergence of Geology in the Scottish Universities', *Transactions of the Edinburgh Geological Society,* XV (1952), pp. 297-316.

Russell, James, *Remarks on the Utility and Importance of Clinical Lectures on Surgery,* Edinburgh, 1824.

Saunders, Laurence James, *Scottish Democracy 1815-1840: The Social and Intellectual Background,* Oliver and Boyd, Edinburgh and London, 1950.

Scott, W. R., *Adam Smith as Student and Professor*, Glasgow, 1937.

Shapin, Steven, 'The Audience for Science in Eighteenth Century Edinburgh', *History of Science*, XII (1974), pp. 95-121.

Shapin, Steven, 'Property, Patronage, and the Politics of Science: The Founding of the Royal Society of Edinburgh', *British Journal for the History of Science*, VII (1974), pp. 1-41.

Simon, S. William, 'The Influence of the three Monros on the Practice of Medicine and Surgery', *Annals of Medical History*, IX (1927), pp. 236-44.

Smart, R. N., 'Some Observations on the Provinces of the Scottish Universities, 1560-1850', *The Scottish Tradition: essays in honour of Ronald Gordon Cant*, ed. G. W. S. Barrow, Scottish Academic Press, Edinburgh, 1974, pp. 91-106.

Smith, Adam, 'An Enquiry after Philosophy and Theology', *Edinburgh Review*, (1756), pp. 3-12.

Smith, Adam, *An Inquiry into the Nature and Causes of the Wealth of Nations* ed. E. Cannan, 2 vols., 5th ed., London, Methuen, 1930.

Smout, T. C., *A History of the Scottish People 1560-1830*, Collins/Fontana, London, 1972.

Somerville, Thomas, *My Own Life and Times 1741-1814*, Edinburgh, 1861.

Statement regarding the New Town Dispensary by the Medical Gentlemen Conducting that Institution, Edinburgh, 1816.

Stewart, Dugald, 'Dissertation: exhibiting the progress of metaphysical, ethical and political philosophy since the revival of letters in Europe', *Collected Works*, ed. Sir William Hamilton, 11 vols., (1854-60), I (1851).

Stewart, Dugald, *Collected Works of Dugald Stewart*, ed. Sir William Hamilton, 11 vols., Edinburgh, 1854-60.

Thomson, John, *Account of the Life, Lectures and Writings of William Cullen*, 2 vols., Edinburgh and London, 1832 and 1859.

Topham, E. C., *Letters from Edinburgh: Written in the Years 1774 and 1775*, Dublin, 1776.

Trevor-Roper, Hugh, 'The Scottish Enlightenment', *Studies on Voltaire and the Eighteenth Century*, cviii (1967), pp. 1635-58.

Veitch, John, 'Philosophy in the Scottish Universities', *Mind*, old series, II (1877), pp. 74-91, 207-234.

Walker, John, *Lectures on Geology: including Hydrography, Mineralogy, and Meteorology with an introduction to Biology*, ed. Harold W. Scott, Chicago, 1966.

Walpole, Spencer, *The Life of Lord John Russell*, 2 vols., London, 1891.

CHAPTER 7. NEW INSTITUTIONS AND THE SCOTTISH ENLIGHTENMENT

Brougham, Henry and Jeffrey, Francis, 'Don Pedro Cevallos on the French usurpation of Spain', *Edinburgh Review*, XIII (1808), pp. 215-34.

Brougham, Henry, 'High Church opinions on Popular Education', *Edinburgh Review*, XLII (1825), pp. 206-23.

Brougham, Henry, 'New University on London', *Edinburgh Review*, XLII (1825), pp. 346-67.

Brougham, Henry and Jeffrey, Francis, 'Parliamentary Reports', *Edinburgh Review*, XVII (1811), pp. 253-90.

Brougham, Henry, 'Society for the Diffusion of Useful Knowledge', *Edinburgh Review*, XLVI (1827), pp. 225-44.

Brougham, Henry, 'Supposed dangers of knowledge', *Edinburgh Review*, XLIII (1825), pp. 242-8.

Caledonian Mercury.

Carlyle, Alexander, *Anecdotes and Characters of the Times,* ed. James Kingsley, London, O.U.P., 1973.

Clive, John, *Scotch Reviewers: The Edinburgh Review 1802-1815,* London, Faber, 1957.

Cockburn, Harry A., 'An Account of the Friday Club, written by Lord Cockburn, together with notes on certain other Social Clubs in Edinburgh', *Book of the Old Edinburgh Club,* III (Edinburgh, 1910), pp. 105-78.

Cockburn, Henry, *Life of Lord Jeffrey with a selection from his correspondence,* 2 vols., Edinburgh, 1852.

Cockburn, Henry, *Memorials of his Time,* Edinburgh, 1856.

Comrie, J.D., *History of Scottish Medicine,* 2 vols., 2nd ed., London, 1932.

Constable, Thomas, *Archibald Constable and his Literary Correspondents,* 3 vols., Edinburgh, 1873.

Davie, G. E., 'Berkeley's Impact on Scottish Philosophers', *Philosophy,* XL (1965).

Edinburgh City Chambers, McLeod's Bundle 16, Shelf 36, Bay C.

Edinburgh Journal of Natural and Geographical Science, II (1830).

Emerson, Roger L., 'The Social composition of enlightened Scotland: the select society of Edinburgh, 1754-1764', *Studies in Voltaire and the Eighteenth Century,* CXIV (1973), pp. 291-329.

Edinburgh University Library, Ms. Dc.6.111. Dc.2.57. College Minutes, III (1812-1824).

Evidence, Oral and Documentary taken and received by the Commissioners appointed by his majesty George IV, July 23rd, 1826; and re-appointed by his majesty William IV, October 12th, 1830; for visiting the Universities of Scotland. Volume I: University of Edinburgh; Volume II: University of Glasgow; Volume III: University of St Andrews; Volume IV: University of Aberdeen.

Eyles, V. A., 'The Evolution of a Chemist: Sir James Hall Bt., F.R.S., P.R.S.E., of Dunglass, Haddingtonshire (1761-1832), and his relations with Joseph Black, Antoine Lavoisier, and other scientists of the period', *Annals of Science,* XIX (September, 1963), pp. 153-82.

Fetter, Frank Whitson, 'The Authorship of Economic Articles in the *Edinburgh Review 1812-1847*', *Journal of Political Economy,* LXI (1953), pp. 233-59.

Fetter, F. W., 'The Economic Articles in the Quarterly Review and their Authors, 1809-1852', *Journal of Political Economy,* LXVI (1958), pp. 47-64, 154-70.

Finlayson, Charles P., 'Records of Scientific and Medical Societies preserved in the University Library, Edinburgh', *The Bibliothek: A Journal of Bibliographical Notes and Queries mainly of Scottish Interest,* I (1958), pp. 14-19.

Fletcher, Harold R., and Brown, William H., *The Royal Botanic Garden Edinburgh, 1670-1970,* Edinburgh, HMSO 1970.

Humphries, Walter R., 'The First Aberdeen Philosophical Society', *Transactions of the Aberdeen Philosophical Society,* V, (1938).

Index to the Transactions of the Royal Society of Edinburgh, 1783-1888, Edinburgh, 1890.

Jeffrey, Francis, 'Cobbett's *Political Register*', *Edinburgh Review,* X (1807) pp. 386-421.

Jeffrey, Francis, 'Craig's Life of Millar', *Edinburgh Review,* IX (1806), pp. 83-92.

Jeffrey, Francis, 'Leckie on the British Government', *Edinburgh Review,* XX (1812) pp. 315-346.

Jeffrey, Francis, 'Millar's *View of the English Government*', *Edinburgh Review,* III (1803), pp. 154-81.

Jeffrey, Francis, 'Political Economy', *Edinburgh Review,* XLIII (1825), pp. 1-23.

Jeffrey, Francis, 'Stewart's Life of Dr. Reid', *Edinburgh Review*, III (1804)
    pp. 269-87.
Jeffrey, Francis, 'Stewart's Philosophical Essays', *Edinburgh Review*, XVII
    (1810), pp. 167-211.
Leslie, John, *Remarks, for a series of years on Barometrical Scales, showing they
    are inadequate to predict the Weather: the results of these observations
    exhibited and corrected upon a new and enlarged plan; as also, an improvement
    proposed on the Rain Gage; with a few hints of the effects on the weather, by
    the different directions of the Wind. Principally intended for the use of the
    Farmer*. Edinburgh, 1814.
Lockhart, John Gibson, *Peter's Letters to his Kinsfolk*, 3 vols., 3rd ed.,
    Edinburgh, 1819.
McCosh, James, *The Scottish Philosophy*, London, 1875.
McCulloch, John Ramsay, 'Rise, progress, present state, and prospects of the
    British Cotton Manufacture', *Edinburgh Review*, XLVI (1827), pp. 1-39.
McElroy, Davis Dunbar, *A Century of Scottish Clubs 1700-1800*, Edinburgh,
    1969, typescript in all main Edinburgh libraries.
McElroy, Davis Dunbar, *The Literary Clubs and Societies of Eighteenth Century
    Scotland, and their Influence on the literary productions of the period from
    1700-1800*, Ph.D. dissertation, University of Edinburgh, 1952.
McElroy, Davis Dunbar, *Scotland's Age of Improvement: A Survey of Eighteenth
    Century Literary Clubs and Societies*, Washington State U.P., Pullman, 1969.
Mackintosh, Sir James, *Memoirs of the Life of the Rt. Hon. Sir James Mackintosh*,
    ed. Robert James Mackintosh, 2 vols., London, 1835.
McLaurin, Colin, *An Account of Sir Isaac Newton's Philosophical Discoveries*,
    London, 1748.
Mather, W. M., 'The Origins and Occupations of Glasgow Students 1740-1839',
    Past and Present, (1966), pp. 74-94.
Meikle, H. W., *Some Aspects of Later Seventeenth Century Scotland*, Glasgow,
    1947.
Millar, John, *An Historical View of the English Government from the Settlement
    of the Saxons in Britain to the Revolution in 1688*, 4 vols., London, 1803.
Morrell, J. B., 'Practical Chemistry in the University of Edinburgh, 1799-1843',
    Ambix, XVI (1969), pp. 66-80.
Morrell, J. B., 'Professors Robison and Playfair, and the *Theophobia Gallica:*
    Natural Philosophy, Religion and Politics in Edinburgh 1789-1815', *Notes and
    Records of the Royal Society of London*, XXVI (1971), pp. 43-63.
Morrell, J. B., 'Reflections on the History of Scottish Science', *History of Science*,
    XII (1974), pp. 81-94.
Morrell, J. B., 'Science and Scottish University Reform: Edinburgh in 1826',
    British Journal for the History of Science, VI (1972), pp. 39-56.
Morrell, J. B., 'Thomas Thomson: Professor of Chemistry and University
    Reformer', *British Journal for the History of Science* (1969), pp. 244-65.
Morrell. J. B., 'The University of Edinburgh in the late Eighteenth Century:
    Its Scientific Eminence and Academic Structure', *Isis*, LXII (1970) pp. 158-71.
Mossner, Ernest Campbell, *The Life of David Hume*, Nelson, Edinburgh and
    London, 1954.
Napier, Macvey, *Selections from the Correspondence of the late Macvey Napier*,
    ed. Macvey Napier, London, 1877.
National Library of Scotland, Ms. 331.
National Library of Scotland, Ms. 755, Correspondence Book of the Academy of
    Physics, Edinburgh.
Newman, John Henry, *Historical Sketches: the Rise and Progress of Universities*,
    London, 1872.
Olson, Richard, 'Scottish Philosophy and Mathematics 1750-1830', *Journal of*

the History of Ideas, XXXII (1971), pp. 29-44.

Playfair, John, *The Works of John Playfair*, ed. J. G. Playfair, 4 vols., Edinburgh 1822. For detailed reference to his many articles in the *Edinburgh Review* mentioned in the chapter, see notes 39 and 46.

Royal Medical Society of Edinburgh, *Dissertations by Eminent Members of the Royal Medical Society*, Edinburgh, 1892.

Shapin, Steven, 'The Audience for Science in Eighteenth Century Edinburgh', *History of Science*, XII (1974), pp. 95-121.

Shapin, Steven, 'Property, Patronage and the Politics of Science: The Founding of the Royal Society of Edinburgh', *British Journal for the History of Science*, VII (1974), pp. 1-41.

Shapin, Steven, *The Royal Society of Edinburgh: a study of the social context of Hanoverian Science*, Ph.D. dissertation, University of Pennsylvania, 1971.

Stewart, Dugald, *Collected Works of Dugald Stewart*, ed. Sir William Hamilton, 11 vols., Edinburgh, 1854-60.

Stuart, W. J., *History of the Aesculapian Club*, Edinburgh, 1949.

Sweet, Jessie M., 'The Wernerian Natural History Society in Edinburgh', *Freiberger Forschungshefte*, C 223, Mineralogie–Lagerstattenlehre Abraham Gottlob Werner Gedenkschrift aus Anlass der Wiederkehr seines Todestages nach 150 Jahren am 30.

Thomson, John, *An Account of the Life, Lectures and Writings of William Cullen M.D.*, 2 vols., Edinburgh, 1822-59.

Thomson, Thomas, 'History and the Present State of Chemical Science', *Edinburgh Review*, L (October, 1829), pp. 256-76.

Veitch, John, 'Philosophy in the Scottish Universities', *Mind*, old series, II (1877), pp. 74-91, 207-34.

Wallace, Robert, 'Memorials of Dr Wallace of Edinburgh', *Scots Magazine* XXXIII (1771), pp. 340-1.

CHAPTER 8. CONCLUSION AND INTERPRETIVE

The Autobiography of Dr. Alexander Carlyle of Inveresk, 1722-1805, ed. John Hill Burton, London and Edinburgh, 1920.

Buckle, H. T. *Introduction to the History of Civilization in England*, new and revised ed., Routledge, London, 1904.

Buckle, H. T., *On Scotland and the Scotch Intellect*, ed. H. J. Hanham, Chicago, U.P., 1970.

Campbell, R. H., 'The Union and Economic Growth', *The Union of 1707: Its Impact on Scotland*, ed. T. I. Rae, Blackie, Glasgow, 1974.

Carabelli, Giancarlo, 'Hume, Scotland and Europe', *Scottish International*, VI (1973), pp. 24-7.

Clark, Ian D. L., *Moderatism and the Moderate Party in the Church of Scotland 1725-1805*, Ph.D. dissertation, University of Cambridge, 1964.

Clive, John and Bailyn, Bernard, 'England's Cultural Provinces: Scotland and America', *William & Mary Quarterly*, XI (1954), pp. 200-13.

Cockburn, Henry, *Journal*, 2 vols., Edinburgh, 1874.

Cockburn, Henry, *Memorials of his Time*, Edinburgh, 1856.

Davie, G. E., 'Hume, Reid and the Passion for Ideas', *Edinburgh in the Age of Reason*, Edinburgh U.P., 1967.

Ferguson, William, 'The Reform Act (Scotland) of 1832: Intention and Effect', *Scottish Historical Review* (1966), pp. 105-14.

Hill, John, *Account of the Life and Writings of Hugh Blair*, Edinburgh, 1807.

Jeffrey, Francis, 'Stewart's Philosophical Essays', *Edinburgh Review*, XVII

(1810), pp. 167-211.

Lockhart, J. G., *Peter's Letters to his Kinsfolk,* 3 vols., 2nd ed., Edinburgh, 1819.

Millar, John, *An Historical View of the English Government from the Settlement of the Saxons in Britain to the Revolution in 1688,* 4 vols., London, 1803.

Phillipson, N. T., 'Culture and Society in the 18th Century Province: The Case of Edinburgh and the Scottish Enlightenment', *The University in Society,* ed. Lawrence Stone, 2 vols., Princeton U.P., 1975, II, pp. 407-48.

Phillipson, Nicholas, 'Towards a Definition of the Scottish Enlightenment', *City and Society in the 18th Century,* eds. P. Fritz and D. Williams, Toronto, 1973, pp. 125-47.

Redwood, John, *Reason, Ridicule and Religion: The Age of Enlightenment in England, 1660-1750,* Thames and Hudson, 1976.

Smout, T. C., *A History of the Scottish People 1560-1830,* Collins/Fontana, London, 1972.

Stewart, Dugald, 'Dissertation: exhibiting the progress of metaphysical, ethical and political philosophy since the revival of letters in Europe', *Collected Works,* ed. Sir William Hamilton, 11 vols., (1854-60), I (1854).

Trevor-Roper, Hugh, 'The Scottish Enlightenment', *Studies on Voltaire and the Eighteenth Century,* cviii (1967), pp. 1635-58.

Webster, Charles, *The Great Instauration: Science, Medicine and Reform, 1626-1660,* Duckworth, 1975.

INDEX